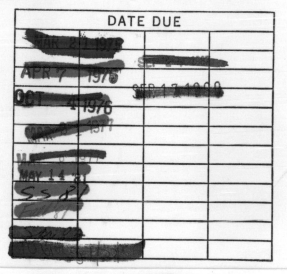

THE POET AND THE POEM

BY JUDSON JEROME

Writer's Digest, 9933 Alliance Road, Cincinnati, Ohio 45242

Books by Judson Jerome

Light in the West (poetry)

The Poet and the Poem (essays)

The Ocean's Warning to the Skin Diver and Other Poems (poetry)

Serenade (poetry)

Poetry: Premeditated Art (text)

The Fell of Dark (novel)

Plays For an Imaginary Theater (verse drama)

Culture Out of Anarchy: the Reconstruction of American Higher Learning (social criticism)

I Never Saw (poetry for children)

Families of Eden: Communes and the New Anarchism (social criticism)

Communal Living (social criticism)

The Poet and the Poem, much expanded and revised (essays)

Library of Congress Cataloging in Publication Data

Jerome, Judson.
    The poet and the poem.

    1. Poetics. 2. Poetry — Authorship. I. Title.
PN1042.J45   1974   808.1   74-9968
ISBN 911654-25-9

To Jenny —

whose poetry has no language

Acknowledgements

Most of this material appeared in Judson Jerome's monthly column, "Poetry: How and Why," in WRITER'S DIGEST. Other material, in slightly different form, has appeared in YALE REVIEW, COLORADO QUARTERLY, WRITER'S YEARBOOK, THE ANTIOCH REVIEW, and CONTACT. Poems by Judson Jerome have appeared in BELOIT POETRY JOURNAL, COASTLINES, A HOUYHNHNM'S SCRAPBOOK, and SHENANDOAH.

"The Fish" by Elizabeth Bishop © Houghton Mifflin Co.; "The Second Coming" reprinted with permission of the publisher from Collected Poems by William Butler Yeats, © 1924 by the Macmillan Co. Renewed 1952 by Bertha Georgie Yeats; "Leda and the Swan" and "Among School Children" reprinted with permission of the publisher from Collected Poems by William Butler Yeats, © 1928 by the Macmillan Co. Renewed 1956 by Georgie Yeats; "For Once, Then, Something," "Mowing," "Directive," and "Meeting and Passing" from Complete Poems of Robert Frost. © 1916, 1921, 1923, 1934, 1947 by Holt, Rinehart and Winston, Inc., © 1936 by Robert Frost. Copyright renewed 1944, 1951, © 1962 by Robert Frost. Reprinted by permission of Holt, Rinehart and Winston, Inc.; "Naming of Parts" by Henry Reed reprinted with permission of Harcourt, Brace & World, Inc.; "The Love Song of Alfred Prufrock," "The Waste Land," and "Gerontion" by T. S. Eliot reprinted with permission of Harcourt, Brace & World, Inc.; "For A Dead Lady" and "Miniver Cheevy" reprinted with permission of the publisher from The Town Down the River by E. A. Robinson; © Charles Scribner's Sons; "Fern Hill," "Alterwise by Owl Light" and "Light Breaks Where No Sun Shines" by Dylan Thomas, © 1957 by New Directions; "anyone lived in a pretty how town" by e. e. cummings; © Marion Cummings; "The Red Wheelbarrow" by William Carlos Williams; © 1938, 1955 by William Carlos Williams. Reprinted by permission of New Directions Publishers; "Home" from Collected Verse by Edgar A. Guest; © 1934 The Reilly & Lee Co.; "Blue Girls" from Selected Poems, revised edition by John Crowe Ransom; © 1927 Alfred A. Knopf, Inc. Renewed 1955 by John Crowe Ransom; "The Return" © 1926, 1954 by Ezra Pound. Reprinted by permission of New Directions, Publishers; "Digging For China" by Richard Wilbur reprinted by permission of Harcourt, Brace & World, Inc. Howard Moss, "Waterfall Blues" 1st and 2nd stanza, Modern Poetry, American and British, Appleton-Century Crofts 1951; James Tate, "Amnesia People" first 8 lines, Yale U. Press; W. S. Merwin, "The Animals" from The Lice, Atheneum, 1967; Phil Fried, "Neighbor, Arise" North American Review; James Dickey, "The Beholders" 1st stanza, Poems: 1957-67, Wesleyan U. Press, 1967; Peter Viereck, "Kilroy Was Here" 1st stanza, Terror and Decorum, Scribner, 1948; John Crowe Ransom, "Equilibrists" Selected Poems, Knopf, 1963; e. e. cummings, "plato told," Poems 1923-1954, Harcourt Brace & World, 1954; Robinson Jeffers, "The Purse-Seine" Collected Poems, Random House, 1959; W. H. Auden, "In Memory of W. B. Yeats," Part II only, The Collected Poetry of W. H. Auden, Random House, 1945; Amy Lowell, "The Taxi," Selected Poems of Amy Lowell, Houghton-Mifflin, 1927; John Ciardi, "Thoughts on Looking Into a Thicket," As If, Rutgers U. Press, 1955; Wilfred Owens "Dulce et Decorum Est" Collected Poems, New Directions, 1963; Gerard Manley Hopkins "Spring and Fall (To a Young Child)," Collected Poems of Gerard Manley Hopkins, Oxford U. Press, 1931; Stephen Spender, "The Express" Poems by Stephen Spender, Random House, 1954; Minou Drouet, "Tree that I Love" First Poems by Minou Drouet, Harpers, 1956; Aliki Barnstone, "The Real Tin Flower," The Real Tin Flower, Crowell-Collier, 1968; D. H. Lawrence, "The Elephant Is Slow to Mate," Portable D. H. Lawrence, Viking, 1947; Wallace Stevens, "Anecdote of the Jar," The Collected Poems of Wallace Stevens, Knopf, 1954; W. B. Yeats, "Easter, 1916," lines 17-20, "Sailing to Byzantium," "Long-Legged Fly," The Collected Poems of W. B. Yeats, Macmillan, 1951; Denise Levertov, "Life at War" lines 1-2, 12-31, 33-34, 38-39, and 45-47, The Sorrow Dance, New Directions, 1967; and "An Interim," pt 1, lines 1-6, pt 2, lines 24-5, pt 3, lines 7-8 and 15-23, pt 6, stanzas 4 and 5, stanza 7 lines 6-10, stanza 10, lines 2-3, and pt 7, lines 2-4 and stanza 4, lines 4-5, from Poetry, November, 1968.

Contents

Preface

Books, conferences, magazines, courses, even degree programs in colleges, intended to teach people how to write are a peculiarly American phenomenon. Perhaps this has something to do with the value Americans place on individual experience. We seem to believe each person has a book in him, and we set about helping him get it out. If we stopped searching out and encouraging writing talent, our literature might lose much of its breadth and depth and crazy vitality.

It would be interesting to know what percentage of those who eventually make a name as writers have been helped by the plethora of "how to" resources available. I know I had courses in journalism and creative writing in college, subscribed to a writer's magazine for a while, and though I never went to writers' conferences until I was invited to them as a staff member, I can see how they would have helped at critical stages of my career. First-hand contact with established writers, even in brief conversations, was immensely influential in my development. Some writers dismiss such help as useless — but that may be like climbing up on the barn and kicking the ladder away, making it seem that one flew.

Most who read such books and magazines and attend conferences and take courses never, of course, publish a thing, but their time and energy are not necessarily wasted. One teacher said that in any of his creative writing classes there might be four or five learning to write and another fifteen or so learning to read — a valuable end in itself. Similarly, I hope this book will be useful for readers as well as for writers (and that it will help writers become better readers). Another often disguised motive is personal therapy: many study writing as a means of psychological development, a way of coping with inadequacies they cannot name. Some simply enjoy reading and talking about literature — and find the workshop atmosphere less stultifying than books of literary criticism or courses in literature. Some like to associate themselves with the glamour and gossip of writers (as others read movie magazines). Some are escaping a vacancy and weariness in their lives. Such motives are neither superficial nor ignoble.

Some, especially some writers, repeat too glibly that cliché that writing cannot be taught. They may feel honestly guilty about participating in exploitation of the lonely housewife in Duluth who retains her grasp on dignity by believing that after the diapers, after the dishes, after the vacuum that trails along the floor, she will somehow discover meaning in her life and express it in poems to go on the shelf alongside those of Keats and Miss Millay, evidence that she, too, lived and felt and mattered. But the myth that talent is purely God-given is also part of the writer's bag of tricks. As the ballet dancer learns through long and sweaty hours to appear at ease, so the poet labors to seem spontaneous, possessed of a mystery beyond his comprehension. A magician might say magic cannot be taught. He for damned sure doesn't *want* it taught to all and sundry. Someone has to sit out in the audience.

I call it the myth of talent because the innate differences between people are remarkably slight, once we correct our measurements for whatever cultural bias or snobbery colors the test and makes it easy for the privileged to come out on top. Whether writers are born or made, they are at least susceptible of growth.

When the Editor of *Writer's Digest* asked me, in 1959, to begin a monthly column on writing poetry, I suffered most of the misconceptions I have mentioned here. I accepted the offer in what I now recognize was a spirit of defiance. I couldn't quite believe that the magazine really wanted an honest discussion of what writing poetry involved — writing *good* poetry, I mean. I thought such magazines were concerned only with breaking into markets, with gimmicks, trends, slickness and success. Well, I would show them. I'd write a column or two which did not show you how you and your Uncle Ebenezer could write poetry and *sell* it, but which argued, instead, that to write good poetry was nearly impossible and offered almost no chance of success and less of profit. I thought a dose or two would be too much for the editors and readers, and I could resign with a fine gesture, my cynicism intact.

To my astonishment, both the readers and editors showed an appetite for these bleak views; and as I warmed to the task, I became, if not less bleak, at least passionately concerned to discover whether it were possible to say anything really sensible about the mysteries of the art. I had read handbooks giving verse forms and the rest;

but how do you get from knowledge of what iambic pentameter is to *Lycidas?*

I am not likely ever to know; but the opportunity offered by the column, eventuating in this book, has allowed me to explore rather unremittingly the highest standards we can bring to bear on poetry, assuming my readers to be in some sense in competition with Shakespeare. No one sets out to be second-rate, but many exposed to success and disappointment learn to accept that limited objective as not only sufficient but even itself beyond all reasonable hope of fulfillment. For the poet, adjustment to his own insignificance can be chastening — if it is not absolutely debilitating.

But modesty allies itself with realism and sloth to encourage us to settle for publication rather than poetry. Consider the second-rate poets — the Surreys and Shelleys, the Patchens and Pounds — and tremble. Which of us thinks he has more to offer the world than these, and that he has the energy, skill, connections, luck, and vision to hope ever to measure himself against them? Why go on? I find myself tucking my manuscript back between my legs and asking the way to the third-class compartment.

Curiously, the prospect of the heights is not so discouraging. We can live in the shadow of Chaucer, Shakespeare and Milton (so old, after all, and so permanent), of Keats and Yeats and Frost, with the fond indifference of Alpine peasants for their surrounding peaks. It is hills that make us nervous — or even hummocks like the poet next door. Someone (worst of all we ourselves) might expect us to work at such altitudes. You can break a leg in a ten foot fall — never mind the crevasses beyond the timberline.

We know the conventional responses. "I do it for money," one says, disclaiming thus any responsibility for quality (and ignoring for the moment that there is no more inefficient way to make money in the world). Or, "I want an audience," as though the way to get one were by speaking through a garden hose into a tomb. Or, "Look at the junk that gets published," as though the domains of poetry were best conquered by contempt. Or, "Poetry, after all, is just writing," as though it were. Or, "I'm not a *poet;* I just write verses," as peeping Tom said when he was hauled down from the lamp-post. Or, with endearing giggle, "I just write light verse," as though your squibbles were not to be compared (they will not be) with comic masterpieces such as "The Miller's Tale," or "Absalom and Achitophel," or "The Dunciad," or Byron's "Don Juan" — or even with the work of Phyllis McGinley or Ogden Nash, whose brows were sometimes threateningly high. In abysmal states of self-hatred one utters the most pathetic rationlization, "I don't write for anybody — just for myself," (demonstrably true: look at the rejection slips).

I have lived with these attitudes both as poet and editor. As the first I know the temptation to let a line go which "will do," a word which may fit but suggests little, a lame rhythm which I know most readers won't hear anyway. On the other hand, as editor, I have waded in the sea of manuscripts to which we all contribute, and I have wished that stamps cost even more than they do. I suppose that one should be astonished that sheer creativity manages to make verses from nothing, that so many thousands of people can start with a blank page, without an idea, observation, emotion, or cleverness, without a sense of language or knowledge of technique, without even the skill to come out of a complex sentence right side up, and emerge some moments later (I can't believe it takes long) with a composition they are not embarrassed to post successively to every professional judge of poetry in the country. But astonishment wears off. I wish poets would apply one minimal criterion: that they refrain from sending poems which they themselves would not be interested in reading, if the poems had been written by someone else.

People believe what Edison said about genius — that it is one percent inspiration and ninety-nine percent perspiration, and think they might be willing to put in the perspiration if they could be assured they have the essential one percent inspiration — or what is commonly called talent. They come to us asking to be told: "Have I got it?" I think the most painful thing I have to say might as well be said at the outset. I do not believe in that one percent. I believe it is *all* perspiration — but of a quite different sort than Edison meant.

To become a poet a person must change — radically, to the roots. The sweat required is the cold sweat of terror, among other things. At times it is a more passionate sweat of love. By dint of application you may learn to write verse that meets all technical specifications, but the difference between published and unpublished poets (aside from luck) and, more importantly, the difference between merely published poets and those who have some lasting significance in literature, has to do with their most intimate personal psychology, their world view, their social and political attitudes, their willingness to take risks, to explore, to permit their imagination to pursue the anguishing and difficult and forbidden.

The term *vision* describes that complex of personal outlook and style and grasp of wide significance which characterizes the work of a Dante or Whitman or Emily Dickinson or Sylvia Plath. It is not necessarily what the world regards as a state of sanity or health (though it is not necessarily insane or unhealthy, either). It is what is meant when we speak of a person as being "very together," which does not mean "well-adjusted." It means having discovered some source of inner coherence which enables one to function — minimally to survive in an all too intensely vivid world, maximally to achieve greatly, as in great art.

Such vision cannot be deliberately acquired, yet, paradoxically, it can arise from work, thought, suffering, ecstasy, willing surrender, courageous engagement, and solitary facing of self. When achieved it may impel a person to reject all I say here — and that may be exactly the route one must follow to become a poet. When people say that writing cannot be taught they mean that one cannot give another person vision. It must be discovered in and wrought of self.

What one can do — and what I have tried to do here — is continually raise the kinds of questions which lead to (perhaps the word is provoke) such metamorphosis. In discussing poetry I have tried to show that there is no way it can be separated from philosophy, faith, politics, social criticism, personal and social psychology, individual experience and commitment, from all the rest of human culture. Simultaneously I have tried to offer specific, realistic, and practical advice about how to make poems work once one has achieved something like personal vision.

In this new edition I have retained most of the first edition's chapters, adding new material, on the more technical matters of verse writing. But I have supplemented this material with chapters which bear more directly on the process of becoming a poet — specifically a poet for the seventies and eighties. In one of these I describe the end of the era in which I myself came to such maturity as I have:

> We went through a period in the fifties and early sixties in which poetry became professionalized. The routes to publication and reputation were laid out and paved, and droves of the talented button-down breed of young writers began developing their sophistication and skill in poetry (and, always, criticism) in much the same way they might pursue a career in sociology and physics . . . . But that's all over now. Rather, it dribbles on, but it is not important.

It will still be true, as it has always been, that one may hew out a kind of profession (if not a living) as a poet, but I expect poetry in the next decades to take on a different function for society and to achieve a new centrality in people's lives. And I believe that to be a poet will mean something quite different in the future than it has meant in the past.

Today new echelons of artists are painting murals on board fences and crumbling brick walls, indifferent to whether they are Sunday or Monday painters, to whether they are professional or amateur, to whether or not they are paid. If novels give way to films, and correspondence to the telephone, and other means of communication meet our needs for information and personal encounter, there may be little need of writing anything *but* poetry (and I think people will continue to write). I predict that active involvement in the arts of all sorts will increase if leisure (perforce or by fortune) becomes the business of our lives. There are probably already more people whose mental health is endangered by idleness than those who suffer from overwork.

This may not result so much from abundance or an all-competent technology as from poor social organization and poor distribution of wealth. But unrest and unemployment may combine to foster arts of a new kind. (Consider the renaissance in popular music — with its potent lyrics — which has welled out of the youth rebellion.) The techniques and values of older poetry will not be irrelevant. Invention is never from ground base zero, but it is a transformation and modification of the past. As always, good poets of the future will have to absorb the past; but they may find the time and means and, most important of all, the motive for new applications of what they know.

Part One of this book explores in greater depth the various reasons we have for writing poetry — especially now, in this age. It is more directly autobiographical than the rest of the book (though all books are autobiography, if read right), as the only motives I can finally speak about with authority are my own. The bulk of the book is Part Two, which discusses and illustrates in turn the various technical elements of poetry, showing, wherever possible, how they work in well-known poems. (Or poems which should, I think, be well known.) I assume that readers have at hand good anthologies of English and American poetry, since the explications often do not quote whole poems — and these must be read to see the points I am making. For older English poems I most often use the Viking

Portable set of five volumes, *Poets of the English Language,* edited by W. H. Auden and Norman Holmes Pearson, because it reproduces where possible texts as they were originally published — and the spelling and punctuation are closer to the authors' intent. For modern poetry the anthologies are too numerous, and change in content too rapidly, to warrant a recommendation. Most of the poems referred to are also in my *Poetry: Premeditated Art,* available in paperback from Houghton-Mifflin, a text which also contains more explications and extended discussion of technical elements, generally not repeating material in this book. Again and again the advice I give aspiring poets is simply to read poetry — carefully, analytically, looking for tips, techniques and insights as well as vision. A book about writing poetry which was not in large part a book about reading poetry would have to be a hoax.

Part Three is more directly concerned with problems of revision and publication, the nitty-gritty of the profession. And Part Four returns to and expands the concerns of Part One: what it means to be a poet in our age, particularly in view of the massive cultural change we are experiencing (which I believe will prove to be one of the major watersheds of human history). Though I write as a poet and for poets (and prospective poets), there is no real separation possible between poetry and life — and the interpretation of our contemporary world and my personal experience in it seems to me as intrinsic to the craft as discussion of diction, meter and figurative language. Nothing in this book is elementary. My fear is, rather, that I haven't sufficient profundity to respond to the staggering question of what it means to be a poet and thus to participate in building the most towering yet most delicate edifice in human history. I have sat spellbound contemplating the imagination, technique and expenditure of resources involved in sending our astronauts into space. Yet when I see those intricate craft drifting beyond gravity I want to ask the spacemen, "Have you read Shakespeare's Sonnet 129?"

PART ONE:

FOOTHILLS OF PARNASSUS —
OR
WHY BOTHER?

shucks, ma,
I wrote a pome

Horace drew attention in verse to a problem which has existed as long as there has been such a thing as a literary reputation and a horde of aspirants desiring one: the plague of non-professionals descending on professionals in search of attention, advice, and promotion (much more of the first and third than of the second). Along with tales of losing one's virginity or learning about Pearl Harbor or the assassination of President Kennedy, almost anyone might tell about his experiences trying to get well-known writers to read and comment on work. It seems that everyone has at one time or another thought he might be a writer; in some fashion he tried to get an authoritative judgment on his chances of success. On one hand are the stories of the rudeness, vanity and fallibility of the professionals; on the other are the complaints (such as that of Pope in his "Epistle to Dr. Arbuthnot") about the naivety, persistence and self-centeredness of neophytes who line up outside the homes of writers like bill collectors.

There is no way to avoid the problem, for, surely, everyone must start somewhere, and that means getting someone to read his work. The opinions of family and friends are eventually unsatisfying (no matter how encouraging). Rejection slips are uninformative. Teachers of English are undependable as sounding boards. Inescapably beginners haunt published poets with their sad and desperate question: "Shall I go on?" Dryden told his cousin Swift that Swift would never be a poet (and, in spite, Swift became a good one). But no matter how confident we may be of negative predictions, they serve little purpose. The question permits only one answer — and one may give it without ever seeing the beginner's work: "Of course you should go on, if you really want to. But do you know what you're in for?"

To be a poet is, of course, to transcend such categories as "amateur" and "professional." A professional poet is, in a sense, a contradiction in terms. In the first place poetry is not something at which one can make a living. There is no agreed-upon body of knowledge, no set of methods or principles, nothing much to profess. But it is possible to make a career of sorts out of writing poetry and engaging in the activities which pertain to or grow out of writing poetry — giving readings and lectures, editing, teaching, engaging in scholarship and other kinds of writing. A reputation as a published poet opens doors which lead to other things which generate a little income. And in spite of coy denials and the lack of absolutes, there is more agreement than we often admit about necessary knowledge, techniques, bases of judgment, goals and steps of advancement. Knowing all that will not make one a poet, but if one becomes a poet there is a high probability that he will learn these things.

Becoming a poet is, however, another matter. Experienced writers talk a lot about discipline, but they do not often talk about the motivation which underlies discipline. A young man shared my study recently for a couple of days and marveled at my capacity for staying right here at my typewriter hour after hour. I said it was easy — easier than doing anything else — because I loved it. It is like fly-fishing or skiing or sailing or making love: one does not do it primarily to get somewhere. One does it out of commitment to the activity itself. Getting results is satisfying, of course, but one learns (particularly in writing poetry) to minimize that motivation. The time and uncertainty between writing a poem, revising it, sending it out, having it accepted, seeing it in print, and having it read by others, and the goal — having it influence their lives — all this is too tenuous to operate effectively as a driving force.

The questions one must ask himself open up chasms: Why am I doing this? What am I looking for? How will I know when I have found it? What would I consider success? What relation has my opinion to that of others? Those who become poets find ways of answering or coping with such questions which motivate them to dedicated work. They discover appropriate stances toward themselves and their art. All the practices and lore and rewards of the non-profession are secondary to discovering motivation.

At a writer's conference I heard John Frederick Nims tell how to become a poet. "It's easy," he said, "to tell you. It's like teaching you to ride a bicycle across the Grand Canyon on a cable, balancing bowls of fish on either end of a long pole. First, stretch a cable across the canyon. Get a bicycle which will roll on the cable. Balance the fishbowls on the pole and mount the bicycle, being careful not to spill the fish . . . ." The audience was breaking up with painful laughter. "No," he said, "that's wrong. To become a poet, get a bottle of whiskey and go off in the woods and drink it in one evening. Have a tragic love affair. Converse with God . . . ." Though both lines of advice are reductions to absurdity of the question, both contain much truth. There is no formula. It sounds impossible, but clearly it is not.

Part One explores the questions surrounding that discovery of
stance (and distinguishing it from mere posturing — as those would-
be poets engage in who buy their wardrobe and start practicing
their autograph without undertaking the preceding steps). How
does one acquire the readiness, the strength, the serious purpose?
I can't tell you — but I can say something about what these questions have meant to me and to others I have dealt with.

on mountain fork

discipline: the whispering S of line
above the canoe, the weightless fly thrown through
a gap in the branches, spitting to rest
on the still pool where the bass lay,
                                    wrist true
in the toss and flick of the skipping lure.

love: silence and singing reel, the whip
of rod, chill smell of fish in the morning air,
green river easing heavily under, drip
of dew in brown light.
                        At the stern I learned
to steer us — wavering paddle like a fin.

art: tyrannous glances, passionate strategy,
the hush of nature, humanity slipping in,
arc of the line, ineffectual gift
of a hand-tied bug, then snag in the gill, the snap
and steady pull.
                        His life was squalid, his

temper mean, his affection like a trap.
I paddled on aching knees and took the hook.
My father shaped the heart beneath my skin
with love's precision:
                        the gift of grief, the art
of casting clean, the zeal, the discipline.

CHAPTER ONE

Are You a Poet?

Of course, you think you are.

I have never met a person who has never written a poem.

Scratch your cowboy, you will find a Sandburg; scratch your engineer, you will find Hart Crane; scratch your mother, you will find Millay. The bourgeois gentleman may have spoken prose all his life, but he writes poetry, saves it for years and then sends it to me. He goes at it like Don Quixote at the windmill or, in a more American spirit, he gets in there and *tries*.

He doesn't write jingles, by the way. Jingles require too much skill. He writes, almost invariably, free verse. He isn't superficial; he is always fantastically profound, as he will explain, and what looks like foolishness is simply more advanced than the reader. He isn't childishly simple; he is always obscure and difficult. No poetry is more obscure and difficult than amateur poetry. He has unshakeable faith in the validity of his thought and the significance of his emotion; if he writes it down it must be *so*.

And he has faith in the value of expression for its own sake. He doesn't save his nail parings in his jewelry box. If he expresses himself into a Kleenex he doesn't hang it on the wall. If he belches, he does not record it and play it on hi-fi. But if he finds what seem to him verbal equivalents for internal exudations, he has a touching confidence that he has produced something to be revered and shown in public.

I speak of the amateur, but there should be a more accurate word. *Amateur* comes from *amare,* to love, implying, true, that there is more infatuation than wisdom, more enthusiasm than skill, about what he does. But, unfortunately, many amateur poets hate poetry, never reading any except their own, never thinking about it, hearing it, seeing it, above all never buying it. Poetry is their personal vengeance on the world of literature, or, more specifically, on their highschool English teachers.

Such a poet preserves his amateur standing with vicious jealousy. Poetic license, for him, is tacit permission to indulge in an emotional range from infantile display to adolescent sentiment. His inspiration excuses all; he believes Art is Divine — by which he means it is free from the ordinary considerations of common sense, utility, improvement by practice, decency, relevance and intelligence. Poetry is, by definition, thus, lacking in common sense, impolite, useless, of no conceivable importance to human life, and produced by a half-wit without much preparation, effort or care. An amateur of this kind does not want to lose his inalienable right to participate in such an orgy.

An exceptionally able pianist I know practices for pay in bars. He hears there some of the premises ordinarily suppressed or more carefully disguised. He recognizes two basic attitudes toward his profession. The first goes, "I took piano lessons when I was a kid. Wish I had kept it up, but you know how it goes — no time." This can be translated or expanded: "If I were to practice I would be as good as you are. But I have *important* things to do." The second attitude is expressed as, "You don't know how lucky you are to be given a talent like that." This means, roughly, "The only difference between you and me is luck. You got it; I didn't. I am not too lazy to practice six hours a day for fifteen or twenty years, nor too dedicated to other satisfactions to give my time to so unprofitable a pursuit. Only the rare person is gifted — as it were like a divine teacher's pet. We normal folk can be thankful we aren't queer."

The first of these attitudes underrates the natural differences between people (I am avoiding the abused word *talent,* which smacks of the mysterious); the second underrates the slow, onerous development of skill. Neither, notice, gives any credit to the artist nor to his art. Both are rationalizations of non-artists, and they are born of a curious but common mixture of envy and contempt.

But these are the ways many amateurs look on professionals. They consider their own innocence and spontaneity as at least the equivalent of knowledge, probably superior in the long run. Moreover, they feel there is something corrupt or evil in art if one knows what he is doing. They look on professionals as sweethearts look on courtesans. (And, actually, the analogy is illuminating in many ways.)

A hack is more nearly a poet than that kind of amateur. Like courtesans, poets come in all degrees of competence and natural endowment; only a few are great. But the hack, unlike the amateur, has cleared his mind of basic distortions of the artistic process. He knows, for example, that his first obligation is to make himself understood. He does not confuse carelessness with creativity. He recognizes external demands on his work, the necessity of making his product fit into a pattern of needs and interests outside himself. He values sensitivity less than sense. He is not an intellectual hoodlum, attempting to browbeat his audience with pedantry or haughty subtlety. He would rather be wrong than be dull. He may have more craft than conscience — but that hardly matters, for, above all, he is an artisan, concerned with doing a job well. He has little interest in expressing himself.

So far, his qualifications are exactly those which were essential to Homer, Dante, Chaucer, Shakespeare, Milton, Dryden or Goethe. Our hack may lack the largeness of mind of the great ones, their depth and scope, their dedication, their capacity for hard work, their capacity for life. But he is straight on many of the basic principles; he differs more in degree than in kind.

an ear for poetry

Aside from these essential attitudes, the most important qualification you must have as a poet is what is called "an ear" — a sense of rhythm and sound relationship. Like most talents, your ear for poetry is partly gift and partly acquisition. The best training for it is analysis of great poetry. Much of what I have done in this book consists of analyzing passages of poetry in great detail, as I hope to encourage readers to insist upon a sensitive and detailed understanding of what goes on in poems. At this point perhaps the nonconformist rebels. He wants to do something *different*. But he would probably not be concerned with poetry at all unless he had developed a love — based on knowledge — of the fine points of the art. Analysis (which is sometimes seen as the opposite of creativity) can be tender as well as penetrating. It requires learning to care about the right things.

When you sense that something about a line or a passage is

particularly compelling, that its effect is indelible, stop, take it apart and examine the pieces.

>Was this the face that launch'd a thousand ships
>And burnt the topless towers of Ilium?
>Sweet Helen, make me immortal with a kiss.

Listen to the sounds one by one in their interweaving patterns: the *s's*, *l's*, *t's*, the nasals, but, above all, the short *i's* in *this, ships, Ilium, immortal, with* and *kiss*. The powerful climactic effect of that word *kiss* arises partly from this repetition of the vowel sound, particularly as it rhymes with the first beat in the passage, *this*, and strongly echoes the last word of the first line, *ships* (which, by the way, suggests *lips* — but more of that later). Outright alliteration *(topless towers, make me immortal)* is a rather obvious device, but much subtler are the modulations from one sound to another and the playful and minute echoes. For example, in the last line, the long *e's* in *sweet* and *me*, subdued because *me* is unaccented, or the consonance of the *k* in *make* with that in *kiss*, or the movement from the high bright vowel in *sweet* down to the dark *o* in *immortal* back up the scale to the two short *i's* at the end of the line.

Now look at the rhythm. It is perfectly regular through the first two lines until the last light beat in *Ilium* (and note how the light beat on *um* pulls against the voice which is rising to complete the question). Then the astonishing third line:

>*SWEET HEL*| en, *MAKE*| me i *MOR*| tal with a *KISS.*|

In conventional terms, the five feet are a spondee, iamb, anapest, pyrrhic and iamb — not a particularly unusual line of iambic pentameter. But the dramatic appropriateness of the initial surge, the stagger of the anapest and succession of three unaccented syllables resolving almost passionately on the word *kiss* can hardly be accounted for in conventional terms.

One's ear for rhythm is not an ear for regularity: anyone hears a metronome's steady throb. Rather, it is the ability to hear the dance of variation, the pulse and lag of beats syncopating over the established base. *Poetry is order threatening to become chaos — just as the best prose is chaos threatening to become order.* You have an ear if you hear both the order and artful disorder simultaneously.

These lines, of course, are spoken by Marlowe's Dr. Faustus at his moment of triumph before his commitment to Hell begins to press its horror to his heart. No amount of management of vowels, consonants and metrics could make the lines as imperishable as they are if it were not for their dramatic setting, for their tone of exuberance shaded with poignant irony. This is the face for which the towers were burnt, the Greeks were embroiled all those years, and for which Faustus will willingly go to damnation. Immortal he wants to be? He cannot avoid an immortality of punishment. With a kiss? That briefest of experiences is cast against the yearning for timelessness — and, additional irony, the kiss *does* make him immortal, for the fictional Dr. Faustus steps with these three lines into the permanent memory of the world and assumes a reality no actual magician could ever achieve. He goes on to say (and notice here the double occurrence of the word *lips* for which the previous lines have prepared us):

> Her lips suck forth my soul; see where it flies!
> Come, Helen, come, give me my soul again.
> Here will I dwell, for heaven be in these lips,
> And all is dross that is not Helena.

The meaning of the play is crystallized in this passage: he does indeed lose his soul for Helen, and for the other pleasures which he has bought by his contract with Mephistopheles. But the moment is exquisite — and Marlowe almost convinces us that for such a moment we would also sell our souls. How much (given the situation) that experience owes to the handling of the short *i* sound, to the surge and limp of a meter in a single line!

That is a poetic ear — the ability to hear and select language for its sound — not pretty sound, but *right* sound; not stability, but pattern always seeming to dissolve.

I have suggested other aspects of poetic talent which are just as essential as the ear, but they are equally essential in all writing. I mean control of language, drama, of idea, of tone, of fictional reality. The difference is that in poetry *every* element is so much more intense, has so much attention thrown onto it, that the demands are incomparably heavier on the poet than on the writer of prose. Unless you care as much or more for your syllables and sounds, for your beat, for your line shape, for the details of your pattern, as you do for your meaning, you may as well write prose. You are not a poet.

Form is the poem; form cannot be paraphrased. And form is as simultaneously rigid and supple as a skeleton. Nothing about the poet can be soft: poetry is the toughest of arts, and you must be tough to practice it. Lines will go dead on you if you relax, your words will drown if you water them. The plunk of hard syllables, knuckles of sound, ribs of meaning — these are the stuff of verse. You must yearn for the solid, the irreducible, for the hard and lasting. I am not speaking of hardness in the sense of being difficult to comprehend: such difficulty grows more often in fuzziness, confusion, the smog of thought, than it does in the weathered language of poetry. Your concern is not to be difficult, but rather, to give to airy nothing a local habitation and a name, to put real toads in imaginary gardens, to discover bone and build outward. Have you the courage to be a poet? To step beyond the easy answers?

rivalry with madmen

I take that title from Plato, who, in the *Phaedrus,* speaks of "the madness of those who are possessed by the Muses." This madness, he says, "enters into a delicate and virgin soul, and there inspires frenzy, awakens lyrical and all other numbers; with those adorning the myriad actions of ancient heroes for the instruction of posterity. But he who, having no touch of the Muses' madness in his soul, comes to the door and thinks that he will get into the temple by the help of art — he, I say, and his poetry are not admitted; the sane man is nowhere at all when he enters into rivalry with madmen."

If what I write is poetry, *if* my experience is that of a poet, what I say may have some relevance. But there is a risk in the assumption; my frenzies do not produce poetry; when not frenzied I am, I hope, sane — which is to say, if Plato is right, I am nowhere at all as a poet.

No one sits down to give a public performance on a piano unless he has had some instruction and practice, unless he has learned something about the craft. Seizure, frenzy, he considers not enough — just as it is not enough to enable one, for example, to pilot an airplane. I used to sneak into cockpits of airplanes at an airfield near home and pretend to fly. I *wanted* to fly, as badly as can be. I was inspired to fly. But I had so little faith in my inspiration that I would not turn the switch. Faith about poetry comes more easily, though. Thousands of people turn the switch every day producing writing ranged irregularly down the page, and preparing any captive reader with the proud preface that he never wrote poetry before, doesn't know anything about poetry, and, in fact, doesn't read and doesn't *like* poetry. Unembarrassed, proud of their innocence (or, as Plato says, their delicacy and virginity), such poets consider ignorance positively a recommendation. The results are usually comparable to what would have happened if I had turned the switch in the airplane, or if I were to sit before you in my musical ignorance and attempt to entertain you on the piano.

A character in Steinbeck's *Of Mice and Men* says something to the effect that one should never fight with little guys; they are excused if they lose and get too much credit if they win. The novice approaches art, I think, as a little guy, knowing he is insured either way. If he loses, he expects patience, understanding, and praise for a noble attempt. If he wins, he expects immediate immortality. Although no art is immune from him, he usually tries poetry.

That a little child shall lead us is one of the great delusions of Western civilization. Idiots, dogs, children, monks, and condemned men share with poets and other artists a reputation for uncanny wisdom. It is our favorite story: how one learns about life by being cut off from it. God appears to the blank mind. It is popular to praise the barefoot or backwoods artist, the unspoiled child of nature, because it is assumed he has a freer access to his subconscious than other people; that is, that he lacks the controls of behavior and expression which are induced by civilized commerce. He is like the child, untarnished, nearer truth than those of us who have labored to discover it.

The popular view is that intelligence is regarded as an absolute disadvantage to emotion — whereas in good art they are not only compatible but intensify one another. Art, insofar as it is a celebration of or uncritical indulgence in feeling, is one of the most attractive forces of anti-intellectualism at loose in the world. We may be glad so few people pay attention to it.

I will illustrate how feeling and reason work together with one of my poems:

AUBADE

That is dawn, that light in the west
brighter than lead dropped scalding on the eye,
breaking the day of silence on the nest
untenanted — and strewn from the naked tree

or atomized. Across the new white land
no bough holds any dew, nor leaf, nor must
any angled arm of wood make shadow; wind
must not stir the unreflecting, hanging atom dust

in that white land of final dawn. If we,
my loving flesh, could but prolong our night!
But no cloud crosses the coming of the light;
no birdsong shrieks that instant breaking,

that day of terrible mind. In a granule, borne by
a wheel grunt? shield clank? clatter of chariot wheel?
on covert piston slipping steady lechery?
Will silver hollow whistling sky fish carry it?

Or will some draftsman, coat on a nail,
switching his steel-beaked compass, setting a thumb-screw,
drain the last black drop? What bestial hand, like mine,
will turn the last dial to the point marked TRUE —

searing the skyline with a flameless fire,
powdering all the antique ways of blood,
cauterizing bed and loin and mire
and drying dark in dawn's pure, pure still flood?

(*The Nation,* September 10, 1955)

The poem is about the bomb. Light is a familiar symbol for
intelligence or reason. The West is not only the Pacific bomb
range; it can be taken as both death and the Western world. The
speaker is singing a traditional love song on parting from his mistress
at dawn. In this case his mistress is his flesh. The dawn which
separates them is the enlightenment of Western culture, which
reaches its apotheosis in the explosion of the bomb: both the
height of achievement and the end. For it is still a bestial hand
which turns the dial of the machine produced by the mind; enlightenment cannot come to the body. The results are inevitable as truth.
The body, when products of intelligence have final sway, is obsolete,
antique, and the landscape is that of a waste land, without foliage,
shadow, or dew. Life is, as it were, a darkness, a disease, an im-
perfection, which enlightenment will cauterize. The speaker sees the
end of life tragically, preferring the disease to the cure.

We were discussing inspiration. Was I seized to become the mouthpiece of the supernatural? Did I plumb my subconscious, ripping through the barriers of my civilized overlay? Well, I remember very clearly that I was scrubbing my back in the shower when it occurred to me that it would be amusing to see the sun rise in the west rather than the east. I began, soap in hand, orating to the shower curtain, "That is dawn, that light in the west," delighting in the absurdity of the pronouncement. Then I began to take myself seriously, as I frequently do when absurdities engage me. "Brighter than . . .," I added, and tried to think of intense brightness, blinding brightness, and imagined the sensation (note: sensation) of burning out an eye. With a poker; with boiling oil; finally, with molten lead. My notion was of something like a prisoner in a movie thriller tied to a table with Chinese pirates dropping hot lead, drop by drop, in his eye. What *is* that bright? An image came to me of people watching a bomb test through smoked glass, and then I was off. All the humanitarian, social concern of the poem came as an afterthought. I needed a "subject" strong enough to justify the startling beginning I had conceived. Still dripping I began working on the poem. Although I wrote the poem very quickly (it was substantially as it stands in half an hour), I was not, I underline, inspired. I was *working,* consciously and carefully on the symbolic meanings of light, darkness, flesh, dawn, the West; consciously varying meter, searching for discordant rhymes, hunting for dramatic hesitations for line endings — all the conscious concerns of craft. If I worked quickly it was because I had been preparing for the job for several years: reading, analyzing poetry, and practicing its composition. I had a reservoir of skill to draw on. A farmhand milks a cow faster than I do because he has developed the muscles, and, besides, he knows how. I do not accuse him of inspiration. It is an activity of sanity, not of madness.

The emotion is approached, I think, rationally. For example, there is throughout a conscious, careful imitation of oracular statement, the rhetoric of prophecy, vision, dire revelation. I did not *have* such a vision; I created it. Let me call your attention to some of the details of organization you might not have noticed. The poem opens with a paradox stated as a simple fact. Dawn usually has good connotations, but these are immediately reversed by the second line, and an ominous sense is (or should be) created by the phrase "day of silence" and the stark images. The final word of the first sentence, *atomized,* comes, I hope, as something of a surprise, dropping down into the second stanza. This word suggests the meaning of this dawn, at least on the level of the bomb. There follow more stark images, negatives, in the next sentences, and repetitions of the word *must,* suggesting "do not disturb" — as though things were as they should be, or inevitable, final, and to be respected.

The title has suggested a love song, but it is not until the third stanza that the theme of love emerges, and then in a single, futile apostrophe. No use. And the next line, beginning with a series of heavy stresses and ending with a hard and sudden rhyme, hinges the poem, turns us immediately back to desolation. In the fourth stanza a series of short questions is meant to suggest the steady implacable steps of progress, stages of civilization, one means of war after another. The third line, the machine, the combustion engine, is associated with sex; not love but lechery, and with the cyclical untiring movement with which machines replace human functions. The final horror in this gallery of horrors is the jet, with its spinning turbine, deadly in the sky, and associated with a fish, another sexual symbol. If this stanza works, in evoking the full sweep of civilization and progress, the poem has moved to another level of abstraction; it is no longer merely the bomb we are talking about, but all civilization which threatens "my loving flesh." "That day of terrible mind," we see now, means not only "terrible to think of," but the day when our mind triumphs over flesh entirely.

The fifth stanza suddenly drops back several notches of emotion. The word *draftsman* is quite different from those used so far in the poem; it is more familiar, more technical, more specific, closer to everyday experience, and "coat on a nail" reinforces this homey tone. We should relax for a moment with that line, but "steel-beaked" in the next line sounds sinister, and, though a draftsman's compass has a "thumb-screw," that term should recall a device of torture. Innocent ink in the next line becomes "the last black drop," suggesting the last drop of blood, and the significance of this relaxation to a conversational level now should be clear. The innocent act of the technician in a complex, interlocking, impersonal civilization may, with no one's knowledge, be the final detail in the blueprint of disaster, as a sailor punches a button in the belly of a battleship, firing a gun on deck which destroys a plane in the air, a plane the "gunner" never saw. Another function of the draftsman image is to imply a fellow like you or me; and this is picked up by "bestial hand, like mine" which in its hairy-fisted way turns some scientific knob, and bang: truth is horribly, inevitably upon us. The last stanza employs closed lines, complete (that is) in themselves, describing the results 1, 2, 3, 4, recapitulating the themes, symbols, and ironies established earlier in the poem. The rhyme pattern which has been trying to assert itself in the other stanzas materializes here, and the assertive, final lines work against the question-mark; is there, at this point, any question at all?

Most poets, I think, do not dedicate themselves to programs but to themes; they come back to the same problems or questions again and again from all different angles. The theme of this poem, the antagonism between reason and feeling, is common to hundreds of poems, including many of my own. But now I would like to contrast that poem with a later, very different one, also mine, also about the bomb.

GRANDSONS OF GRENDEL

Older than English: how evil emerges
on a moor in the moonlight, emotionless, faceless,
stiff-kneed, arms rigid, and stalks through the fog field
until finally its fist falls, forcing the oaken door
of whatever Heorot harbors the gentlefolk.
In movies, a scientist, satanic with a spark gap,
his power and intentions plainly dishonorable,
releases a monster with electronic instincts:
Hollywood's pronouncement on the nature of evil.
Whom shall we send for? How shall we meet it?

In dark times when warriors wassailed one another,
banged cups in the meadhall, then crumpled like heroes
till Grendel (they called it) gobbled them, unwashed,
they stared in the daylight, dumbstruck, religious,
their hall all a shambles, their heads hurting,
and easily believed an evil wyrd
(generated in a fen not far from Heorot)
molested mankind. Such mornings we all have.

A blond boy, traveller, Beowulf, bear-boy,
sparing of word-hoard, spunky at swimming,
arrived like justice (riding Old Paint),
had to be wakened to harry the hairy one,
grappled in darkness, grunted and clung
and unstrung the monster, as one masters a toy
by mangling the machinery. Men of the warrior breed
approach the irrational rippling their muscles,
relying on wrestling to reckon with angels.

Grendel in our time goes by a new name:
Old Mushroom Head, the Mighty Bomb,
nightly distilled from seeping chemicals
in coils of our brain-bed, composite monster
fashioned of guilt and our most fearful urges.
Blame it on physics; feign that evil
is external, inhuman! We turn to our warriors,
hating all Science, harboring our mead-dreams,
hating intelligence, terrorized by instinct.

Send me no bear-boys when the brute crashes oak doors.
Although he goes howling, holding the socket,
bleeding and armless, back to his mother,
Grendel returns, trailing our fear-scent.
As the movies will tell us, tatters of bullets
rip Grendel's chest as rain rips a snowbank,
yet he comes plodding, impassive, stiff-necked . . . .
We are his Mother, his mate and his offspring.

                                    (*The Humanist,* No. 6, 1958)

　　Still there is a monster approaching with steady step; but now
it is unreason, and the poem appeals for enlightenment to save us.
Grandel, our Frankenstein's monster, is an imaginary creature,
really; we make up such horror to pretend that evil is outside us,
whereas actually, the poem says, it is within us, our guilt and most
fearful urges.

　　This poem begins with an image of horror comparable to the
molten lead; but here I am making fun of the horror. The alliterative structure of the verse (imitating the Anglo-Saxon pattern)
emphasizes the slightly satirical intention. Throughout, the language
is much nearer conversation. No prophecy, no vision. There is

less use of paradox, of symbol. The meaning is on the surface. I mean what I say. The poem uses humor, contemporary reference, is more relaxed, and, I think, more earnest. I don't want to astonish you in this poem. I want to tell you something, and I want very much for you to understand me. The poem is didactic. I hope it amuses and interests you along with the preaching, but the chief end is to make a point. In writing it, I was not in rivalry with madmen. It tries to examine and understand the subconscious, not merely submit to it. It regards the primitive as primitive. I think it moves in the direction of civilization rather than against it. It may not do this well, but it does it deliberately, consciously. It is premeditated: an effort to apply my best skill and knowledge to a task in a professional way, to manufacture a product which will be useful and applicable to human life. If Plato is right, this poem is moving away from rather than toward art.

I can't imagine that Chaucer or Shakespeare or Milton or Dryden could have afforded to have what is called artistic sensibility. They were busy turning out useful products for which, like professionals, they were sometimes hired. They could tell a story you wouldn't mind reading, or damn or praise or comfort or unsettle or advance ideas or defend values. They learned their craft and worried less, I think, about their integrity as artists than about the integrity of their products; if the damned thing won't hold together it won't sell.

Now, of course, craft isn't ever everything. There are differences among people. Shakespeare had something I haven't got. Whatever it was, I suspect it was more nearly intelligence than madness. He was smarter than I am, and worked harder than I do. How much easier would it be for my ego to pretend that he was more inspired.

amateur, tradesman, professional

I have talked about three kinds of poets — amateurs, hacks (or, more kindly, tradesmen), and professionals. All, of course, start as amateurs — but some aspire to no other status and, in fact, associate their integrity with their freedom from the contamination of trade or the profession. Many amateurs publish — in newspapers, organizational publications, or in the many little magazines sponsored by "poetry lovers," appearing and disappearing like seasonal flowers. If they decide to go into the trade or the profession (and there is a distinct difference), they begin to seek remuneration or honor in ways that are fairly clearly established.

There is little help or guidance one can give an amateur, since his own satisfaction with his work is the only relevant criterion of judgment. If a poet wants to go into the trade, there is much material available about writing light verse, greeting-card verse, and other verse for remunerative markets. The only relevant criterion here is whether — and how much — it pays. This book may interest all three, but I assume that the reader's primary concern is with the profession. Professional poets publish in the quarterlies and periodicals read by literary intellectuals, bring out books which will be reviewed in those periodicals, seek recognition by other professionals — and by the reading public — e.g., through the medium of anthologies. To put it operationally, a professional might aspire to be represented in the next edition of *Modern American Poetry* or a comparable collection which seeks to sift out the poets who will make up the literary canon in years to come.

I do not mean to imply that the professional route is the only valid one; it simply has a different destination from the other routes. One cannot make a living from it, for the most part. Professional poets survive not on the basis of direct sale of their work, but on the tangential support which accrues as their reputation develops. *Poetry,* one of the rather official organs of the profession, pays $.50 a line (e.g., $7 a sonnet). A poem in *Saturday Review/World* or *Harper's* may draw anywhere from $25 to $75. A professional poet might hope to appear half a dozen times a year in such periodicals — and most of the quarterlies and literary magazines pay less, sometimes nothing at all. If a poem is picked up by an anthology, the poet may reap another $10-$50 as a permission fee. If a major publisher brings out a book (professionals tend to publish a book about every five years), the poet may get an advance — say $500. But he is unlikely to get any royalties, as few poetry books sell enough copies to make up the advance. On the other hand, his publications may bring him grants (e.g., a Guggenheim award, enabling him to live for a year), may bring him advancement in a professorial job, may bring him reading engagements (e.g., at $200 or more per performance). Most poets write prose as well — e.g., criticism, personal essays, fiction — which brings them more than their poetry, but it may be their stature as a poet which brings good prices for their prose. Many of them today are or have been, in one way or another, professors; the academy thus supports creative work in the way the Church supported creative monks in the Middle Ages. I do not pretend that this is how it ought to be; I am telling you how it is. If you are thinking of becoming a professional, that is what you will be getting into.

And, of course, the profession is riddled with corruption. Because the number of poets who are more-or-less "recognized" at any given time — be they Gary Snyder, Allen Ginsberg, Howard Nemerov, or Denise Levertov — is very small (perhaps a hundred in the United States might claim that status today), they tend to know one another and to favor one another, to prejudge one another, to give their critical attention — which helps, even when abusive — to one another. Thus, whether they like the idea or not, they constitute an informal Establishment. It is their opinions which are sought when awards are given, books are published, appointments are made. A good example of how the profession operates is an issue of *The Beloit Poetry Journal* devoted to "Discoveries," published under a matching grant from the Wisconsin Arts Foundation and Council. The editors explain, "we wrote to 40 poets who, in a sense, were our own past Discoveries — at least we published poems of theirs before they achieved reputation. We asked them to recommend to us upcoming poets who in their judgment were worthy of greater recognition than they had yet received." The currency, notice, is "recognition." No one but the printer gets any cash out of this endeavor. Three poets I recommended are included — as well as those recommended by such people as Galway Kinnell, X. J. Kennedy, James Schevill and Charles Philbrick. The three I recommended were young people I met at Bread Loaf Writer's Conference — knew as persons first, as poets second. My recommendations were, as I am sure all the recommendations were, conscientious: I truly respect the work of these poets and believe they deserve more prominence. But you can see that the profession is somewhat ingrown — and it is natural in such a cultural situation that politics would have as large a part as merit in determining advancement.

I am sure the same conditions exist in professional music, art, theater — and, indeed, in professional medicine, law, teaching and the ministry. But where the numbers are smaller, as in poetry, the effects of personal relationships are likely to be more intense — and more bitterly resented by those who are not "in." In a gathering of poets there is likely to be enough buttering up and putting down, jockeying and back-stabbing to make the National Association of Manufacturers seem a convocation of saints.

Nor does the Establishment do its job really well — i.e., the job of selecting and promoting poetry of enduring merit. The world of poetry is very nearly as subject to fads as the world of fashion. For example, the favorite critical term, I understand, at the Iowa Poetry Workshop — a kind of West Point of the Establishment, was, for a period, "strange." There was a wave of poetry in the mails and in the magazines which sought to evoke wonder, a sense of the uncanny, the incongruous, the surrealistic; and all poets who do that sort of thing well (e.g., Mark Strand, Louis Simpson) advanced two spaces, while others rapidly retooled their imaginations to fit the fashion. Robert Lowell published a couple of poems which quite literally, simply and painfully recounted his experiences in civil rights demonstrations, and poets began muttering that "statement" is "in," that social consciousness is "in," and some painted signs and set out marching. I may be exaggerating, but it would be foolish to contend that we base all our judgments on the immutable standards of excellence we expound. All of us use language like this, from that same *Beloit Poetry Journal:* "As far as we're concerned, it is the function of a little poetry magazine to print good poetry and to discover new poets. In our daily mail we look exclusively for good poems," but that word *good,* which appears to come from Plato's Heaven of Absolutes, is likely to refer, in practice, to what is fashionable or what is recommended by those one recognizes as having made it.

All these disclaimers are intended to help you feel better if you do not really care to join the professional rat race. If that is the sort of thing you like — or can tolerate along with your private search for excellence — the professional route may interest you. But I would not be surprised if many find it too repugnant to undertake it.   ,

I know very little about that kind of poetry (or, as it is usually called, verse) produced in what I call "the trade." My attitude is not one of contempt: it is simply a field which does not interest me much. I should think it would hardly be worth taking up unless one could expect regular sales at, say, $5 a line or more. (Compare that with *Poetry's* $.50 a line.) I gather that much greeting-card verse is written in the office, by people on salary — a kind of security unknown in the profession. Most of the magazine verse which pays well is "light verse," though serious verse is sometimes used as well. And there is not always a clear distinction. I have sold one poem to *Mademoiselle* for $5 a line, another to *Ladies' Home Journal* for $10 a line, and these were poems I am happy to keep and use in a book, poems which might just as well have been published in a quarterly for $5 a page. I would have no shame in selling all my poems for $10 a line, but few of them are acceptable in the verse market — and rather than change my style in poetry, I'd rather put up with the indirections and collusions of the professional game, earning my living in other ways. The "trade" is to the "profession" as "commercial art" is to "fine art," or as "pop" music is to "classical." In all these areas, the lines are blurred; high quality is possible in each; sometimes the same practitioners produce both. But the aims are quite distinct. Verse writers are often talented verbal craftsmen — often better craftsmen than are the professional poets. But they have little interest in getting their names on the library shelves alongside Keats and Chaucer.

CHAPTER TWO

The Vanity of Print

Let me draw a picture which many a young man and woman, and some no longer young, will recognize as the story of their own experience.

He is sitting alone with his own thoughts and memories. What is that book he is holding? Something precious, evidently, for it is bound in "tree calf," and there is gilding enough about it for a birthday present. The reader seems to be deeply absorbed in its contents, and at times greatly excited by what he reads; for his face is flushed, his eyes glitter, and — there rolls a large tear down his cheek. Listen to him; he is reading aloud in impassioned tones:

> And have I coined my soul in words for naught?
> And must I, with the dim forgotten throng
> Of silent ghosts that left no early trace
> To show they once had breathed this vital air,
> Die out of mortal memories?

His voice is choked by his emotion. "How is it possible," he says to himself, "that anyone can read my 'Gaspings for Immortality' without being impressed by their freshness, their passion, their beauty, their originality?" Tears come to his relief freely, — so freely that he has to push the precious volume out of the range of their blistering shower. Six years ago "Gaspings for Immortality" was published, advertised, praised by the professionals whose business it is to *boost* their publishers' authors. A week and more it was seen on the counters of the booksellers and at the stalls in the railroad stations. Then it disappeared from public view. A few copies still kept their place on the shelves of friends, presentation copies, of course, as there is no evidence that any were disposed of by sale; and now, one might well ask for the lost books of Livy as inquire at a bookstore for "Gaspings for Immortality."

All you have read in this chapter so far is quoted word-for-word from Oliver Wendell Holmes' *Cacoethes Scribendi,* written some hundred years ago. As I read it, my first laugh was at the poets who, today as a century ago, pour their hearts into pamphlets and are astonished that the world takes little note, nor long remembers. My second laugh was at myself, for Holmes might, indeed, have written this book for me, so little has the poetic situation changed. If it is vain to write poetry, have it printed, send it to critics, it is equally vain to rail against the human habit. Holmes says:

> For the last thirty years I have been in the habit of receiving a volume of poems or a poem, printed or manuscript — I will not say daily, though I sometimes receive more than one in a day, but at very short intervals. I have been consulted by hundreds of writers of verse as to the merits of their performances, and have often advised the writers to the best of my ability. Of late I have found it impossible to attempt to read critically all the literary productions, in verse and in prose, which have heaped themselves on every exposed surface of my library, like snowdrifts along the railroad tracks, — blocking my literary pathway, so that I can hardly find my daily papers.
>
> What is the meaning of this rush into rhyming of such a multitude of people, of all ages, from the infant phenomenon to the oldest inhabitant?

Hello, Oliver! I shout through the catacombs of the years. It is much the same now — as it was for Horace and Catullus, as it was for Pope:

> Shut, shut the door, good *John!* fatigu'd, I said;
> Tye up the knocker! say I'm sick, I'm dead.
> The Dog-star rages! nay, 'tis past a doubt,
> All Bedlam, or Parnassus, is let out:
> Fire in each eye, and papers in each hand,
> They rave, recite, and madden round the land.
> What walls can guard me, or what shades can hide?
> They pierce my thickets, thro' my Grot they glide,
> By land, by water, they renew the charge,
> They stop the chariot, and they board the Barge.

No place is sacred, not the Church is free,
Ev'n Sunday shines no Sabbath-day to me:
Then from the Mint walks forth the Man of rhyme,
Happy! to catch me just at Dinner-time.
   Is there a Parson much be-mused in beer,
A maudlin Poetess, a rhyming Peer,
A Clerk, foredoom'd his father's soul to cross,
Who pens a Stanza, when he should *engross?*
Is there, who, lock'd from ink and paper, scrawls
With desp'rate charcoal round his darken'd walls?
All fly to *Twit'nam,* and in humble strain
Apply to me, to keep them mad or vain.
Arthur, whose giddy Son neglects the Laws,
Imputes to me and my damn'd works the cause:
Poor Cornus sees his frantic wife elope,
   And curses Wit, and Poetry, and Pope.

It would be funnier if it weren't so true. At two in the morning, when I was out of town, an angry husband called my wife to find out where I was. His wife had disappeared, and he thought I might know something about it. The extent of my contact with that woman had been when she called me on the telephone some weeks before to ask me to read her novel based on her adventures as a male-impersonator on a battleship — and I had refused. The literary life is full of strange hazards.

When I was a professor, I posted on my office door this motto from Pope (taken, as was the last quotation, from his "Epistle to Dr. Arbuthnot"):

Seiz'd and ty'd down to judge, how wretched I!
Who can't be silent, and who will not lye;
To laugh, were want of goodness and of grace,
And to be grave, exceeds all Pow'r of face.
I sit with sad Civility, I read
With honest anguish, and an aching head;
And drop at last, but in unwilling ears,
This saving counsel, "Keep your piece nine years."

I took it down after awhile because it seemed unkind — and because, as a teacher, I had no right to abuse those whom I invite to come to me for criticism.

I am not complaining about students and magazine contributors, however; one asks for what one gets in those quarters. But how should I have reacted to this conversation, back in the days when I was poetry editor for the *Antioch Review?* I was sitting in my study, work in my typewriter, people gathered for a meeting, when a young man called from a distant city.

"I wonder if I could have your opinion of my poetry?" he asks.

"Have I seen it?"

"No, I haven't sent it to you. I was wondering what you would say."

"Well, I can't say anything without seeing it."

"I don't have but one copy. Will you return it?"

"Do you mean to submit it to the *Antioch Review?*"

"What's the *Antioch Review?*"

"That's a magazine. I'm the poetry editor."

"But I'm not sure whether my poetry is good enough to be published."

I am twisting on my chair, smiling and shrugging at the people in the office.

"Why did you call me?"

"A friend told me you read people's poetry."

"I read quite a lot of poetry, but I'm not in the business . . ."

"But I heard you do sometimes tell people what you think of their work."

"Sometimes I comment on work submitted to the *Antioch Review,* if I think it is particularly promising and I would like the poet to send more or to revise."

"Will you criticize mine?"

"If you submit it in the usual way, with a self-addressed, stamped envelope, and if it seems close to being publishable . . ."

"But I just want to know what you think . . ."

I am abbreviating this conversation which, literally, went on for twenty minutes, long-distance. Among other things the poet told me he didn't have any money so could not afford to have his work typed.

On another occasion I received a packet of poems, addressed to me personally, with this note: "Please publish these poems. I am not enclosing a return envelope because I am running away from home and will not have any address. But I'll look you up in Cincinnati and collect the money for the poems in person." Luck had it that I was nowhere near Cincinnati.

Nor am I, any longer, poetry editor for the *Antioch Review.* After finding that I was destroying friendships with poets by reviewing their work, I have resolved to do no more book reviewing.

I am trying to discipline myself to make no comments whatsoever on most work sent me or handed me. I insist that it be a professional relationship. Just as it would be ridiculous for a doctor, whom you pay for advice, to spare your feelings and be falsely encouraging or deceptively genial, it would be a waste of your time and mine for me to coddle you when you seek professional advice.

What does "professional advice" mean in regard to poetry? In my view it is an experienced judgment as to whether the work in question is likely to be accepted for publication in a quality periodical or by a reputable publisher, and, if not, why not. It includes saying what, if anything, could be done to the work to increase its chances of acceptance. This has, notice, very little to do with whether I, personally, "like" the poetry. Much is published which I dislike intensely. Nor has it much to do with whether the poet has "expressed" himself or said what he really wanted to say. That is a matter for the poet himself to judge. Nor does such professional advice attempt to determine whether the poetry is "good" for the ages, regardless of the fashions of the current publishing scene. If I were to encounter a poem in manuscript — my own or someone else's — which I thought might take a place on the immortal bookshelf alongside work by Shakespeare and Donne and Milton and Pope and Keats and Browning and Yeats and Frost, I would undoubtedly say so, before fainting. But I have never had that experience.

Oliver Wendell Holmes reminds me:

> The authors of these poems are all around us, men and women, and no one with a fair amount of human sympathy in his disposition would treat them otherwise than tenderly. Perhaps they do not need tender treatment. How do you know that posterity may not resuscitate these seemingly dead poems, and give their author the immortality for which he longed and labored? It is not every poet who is at once appreciated. Some will tell you that the best poets never are. Who can say that you, dear unappreciated brother or sister, are not one of those whom it is left for after times to discover among the wrecks of the past, and hold up to the admiration of the world?

What will be, will be. I doubt that I, personally, can extinguish

any truly immortal flame. I can't even put out a grass fire. Pope
wrote:

> Who shames a Scribler? break one cobweb thro',
> He spins the slight, self-pleasing thread anew:
> Destroy his fib or sophistry, in vain,
> The creature's at his dirty work again,
> Thron'd in the centre of his thin designs,
> Proud of a vast extent of flimzy lines!
> Whom have I hurt? has Poet yet, or Peer,
> Lost the arch'd eye-brow, or Parnassian sneer?

One of the things talented poets and, as Pope calls them,
scribblers have in common — which makes them hard to distinguish — is an irrespressible, stubborn, almost desperate will to
write. Poetry is such an unlikely way to gain fame or fortune or
any external and practical award that those who go into it at all
are beyond ordinary forms of dissuasion. I do not say this cynically:
it is testimony to the deep-rootedness of our need that we write
poetry at all; and I believe that bad and good poetry have the same
mysterious and powerful source. We draw, in fact, on the deepest
spring of all — the instinct for survival. Recognizing the futility of
most means of escaping death, we try to embody our most intimate
and valuable and essential self in language, to shape that language
to endure beyond our physical selves. The scribbler spinning his
web and fevered Keats on his death bed are similarly driven to record
themselves in shapely phrases, steadier than the inconstant heart
which gave them birth.

enter the critic

Who needs him? Most of us who write have less desire to be
instructed than to be recognized. I still, myself, fall into the trap
and delusion of asking people for their opinion of my work. I set
my face in a studious, receptive way and listen. I pretend I am
asking for help. But the only opinion I am listening for is one
or another form of Wow! If a poem "works" for a reader, I am
acknowledged — and get a brief bath of celebration. If it does not,
no amount of fiddling or explaining or justifying is likely to make
it work. I may go back to the study to write another poem or start

again — or I may wait for another reader, more able to respond to what I have done. But detailed "criticism" is usually beside the point: it only says, repeatedly, this didn't work for this reader. Cutting and pasting won't help.

I realize that this confession contradicts the dogma of writing teachers. In a sense criticism and revision are always helpful, and, certainly, most good poets revise many times. But the best criticism always comes from oneself. The scribbler is likely to be so carried away in admiration of the phenomenon of his creativity that he is unable to act as critic for himself. But the criticism of others won't reach him either. The good poet learns a lot from general discussions of poetry, and "workshop" discussions of specific poems may help sensitize him to problems in his own work. But he is not likely to make a good poem out of a bad one by changing words and correcting weaknesses critics perceive. After all discussion is over, he will have to start with himself again, start from scratch, come up with something new in hopes that *it* will shimmer in wholeness.

(The opposite, in my experience, is true of prose. Detailed criticism and discussion can often help a writer redeem a poor piece with a good idea behind it. But in a poem the conception and performance must be so totally of a piece that this whole process is much less helpful.)

All of which is to say that when people ask for criticism of their poetry they very often are asking for something else entirely, such as personal attention, affection, respect — and the poem is a kind of token to sanctify and neutralize the request. The poets who clamor for commentary probably do not understand their own needs very well. If they get the kind of professional criticism they seem to be requesting, they are only hurt and indignant, as one would be who offered a kiss and received a critical analysis of the way he puckered.

For example, a woman shyly hands me a manuscript, saying, "I don't know if it's poetry or not":

> 'Twas like the dawn,
> Meeting you.
> The night had been dark and chill
> And lonely.
> Though I could not say it
> Except with my eyes,
> For others were there and the rules dictate
> That girls upon men's will must wait,

I felt the warming rays
And clarity of vision
And communication with another
Which brought the joyful thought:
'Twas like the dawn.

Well, if it isn't poetry, most of what people write as poetry is not poetry. One could quibble about definitions forever and never get around to discussing what matters, the human significance and quality of the words on the page. When she asks me if it is poetry I think she is really asking for something other than a classification. Suppose I answer *yes*. Suppose I answer *no*. What will I have told her? What does she really want to know?

Though I have just met the woman, I make some guesses about her. This writing is not fiction. Probably she recently met some fellow and had an instantaneous sense of awakening, of joy, hope and expectation. She couldn't let on. Others were around, as the poem says. Moreover she had been conditioned to accept a woman's passive role. All she could do was hope he noticed the sparkle in her eye and that he would take some initiative. I would further speculate that he did take that initiative. They must have begun dating, perhaps became lovers. At some point she felt that it was important to write something down on paper about what had happened. Subsequent experience had verified something about that first instant of her meeting. She had been right in her intuition. It *was* a kind of dawn.

My guess is that she has given the poem to him as a way of saying that their relationship is special. And I would bet that he got the message. He thought "She cares. She went to a lot of trouble to write this. And there must be something special about me, or magical about our coming together, if she had these feelings at the very first moment of our meeting. Something was going on behind that passive face."

If the poem did all that, it must be a good poem. It served an important function for her and for him. It may have provided a little glue (if not cement) for a rewarding relationship. It brought greater clarity and warmth to a pair of human beings. Why demand anything more of it?

Why bring it to a third party, a stranger, and ask if it is poetry? I once thought she wants to know whether there is any chance of publishing the poem, as in a magazine. Perhaps she wants to know whether she should spend more time writing poetry — completely aside from her relationship with the young man. She may wonder whether critics would notice her, whether she might publish a book or books of poetry, be represented in anthologies, become a part of literature.

That is too much freight for the poem to bear. I would point out the virtues of the poem. First of all, it has a neat design. The central image is carried through consistently. The three qualities of the night — dark, chill, loneliness — are matched by three qualities of the dawn — warmth, clarity, communication. The poem is direct and evidently sincere. The rhymed couplet in the middle approaches wittiness.

On the other hand the poem has certain defects — and these are more difficult to describe, but immensely more important in determining whether, for instance, the poem stands a chance of publication and whether the poet stands a chance of a professional career in this realm of literature. The defects are difficult to describe in the same way that it is difficult to tell a person that he is uninteresting. He may not do anything particularly wrong. But he is just dull. Somehow he doesn't matter — at least to you. How can you tell him that? While this poem can be tremendously meaningful and even exciting as communication between two people, the odds are that it will not much interest a wider audience at all.

Why? I can point to some specifics, but I am not sure that, in sum total, they answer that question. For example almost any poem which uses a contrast between night and dawn as its central metaphor is doomed. The idea is simply too easy, too often used. (But, one may object, if it is used that often, it must have some universal appeal!) The poem is too prosy: it just says plainly what it means. (But, says the objector, you just called its directness and sincerity virtues.) Archaic devices such as " 'Twas" and the inversion in the eighth line (that is, use of an unidiomatic word order to make the rhyme come out) mark the poem as amateurish. It is extremely difficult to make abstractions such as "clarity" and "communication" work in a poem. The cleverness of the couplet is, in the first place, not all that clever, and, in the second, is out of keeping with the tone of the rest of the poem. Nothing interesting is done with rhythm, with line division, with imagery. The basic idea is commonplace.

But what do these criticisms mean in regard to the question asked? Each criterion can be argued: a case can be made for plainness, for mixed tonality, for dwelling on the commonplace, etc.

But arguing over such details is beside the point. Just as you can't argue a person into liking you by justifying the length of your nose or your lack of humor or your paunch, you can't save a poem by defending its parts. If it doesn't work, it doesn't work. This poem probably worked for its one-man intended audience. It doesn't work for me, and I would guess it would not work for most readers, who would find it pleasant, inoffensive, but not memorable. I would guess it would not work for most editors who simply have too many poems on their desk, competing for the same space, which have more sparkle, profundity, individual style, which are more moving or amusing or just plain more interesting.

For years I responded very stupidly to such questions as this woman raised. I tried to advise such people as though they had intentions of revising the poem or writing other poems for the market. That is not only hopeless, but is very punishing for the person who has to sit and listen to herself being measured against Sylvia Plath or Edna St. Vincent Millay or Emily Dickinson. For the truth is — though she would never say this nor can one say it to her — she has no serious intention of writing poetry which can be evaluated as literature or even for publication.

An easy dodge is to say she has no talent. I don't believe that. Does she have talent as a thief, as a whore, as a welder? She could probably do very well at all those vocations, and at being a poet, too, if she really wanted to; but she doesn't. Consequently the advice I might give her about becoming a better poet would fall on deaf ears.

But somehow it is easier for a woman to admit that she has no serious intention of becoming a thief, whore or welder than that she has no serious intention of becoming a poet. This woman was using poetry as a means of reaching or searching for something else, something which is difficult for her to understand or name.

She gives us the clue in the poem when she says that "rules dictate/That girls upon men's will must wait." What she seeks is love, recognition, approval — not of her poetry but of herself. But the rules of society have made it necessary for her to be devious. This is true not only for girls. I have learned that society often disapproves of direct expression of needs and desires. I cannot get what I want by asking, by being honest. It is very difficult even to be honest with myself about my needs. The needs and desires are real and powerful, however, and I engage in all variety of games to achieve them.

So I do not blame her for asking me if her poem is really poetry.

She is not a fool. She is not dishonest — except in the way most of us are dishonest, inescapably. Nor do I want to hurt her. I especially do not want to score some mythical points in some mythical game by demonstrating to her my superior knowledge of poetry.

What *do* I say to her, however? (For she will come; she will come again; they come to me in droves with such poems and such confusions.) What I can do is accept the token for what it is — a way of gaining entry. Yes, I know what it feels like to want to write a poem about what you are feeling. I know how good it feels to give expression some form, some dignity, some beauty. I know how language itself is beguiling, and how one is drawn on and satisfied by the exercise of imagination. I know how art can be a way of storing up something of semi-permanence against the transient and ephemeral quality of life and, especially, tender relationships. I know what it feels like to want to be respected by others, even strangers, even poet-critic-writer-professor types like myself. I know especially how frustrating it is to know that "rules dictate" that we not speak out what we are and what we feel. I know the little spurt of satisfaction that comes of making that rhyme, awkward as it may be. I say these things honestly — not because I know they are what she wants to hear, but because I identify with her and believe that such mutual affirmation is the most important thing we can do for one another.

But if she wants my severity, she should come again and give me the freedom to exercise it. Real artists, real poets, are not hurt by negative criticism; they learn how to ignore what is irrelevant to their vision, what is superficial and merely mean, and to hear that which will help them do better work. The need for survival teaches them these listening skills. Especially, they do not need to ask whether what they write is poetry. It is what it is. It is what it has to be. That is not to say it cannot be improved. The comments of others who understand the basic vision and who share a love of fine craft and profound poetry can be especially helpful. But the one thing they know as surely as they know their own hunger is that what they are doing is essentially necessary and right, whether one chooses to call it poetry or not.

Most pathetic are those so deeply confused that they pay to have a collection of their poems printed. I receive, weekly, three or four such collections, usually in pamphlet format, usually inscribed somewhat as follows: "Dear Dr. Judson, I have long admired your column and hope these modest efforts bring some joy into your life."

I wish I could say my heart was big enough to be moved, my leisure sufficient to enable me to respond to such gaspings for immortality. I wish I even had bookcase space to store them, but, alas, I can only drop them in the wastebasket. It is expensive and sad.

And the view it evokes of the human condition is sadder still. Who *are* these poets? I wrote a poem about them:

POETRY EDITOR AS MISS LONELYHEARTS

Round the horizon I see silhouettes
of sweet old ladies who live with their pets,
parents neglected by their children, scholars
bullied by schoolmates, men in starchy collars
whose daily wisdom always falls among swine,

girls who read on Saturday night, fine wine
merchants, inmates, shut-ins, neglected wives.
Love is a seller's market. Hope arrives
in bundles on my desk, those poems blest
with kisses, tears, stamped envelopes — self-addressed.

Is there not love enough in the world to go around? Have we not succor more sustaining than the printing press for people gasping in their loneliness?

the publisher's role

On the other hand, a poet seriously seeking to enter the profession cannot expect compassion, love, or even much understanding. Editors are not likely to finish a manuscript — or even a single poem — which begins badly. As John Ciardi has said, if a performer plays half a dozen bars badly on the piano, you don't have to listen to a whole recital in order to know what to expect of him. Often an editor judges from the first line whether to read another — thinking that a poet who turns out one monstrosity is not likely to produce a publishable poem.

For example, a rather curious collection of poems begins with a line which might cause any professional editor to reject the whole packet without further consideration: "From fairest creatures we

desire increase." The language is abstract, colorless. The stance
seems a trifle pompous — telling us what "we" desire. But I am
put off most by the imprecision of that word *increase*. He means
something like *abundance, progeny, reproduction,* I gather, and
increase is simply a vague stab in the general direction. He goes on:

> From fairest creatures we desire increase,
> That thereby beauty's rose might never die,
> But as the riper should by time decrease,
> His tender heir might bear his memory:

The rhymes are abominable: *die-memory* is called an eye-rhyme,
which only serves to bring attention to the dissimilarity in the sounds
of the words; but *increase-decrease,* an identical rhyme, is much
worse. The sure sign of an untalented poetaster is the rhyming of
words differing only in unstressed prefixes, such as *enable-unable-
able, light-delight, inform-uniform-reform,* etc.

Notice the grammatical imprecision of "beauty's rose." He might
mean that the beauty of the rose might never die, or that the beautiful
rose might never die; but it does not make sense to say that the
rose belongs to beauty. There is similar awkwardness in the use of
riper to mean an old, or aging rose. *Decrease,* an odd word for
wither or *fade,* seems to be used only for the sake of that bad
rhyme. Everything — grammar, diction, rhyming, imagery — seems
wrenched, strained, artificial. We know at once the poet is an
amateur — and not likely at this stage of his career to produce
a publishable poem.

The complete poem is a sonnet. The next quatrain is this:

> But thou, contracted to thine own bright eyes,
> Feed'st thy light's flame with self-substantial fuel,
> Making a famine where abundance lies,
> Thyself thy foe, to thy sweet self too cruel.

In spite of his use of the archaic second person forms, we can see
that this poet is addicted to many of the worst faults of modern
poetry. First we notice, in the second line above, rough meter combined with heavy *f* alliteration, resulting in a line almost impossible
to pronounce musically. Secondly, as is characteristic of much
modern poetry, there is a bewildering inconsistency of imagery, or
what is commonly called "mixed metaphor." In the first line the
person addressed is engaged (as to be married) to his own eyes.
Ignore for a moment the grotesqueness of that fanciful notion and
look what becomes of it. *Bright* suggests *light,* so now this man
engaged to his eyes is feeding his "light's flame." Compare that

phrase with "beauty's rose," above: does the flame belong to the light, the light to the flame — and what relation has either notion to "bright eyes"? The fuel is "self-substantial" in one line — suggesting that it is inexhaustible; but, no, in the next it is "Making a famine." The first two lines suggest that he is sustaining himself, the next two that he is destroying himself. Fantastic and purely cerebral analogies are piled on one another until they make very little sense at all — and bear almost no relation to concrete, felt human experience.

It would be only fair to show you the conclusion of the poem:
> Thou that art now the world's fresh ornament
> And only herald to the gaudy spring,
> Within thine own bud buriest thy content
> And, tender churl, makest waste in niggarding
>> Pity the world, or else this glutton be,
>> To eat the world's due, by the grave and thee.

The man addressed was formerly a rose; now he is a bud, an early bud of springtime. The poet is telling him to have an heir to carry on his beauty — unlikely advice to a man, or to a rose, but almost ludicrous when addressed to a bud. Notice the confusion in the third line above: *content* seems to mean *contentment,* and the idea of being contented with oneself is mixed up with that of burying one's attention in oneself — which is not a matter of burying contentment. The last line is almost completely obscure — not with the difficulty of concept which sometimes characterizes great poetry, but with sheer ineptitude of phrasing, which characterizes the posturing of an amateur. The final couplet seems to mean, "Either take pity on the world (by perpetuating your beauty in offspring), or you will be the sort of glutton which devours that (your beauty) which belongs to the world. You will devour your beauty until the grave finally devours it." That last idea is not actually expressed in the poem at all; I have generously supplied it as the only conceivable way of making sense of the poem's last phrase.

But the general intent of the poem is clear enough — and it is certainly strange. Moreover, the next sixteen poems in the collection repeat the same message. A male poet is asking a young man to have children so that his beauty can be preserved. It is difficult for any reader to identify with the implied dramatic situation. Before we can care about a poem we must recognize in it some valid, humanly important *raison d'etre.* Seventeen sonnets telling a young friend to have children seem merely impertinent.

No editor is likely to give as much thought and attention to that poem as I have here; it is a clear case of premature submission — and it can do a neophyte more harm than he knows, for an editor just might remember his name the next time a packet of poems comes in, and brush it by hurriedly. In this case, that would be a pity, for I have gone over this collection with some care — and see evidence of what might prove to be considerable talent. Even in those first seventeen poems there are phrases and turns suggesting latent ability. There is, for example, a certain intensity in this poem, gleaming through its crudities:

> When I do count the clock that tells the time,

(I must interrupt to point out that the expletive *do,* simply to fill out meter, is a dead giveaway of the amateur poet.)

> When I do count the clock that tells the time,
> And see the brave day sunk in hideous night;
> When I behold the violet past prime,
> And sable curls all silver'd o'er with white;
> When lofty trees I see barren of leaves
> Which erst from heat did canopy the herd,
> And summer's green all girded up in sheaves
> Borne on the bier with white and bristly beard,
> Then of thy beauty do I question make,
> That thou among the wastes of time must go,
> Since sweets and beauties so themselves forsake
> And die as fast as they see others grow;
> > And nothing 'gainst Time's scythe can make defense
> > Save breed, to brave him when he takes thee hence.

But at critical points the poem simply fails to come across. "Past prime" gives us no vivid image of the wilting violet. *Silver* and *white* either fight each other or are redundant in the fourth line. I like that mid-line trochee, *barren,* in the fifth line — but notice the awkward *did* in the sixth. The image of the frost-covered sheaves of grain in the seventh and eighth lines is the strongest detail in the poem — and a good conclusion for the octave. But how pathetic the poem becomes when it returns to that dreary theme running through these poems — the problem of the survival of the young man's beauty. "Do I question make" is a completely impotent and clumsy phrase for introducing the poet's concern. The sestet limps into an absurd couplet. The enjambment, or runover line, leading to "Save breed" is a powerful device, but it only points up the awkwardness of "breed" used in this sense. An image of screaming youngsters is evoked, hurling taunts at Time as he carries off the young man. The use of *brave* in two senses (in lines two and fourteen) seems to be merely careless, not a meaningful association. And, of course, braving time is not, after all, a defense against his taking one hence; the problem the poem introduces remains unresolved.

Finally the poet gives up on the idea of the young man's immortalizing himself through progeny and decides, rather vaingloriously, that his own poetry will immortalize his friend's beauty. Here is one the *New Yorker* should print with a sarcastic remark about the short time remaining for men to breathe and see:

> Shall I compare thee to a summer's day?
> Thou art more lovely and more temperate:
> Rough winds do shake the darling buds of May,
> And summer's lease hath all too short a date:
> Sometime too hot the eye of heaven shines,
> And often is his gold complexion dimm'd;
> And every fair from fair sometimes declines,
> By chance or nature's changing course untrimm'd;
> But thy eternal summer shall not fade
> Nor lose possession of that fair thou owest;
> Nor shall Death brag thou wander'st in his shade,
> When in eternal lines to time thou growest:
> > So long as men can breathe or eyes can see,
> > So long lives this, and this gives life to thee.

If the young man has to depend upon progeny or such verse as this to make him immortal, he'd better stick to breeding! Such sentimental words as "lovely" and "darling" are the weak efforts of the amateur to make up for lack of craft with feeling and sincerity. "Short a date" is wordy and inexact. The "eye of heaven" for sun is a trite circumlocution. "And every fair from fair" — meaning something like "every fair thing from its state of fairness" — is one of those pieces of cleverness which a good poet learns not to be tempted by. I know what it means to trim a sail, but I cannot imagine what an untrimmed course is. And what does it mean to *grow* to time in eternal lines? "So long lives this"? I wouldn't count on it!

One would gather that this collection, which consists of 154 poems (all of them presumably intended as sonnets, though one has only twelve lines and one is in tetrameter) was written over a period of years. A kind of narrative is implied. The first 126 sonnets appear all to be addressed to this tiresome young man, who emerges as extremely vain, cold and disloyal. It is implied that the poet is a playwright — and is jealous of another poet and/or playwright, who is also writing poetry to the young man. He is also jealous — both ways — of his mistress, who seems to be having an affair with the young man. It is a sordid tale which might make a better novel than material for a sonnet sequence, but our concern is with poetry and the evidence of poetic talent buried in a collection of largely misbegotten poems. There is, indeed, reason to believe that the poet was maturing both as an artist and a man during the period in which the poems were written. The man who wrote the following, for example, may yet develop true poetic craftsmanship:

> When my love swears that she is made of truth
> I do believe her, though I know she lies,
> That she might think me some untutor'd youth,
> Unlearned in the world's false subleties.
> Thus vainly thinking that she thinks me young,
> Although she knows my days are past the best,
> Simply I credit her false-speaking tongue:
> On both sides thus is simple truth suppress'd.
> But wherefore says she not she is unjust?
> And wherefore say not I that I am old?
> O, love's best habit is in seeming trust,
> And age in love loves not to have years told:
> > Therefore I lie with her and she with me,
> > And in our faults by lies we flatter'd be.

The paradoxes are piled skillfully upon one another to create the fabric of deception, self-deception, hypocrisy and disgust climaxed by that grossly simple pun on lie, capturing the pathetic sensual dependency of the lovers upon one another which makes them endure their vain flatteries. Compared with the other sonnets we have looked at, the language here is relatively plain and idiomatic, the diction unadorned but accurate. For me the eye-rhyme of *lies* and *subleties* works effectively, as it draws out the last syllable of the second word in a sinister hiss. The weak phrase, "past the best," seems right to me, also — a kind of frank understatement which disguises as it reveals the poet's melancholy acceptance of his age. "Unjust" is somewhat strained — meaning "disloyal." And the inversions — "says she not" and "say I not" — are rhetorical flourishes which seem slightly out-of-place in the context of the relaxed, natural language of most of the poem. "Habit" — meaning both customary behavior and garment — enriches the implications. And the ingenious "love loves" does not seem mere cleverness; it is saved by its bitter tone. A better poet would try to figure out a way to avoid the final inversion, "flatter'd be," which is even ungrammatical (it should be "flatter'd are"). But the defects are minor in a poem which brilliantly illluminates the poignancy and *Weltschmerz* of illicit love. The word *love* of the first and eleventh lines rings hollowly. *Think, thinking* and *thinks* bang against one another with a sickening echo reminiscent of *Othello:*

Othello. What dost thou think?

Iago.   Think, my lord!

Othello. Think, my lord! By Heaven, he echoes me

    As if there were some monster in his thought

    Too hideous to be shown. Thou dost mean something.

Simply and *simple* play against one another, glimpses of the innocence which lies beyond the web and can only be feigned in its trammels. Were this poem to come to me in an envelope, unencumbered by the lumbering efforts which surround it in this collection, I would probably write the author encouragingly and suggest that with a few revisions it might be published.

Imagine my surprise, then, to discover that not only this poem, but the entire collection, had been published in 1609 (which, at least, explained the poet's fondness for archaic forms). We have learned a great deal about poetry in the intervening years, and taste has been considerably refined. Perhaps, too, less poetry was written in those days; publishers may have been forced by shortage to use material they would not consider today.

But that does not explain what I further learned — that this collection of poems has been the subject of more critical discussion than any single literary work, with the possible exception of *Hamlet*. It has been called not only the finest sonnet sequence in English, but the finest collection of lyric poems in any language. Such a thought is staggering when we stop to realize what monumental literary achievements will be forthcoming in the future, now that enlightened critical standards are being exercised.

CHAPTER THREE

Some Autobiographical Notes

the search for form and meaning

One of those questions which keeps coming up in the awkward "discussion periods" after readings — such as, "Do you type or write your manuscripts in long hand?" or "Do you keep a regular writing schedule?" — is, "How did you get started writing poetry?" I've thought about this — and the answer may contain points with which others can identify.

Both my grandfather and father were amateur poets; my grandfather had a collection of poems about his family privately printed in a soft, imitation leather binding, and a number of my father's poems were printed in Oklahoma newspapers. Both were rough, masculine men with streaks of tenderness and weakness which caused both to drink too much and also to write poetry. Most of what my father wrote was dialect verse, influenced by James Whitcomb Riley and Edgar Guest; it was humorous, vivid, and technically competent. It was not unusual for him to come home from work excited, with a new manuscript in his hand — and that sand-colored volume of my grandfather's was always around the house, a reminder that real men wrote poems about the people and things they cared about.

My aunts on my father's side — three young women during my formative years — loved to read poetry to me and to persuade me to memorize it. I remember especially Poe's *The Raven,* another soft leather pamphlet around the house, with eerie illustrations. My aunts read it aloud to me with ghostly drama in their voices. Riley's "The Raggedy Man" and "Little Orphant Annie," Field's "Wynken, Blynken, and Nod," "Little Boy Blue," and, especially, "Jest 'Fore

Christmas," and most of Stevenson's *A Child's Garden of Verses*
were deeply implanted in my mind at an early age — along with,
of course, the Mother Goose rhymes and other familiar, anonymous
verses that are part of the culture of childhood. As I remember,
relatives were always asking me to recite poetry — so I must have
come early to associate it with attention and applause.

Those memories of pleasant associations with poetry end about
the time I began school — except for the continued influence of
my father. Some little poems I wrote during my first years in school
turned up in my papers — very conventional, rhymed, sentimental
poems, but I remember almost nothing pertaining to poetry which
stirred my imagination or deepened my commitment. Our school
system seems designed to curtail and stifle individuality and creativity.
I attended various elementary schools in Tulsa and Oklahoma City
and Houston and grew increasingly alienated from poetry, literature
and reading itself, although I remember the delicious reading of
summer vacations — time stolen from the system — when with
almost the excitement of crime I wallowed through such fat novels
as *Ben Hur* and *A Tale of Two Cities*. In high school in Houston
I began writing stories and developed an interest in journalism,
putting out a little neighborhood newspaper in summer months. If
I read poetry at all it was in the context of grinding out assignments
for effusive lady teachers who tried to persuade us of the morals
poetry contained and seemed oblivious to its power and beauty.

As a freshman at the University of Oklahoma, sixteen years
old, something again awakened my interest in poetry. I wrote one
little poem and submitted it to a poetry magazine called *Red
Earth* — and to my surprise it was accepted and published. I
remember how it started:

> A finger on the window pane
> Sketches in rime that follows rain
> The idle thoughts of a youthful brain.

I remember being very proud of that word *rime,* used as a pun, and
on working the word *ephemeral* (which I had just learned) into the
poem. Poetry was unfortunately all mixed up in my mind with
vocabulary expansion.

One of my professors there (Bob Daniel, now at Kenyon) had
an elegant Harvard accent which I much admired and a poem
published in a soft-cover pamphlet which I admired even more.
Not until working on this book did I make the connection between
that poem and the leather-bound pamphlet of my grandfather's.

Here again was a man in flesh-and-blood, with a family and apparently normal habits, who wrote and published poetry. Consciously or unconsciously we shape much of our lives on living models — and I was lucky to have had a chance to associate with a few men who were unashamed to let poetry be a precious and natural part of their being.

When, at eighteen, I was drafted, I had a month at home of suspended animation between the time I dropped out of college and actually reported for duty. It was a natural time for reflection — and much of my reflection took poetic form. I had no technique. I arranged words around the paper in what might be called experimental ways — though it might be more accurate to say I was looking for a form to contain me. Similarly the poetry I wrote during my year on Okinawa stretched, contorted, shrank, chopped, screamed, whispered, and talked, but rarely sang, as I tried long lines, short lines, rhythm and non-rhythm, typographical tricks, designs, and what have you — all palette work to discover what the medium of poetry was capable of.

I believe that such experimentalism is especially characteristic of that period of a poet's life before he knows what he wants to say. Good poets are continuously experimenting with form, continuously learning and adapting their forms to what they have to say. But when the manipulation of the way the poem appears on the page completely dominates the poem and obscures its content, this is a symptom of confused purpose, confused mission. When a poet finds himself, when he comes to care passionately about *what* he is saying, when he feels his content is urgent and must not be blurred or damaged on its way to a reader's mind and heart, his experimentalism with form becomes much subtler. He does not want the noise of innovation to muffle the music of his intent.

But I was not even aware of such problems while I was in the army. When I was discharged in November, 1946, I began falling in love and found that a great stimulus. I settled into a fairly stable style, Eliotian in flavor, erotic in content — and I still hadn't the least idea what I was doing in terms of form except that I tended to keep the lines on the page of rather even length. I fled the Southwest for Chicago, fell in love with a suitable audience for my poems (she has continued to function well in that respect during more than a quarter century of marriage), and kept playing with line length, punctuation, capitalization, surrealistic imagery, jumbled syntax, graphic design, as I poured out variations on the theme of

"I love you." Some of these I sent back to Bob Daniel, who noted that I must have been reading a lot of Eliot, and who asked me what was perhaps the most shaking question I had tried to deal with up to that time (at least in regard to poetry): "How do you decide where a line should be divided?"

I didn't know. My experimentation had been a wild effort to dodge the question entirely. About the same time I took a poetry course at the University of Chicago with J. V. Cunningham, who asked even more hard-headed questions. If the word *poetry* referred to anything other than metrical writing, he had to be convinced. My form of rebellion against what seemed to be an excessively narrow view was to prove to him that I could write in tight forms if I chose to do so — and I began churning out rhymed iambic pentameter, even sonnets. And, strangely, I liked the experience. For the first time I could put the question of form out of my mind to a large extent, accepting a norm of iambic verse with a limited and recognized range of variations, and I could turn my serious attention to what I was saying.

I will give you a couple of samples of poetry from that period. Here is the first stanza of a long poem I wrote to my Spanish professor, entitled *Insomniac River:*

> Deeply the water worries flinty knots
> that rise like bad springs in its bed
> and turn the troubled surface where it lies
> reflecting garbled visions of the skies.

The pun in the second line reflects an enthusiasm for the metaphysical poetry of John Donne and others. Overall, the poem is thick with words and intellectuality. It is literary in the worst sense — and that is where I was at about age 21, in graduate school, studying the New Criticism. At the same time I hit upon a theme with deep personal meaning for me, one which I thought must have deep personal significance for others. Under the silt of the insomniac river was a clear cold current of conviction, a drive for perfection — which ultimately is a drive for death — "to find where seas their absolutes unfold."

The same theme emerges in a poem I wrote for Prof. Cunningham's poetry class (and which was eventually published in *Epos* and picked up in two anthologies):

MY DOUBT RANGED FREE

My doubt upon the land ranged free; it fed
where others trusted and believed: a child
for lunch, a test tube, home and church were piled
upon its dinner plate alive and dead;
for all was sham except my love and me.

The land was bare; my doubt was fat with pride,
and, ardent beast, it purred at my delight;
but fond of praise and whetted, vain of might,
it looked again; it was not satisfied
until it turned, consumed my love and me.

Again it was the problem of belief. Education seemed the education
of doubt, but skepticism was a corrosive force, a universal solvent —
and the problem with a universal solvent is that there is nothing
to keep it in. As a term paper for a Melville course I turned in a
long blank verse poem called *Ishmael to Ahab*. In it, Ishmael is
speaking from his wallowing coffin on which he floated alone, after
the sinking of the Pequod, to the drowned, fanatic captain who had
led the mad voyage of revenge. Ishmael finds himself jealous of
dead Ahab for the latter's capacity for belief. The poem concludes:

Asea in comprehension, I have none:
no creed of love or hate on which to build;
a moment's thought, and schools of Moby Dicks,
and Christs and countries, mistresses of mind,
suddenly naught.
                    Could I resign my rightness
and my strength to gods to whom they are
not worth the taking, or, like Ahab, thrust
my spear in any clear contention, then
lose scope, be damned to narrow ignorance,
in the closed world believe a fragment of truth,
fragment of nonsense, could I but do this . . . .
did I not comprehend my very wish . . . .
the glory of my chase would soon obscure
the failure of my voyage; no one fails
who, numb to truth, pursues to the last lowering,
and, dying, can mistake his own blood spouting

for the whale's.
Now casual scud clouds
ride low before the wind, besmudged and tattered,
helpless they sail, and fail to fill the sky.
My coffin has no keel; by a dumb gull,
hiding his legs, crossing the moon, am I
mocked, with now foot and now skull at the bow.

After my period of confinement in rhymed, rather strict iambic verse, this venture into unrhymed pentameter seemed like a convalescent's uncertain first walk in the open air. Notice how closely the texture of this passage is woven with alliteration and internal rhyme — a kind of security I needed while working in the scary open spaces of lines without end rhyme. I remember being very proud of the variations in the last line:

<u>MOCKED, with</u>| now <u>FOOT</u>| and now| <u>SKULL</u> at| the <u>BOW.</u>|

The line seems to sway like the coffin on the open sea, the trochees in the first and fourth feet jerking it about like the directionless turning of the floating man. In the preceding lines the gull flaps along on a sure course, the rhythm conveying the lazy evenness of his wing beats:

<u>HID</u> ing| his <u>LEGS</u>| <u>CROS</u> sing| the <u>MOON,</u>| am I|

For the next couple of years after getting my M.A. from Chicago, while working for a doctorate at Ohio State, I wrote very little poetry, but in the course of my study I did a great deal of intense analysis of poetic form, particularly of Shakespeare's verse, metaphysical poetry, and the heroic couplet tradition of the late seventeenth and early eighteenth centuries. I scanned reams of Milton, Cowley, Herrick, Donne, Herbert, Dryden, and Pope. Until I felt I understood what metrical principles underlay a poet's practice, I felt I did not understand his poetry. What little poetry I wrote myself was excessively tight, bottled in short lines, strict meter and exact rhymes. Somehow getting out of graduate school was liberating, and when I started teaching at Antioch College in 1953 I simultaneously began writing in a wilder manner, though I rarely sank into free verse.

And for the first time I began submitting poems for publication. This was my first published poem, after the one published in *Red Earth* when I was sixteen:

THE JITTERY GENTLE SQUIRREL

The jittery gentle squirrel
has no right to such a belly
as hangs on the sidewalk
while he cocks his hind leg
and scratches a flea like some
little old dog with a spring broke.

Besides, the creepy son-of-a-bitch
has long bent black fingers
with no thumbs and when he looks at you
sidewise, his mouth all pulled down
saying I'm Aloysius Something the Goddamned Third
so don't pick on me don't pick on me
HE doesn't think he's cute
and neither would you if he
was a rat which he almost is.

I remember that the squirrel I had in mind was sitting in front of the library at Ohio State — and I wrote the poem up in my carrel, where I was supposed to be working on my dissertation. It was published in 1955.

Never, in all this time, had I regarded myself as a poet. Sometimes I thought of myself as a writer who taught; more often as a teacher who sometimes wrote poetry. At what point does one earn the right to say of oneself "I am a poet?" Perhaps never — but I can pinpoint the time when, whether justified or not, I so began to regard myself.

One evening when I felt like relaxing from my dissertation, I went to my basement study and started writing sonnets. I wrote four of them between eight and midnight, all based on boyhood experiences in the Kiamichi Mountains of Oklahoma. I was a little giddy with my facility, but had no notion whether I should take the sonnets seriously as more than exercises. I sent them, presumptuously, to *Poetry,* and within a month one was accepted, appearing in their May, 1955 issue:

DEER HUNT

Because the warden is a cousin, my
mountain friends hunt in summer when the deer
cherish each rattler-ridden spring, and I
have waited hours by a pool in fear
that manhood would require I shoot or that
the steady drip of the hill would dull my ear
to a snake whispering near the log I sat
upon, and listened to the yelping cheer
of dogs and men resounding ridge to ridge.
I flinched at every lonely rifle crack,
my knuckles whitening where I gripped the edge
of age and clung, like retching, sinking back,
then gripping once again the monstrous gun —
since I, to be a man, had taken one.

When I received that acceptance I said jokingly to a friend,
"Well, if I'm going to be published in *Poetry,* I guess I'm a poet."
And I must have believed it, for from that time forward I began
writing more regularly, submitting more, and adjusting my psyche
and my life to a new identity. The other three Kiamichi sonnets were
soon also accepted by magazines. Most of the poetry I was writing
was getting accepted — and my name began to stare back at me
from dozens of little magazines and some of the big ones. In fact,
I began to be embarrassed by some of the poems appearing in
print, as my own values about poetry were shifting rapidly.

In 1955, when my poetry began appearing in magazines, I was
28 — and more naive, and cockier, than I had any right to be.
I was to learn that it was altogether too easy to get poetry published,
to be a poet in that superficial sense — and that this enables one
to dodge the real question of whether his work is truly good, of
whether he is a poet in any enduring way.

From this brief account I think I can deduce several operating
principles which might apply to the experience of others. I saw
early that poetry was a way of getting attention and affection. It
was something one could do with his familiar and casual experience — besides forgetting it. It was something men do — if not a
career, at least a respected avocation. As I became more sophisticated I began to see literature as the core of human culture. Writing
about one's own life and thoughts was a way of preserving the

ephemeral and enhancing (or discovering) its significance. Similarly, it served that function for mankind as a whole. Growing up meant reading and being grown-up meant writing — contributing to the life stream. Poetry differed from other kinds of writing in its greater emphasis upon form. Understanding it meant in large part understanding the form.

I can imagine mathematics having exactly the same kind of function in a young person's life. He comes to see that underlying all experience are certain abstractions of quantity and relationship, that process can exist and be exciting independent of any particular content. Being a person, participating in humanity, understanding life — all are determined by the mathematical (i.e., logical) skeleton underlying experience. One is impelled not only to learn and use the underlying principles, but to make some personal contribution. Thus he pays his dues and belongs to the human race.

For me literature, and particularly poetry, came to have that almost religious function. It was the substratum of earthly change. It contained the mysteries. It contained the keys. Life is something to be written about. To live is to write about it. I can remember, in my twenties, thinking that writing must surely be the only source of commitment and meaning. I thought that everyone, willy-nilly, was either a writer or a frustrated writer. I can remember, at thirty or so, turning an intellectual corner, new green fields opening up before my eyes, when I discovered that writing was for life, not life for writing.

But though I could turn that corner intellectually, it was too late to turn it in practice. When my sixteen-year-old daughter told me about a rather horrible sexual encounter she had had, my intuitive thought was, "Wow! What a good story that would make!" I had to remind myself that the impact of the experience on her — whether written about or not — was also of importance.

the use of experience

There is something almost chilling about the way writers are willing to use intimate material of their lives for their work. A poet's personal experience is, of course, all he has to work with. But that experience is like lumber stacked in the barn, with the new and second-hand boards all mixed together. Some may still have old nails in them. Some have been sawed crookedly. Much of it comes from old structures now dismantled. It is important that when the poet goes to build something he not moon over the lumber's original use or worry about the trees from which it came. The present work has present demands. If the poet does not find at hand what he needs, he has to make it up or go out and get it. In the finished product it will be impossible or difficult to recognize where all the pieces came from; but if one *can* recognize them, and makes a point of doing so, this will only interfere with proper appreciation of the new creation.

Let me illustrate by a discussion of the relationship of a poem to the facts of my life. Some years ago my wife, Marty, was in the hospital, coming out of anesthesia after a complex operation on the bones of her foot. Recuperation from bone operations is a particularly painful experience, and as she drifted to consciousness she suffered wracking agony for incoherent spells, and then fell back into unconsciousness. It was important that someone — that I — be right there beside her bed to comfort her during those moments of fitful waking. But most of the time she was asleep.

But what was I doing while she was sleeping? Sometimes I read — but I found it hard to concentrate on reading. Sometimes I simply rode the reverie of my mind — but that was a fruitless and frustrating indulgence. Well, I thought, I'll write a poem. How could I write a poem under those circumstances? I found the forced effort of concentration was actually a relief from random musing and random feeling. Was I heartless? Maybe. I decided to write a poem about that very phenomenon. It came out as a sonnet:

COLD BLOOD

Magic is skill. Plunge here in my bare chest
or anywhere. Although you puncture skin,
find gristle, ribs, your blade will never nick
my heart (which like an old frog knows the best
endurance, croaking lamentation or
laughter, remaining unobserved). Once
a nimbler, dumb heart hopped in young response;
a touch could scratch it. Never saber more
shall find it out. My heart has learned to think —
and though I bristle with blades the wise one squats

in a corner, pumping, not in terror but
wary and knobby, its belly chilly pink,
its eyes like seeds, its great mouth tight and tragic.
All hear, none see or feel it. Skill is magic.

As I remember the original, there was a reference to my father in lines 8 and 9, in place of "Never saber more/shall find it out." The poem said, not very clearly, that it was the injury to my heart rendered by my father which caused my heart to wise up. I took that out because I hadn't said it very well — and I wasn't sure it was true: it was too simplistic an explanation (and perhaps too self-pitying). As revised, the poem gives no explanation except natural maturation for the heart's learning to think.

What is the material for that poem? The situation in the hospital is never mentioned, but it was, in fact, the poem's chief instigation and provided its theme. How can one deliberately, in cold blood, sit beside his suffering wife and write a poem — a sonnet, no less? Is it inspiration? Is it magic? No: I had learned at an early age that the magician was a trickster. I remember going to see Blackstone the Magician at a theater in Houston — and from the angle of my view on the first row I could see "behind" a number of his tricks. Besides, he told us himself that there was no such thing as magic. Children are harder to fool than adults, he said, because when he pointed across the stage an adult would look where he was pointing, but a child was likely to look at his pointing hand. For some reason, this discovery was not disillusioning for me but exciting. There was no Santa Claus. Events had explanations. Reason and skill made the world accessible to me, whereas I could never hope to participate in a mysterious and supernatural world unless God began whispering in my ear — which He did not seem likely to do.

Magic is skill. Blackstone or some other magician put the girl into the box and shoved in saber after saber — then opened the lid and showed us how the clever and limber girl was twisted around the blades like a boneless doll. Need one be heartless to write a poem in a recovery room of a hospital? No: but he'd better have his heart under control. Drive what sabers you please through my chest, the limber heart will contort itself around them.

In searching for an image for the heart itself I thought of a fat old bullfrog such as I used to hear croaking through the night when I camped in the Kiamichi Mountains of eastern Oklahoma.

You could tell by the size of the croak that he must be a monster, but if you went looking with a flashlight you would probably never find him. I remember sloshing along the black creeks, little frogs arcing through the flashlight beam right and left, only rarely finding the big ones that made the most noise, bafflingly near, immobile, invisible. The image of the magician putting swords through a box with a girl in it fused with that of searching the night for a bullfrog. Also, I remembered that I had been told that children were to be seen but not heard. As a man, particularly as a poet, I preferred to be heard but not seen, like the bullfrog. If my heart was truly to croak its lamentation or laughter, it needed some survival tactics. It had to remain unobserved. It had to learn how to think.

But an element was still missing if I wanted the poem to be true to experience. That responsive, "nimbler, dumb heart" of youth participated in a world which reason could never comprehend and contain. In his secure isolation the old frog comes upon a lonely and tragic truth. Paradoxically, the very wisdom which enables him to survive in the world cuts him off from its essential spirit.

It is, after all, cold-blooded to be able to write that poem under those circumstances. Could I be *with* Marty in her suffering, feeling what she was feeling, writing the poem would be as unthinkable for me as it was for her in her burning twilight of consciousness. I would be more miserable, perhaps, but neither of us would be so lonely in our experience. My presence there was itself an effort to combat that loneliness.

As I remembered the bullfrogs I had seen — their cold eyes intent and fearful, their wide mouths clamped, their soft throats pulsing — I thought of a pathetic, puppet, tragic mask. So it was *you* making all the noise in the night. Only you. I was back into the child's world from which Blackstone had delivered me. The universe is at least paradoxical. Nature is supernatural. Mystery does after all haunt our darkness. Even the awesome skill of the magician is ultimately inexplicable. Skill is magic.

That is the kind of thinking that went on as I sat there, interrupted by Marty's moans from time to time. I want to tell one other anecdote about that poem. John Ciardi had recently taken over the job as poetry editor of *Saturday Review,* and in his initial editorial statement he said, in effect, that if any sonnets were thereafter accepted for that magazine it would be over his dead body. I had not published much poetry anywhere and none in *Saturday*

Review, and I did not know John Ciardi, but I took that statement as a kind of personal challenge. I sent him half-a-dozen sonnets in a row, and finally he accepted "Cold Blood," the first of many poems he was to accept. Was it the poem's magic or its skill? Or neither? It may have been nothing more mysterious than my perverse persistence.

If I had not told the autobiographical facts surrounding that poem there is no way they could be derived from the poem itself, and when I read interpretations speculating on a poet's life on the basis of what he says in his poetry I am reminded of that gulf which I know exists inevitably between even very explicit autobiographical statements and actual autobiography. It has to be that way. If a poet, while he is writing, worries about what people will think of *him* he will not have the necessary freedom to make an excellent poem. He has to ignore all distracting temptations — to "get" someone, to psych out someone (or himself), to preserve precious moments (as in snapshots — which are not likely to be works of art), to re-live life.

Poetic license should somehow protect poets even from being asked — and should protect them from the impertinent speculations of their biographers and critics. For example, in creating a character, a writer (or poet) may draw substantially upon someone he knows. But the demands of his story or his poetic form may cause him to pick up characteristics from other people he has known or read about or from pure imagination (if there is any such thing). He cannot run along after his fiction to explain all this in detail so that no one will be hurt, offended, or misled — and if he even worries about that problem his work will suffer. Frequently I write about sexual experiences, some of which I have had, others I have heard or read about, others I have merely wished I had or imagined. In writing, I try to make these as convincing as possible. I hate to think (I won't bother to think) what kind of biography someone might put together on the basis of things which I have said in poems have happened to me. With friends and family the policy is clear: if you want to know what I think or what I have actually done, ask me, and I'll tell you as best I can. But please don't try to figure it out from what I have written. That may or may not be thinly disguised experience, but the mixture of fact and fancy is so bewildering that I would have a hard time sorting it out myself, and certainly no one else could begin to do so.

The basic and most destructive confusion is between the value of the work of art and the personality or history of the person. We are lucky to know so little about Shakespeare, and the many efforts to extrapolate a biography from his plays are deservedly laughable. Suppose we were able to reconstruct a convincing portrait of a man by this method. What would we have? Lacking any real evidence, we are forced to be satisfied with something which matters a great deal more than an account of any individual life: a body of great literature.

In fairness it must be acknowledged that many poets contribute to the confusion, particularly in our publicity-minded times. If you watch the talk-shows on TV you realize that for the sake of success it is almost essential today that a writer be a "personality." The writer who simply writes good books and refuses to make public appearances (or who comes across poorly in the media) is doomed to obscurity. To some extent this is true in the much less publicized world of poetry: it is much more important that a poet be somehow spectacular in his public appearances and in his private life (his political activity, his costume, his sex life) than that he write well, if fame is his objective. In this context it is not surprising that a good deal of modern poetry is autobiographical and confessional, and when a poet is saying in his verse that he has had sexual intercourse with his mother (as one has), only the coolest reader will be attending the quality of the expression and aesthetic value or general wisdom of the work. The public is much more likely to be interested in gossip about personalities than in more enduring poetic values. The poet who takes advantage of that propensity perhaps should have his license revoked.

A somewhat different but similar problem concerns the poet's beliefs and attitudes. For example, one of the reasons for the great popularity of poetry in the Soviet Union is that poetry is recognized as a medium for more-or-less cryptic political utterance. People line up at the bookstores to find out what poets will dare say. And certainly we would not want to operate under aesthetic principles which denied the importance of the content and personal expression of poetry. Poets use their medium to say things they have thought about and cared about very deeply; it would be a perversion to ignore that aspect of literal expression in reading and judging them.

But it is just as serious a mistake, I believe, to lift a statement out of a poem and to regard it as a plank in an ideological or political platform as it is to take personal details as factual autobiography. In an art work all things must be understood contextually, and whatever statements of belief may mean about the actual beliefs of individual poets, they function primarily as pieces of an aesthetic whole, often one which modifies or even contradicts particular statements. Do I believe that magic is skill or that skill is magic or both or neither? I hope my discussion of the poem has convinced you that any honest answer would be very complex and deeply interwoven with experiences inside and outside that poem, not to mention the sheer element of design which brings the two faces of the paradox into relationship with one another.

Just as it hardly matters what my actual experience may be, it hardly matters whether I happen to believe this or that. I am a highly fallible and rather accidental organism in human history. If the poem has any value what matters is whether in any sense it is true or casts light on truth which it cannot hope to contain. It is important that we read poetry, in part, to acquire wisdom, to think profoundly, to experience deeply, to cultivate our own ethical sense. But it is a distortion of that process to concern ourselves literally and explicitly with what particular poets happen to believe or to have done or think good.

Misunderstanding of this principle, both by poets and by readers, makes for a lot of bad poetry. Often when talking to beginning poets I find that passages are obscure or abstract or convoluted because the poets could not bring themselves to say outright what they wanted to say: they feared personal exposure, or they didn't want to hurt someone's feelings, or they were for some other reason afraid of being taken literally. Sometimes, it is true, very powerful work emerges from just that struggle against repression. But most often the effect is to make the poetry unreadable, dull or vague. It is as though the potter were afraid to touch the clay. There is no way to be a writer without using life, and especially one's own life, as material. If you can't do that comfortably, mingling fact and fiction as needed, without a paralyzing regard for what people will think of you personally, perhaps you should write music or take up some other less revealing art.

the new culture

Much of what I have said implies a kind of "executive privilege" for poets — and recent history has shown us the danger of that view of inviolable domain. Since I have started writing my column in *Writer's Digest* I have found myself moving farther and farther from elitist views of art. I once thought that some few readers out there might have something significant to say and that I might help them refine their techniques in order to put that content into memorable poems. In recent years I have been less concerned with helping a few good poets than with encouraging people generally to build a nation that shares a poetic vision of life. That is in part a political aim. It has taken the form of my retiring from "professional" life to live and write on a communal farm — and that transition probably reflects a response many poets and other artists are having to the world situation in which they find themselves.

I don't think it is ostrich escapism which leads many of us these days to try to go back a little, to discover what went wrong, as a prelude to trying to discover what might be done to renew our culture. I was recently rereading a poem of mine written in 1955 (published as "Servos" in *Epoch,* Fall, 1957). It grew out of a visit with my father-in-law, a research professor of physics at Harvard who worked with Norbert Weiner on *Cybernetics.* I looked at the odd, thin volume, full of abstruse mathematical formulae, uncomprehendingly. The physicist told me something about self-correcting devices, servomechanisms, and the possibility of totally encompassing self-correcting systems, and I had a glimpse even then of the computerized civilization which now, nearly twenty years later, is our daily experience.

SERVOMECHANISMS

AS WHEN the tires pull on the pavement like
a dry palm rubbed on window glass, the whole
weight on the springs swings and it gives, just the turn
of your wrists at the wheel pulls after it everything,
then, when with tremor of pedal you startle the fact,
you butterfly guiding a cannonball, all-wise and all-
powerful (hinting the brake now, holding the one
right speed and judging just how much push you
will need to take a coming hill) and you

bring all complexity to bear on holding
Nature in firm yet giving grip (unless
bothered, tired, or in a mood)
                              SO DOES
the spinning governor with two brass balls
suspending weight on the thin edge of speed,
correcting steam, saddling expansion, resting
when deep heat rests; and aiming devices know,
and telephone exchanges know their navels,
know what is right, and what minute adjustments
keep it so. *They* have old Nature where her silken
hair is short. *You,* moody one, beware!

Bottling works shortly will shiver when beer is uncapped
in Moline. Any highway disaster will jiggle a lever
affecting production at Ford. And mechanical mice
will invent their own traps, perhaps, to avoid being bored.
The sealed and silent factories, soft lit
by the low glow of circuitry, will know,
and what they know they can perform. Infinite
self-knowledge = maximum control. And where
filaments pulse, distinctions disappear,
and things and thoughts of things all one, and seeds
and needs and gears and mica plates, or mass
and energy, virus and protein, all one.

And meanwhile you there at the wheel are clever
(as you calculate a curve), make consummate
use of the chemicals at your command.
But now the time demands you find a way
to live with interlocking servos down
the line. Like any electric eye, flooded
with light, you can switch off, or else, renouncing
knowledge and power, mutate, become beautiful
and good until you die.
                              Drop out. Retire
like a sponge on a rock, and then when the ships shudder
shadowy overhead, lie still, lie still, and let
the brass balls whirl, and never be distracted.

It took me many years to take my own advice. The term "drop

out" was not used in those days, but by now has become common
parlance. (I prefer the term "peak out," for many to whom it
applies have, as it were, reached their limits in the straight
world before taking radical steps in their own lives to discover
alternatives.) And I may well fail to become either beautiful
or good before I die. But, however dimly, I recognized even then
that working within that system only strengthened it, and that
there was something basically incompatible between the system
and myself — or, better, the system and poetry.

And so, indeed, I retired. At forty-five. I have cashed in my
chips, taking the small annuity earned during twenty years as a
college teacher, and putting all my assets into a hundred acre farm
in the Allegheny mountains, where I now live with my family
and about (the number changes from time to time) ten other people.
We live communally. We farm. We have started a small business
to earn the little cash we need to live at a minimal rate of consumption. A passage from another poem, written in 1970, expresses
the kind of ideal we have in mind. It was written after we took
our brain-damaged daughter to a residential school, which happens
also to be a religious commune: Beaver Run, one of the Camphill
Special Schools. I found myself yearning for the way of life represented by that little village created to serve brain-damaged and
retarded children:

<pre>
                          suppose there were
        a village just for people who lived in care
                                              of one
            another where
                      differences were expected
                                              judge
        not
            with what one has make do
                                        I see a village
        spreading its cottages and economical gardens
        on the verdant hills
                        people sharing whatever
                                                coming
        together to work play learn worship in joy
                                              no last
            names
                    ages all relative
</pre>

                         the sexes mingling
                                             the point
        of life being
                     nurture fulfillment happiness
        I try to imagine yearning for nothing having enough
        food warmth company
                               reading no ads
                                          imagine making
              our own music bread and love
                        have we brains enough among us?
        imagine congruence of need and delight
                                                imagine
        sinking into the downy bed of the earth's abundance
        letting now be adequate
                                   there is nothing but now
        I dream a village
                          rooted and spreading
                                                 ready
        for seasons
                        riding the earth round steadily into
          the dawn

Today's communes have little to do with Communism; in fact,
they are in many respects the opposite of massive statism, particularly insofar as Communist states identify human progress with
industrialism and scientific materialism. They tend to be small
domestic units, a dozen or so people who have chosen to live
as a family, often on marginal farms abandoned by farm families
in the past. It has never seemed to me an adequate response to the
world to seek individual salvation. The history of revolutions
seems inevitably to suggest that they succeed only in putting new
pigs in power. A third alternative — reform — simply helps the
system grow more and more sophisticated, powerful and engulf-
ing. It is after having rejected these three responses that people
have perennially turned to communalism in an effort to create alternative models for human welfare and happiness. It is a kind of
politics which "left" and "right," "radical" and "conservative" do
not describe.

One of my primary motives (along with getting closer to my
family and other loved ones, reducing consumerism, helping to
revitalize rural America, and so forth) was to center again on

poetry. For many years I dreamed I could have it both ways —
being both a professional educator in the system and (as it were,
on weekends) a poetic rebel against it.˘ But one way of life invalidates the other. If you are tottering on the brink, take my word
for it that you cannot inhabit both worlds. Don't tell me again
that Wallace Stevens was an insurance executive, William Carlos
Williams a doctor, T. S. Eliot a banker and publisher. Such dual
lives may have been possible for some in some times — but even
so I am not sure that poetry gained or that their authenticity as
artists was not compromised. Don't tell me further that we all
make compromises. Of course we do — but we needn't elevate
that necessity to a principle. Compromise we must; but we needn't
make it central in our lives.

I don't know what effect this change will have on my poetry
or my writing about poetry, but I hope to recapture for myself and
for others some of the vision that has been tarnished and neglected
in recent years. I have learned a lot. For example, I have learned
that publication and "success" are not nearly so important as I
once thought they were. I have learned that the "profession" of
poetry is about as ugly an exercise in self-seeking and competition
as any other profession, and that if one is serious about poetry, he
had better be very clear about separating it in his mind from fame
and fortune (and advancement). I have learned to respect the
promptings, however unskilled their expression, of people who
use poetic form to reach out to others. Whether their poems will
become immortal contributions to our literature is entirely another
question — and not one of much immediate concern. (To write for
immortality is probably as corrupting to the poetic impulse as to
write for cash.)

Above all I have learned that recovering poetic vision is more
important, even, than writing poetry. I use the term *recovering*
because I believe that vision is normal to humankind, that it is
evident in children and primitive people, and dims but does not
disappear as we are absorbed by a civilization that systematically
alienates us from ourselves, our dreams, one another, and the
natural world around us.

poetry and community

It is too early to assess what effect the new culture that is emerging will have on poetry, but perhaps there are some clues in an experience I had in what, a few years ago, would have been described as a "hippie pad," though in current language it is the "space" of one of a new breed of communards. A section of the cement floor of a former factory had been walled off to provide living quarters and studio for the young man who sat cross-legged on the bed. His blond beard and long curls were those of General Custer, but his head band and leather vest were more suggestive of the General's victims and enemies. Six or eight other men and women shared the large mattress with him, lying or leaning against the wall, and fifteen or so of the rest of us were sprawled around the space on its ancient but comfortable carpet. We had wined and dined together there; ceremonial joints, like peace pipes of yore, had been passed around, and we were ready for the announced purpose of the gathering — a poetry reading. All had been invited to bring poetry (or anything else) they wanted to read to the group — their own writing or that of others. Our host cleared his throat to begin.

What would he read? Conditioned by years of such gatherings on college campuses, I considered myself prepared for whatever obscurity, mysticism, obscenity or angry anti-Establishment tirade might ensue. The young man was, I knew, a devotee of the *I Ching,* and I thought he might share some Orphic haiku with us, or other Oriental illuminations. I was in a mood for erotic titillation, if that was on his mind. And since, during those very days of my visit, buddies of his were getting busted for anti-war activity on the streets of Washington and San Francisco, I was disposed to sympathize with a tempest of political anger. Psychedelic, orgiastic or militant, the poetry of the new culture would not catch me off-guard.

But I was astonished to see him open a very familiar *Complete Poems.* He said, "I am going to read a poem by Robert Frost," and proceeded to share the two quatrains of "The Pasture," a simple invitation to participate in joy and work combined; here is the first of the two:

I'm going out to clean the pasture spring;
I'll only stop to rake the leaves away
(And wait to watch the water clear, I may):
I sha'n't be gone long. — You come too.

Such poetry readings are carried on like Quaker meetings: one speaks when so moved. After an appreciative silence, another hairy young man spoke from his lotus position across the room. "I would like to read 'Mending Wall,'" he said, and I could see that he, too, had a volume of Frost's *Complete Poems.* There aren't many books (or other possessions) around the commune — and I was struck by the fact that two people owned hard-back collections of Frost — a book which is not likely to be a left-over text from a college course. The next poet to be read was e. e. cummings. The next was Kahil Gibran. I was dazed to discover, in the course of a long evening, that the poetry of this community, at least, was that of nearly half a century ago. There was nothing read all evening that could in any way be described as *avant garde.*

I was intrigued by the special function of poetry in this commune — and wonder whether it is not an index of things to come. Alvin Toffler, in *Future Shock,* dismisses interest in communes as revealing "only a passionate penchant for the past," but it may be that the past gives us some good indications of waves of the future. The cycles of history, of course, are always spirals: the past is never repeated exactly, though there are always fascinating parallels. Right now we are watching Utopian visions of the Great Society — a gleaming, seamless, cybernetic, electronic complex of perfect, all-comprehensive institutions — fall apart, and the emergence through the broken parts of rusting machinery of Edenic visions of new community, a recovery of familial and communal values, a rediscovery of the satisfactions of toil for survival, a rejection of the profit motive and tragically illusory promises of progress, of Systems and Roles and Degrees in the meritocracy, and a recurrence of simplicity, individuality, self-determination, and self-sufficiency, above all of self-actualization, as primary drives and values. Along with granny-glasses and granny-skirts come some of granny's tastes and concerns. Could it be that it is more nearly Robert Frost than Ezra Pound who speaks to our condition?

Only a few years ago I was asking where were the poets of the new age, at that time straining to accept a civilization with which I could not identify. I predicted a society of anonymity, in which we must "lay our names, as we must lay our prejudices and our nationalities, on the altar of the planned society." Today the possibility — let alone the desirability — of a planned society seems much less apparent; and the inevitability of a world-wide megaculture seems a ludicrous, somewhat quaint concept. The key term of the civil rights struggle in the fifties and sixties was *integration;* it has been replaced by *pluralism.* Our efforts now are to enfranchise the oppressed — be they minority races, women, children, the aged, the deviant — and to cherish our differences from one another. Ultimately the oppressed minority is the individual self, that very self which Kennedy asked us to commit to the nation. Our young people gladly call themselves "freaks," and they ask us to discover and celebrate our freakiness. Once a taste for liberation becomes endemic, and each person demands and finds the way to his own fulfillment, all possibility of a Brave New World of absolute order and human-dominating technology disappears.

I believe we are experiencing a major cultural shift, moving from mechanistic models of truth to organic ones. My wife once took a biology course in which the text was entitled, *The Machinery of the Body,* the cover showing a man reduced to diagrams of levers and pumps and electrical systems. For about three centuries it has been useful to Western Civilization to understand nature by comparing it with machines, and our astronomy, our biology, our structures of political organization, our economics, even our psychology reflected this way of thought. Today, with computers developing psychoses from information overload, we sometimes need to refer to organic processes to understand mechanical ones. It may be that the metaphors drawn from the natural world will again become (as they have more-or-less always remained) the sources of richest meaning for poetry.

It is interesting that the Great Society never caught on as a source of inspiration for poets. The response of artistic sensibility to a civilization which was increasingly organizational, institutional, technological, "planned," has largely been to produce distortion, obscurity, exoticism, even perversion, like fevered dreams in a sterile hospital in which clean sheets and aseptic nurses and buzzing equipment and wonder drugs bring no comfort. A kind of artistic snobbism emerged as Modern Art, a contemptuous rejection of the values and interests of "common man," a desperate pedantry and obscurantism and conscious ugliness were used to protect the individual imagination from absorption in the mass mind. The public and art became mutually inimical. And while poets and artists enjoyed unprecedented prestige and worldly success, they lost all real popularity, all sense of speaking from a central position in their culture, all loving relationship with their audience. To be a poet in the past few decades has been somewhat like being a nuclear physicist; one might be honored, but not revered, listened to, but not comprehended. The Great Society produced museums and libraries and concert halls just as it produced welfare programs and space programs and economic flow-charts; and high culture (LP's, reproductions of art works, book-club editions of intellectual masterpieces) was mass-produced to adorn every middle-class home. Poetry readings — auditorium performances of unintelligible eccentricity — spread like Chautauqua over college campuses.

Opposed to the idea of *society* is that of *community*. Every social institution — be it jail or hospital or library or school — represents some failure of community, some instance in which people could not cope, in which they felt it necessary to mobilize and mechanize their resources to meet some human need. The prevalence of communes is only one indication that people today are trying to recapture from society some of the functions of community and family. The attraction of rural life (with all its hard terms of survival), of relative poverty, of scruffy clothes and old cars (or none), of long hair and unpainted skin, of crafts and baking and organic gardening and diets, of Eastern religion and even of primitive Christianity, is not merely the attraction of romanticism and nostalgia. It is, I believe, an intuitive, corrective movement in a society which went overboard for urbanization, prosperity, hierarchy, style, mass production, chemical facsimiles of food, materialistic, mechanistic and rationalistic responses to spiritual questioning, and a faith in social organization as the guarantee of human welfare.

And as people move tentatively, yearningly and often incompetently into new extended family arrangements and new communities, they are likely to discover a new poetry of community (and rediscover such poetry in the past). Ironically, individualism and community go very well together: a community is, as two of Frost's characters defined home:

> ". . . the place where, when you have to go there,
> They have to take you in."
>> "I should have called it
> Something you somehow haven't to deserve."

Community assumes the unconditional right to be oneself; the non-judgmental acceptance of differences. In community, a living is not something to be earned. Sustenance, survival, acceptance, even a certain amount of affection are guaranteed. All the game-playing of taste and hierarchy and measures of human worth are abandoned. And poetry flourishes there as a way of binding and relating and being oneself. In that context it may be that, finally, even Robert Frost can have his day.

my competition with Shakespeare

Although to be sociable, I am willing to gripe along with the next guy, my heart isn't in it. I must admit, unfashionably, that I'm really very happy. Mostly this is because of my competition with Shakespeare.

As regularly as man sleeps and wakes he cooperates and competes in complementary phases. Both phases are essential, but people disagree as to the proper proportion and emphasis in the formula for happiness. Conservatives contend that life is getting ahead, liberals that it is getting along. Husbands take one side, wives the other, as do winners and losers, hunters and farmers, children from square table nurseries and those whose tables were round. One sets out, unprepared, to *live;* the other orders from Society a Universal Do-It-Yourself kit and makes life a family project. One cries in the wilderness; the other finds Truth with a committee. Satan is for achievement, God for security. One loves himself, the other — nobody in particular.

Both, of course, find both misery and happiness.

The competitive fellow frets himself to glory. His lonely tower stands against the sky and his watch on its battlements is nervous, tireless, his naps restless, his mind gnawed by the friendly mice: fear and desire. Even his children, he thinks, are out to get him; but his art and science, his defense and offense, curiously remain on the desert after he has been forgotten. In trying hopelessly to save himself he has made the world worth saving.

The cooperator saves the world, a fond task of a mother collecting scattered toys. He knows that if the bread truck did not arrive at its appointed hour, if the traffic did not observe its lanes and stop at the lights, the world would collapse like any house of cards in which the chief virtue is stillness. He is in favor of progress, of course, but knows you cannot build the house of cards un-equally; we all become happier together. His love is benign; he goes to bed like a heating pad, and dreams no dreams. If, in his sea of satisfaction, he feels an aching heart, it is because some boats somewhere are sinking. Or, sometimes, because beneath the excite-ment of the surface, the pitching waves and weather, there is no flow; he hasn't even the illusion that he is going anywhere, really.

My way, and I recommend it, is to compete with Shakespeare. I will not keep up with nor surpass the Joneses because that contest has no relevance to my real engagement. I cooperate as an interim measure — not because I have much faith in cooperation but because it makes my only competition possible.

I will not twitch with envy or despair *because* I see no possi-bility of winning and never dream of what it would be like to win. Moreover (and this is, in my game, easy), I love my enemy, Shake-speare, more than myself. I play against him in admiration; there is no question of vanquishing. Also, there is no question of giving up. I enjoy the fight, the better my performance the better I enjoy it, and the sense that it can never be won is exhilarating.

One is in the ring with Shakespeare, whether he realizes it or not, just as he is with Hitler. The peaks and chasms of human achievement are the borders of our field. We create meaning and direction by exceeding the meaningless, by exceeding our lostness. Sure, we are born into a world we never made, jostled to walk into the wind with no notion of where we are going, howling in the chaos of the given. Sure, we must say patiently — sure. There is no sense we do not make. But we *can* make. Shakespeare made. Whatever misery he may have suffered, his private self, his very identity has been rubbed away. But his work stands impassively, bigger than anyone's understanding of it. He shows up in our confusion and tears. Clearly one can do something about life, and until he *has,* until he has accepted the challenge of Shakespeare, his blows are random, his wailing has no hearers.

Nothing matters but the competition. One is free to be kind because there is no threat from others. One is free to draw a breath of indifference because the embroiling affairs, the petty slights and impermanent victories, because all the vexatious details with which existence is riddled, are nothing to that serene and long engagement. It means nothing to beat those who have beaten you: only to beat Shakespeare. There are no secondary successes. Get along. Compromise. Cajole. Mere affairs of neighbors and friends, mere hot little hostilities of cross men confused, do not deserve the energy they seem to demand. Save all for the battle. We may draw a breath and lift our sights. Surpassing Shakespeare would be an act with definition. Short of that our infinitesimal acts are so nearly alike one need not pick them out and give them names. Oh, love your neighbor and he will distract you less; forgive your enemy and he will tire of flailing the air; accept the blame, no matter how unjust, and they will let you get back to your work.

Free of fashion, free of resentment; except for the most presumptuous ambition of all, free of ambition; except for the only sustaining desire, free of desire — all this when you compete with the best you see in your longest view. Pity Shakespeare, who had no Shakespeare to compete with; his achievement is all the more remarkable. If one really were condemned to listen to the critic of the moment, to perfect his paltry loves or rely on the value of his paltry deeds, he would, indeed, despair. Some seem to take their life in the current very seriously, but I cannot believe they commit themselves totally to it. They could not bear to live. Some strand from their mind must anchor in the rocks. If they strengthened that tie, if they knew where it was anchored, they could more certainly ignore the stream.

God will not do. It must be Shakespeare. Partly because he is *not* God. Not a single one of his works is perfect; his whole production is ragged with flaws and inconsistencies that you can see and I can see and to which Shakespeare must have been sublimely oblivious. (Surely there *was* some Shakespeare with whom he was competing, some struggle that made trivia seem trivia.) He was professional; he went in, taking what he could get his hands on and slapping in into meaning, rough-hewn — as divinity shapes our ends. His human imperfections make him all the more imposing as an adversary. Like Moby Dick, he sounds, bearing his harpoons and fouled lines indifferently down and rips free as one irritably breaks through a web. Nothing divine about him. No excuses for us, denied that rationalization that we are a different order of being. He did what we would do if we could, and left no Taj Mahal behind him, no polished tomb, but a rambling rabbit-warren of creation, a ramshackle monstrosity bustling with life. And it is the greatest edifice of the human mind.

That is, until you, until someone, whips the old battler at his game (which is not, basically, poetry, but creation). That victor will have to keep his wits through every distracting moment, will be lost in no critical quarrels, will have rested on no minor successes, will not have bothered to measure himself against his mere contemporaries, will never have lost sight of the single object that could give his efforts dignity. He competes, but only with the best; he cooperates because that frees him for his struggle. But, above all, his is a happy fight, good all the way, and good to win, and the giant, if vanquished, will go down gladly. This kind of progress draws the world along behind.

PART TWO:

MAKING POEMS

first, stretch a cable across the canyon

The absurdity, illustrated in Chapter Two, of attempting to evaluate Shakespeare's sonnets by detailed analysis of their technique serves as a warning to any who hope to write poetry by studying the details of poetic form. We look back with amusement now at those historical periods when critics thought they had discovered the formulae of excellence. Dryden rewrote several of Shakespeare's plays, admiring their barbaric beauty and strength, but believing he could do Shakespeare a favor by polishing up his work for a more refined age. The results, as you might imagine, were abominable: he vulgarized, coarsened, demolished — and failed to grasp the meaning and the power of the poetry.

We have in this century suffered through another period of enlightenment called that of the New Criticism. Hordes of academic critics, hoping to follow the example of men such as John Crowe Ransom, I. A. Richards, William Empson and Ivor Winters, attempted to arrive at accurate judgments of a poem's worth by close analysis. Cleanth Brooks and Robert Penn Warren embodied this approach in a popular textbook, *Understanding Poetry,* which revolutionized the teaching of literature as it taught the teachers (and some of their students) to dissect poems relentlessly, tally their qualities and arrive at absolute judgments about their value. When I was a graduate student in the late forties and early fifties it did, indeed, seem that we had in our literary test tubes unlocked the secrets of literary quality — and I can imagine our thinking quite seriously of the "monumental literary achievements" which would "be forthcoming in the future, now that enlightened critical standards are being exercised." The irony was that a judgment was made on the basis of the poet's name before the critical scalpels were honed, and the same tools were used to rationalize and justify a crabbed and clumsy poem of Shakespeare's, "The Phoenix and the Turtle," and to tear to tatters a moving but unfortunately popular poem by Wordsworth or Tennyson. The seventeenth century was "in" and the nineteenth was "out." I can assure you no New Critic ever trod so indelicately as I did in Chapter Two on the sonnets of Shakespeare. Every last ineptitude would have in their analysis some metaphysical justification.

On the other hand the New Criticism was a healthy reaction against the uncritical impressionism and sentiment of literary criticism ᴼf the immediately preceding period. The real target was the know-nothingism of practitioners and admirers of popular poesy, typified by Edgar Guest (discussed in Chapter Nineteen), or the gushy romanticism which resisted all rational discussion of poetry, attributing everything to inspiration and feeling and denying that there was any worth in learning or analyzing technique.

My frustration in Part Two is that I know, on the one hand, the futility of trying to teach architecture by concentrating on brick laying, and, on the other hand, the vanity of imagining that a building can stand if its bricks are improperly laid. There is a great deal which can be said with precision about prosody, rhyme, diction, the lyric mode, blank verse and other aspects of poetic form. But having said all that can be said, we will still not have explained the greatness of great poetry, nor will we have taught ourselves to write it.

My temptation is to beg your patience as we wade through the details but that would be dishonest. Rather, I will suggest that you use Part Two as a test of your own interest. I will not pretend that I am bored by these technical elements. They fascinate me, as the differences in lenses and filters and types of film and paper fascinate photographers, as a musician is intrigued by the intricacies of rhythm and harmony and the qualities of instruments. I can't imagine how any person can be an artist without loving the nitty-gritty of his art. Chapter Four speaks of personal attributes lying somewhat beyond the range of technique. The subsequent chapters discuss, one by one, technical elements, illustrating them through analyses of poems. But it is important to remember that all the elements are interdependent upon one another, and upon the six senses embodying the poet's understanding of life.

Six Senses of the Poet

sense of self

By saying the first sense of the poet is a sense of self, I do not
mean that he should have a large notion of his own importance
or a preoccupation with his own psyche, making himself his own
chief study. Nine-tenths of our perception is by means of our eyes.
This does not mean that we are eye-otists or spend our ratiocinative powers analyzing the phenomenon of sight. Because sight *is*
a sense, we may usually take it for granted. Similarly, a sense of
self need not be articulated nor dissected. The poet who uses his
navel as his theme might be accused, in fact, of having very little
sense of self. Need he keep feeling himself to be sure that he is
there?

The poet perceives *through* or by means of himself; he then
speaks through himself. Self transmits the world to him, transmits
his vision to the world. He must preserve the sharp, defining
line marking where he leaves off and others begin.

Separateness, the physical fact of selfness, we are given. By the
snip of the doctor's scissors we are cut loose to drift as a distinct
glob, to take up a seat on the bus, to sign petitions, to receive allot-
ments. Instinct, however, leads most of us to try to overcome that
lonely distinctness as best we can — to climb back into the womb
dragging our umbilical cords behind us. We learn to look anonymous when the sergeant asks for volunteers. We dull our sense of
self by continually comparing our perceptions with those of others
and bringing ourselves quietly in line. We learn to say we see the
emperor's clothes whether we do or not, to blur our personal
accent, knock off the corners of our vocabularies hoping as we

step out on the street in the morning, unobtrusively attired, that we may slip by one more day unnoticed. This may, of course, be a means of gaining privacy — an outward conformity for the sake of purple nights of the mind; or it may be, as it usually is, glad sinking back to soil, death on our feet and sweet oblivion.

Though it pains him, the poet must stay alive — which means preserving his original distinctness. He has a voice; his lines are as purely shaped by it as his trousers are by his posterior, as his hat-band bears his odor. He needn't labor to be individual; he needs labor only not to die. His stride will take on a particular tilt, his hands lie in a particular curl of repose, his eyebrows rise at characteristic moments, as he learns how he best can stand against the wind of circumstance. His style, then, the pattern of his individual characteristics, will emerge naturally out of his self-hood. Beware the poet who adopts a style like a new fall fashion. Beneath that tweed there is probably no chest.

When we read his words we will recognize him, hearing him like a familiar voice in the dark with a unique combination of pitch and emphasis and tone. Voice, selfness, is independent of form and subject matter. One would think that the Neoclassical closed couplet would, if any form could, force poets into sameness. Each line is iambic pentameter, each pair rhyming, a tight, balanced unit of sense. And it is true that many versifiers of the seventeenth and eighteenth centuries are indistinguishable, their authors lacking voice. *Poets,* though, speak distinctly. Hear Dryden and Pope on the subject of dullness and darkness, wit as light. Dryden says:

> Some Beams of Wit on other souls may fall,
> Strike through and make a lucid intervall;
> But Shadwell's genuine night admits no ray,
> His rising Fogs prevail upon the Day:

and Pope's Theobald, in the *Dunciad,* addresses the Goddess of Dullness:

> O! ever gracious to perplexed mankind,
> Still spread a healing mist before the mind;
> And, lest we err by Wit's wild dancing light,
> Secure us kindly in our native night.

Dryden's voice is gravelly with certitude, solid, masculine, speaking in a constant sun of reason and moving us to laugh at Shadwell's divergence from the norm. Behind Theobald's prayer to Dullness, however, we hear Pope's thinner, more musical voice, suggestive of lurking meanings left unsaid, coolly involving us all in darkness. Dryden speaks of a genuine night, Pope of a native night, Dryden of fog, Pope of mist, Dryden of wit's lucidity, Pope of its wild dance. Dryden's cadence is the steady stride of denunciation; Pope's meter bunches and subsides, nervously darting with an irony that bites its master's hand. Even the most rigorous of traditional forms could not suppress their personalities. The sense of self, when strong as it was for them, wears tradition comfortably, knowing it cannot be quelled. The poet may or may not be *aware* of self; the important thing is that he *have* a self through which he can be aware.

sense of fact

Of what? Chiefly of the objective world outside his skin. And for this he needs a second sense, a sense of fact. Much more than the ability to distinguish sense from nonsense, to know fact when it presents itself, a proper sense of fact causes one to *love* the actual, to accumulate details in every corner of the attic of the mind, very little of which is useful. He is not, however, a pedant, a gossip or a quiz-kid. He may not even have much of a memory in the usual sense. His sense of fact is apt to produce ecstasy over isness, fascination with the world that happens. But often he has no file-clerk, and the walls bulge and rafters sag with experience in inaccessible confusion. The only value of such a collection is as material for rainy days of creation, when he sorts, and never knows what he will find.

If he reads (and most poets do), it is with the skepticism of a gourmet who wants no pulpy vegetables foisted on him, who loves fact too much to accept substitutes. Poets are, therefore, often anti-literary; they have no patience with lies other than their own, they shy away from discussions of "meaning," they are amused or anguished to find people taking fiction seriously. They love innocent books by people with names like Edwin Sethington Cronk, M.A., on strip mining, or swamp flora, or Zuni pottery. They believe travelers before anthropologists, accept generalizations tentatively and uneasily, puzzled by metaphors, gagged by beautiful language. Literature, of course, has even more of the stuff of life than science, but when poets read literature, it is with the curious detachment of someone looking on from the wings, not laughing at the jokes (which are for the customers out front), but sympathetic with the performer when his voice cracks, elated with him when the show is going well, envious as he bows in the slanting spot, the dark house exploding in applause. Poets say poets are the best critics. Nonsense. They see only what they can learn by, condemn what they cannot do or would not be interested in trying. Poems are for readers. Poets prefer journals of explorers, figures in world almanacs, laboratory reports (but not the generalizations drawn from them), or little items in the backs of newspapers.

Actually, the poet would not read at all except that life is so short. He much prefers the facts of direct experience, the hot pipe smoke on his tongue, the water pouring from coastal rocks, the knocking of the radiator, the grip of the rake handle, the scent of mushrooms. His sense of fact makes him an observer of the absurd and trivial, the comic cat shaking its wet paw, the bird regaining balance on a wind-tossed twig, the bounce of rain on asphalt, the rusty squeak of the pump, the exact sound of a screen slamming behind a nine-year-old boy flying out for a last hour of summer play after dinner, whose feet will delight that the sidewalk has cooled and who will hear, as the sky swallows its last pink streaks, the insects start to sing in the vacant lot. Books? If he were reading the solution to the riddle of life, and the spine of his book cracked, he would stop to contemplate the sound.

This yearning for concreteness, for truth that can be felt between the fingers and counted, has particularly been the obsession of poets of our time — as when Elizabeth Bishop looks at a fish, half out of the water:

> I admired his sullen face,
> the mechanism of his jaw,
> and then I saw
> that from his lower lip
> —if you could call it a lip—
> grim, wet, and weapon-like
> hung five old pieces of fish-line,
> or four and a wire leader
> with the swivel still attached,
> with all their five big hooks
> grown firmly in his mouth.
> A green line, frayed at the end
> where he broke it, two heavier lines,
> and a fine black thread

> still crimped from the strain and snap
> when it broke and he got away.
> Like medals with their ribbons
> frayed and wavering,
> a five-haired beard of wisdom
> trailing from his aching jaw.

She makes certain that we know what she calls a lip is not a lip, exactly, that there are not actually five pieces of line, but four and a wire leader. This is symptomatic of a cultural state of mind — a world which has taken one too many wooden nickels and therefore moves from fact (the particular sense data of experience) to truth (the theorems data lead to) cautiously if at all. She lets the fish go — not exactly *because* he was old and wise and had suffered. She saw details which suggested age, wisdom, suffering, and, as a separate fact, she let him go.

But although we cling, now, to fact with neurotic desperation, no poet ever wrote who did not relish the still moments of experience, the snowy woods, for their own sake. When a reader objects that poetry is too abstract, he usually means it is too concrete, that poets, veritable pack-rats of experience, would rather collect facts than interpret them; they would go so far as to arrange them in suggestive ways, but are sometimes impatient of making their meaning clear.

sense of language

Sense of self for the inside; sense of fact for the outside; sense of language, then, for a medium of exchange. Poets love words, of course; but this love may be misunderstood. In the Renaissance, when the vernacular needed conscious enlargement, poets like Spenser, Shakespeare, and Milton made deliberate efforts to be fancy, to invent new words and use big ones. In other periods, however, the sense of language tends to lead them quite the other way — to leave the big words for the preachers and professors, to savor the little ones, the slats, chunks, webs, bricks, trunks and boughs of language — or even the twigs, but not the extremities, ramifications or appurtenances. For one thing, such words don't fit very well in meter; they take up too much room to get one thing said. Also, they tend to lead one away from experience, fact, rather than toward it. Even the poets I mentioned recognized this, and the sinews of their poetry are the homiest sort of words. Their seas are rarely multitudinous, and blood is not often apt to incarnadine them. An unfortunate aesthetic caused some poets of the Renaissance and Enlightenment to confuse eloquence and poetry; but poets were never much for theory, anyway. In practice they wrought their strongest lines from iron, not brass.

The two chief veins in our language are the Anglo-Germanic and the Latin. Poetry must be dug from the core; and the poet's sense of language leads him to sweat rather than perspire, to love rather than experience affection, to eat bread rather than consume comestibles. But it may also lead him to be fascinated by juxtaposition of Latin and Saxon words, the ripple of a polysyllable in a stark blunt line, the "synagogue of the ear of corn" (as appears in a poem by Dylan Thomas). Above all, he is concerned with exactness, distrustful of the vague, general, overbloated, the needless multiplication of syllables. The most unpalatable words of all are the barbarisms of over-education: *utilization, analyzation, orientate,* where *use, analysis, orient* do as well. The sense of language aches at advertising, in which things are somethingorotherized, word-wise, I mean, in which comparatives give you nothing to compare with, superlatives superlatize one another, and adjectives and adverbs gum up the wheels of thought. In general, descriptive adjectives and adverbs are poison to the sense of language. The poet prefers to play with nouns and verbs — and no cards wild.

But words alone are a minor concern of the sense of language. To flutter like a butterfly over an individual word is precious and, ultimately, pointless. Rather, the poet's instinct is for phrases; with these he names and remakes the world. The poet's chief work, one might say, is to give the world units of speech which enable it to express its thoughts: "the primrose path," "though this be madness, yet there is method in it," "protests too much," "something is rotten in the state of Denmark," "mirror up to nature," "sick at heart," "Hyperion to a satyr," "in my mind's eye," "more in sorrow than in anger," "neither a borrower nor a lender be," "to the manner born," "more honored in the breach than the observance," "at a pin's fee," "unhand me, gentlemen," "my prophetic soul," "Leave her to heaven," "smiling, damned villain," "more matter, with less art," "easy as lying," "speak daggers," "the hey-day in the blood," "coinage of your brain," "cruel, only to be kind," "hoist with his own petard," "Sweets to the sweet," "yeoman's service," "A hit, a very palpable hit," "Absent thee from felicity awhile," and "the rest is silence," are but a few of the hundreds of such units the world has taken from one play and turned to its service in grappling with experience. Some are catchy; some are euphonious; some are penetrating bits of analysis of common situations; some recommend themselves by their brevity, which is, after all, the soul of wit, in evoking a full range of associations with an instantaneous touch. For the most part, there is nothing unusual about the individual words. But each phrase is a nugget on the pebbled shore of language, selected by the poet's special sense and given its perfect dramatic setting.

sense of art

This requires a fourth sense, a sense of art, the most abstract of the poet's faculties: his concern with pattern, design, dramatic sequence, proportion, his willingness to invent arbitrary limitations and then take them as seriously as any of life's demands. Another term for it might be his sense of play.

A popular song of the Fifties contained the line, "Get out of here with that *thump, thump, thump,* before I call the cops," in which the *thumps* were sound effects, non-words. One might say that the *thump, thump, thump* is definitive of the sense of art: it doesn't matter, really, what it is, but something is *there* which makes a difference. To illustrate this I would like to discuss one of the most powerful and important poems of the twentieth century, W. B. Yeats' "The Second Coming." There are difficult phrases, allusions to Yeats' private system of concepts and symbols, which make the meaning less accessible than the direct aesthetic experience. That experience, I believe, can be abstracted and discussed as a series of overlaid patterns. I would go so far as to say these patterns, not the meaning, are the essence of the poem.

The first strophe is devoted to setting, to establishing the atmosphere appropriate to uncanny events. We might compare it with the familiar opening of Poe's "The Raven."

> Once upon a midnight dreary, while I pondered, weak and
> weary,
> Over many a quaint and curious volume of forgotten lore —

Yeats does not give us his personal situation, but, rather, a series of suggestive statements about the times in which he lives, be-

ginning with a symbolic representation of disorder, the falcon, bird
of prey, on the loose, out of control. He follows this with several
quite literal statements analyzing a world in disorder, the ground
prepared for violence.

> Turning and turning in the widening gyre
> The falcon cannot hear the falconer;
> Things fall apart; the centre cannot hold;
> Mere anarchy is loosed upon the world,
> The blood-dimmed tide is loosed, and everywhere
> The ceremony of innocence is drowned;
> The best lack all conviction, while the worst
> Are full of passionate intensity.

All that can save us is some form of divine intervention.

> Surely some revelation is at hand.
> Surely the Second Coming is at hand.

Now I would suggest that for "Second Coming" you substitute
in your mind the *thump, thump, thump* metrically adapted. The
particulars of the apocalyptic experience he is about to share with
us may cause interpretational difficulties. All I am interested in,
for the moment, is the *art* of the poem — and it may as well be a
corpse walking at the wish made on the monkey's paw, or a
taciturn raven, or any other *thump, thump, thump* which is "at
hand."

Notice the ineffectuality of that phrase, "at hand," repeated at
the ends of two lines. Then "The Second Coming" is repeated.
These two and a half lines constitute the still before the storm,
the heavy moment of stasis, the tense readiness. The art is in conveying the shape of experience — no matter what is coming. He
wants us to feel: Look out!

> The Second Coming! Hardly are those words out
> When a vast image out of *Spiritus Mundi*
> Troubles my sight: somewhere . . .

(And don't worry about what *Spiritus Mundi* is for now; it might
as well be the foggy fens near Heorot, Delphic caves. Note the
vagueness; it might be *anywhere*. Right *here!*)

> somewhere in sands of the desert,
> A shape with lion body and the head of a man,
> A gaze blank and pitiless as the sun,
> Is moving its slow thighs, while all about it
> Reel shadows of the indignant desert birds.
> The darkness drops again;

That was it. The vision, the *thump, thump, thump* is a monster, beast of body, governed, though, by implacable intelligence, its gaze blank and pitiless, its stride deliberate and powerful, as though the sphinx had gotten heavily to its stone feet to walk in the screeching whirl of birds (outraged, but not, as man might be, fearful) at this disturbance of nature. The sun, the "lone and level sands" as Shelley described them, the monster, the flit of shadows of mysterious birds; these are all the ingredients of horror pure and simple, a ghost story if you will. That *thump, thump, thump* will get you if you don't watch out.

          The darkness drops again; but now I know
is a hinge-line, changing the scene, resolving the vision, returning us to stasis, but no longer tense expectation — rather a stasis of nervous knowledge, a moment of relief, disturbed, though, by awareness that even more terrible experience lies ahead. This is the eye of the storm, the moment of dead quiet before the hurricane blasts back from the opposite direction. Interestingly, although the whole poem is in iambic pentameter, with normal substitutions, this is the first and only completely regular line, the solid tick of the meter like the clock in a still and breathlessly waiting house.

    What does he know?

                          but now I know
      That twenty centuries of stony sleep
      Were vexed to nightmare by a rocking cradle,

It is a riddling sort of knowledge. The monster slept uneasily, vexed — for so powerful a being could hardly be more seriously disturbed than that rather irritated word implies — but vexed to nightmare. Here is motivation: the *thump, thump, thump* is angry, his restless sleep finally having become even for him a horror. What horror? The state of the world, as described in the opening strophe — the disorder that developed from rule by a mild god, a rocking cradle. The day of vengeance is at hand, Christ the tiger walks; or, at any rate, if the substitution is too puzzling, the *thump, thump, thump* is clanking into action to wipe out with his paw the source of the irritation. In the starkest terms, a lion-like monster is presented to our imagination as being stirred to fury by a baby. What could be a more melodramatic situation? At such moments adventure serials at the movies used to leave one waiting for the next episode the following Saturday.

    We do not get that next episode in this poem. Rather, it is left to us to fill in — with the poet's canny knowledge that the reader will supply his own catastrophe, that it will be much more ghastly than anything the poet himself might say. He closes with a teaser, a question, to stimulate our bad dreams:

> And what rough beast, its hour come round at last,
> Slouches towards Bethlehem to be born?

Again, consider the combination of suggestive elements in those lines. The question with three stark accents, "what rough beast" — the simplicity of the word *rough* (do we need any more reminder of the implicit horror?) — the ominous note of fate, "its hour come round at last," the almost restful certitude of that phrase, "at last," implying a kind of relief. But the cure will be as bad as the disease described at the beginning of the poem, and we are left, finally, contemplating it. The beast "slouches" — no hurry: another word, like "vexed," like "slow thighs," to suggest magnitude, imperial self-possession, huge authority, knowledge, and power. "Bethlehem" connotes, of course, a place of gentleness, the sleeping city, the cradle of love. And what will he do there? Finally we are told: "to be born" — and the ultimate horror is the identification (we can no longer avoid it) between the monster and Christ. His last incarnation, symbolized by the cradle, was forgiving, mild. But the twenty century dominion of that symbol was like a bad dream to God — and the next incarnation, the one immediately due — well, gentle reader, imagine it for yourself.

I am trying to emphasize in this discussion the sense of art — the sequence of dramatic instances in this remarkably short poem which prepares us, holds us trembling in the paralysis preceding vision, astounds us with a classic *thump, thump, thump,* carries us, then, on, on, with building intensity to a final experience which we must supply ourselves, so guided by the poet. The art is in the arrangement, the dropping of hints, the precision of details, the calculation of rhythm, sound, pace, symbolism, to create for us a pattern of emotional reactions which may or may not *mean* something in the real world. You are free, after you have read the poem, to say Yeats made it all up. He never saw any such vision. No such monster stalks any such desert. Okay. But this is like pinching yourself in a horror film to remind yourself it is all fiction. You do it because you *believe.* You do not believe the "message," necessarily. You believe the art.

Rhythm works so subtly on the consciousness that we have to make some effort to see it; but it is the fabric of the poem. I said that the poem is fairly conventional blank verse, unrhymed iambic pentameter — but with only one line which completely conforms to that pattern, coming at a crucial moment in the poem. Elsewhere, as in all blank verse, we have numerous substitutions of other poetic feet for iambs, and these set up counter-rhythms and emphases which employ — rather than surrender to — the normal grain of the canvas.

The first line is metrically one of the most bizarre:

TURN ing/ and TURN/ ing in/ the WID/ en ing GYRE/

I have provided a conventional analysis: the line consists of a trochee, iamb, pyrrhic, iamb and an anapest. (An iambic line with only two iambs is not uncommon; the first line of the quotation from Pope above is a spondee, iamb, pyrrhic, iamb, spondee.) But Yeats' arrangement creates a superimposed rhythmical unit, DUM da da DUM, which re-echoes throughout the first strophe, sometimes with two, sometimes three, once with four light beats coming between the heavy beats which open and close the unit. Thus the turning motion of the first line is continued by metrical echo in such phrases as:

> FAL con can not HEAR
> CEN tre can not HOLD
> LOOSED up on the WORLD
> CER e mon y of INN o cence is DROWNED

and, to a lesser extent, in the second strophe:

> TROUB les my SIGHT
> SANDS of the DES ert
> HEAD of a MAN
> PIT i less as the SUN

This particular metrical figure reaches its climax in the last line. Notice the weakening effect of the pattern, like the unsteady beating of a heart, the intervals between beats being moments of anxious waiting — as for the other shoe to drop, the heart to beat once more. The more little syllables we rush through before a beat the more tense we become — as in the ceremony line. The next to last line of the poem is firm, using the spondees (which, notice, are common throughout the poem and are particularly associated with the progress of the monster, with GAZE BLANK and SLOW THIGHS, this VAST I mage) of steady cadence, combined with iambs to make three beats in a row:

> and WHAT/ ROUGH BEAST,/ its HOUR/ COME
> ROUND/ at LAST

In the final line we turn from the monster's confident march to our own questioning, fearful perception — and our heart flutters, our knees wobble, and the meter almost falls apart in its uneven tune:

SLOUCH es/ to ward/ BETH le/ hem to/ be BORN.

Of course it is highly unlikely that Yeats planned these effects in any conscious way. A *sense* of art, like any sense, works beneath the level of conceptual thought. In this poem it made him aware that he needed some familiar meter in order to have something to vary. And it caused him instinctively to make each variation emotionally significant.

sense of the age

The last sense I would include in the poet's five ordinary faculties (the sixth, of course, is extraordinary) is a sense of the age. Yeats' poem, again, may serve as an illustration. Regardless of what seems at times in Yeats his spiritualistic hokey-pokey, he heard the heart-beat of the world and knew what it meant; and this knowledge informs the poem and gives it greatness in excess of its art. He claimed in 1939 that the poem (which appeared in 1920) foretold the second World War. Prophecy — prediction of the future by supernatural revelation — suggests magical power; but the real power of the poem is in its very realistic reflection of the possibility of catastrophe inherent in the civilization Yeats saw around him in 1920. The blood-dimmed tide was loosed even before it broke over Poland. As Yeats makes clear in other poems, the ceremony of innocence had washed under with the Enlightenment, after which there was little innocence as there was ceremony; progress had meant the passing of certain beauties from the earth. Virtue had lost its nerve, and the passionate intensity of Hitlers in every walk of life has long since intimidated any faith which reason or goodness may have had in eternal values. All this is in the first strophe: it is time for a change. He claims in the second strophe that a God of Vengeance will replace an ineffectual God of Mercy; but this has not, to my knowledge, taken place. Perhaps the prophecy of Yeats was the wishful thinking of an old man calling a curse down on a generation which had disappointed him. But his sense of age is revealed not in the prophecy but in his knowledge of the world's ills — which he defines in general but precise terms. Love, he would say, has demonstrably failed to hold the world together, and perhaps another means, however unwelcome, will replace it.

Such a sense of age does not necessarily come from reading the newspapers. The poet needn't be socially conscious in the usual sense, i.e., dedicated to a program for social betterment. Yeats was more or less a fool when it came to programs — suffering some terrible delusions about fascism. But the poet's faculties should include an instinctive awareness of where he stands in the history of the world, the history of the culture, the history of poetry. Even a traditional *carpe diem* poem (meaning "Seize the day," or "Eat, drink and be merry, for tomorrow we may die") such as Marvell's "To His Coy Mistress" breathes a sense of the age, the prospect, in mid-seventeenth century, of a purely material existence in which the grave, that "fine and private place," meant not only the end of loving but of everything. That particular perception is, of course, derived from the classics, but the note of desperation in Marvell's poem, the macabre view of a surrealistic landscape of tombs and worms, the interpretation of pleasure not as delight but "rough strife," the sense that sexual indulgence isn't really very much but all we have, if what they say is so — these elements arise from Marvell's Puritan temperament interacting with the discords of his times, the wreck of the Middle Ages on the shoals of modern rationalism. I know of no other *carpe diem* poem with such unsettling tragic force.

The poet, then, has five ordinary senses: he has a sensitive and individual self, an alertness to the facts of experience, a fascination with the sounds and meanings of his language, a highly developed consciousness of arbitrary form, of the artificial, of art, and an awareness of the plight of mankind in his own time.

sense of mystery

These are, however, not enough. His sixth sense must be a hyper-awareness which enables him to exceed all that is explicable in terms of reason and human perception, a sense of mystery.

Hamlet, you know, sees ghosts, and the experience leads him to say:

> There are more things in Heaven and earth, Horatio,
> Than are dreamt of in your philosophy.

The sixth sense is precisely what Hamlet exhibits here. I call it modesty on the brink. We can make our way on solid ground to the very edge of knowledge; but then, looking off at the deep, I think we must be modest. The poet habitually sees ghosts. That is not to say he is a mystic; some are and some are not. Mysticism implies communication with the beyond, and if you can communicate with it, it is to some degree less of a mystery. Hamlet talks with a ghost, all right, but doesn't trust what he has heard. Revelation, in his case, did not stop research.

What I regard as the properly skeptical attitude of the poet toward mystery — and yet his yearning for it, his longing to understand something besides his own reflection in the world, is defined by this poem of Frost's:

FOR ONCE THEN, SOMETHING

> Others taunt me with having knelt at well-curbs
> Always wrong to the light, so never seeing
> Deeper down in the well than where the water
> Gives me back in a shining surface picture
> Me myself in the summer heaven godlike
> Looking out of a wreath of fern and cloud puffs.
> *Once,* when trying with chin against a well-curb,
> I discerned, as I thought, beyond the picture,
> Through the picture, a something white, uncertain,
> Something more of the depths — and then I lost it.
> Water came to rebuke the too clear water.
> One drop fell from a fern, and lo, a ripple
> Shook whatever it was lay there at bottom,
> Blurred it, blotted it out. What was that whiteness?
> Truth? A pebble of quartz? For once, then, something.

One of the simplest mysteries is love — insofar as that experience exceeds all that is known of sex or dependency or security, insofar as it cannot be explained by identification, the myth of Oedipus, guilt, death-wishes or what have you. Love of an individual, love of people in general, love of children, love of animals — don't we all recognize something about it that makes no sense? Half of the world's poetry is about love. The other half is about death. Half of the sum total is about the two in combination. Even a rattling good rationalist like Bernard Shaw said that he had no respect for a person incapable of religious feeling. I am sure he did not mean by that identification with any known religion, not theism of any sort, nor nature worship, nor political fanaticism, nor the *hubris* of the humanist which leads him to celebrate his own kind with almost clerical dogmatism. Poets, it is true, have these attitudes and have worshipped at the shrine of every god from God to gin. But worship and faith seem to me almost the opposite of religious feeling in the sense I am trying to define. Poets wouldn't write so much about love if they had faith in it.

The poem is a speculation; if it asserts, it begs also to be disproved. Some sense in the poet keeps him from final commitment. He is, on this dark level of his soul, amoral, agnostic, even blasphemous, but no more certain of his disbelief than of his belief. In the poems of greatest religious feeling this sense of mystery emerges quite clearly; they are poems not of faith but of doubt — poems like the sonnets of Donne or Hopkins.

I suggest these six senses as a means of measurement. To illustrate from twentieth century American poets, e. e. cummings might receive a A for sense of self, not, I remind you, because he wrote so much about himself but because he saw so individually whatever he wrote about. I would give an A to William Carlos Williams for his sense of fact, to Marianne Moore for her sense of language (albeit she tends rather more toward the ornate than a poet ought), to John Crowe Ransom for his sense of art (for, that is, the infallible strategy of his poems), to Archibald MacLeish for his sense of the age. These are five of our good grey poets; I would go to a sixth to give an A for the sense of mystery — Wallace Stevens. Several are missing from the list, but one in particular — the only one to whom I would give straight A's: Robert Frost. He kept all six senses alert, the acute, strong senses of a major poet.

Notice that I do not demand of the poet what is usually called imagination (which can be a great burden and disability). Nor do I demand emotion, philosophy, not even humanity. I nearly included a sense of humor as essential — if for no other reason than to save poets from posturing; but I suppose the posturing of Yeats was necessary to his poetry and when his sense of humor overtook him he was evacuated of poetry (as he says in "The Circus Animals' Desertion"). Besides, seven is an awkward number for senses.

Readers, of course, must have these senses too in some degree. The poet combines his faculties to produce a poem; but nothing happens, really, until a reader's senses vibrate in response. The poem might be said to happen between us and the poet. When he writes and we read successfully, we take hold of one another with all six hands.

CHAPTER FIVE

Meter

the strain of stress

Once I had the delightfully terrifying opportunity to analyze a poem before a class with the poet, Alastair Reid, listening to me, preparing to follow my comments with his own. Among other things, I considered meter in detail, scanning every line, showing that each had five feet but that only one in the rather long poem was perfectly regular iambic pentameter, and this one, the hinge-line (like that in "The Second Coming" discussed in the last chapter) came at just the moment of rest between the exposition and resolution. I was lyrical in my elaboration of the implied strategy: the ear expects iambic pentameter, but it is systematically frustrated, teased, put off, until the precise moment that the poet wants his reader to relax a moment, satisfied. Tension is maintained while the experience is conveyed, relaxed for a moment so that we may draw an even breath, then tension of another kind is introduced as we are forced to ask what the experience meant, to wonder how it affects us.

When I finished, the poet commented that the metrical analysis was very interesting; he hadn't noticed that before.

The class took this as a denial of all that I had said. If the poet didn't know about the strategy, could it properly be called strategy? He said, further, that he had never scanned one of his poems and was unaware of meter as he wrote. The class — perhaps even the poet himself — was eager to keep the filthy hands of intellect off the pristine integrity of the poem. But let us not kid ourselves now. That is not how poetry works.

Of course the poet doesn't think about meter as he writes — any more than he thinks about gears as he drives a car. A surgeon doesn't need to know the names of organs to cut and patch them effectively; but most surgeons do. Names make things easier to think about. The surgeon must also be aware of the limitations of names. A distinction between heart and artery may sometimes be impossible to make. But he doesn't, faced with ambiguity, throw up his hands and abandon knowledge. Poets sometimes do, disdaining technical knowledge. Some think they have abandoned meter altogether. Intellect is prone to error, and habit can do much, and do it better, unmolested. But anyone who has read much English poetry has, willy-nilly, some metrical preconceptions, and any experienced poet has long since made much of his knowledge and values habitual. This does not mean, though, that his poetry is without meter. If he hadn't been able to get into gear, he would never have arrived.

The peculiarly difficult and enchanting characteristic of most English poetry, which uses what is called accentual syllabic verse, is that (owing to its wedding of Germanic and Romance languages) its usual metrical units mingle syllables and stress in a way that is often mysterious. Syllables are easier to deal with than stress; the dictionary enables one to count them mechanically. But poetry is an oral art, and in speech even syllables lose their identity, so that some long and slippery ones, like the word *choirs,* divide into two, and others blend so easily, like those of the word *ruined,* that two sometimes sound as one. I select those illustrations because they occur in one of the metrically most confusing lines in English verse — a line I will analyze later: "Bare, ruin'd choirs, where late the sweet birds sang." Technically there are ten syllables there, but the first three words all linger on their sounds so delicately that each might be regarded as either one or two syllables in pronunciation.

But what is stress, and how do we know when we have heard it? A sound — or syllable — has three characteristics: volume, pitch and duration. Any of the three may create stress; but determining stress is even more complicated than this breakdown suggests. Meaning determines volume, pitch and duration, which is to say that how a poem sounds (and how it is to be measured if stress is the key) depends upon what it says; and that, we can see easily, might be difficult to determine with any exactitude. You may stress a syllable by whispering it, shrilling it, growling it, extending it or cutting it off sharply.

Moreover, stress of a syllable has meaning only in relation to the syllables before and after it. The middle syllable in *completely* is stressed — even in the phrase *completely worn out,* although it is obvious that the last two words receive more emphasis than *plete.* Which of those two words receives more stress? It is possible to stress them equally: WORN OUT; or to stress the second only: worn OUT; but, notice, you can't do it the other way around: WORN out — unless *worn* is clearly antithetical to some other word: "I didn't say I was born out of wedlock; I said I was worn out with wedlock" — a sentence requiring displaced stresses on both *worn* and *with.*

The very complexity of the problem of stress sometimes causes a haunting tension in our verse, as in the line I quoted earlier: from a sonnet by Shakespeare:

> That time of year thou mayst in me behold
> When yellow leaves or none, or few, do hang
> Upon those boughs which shake against the cold,
> Bare ruin'd choirs, where late the sweet birds sang.

Notice the absolute regularity of the first three lines, the even alternation of stressed and unstressed syllables, a cadence emphasized by the hesitating parenthetical phrases in the second line. How, though, are we to scan the fourth? Strict alternation would make: Bare RU in'd CHOIRS where LATE the SWEET birds SANG; and surely we hear that rhythm, although we wouldn't read the poem that way. Let a drum in your imagination keep the ta-TUM beat while you read against the background with the stresses sense demands: BARE RU in'd CHOIRS where LATE the SWEET BIRDS SANG. But notice that *ruin'd* almost slides together as one syllable (completely in New Jersey). In effect, the line begins and ends with groups of three beats together: BARE RUIN'D CHOIRS where LATE the SWEET BIRDS SANG. Let a second imaginary drum play that rhythm in counterpoint to the first. Now look again at that first astonishing phrase. *Bare* and *choirs* are both long syllables, ending in a resonating *r* sound that lingers like the sound of a struck bell, making them almost trochees, like RU n'd. Can you hear the three contrasting rhythms at once?

> Bare RU in'd CHOIRS
> BARE RUIN'D CHOIRS
> BA-re RU-in'd CHO-irs

The unstressed *where* draws out the effect even further, rhyming with *Bare.* One almost hears the mournful whistling of the wind in the barren trees in the first half of the line — so different in sound from the distinct, sharper syllables of "late the sweet birds sang." It is a line that burns into the mind. William Empson, in *Seven Types of Ambiguity,* showed how the ambiguity in meaning creates tension. (Is "choirs" in apposition to "boughs" — and thus a metaphor — or is it a literal image of the choir lofts of ruined churches?) The rhythm seems to me similarly important. It is the strain on the line that keeps it taut and singing — and the stress that makes the strain. (I will discuss an additional kind of tension in this quatrain in the chapter on tone.)

some definitions

To deal with the complexities of poetic rhythm there has arisen a traditional vocabulary consisting of at least a few simple terms. For example, *metered verse* is that in which the length of the lines is measured by an arbitrary number of units. The language is made to fit some pre-determined design of the poet. Some poets, even, have written on adding-machine tape to impose an arbitrary limit on the number of spaces and characters in a line. Any such measure can be used to meter poetry, as:

> This writin
> g has ten let
> ters per lin
> e but varies
> in the numbe
> r of spaces.

Syllabic verse is the simplest, common type of metered verse. Line length is determined by the number of syllables, as:

> Each of these lines has
> five syllables. Some-
> times that requires di-
> viding the end words.

Some poets such as John Milton and Marianne Moore write essentially syllabic verse.

Accentual verse is that in which line length is determined by the number of stresses, regardless of the number of syllables, as:

*A*nglo *Sa*xons *sang* their *mead* songs
in *lines* of *four* em*pha*tic *feet*
with no *fixed* *pat*tern im*pos*ed on the *num*ber
of *light* *syl*lables, nor *set* po*si*tions —
but the *first* or *second* *stress* in the *line*
had to al*lit*erate with the *heavy* *beat*
in the *third* po*si*tion, *star*ting the *sec*ond half.

As you can see from this example, there is some unavoidable ambiguity about which syllables should receive stresses: in the last line, *half* might as readily be stressed as *sec*ond. Writers of accentual verse have to work at keeping the rhythm strong so as not to lose control of stress placement.

Accentual syllabic verse is the most common — and most complex — form of metered verse in English. Certain fixed combinations of number of syllables and placement of accent are called *feet*. Line length is then determined by the number of feet in a line. For example, the combination of one unaccented syllable and a following accented syllable is called an *iamb*. A line with five feet, most of them iambs, is called a line of *iambic pentameter,* as:

a LA| de DAH| ap PROACH| to VERSE| will DRIVE|
the COM| mon READ| er SCREAM| ing UP| the WALL|

Such a rigid pattern of alternating stresses is almost impossible — and quite tedious — to maintain. In practice, almost every "iambic" line has one or more variations.

Feet common in English and American poetry are the following:

iamb u/   the HILL| is GREEN| and STEEP|

trochee /u   STEEP and| GREEN is| YON der| HILL side|

spondee //   STEEP GREEN| YON HILL|

anapest uu/   o ver THERE| is a HILL| that is SHIM|
                    mer ing GREEN|

dactyl /uu   GREEN is the| SHIM mer of| HILLS at this|
                    AL ti tude|

Another foot, the *pyrrhic,* consists of two unaccented syllables — and cannot be used except as a substitute for other kinds of feet, usually iambs:

i SIGH| in the| en CHANT| ment of| her EYES;|
one SYL| a ble| is ALL| she SAID| to me.|

In the first line, *in the* is clearly pyrrhic. Some prosodists would put a "theoretical" accent on *of* to make that foot an iamb, but as I read it there is no discernible stress. In the second line, the last syllable of *syllable* cannot be accented except in theory. Perhaps the final *me* could bear an accent, but I read that line with the final foot as a pyrrhic.

Rising meter refers to iambs, anapests and spondees — which end with accents. *Falling meter* refers to trochees and dactyls. If a line of rising meter ends with an unaccented syllable (or sometimes two) after the final foot, those syllables are called hypermetrical. Endings with unaccented syllables are called *feminine;* those are *masculine* which end with stress.

Ninety per cent of verse in English is iambic, both historically and currently. Most of the rest is *free verse,* which generally has an iambic base (which I will explain). The rest might be called trick verse, or special effects; it most often occurs in humorous verse or verse for children (i.e., anapestic, trochaic verse, or that in rarer meters). When a poet uses feet such as anapests, trochees, dactyls, spondees, or pyrrhics, they are mostly variations on iambic verse.

Iambic verse is essentially alternating rhythm; every other syllable is stressed. And iambic lines generally end with a stressed syllable. But, as I have said, to follow that pattern strictly would be very monotonous:

> The horses start their day without a plan
> and seem to drift from paddock quite like boats
> released from mooring, munching as they go.

Those lines are blank verse, or unrhymed iambic pentameter, the most common verse in our language, and the medium of most of our verse drama, of such long poems as *Paradise Lost,* and of many short, reflective lyrics (e.g., much of the work of Wordsworth and Frost).

Before we go on, analyze those lines in detail. Note that an iamb has nothing to do with word endings; it is determined by syllables alone. The second iamb in the first line is "es start." Note that all of the lines start with unaccented syllables and end with accented syllables. Many lines of iambic pentameter (or longer) have a natural, medial pause, called a *caesura,* as between *mooring* and *munching* in the third. A caesura can occur, as in the third line, right in the middle of an iamb: *ing,//munch.* Consider the accent on *as* in the third line. The prevailing rhythm of the lines causes us to stress slightly a syllable that might not receive a stress otherwise. In a prosaic context, that *as* would probably not be stressed, and such stresses are sometimes called "theoretical stresses" in analyzing poetry.

Let's find out how alert you are. In the following lines, only one is iambic pentameter, as defined above. Which one is it?

> The land tips steeply to the west covered with
>
> scrub pine and deciduous streaks along
>
> the creeks. It once was cleared for pasture, stripped
>
> of all usable timber; now second
>
> growth is tangled over all as thick as weeds.

I will show how those lines are scanned (i.e., broken into metrical units).

> The land| tips steep| ly to| the west| co vered| with
> scrub pine| and de| cid u| ous streaks| a long|
> the creeks.| It once| was cleared| for pas| ture, stripped|
> of all| us a| ble tim| ber; now| sec ond|
> ˣgrowth| is tang| led o| ver all| as thick| as weeds.|

Such scansion marks are somewhat arbitrary. For example, there might be a theoretical (or light) stress on *to* in the first line. I have left the *with* at the end of the line as "hypermetrical," i.e., it doesn't count. This is customary in scansion of iambic lines — simply to disregard one or two unaccented syllables after the final stress. But one could as easily mark it: co vered with,| which would make the final foot of the line a dactyl. The third line is the one regular line. Some of you might have picked the fifth line as regular, and it is very nearly so. The little *x* before *growth* indicates a missing syllable, and this is occasionally used as a variation on iambic verse. But there are (counting *x growth* as one) six iambs, not five, in that line. To scan it as pentameter, or a five-foot line, would mean calling the first foot or the last foot of the line an amphimacer (/u/), a variation almost never found in iambic poetry.

That last statement suggests, rightly, a predisposition based on statistical probability. To learn to write iambic pentameter you should scan thousands of lines of the iambic pentameter of good poets such as Shakespeare, Milton, Wordsworth, Robinson, Yeats, Frost. You will find many variations, many of them puzzling.

But after awhile you will develop a sense of probability; the variations can more easily be explained one way than another. What I am concerned with here are the easier, more likely ways of analyzing such variations. For example:

o ROM| e o ROM| e o WHERE| fore ART| thou ROM| e o?

de NY| thy FA| ther and| re FUSE| thy NAME|

or IF| thou WILT| not BE| but SWORN| my LOVE|

and I'LL| no LON| ger BE| a CAP| u let|

As I scan it, the first line has a spondee, two anapests, and ends with two hypermetrical syllables. The second has a pyrrhic. The third is metrically regular, but notice how the caesuras break up the line dramatically:

or // IF   thou WILT   not // BE

The fourth ends with a pyrrhic, needed to make up the five feet of the line (and therefore different from the hypermetrical syllables in the first line). This passage is a fairly normal example of iambic poetry.

Music comes from the piano, not the metronome. It is variation, not regularity, which creates interest and the possibility of art (as opposed to mere hack work, or versifying). The most confusing substitutions are those with two accents (the spondee://) and those with no accent (the pyrrhic: uu). These two feet are often used in combination, with the pyrrhic first, as though the accent of one iamb had been displaced to the second (in the dark pit) — a combination called an *Ionic*. Another confusing, and very common, variation is the reversed foot at the beginning of a line, or the substitution of a trochee (/u) in the first foot. This should not be confused with the much less common use of a foot with a missing syllable (called a catalectic foot). Much more often you will find lines beginning this way:

Darkness is all I saw as Mary spoke.

If you learn to recognize spondees, pyrrhics, trochees, and one more foot, the anapest (uu/, ŏr ă foot| with ă limp),| you will have all the equipment you need to scan most iambic verse. One way of thinking of the anapest is that an extra unstressed syllable may be slipped into an iambic line from time to time.

While, of course, there are no "rules" for writing iambic poetry, there are some guidelines that can be derived from the work of great poets which may be useful in predicting what kind of effects are more likely to be successful than others. Let me state them as though they *were* rules:

1. Each line should be scannable as a given number of iambs or standard variations (i.e., trochees, spondees, pyrrhics, or anapests).

2. Never use two of the same variant feet together (e.g., if two anapests are used together, the line begins to trot in anapestic gait: "When we go to the park we like to take a lunch" trots off anapestically at the beginning, and the last three feet rein it back to an iambic walk).

3. Be sure that at least every third foot is an iamb. (There is a limit to how many variations a line can take without losing its iambic texture.)

4. In spite of the above, spondees can be substituted for iambs at any time. (This works because, of any two syllables together demanding stress, one can always be stressed more than the other in reading, so even verse thick with spondees can have an iambic flow:

Corn stalks bend low as the spring winds surge past.

The line is heavy, but works in an iambic context.)

5. Use perfectly regular lines of iambic sparingly, when there is some point in emphasizing the tick-tock steadiness of rhythm, probably with no more than two such lines together.

6. Avoid situations which rely too heavily on theoretical stress. Remember that it is almost impossible to speak English without stressing at least one out of four or five syllables; but poetic lines get shaky when there are too widely spaced stepping stones across the creek:

Ă líne| of pó| ĕt rў| ĭn whích| ăn ín| sŭf fíc| iĕnt ă móunt|
ŏf strés| sĕs áre| prŏ ví| dĕd túrns| tŏ próse| ăs jél| lў góes|
tŏ sú| găr. Sée| hŏw fírm| ĭt stánds| whĕn ác| cĕnts áre| ĭn pláce.|

Notice that as you read the first line of that example there is a tendency to put an artificially strong stress on the last syllable of *poetry* and on *which,* just to keep the beat. Thus the line forces you either to mumble prosaically or to distort natural patterns of emphasis, both weaknesses of verse.

The last point suggests the most important principle of all to remember in writing verse. The major difference between verse and prose is that there is a higher ratio of stressed to unstressed syllables in verse. It is difficult to err on the side of providing too many stresses, easy to err on the side of providing too few. There are, of course, differences in emotional effect related to the number and strength of stresses. The more strongly stressed, monosyllabic words you use, the more intense and emotional the poetry will be. Ratiocinative language tends to be polysyllabic, with relatively more infrequent and lighter stresses. In general poetry is concrete, pungent, strong, compared to prose, which is more likely to be abstract, intellectual, unemphatic. If nothing else I have written in these pages sticks with you, try to require a strong emphasis on at least one syllable out of four. One out of three is better, one out of two a norm, and at least short passages in which every syllable is stressed are not only possible but desirable.

The major difference between *free* verse and metrical verse is that there is no regular number of feet per line in free verse. Other than that, the principles I have discussed here apply to the vast majority of poems written in free verse. The norm is an iambic texture, with such common variations as I have illustrated.

Try your skill at scanning this passage of free verse.

Like an old crone who years ago
gave up sex, the land
responds reluctantly at first as her young lovers
ply awkwardly her drained and unused soil.
At night she remembers:
    There was a time when I was farmed with love.
    A family sucked here: Herb and Sally
    turned my furrows with a horse-drawn plow
    to feed themselves and onetwothreefour kids
    and neighbors, too. They drummed my chest with boots
    in festivals of thanks . . .
                        Then came
    the raper Agribusiness, city slicker, fluttering green
    bills . . . .
Now overgrown with scrub she meditates
in Gothic
reserve,
resents
virile longhaired invaders scraping weakly
at her tired loins.

As I wrote that I deliberately did not scan or count out feet in my head: I let it flow. But the flow was conditioned by years of saturation in the traditions of English poetry, and it is interesting to me, looking back, to see the points at which my intuition drew upon the norms of that tradition. Can you relate these scansion marks to the lines above?

```
uu // u/ u/
x/ u/ u/
u/ u/ uu u/ uu // u
// uu u/ uu //
u/ uu/ u
        u/ u/ u/ u/ u/
        u/ uu/ u/ u/ u
        x/ u/ uu u/ //
        u/ u/ u/ // //
        u/ u/ u/ u/ u/
        u/ uu u/
                        u/
        u/ u/ u/ u/ u/ u/ uu/
        x/
u/ u/ u/ u/ u/
u/ u
u/
u/
x  u  u  u  u  u/
uu //
```

It is as though the norm, the harmonic chord, were iambic pentameter. That norm is strongly affirmed at key points — particularly in the memory of the earth, and in the first meditative line after the memory. Elsewhere, though the number of feet per line varies, all variations from iambic are within the normal range. The poem (I did not plan this) begins and ends with an Ionic (uu //). Three lines conclude with hypermetrical, unaccented syllables (this is called a feminine ending). In four places I indicated a missing unaccented syllable by *x*, but these lines could be scanned in other ways: the important point is that in general there is an alternation between accented and unaccented syllables.

Line length (discussed more fully in the next chapter) is conventionally described by Latinate terms as follows: *monometer* (line with one foot), *dimeter* (line with two feet), *trimeter* (three), *tetrameter* (four), *pentameter* (five), *hexameter* (six), *heptameter* (seven), and *octameter* (eight). Accentual verse is usually classified according to the prevailing kind of foot and line length — as, Longfellow's *Hiawatha* is in trochaic tetrameter.

As you start to write verse, you decide first whether it will be free or metered, and, if metered, whether syllabic, accentual or accentual syllabic. *Units* or *groups* of lines are your next concern.

Verse paragraphs function much as paragraphs function in prose; they are indicated on the page simply by spaces between groups of lines or initial indentation. A long poem such as *Paradise Lost* is broken into verse paragraphs, and a short poem such as "Mending Wall" may be a single verse paragraph.

Strophe is another word for *verse paragraph,* particularly for those units which seem to turn away from the subject matter to introduce a new mood or new dimension of thought.

Stanza is a group of lines more formally determined than *verse paragraphs* or *strophes.* (You might say that the stanza is to the verse paragraph or strophe as metered verse is to free verse.) Stanzas usually have a fairly fixed pattern, or formula, in which lines of the same length are repeated in the same sequence, often reinforced by rhyme patterns. For example, the ballad stanza is usually a group of four lines, the first of which is iambic tetrameter, the second iambic trimeter, the third iambic tetrameter, and the fourth (rhyming with the second) iambic trimeter. When the formula for a stanza is given, repeated lower case letters indicate rhyming lines and superscribed numbers indicate the number of feet in a line. Thus, the formula for a ballad stanza is $a^4 b^3 c^4 b^3$; sometimes the first and third lines rhyme as well, $a^4 b^3 a^4 b^3$:

> He waylays maidens in the lanes
> and wives when they are lonely,
> and little girls with growing pains
> outgrow them with him only.

While there are a number of fairly conventional, standard stanza forms such as the *Spenserian stanza, rime royal, terza rima,* etc. (for definitions, see any desk dictionary), most poets invent their own stanza forms and often do not use them for more than one poem. For example, Shelley's "Ode to a Skylark" uses a stanza which, so far as I remember, he did not use elsewhere: $a^3 b^3 a^3 b^3 b^6$ — the first four lines being trochaic (2 and 4 are truncated, the final unaccented syllable missing), and the last line iambic:

Hail to thee, blithe Spirit!
Bird thou never wert,
That from Heaven, or near it,
Pourest thy full heart
In profuse strains of unpremeditated art.

The release of the long, smooth iambic line suggests flight, particularly after the constraint of the preceding trochees. It is amusing to think of such a carefully wrought stanza being unpremeditated.

A poem is a group or groups of lines. There are some traditional formulae for whole poems, such as the *sonnet,* a fourteen line poem in iambic pentameter, usually with one of several traditional rhyme schemes. Of course sonnets may be linked — in which case they function something like stanzas. But usually sonnets are complete poems in themselves, whether or not they are in a related series.

Fixed forms, thus, are traditional designs for whole poems. The most common fixed forms in English poetry are *sonnets, sestinas, villanelles, haikus* and *limericks,* but there are many other fixed forms deriving from other languages (e.g., Welsh, French) which are sometimes imitated in English. (e.g., the *triolet, roundel, virelay, rispetto.)* Many of these are described briefly in ordinary dictionaries, but for more complete and authoritative references, you might want to own the Dutton paperback, *The Book of Forms* by Lewis Turco, or the useful and comprehensive *Encyclopedia of Poetry and Poetics* published by Princeton University Press.

You can call any piece of writing a poem — and find theoretical support for your contention. A *prose poem,* for example, is one which does not use that most fundamental element of verse, the line; rather, it is written in paragraphs indistinguishable in form from this one. Except for prose poetry, however, poems are pieces of writing in which the physical arrangement of language on the page is a significant and essential element. Poems are sometimes written in shapes — e.g., squares, circles, spreading wings. Sometimes acrostic messages are buried in them. Sometimes, as in *concrete poetry,* typography, color of ink and other graphic considerations may be important ingredients. *Formalism* is that form of decadence in which the artist becomes so preoccupied with playing games with arrangement of words that he forgets to concern himself with meaning.

Versification or *prosody* is the study of these aspects of form. Sometimes one is asked to distinguish between *verse* and *poetry* —

and complex and passionate discussions are likely to ensue. *Verse* can be objectively defined as language which has been versified, or arranged in some premeditated, artful form — particularly if it has been organized rhythmically. *Poetry* is often used loosely to refer to all versified writing. At other times people mean by that term something very subjective: they use it to refer to writing which they find elevated or elevating, inspired, imaginative, etc. Since it cannot be established with finality that any given piece of writing is or is not imaginative — or any of the other adjectives on that list — we may be sure that the discussion of what *poetry* means will go on forever. All that can be defined objectively is *verse*.

feeling your pulse

You need to learn to scan in order to understand the practice of other poets and to develop and extend your own. Paradoxically, over-regularity in a poet's work is usually the consequence of an inadequate understanding of prosody. He doesn't realize what he can do with a line and still have it satisfy the ear. Scanning, like listening to a pulse, is very helpful in diagnosis, both of a positive and negative sort. Infinite refinement is possible (as you begin to distinguish between secondary and primary stresses, long syllables and strong ones, etc.); but too much refinement begins to defeat the usefulness of the analysis. I recommend what may seem a roughshod treatment. Read the passage as naturally as possible — ignoring the underlying iambic pattern — and mark the syllables which *demand* emphasis for sense. Here is an example:

1st foot	2nd foot	3rd foot	4th foot	5th foot
DEATH be	not PROUD	though SOME	have CALL	ed THEE
MIGHT y	and DREAD	ful, for	thou ART	NOT SO,
For THOSE	who thou	THINK'ST thou	dost o	ver THROW
DIE NOT	POOR DEATH	nor YET	canst THOU	KILL ME

All these are disyllabic feet, the most common ones; but occasionally, in other passages, there will be additional unaccented syllables to assign to one foot or another; occasionally the line comes out short, and the only explanation is that one of the feet is monosyllabic, or truncated.

I have indicated stress in the passage above, and ultimately this is subjective. Do the first four syllables of line four receive equal stress? Of course not. No two syllables do; or, anyway, the concept of stress is so hazy that we have no way of determining what "equal" might mean as we juggle volume, length and pitch. The dictionary assigns a "secondary" accent to the first syllable of *overthrow,* but I hear little difference of emphasis between that syllable and those which precede and follow it. Another reader might hear it differently; but surely, it would be a lighter stress than those on *think'st* and *throw.* At any rate, we can deduce a great deal even from this rough sorting out of accents.

The poem is not what the writer writes, but what the reader hears or perceives. As a poet, you want your scansion to be a test: does the passage dissolve into prose? is it unmanageable? and, most importantly, why does it work or fail? In view of this practical purpose, you are justified in taking the more radical of two possible scansions. If you distort in the direction of mechanical regularity, you still have a poem, albeit a dull one. But if, in a dramatically justified reading, the poem loses all metrical organization, it is a piece of writing, still, and possibly a moving or powerful one, but not necessarily a poem. Therefore to test, push away from the regular alternating beat and see whether that leaves you a comprehensible organization. Donne's lines, you see, do.

But there are, as I count them, only ten pure iambs in twenty feet; moreover, it is iambs in succession that remind us of the alternating meter — there are four together in the first line, no two together in the next two lines, and two come together in the fourth. We can depend upon the alternating rhythm being present in the reader's mind, just as the musician can depend upon his audience's familiarity with the diatonic scale (which may be artificial, but it has been around so long that in our civilization it sounds like nature). Donne needn't remind us too often of the steady pulse that underlies his poem. He must suggest it, or the variations would be meaningless, but he keeps our attention on other rhythms.

You will find even less regularity in much verse from Chaucer on, particularly, of course, in modern poetry. I think you may take it as a principle that no more than about fifty per cent of iambic verse need be iambs; but these must be used strategically to maintain the suggestion of background rhythm. The iambs must be used as carefully and deliberately as you use the variant feet. Here Donne wants to create the cadences of a mind working to reassure itself again death (see the discussion of it in Chapter Eleven), emphasizing and subsiding loosely, jerked this way and that by thought. Notice the stresses pile up sometimes three at a time and unstressed syllables (as many as four together) race by in a mumble. Other effects might call for greater regularity (for example melodiousness, driving, steady thought, a lulling, peaceful passage). Iambic verse is flexible enough to permit any conceivable emotional cadence or degree of intensity, and for simple proof you need only read the plays of Shakespeare.

Pentameter theoretically calls for five stresses to a line; but as these lines illustrate, the actual number may vary from three to eight. As I have said, one of the simplest distinctions between poetry and prose is that poetry has relatively more stresses. There are forty syllables in the four quoted lines, of which twenty-one are stressed. In my last two sentences of prose there are forty-eight syllables, in which I count thirteen stresses. As language becomes more intellectual its words become polysyllabic, its connectives or "business" words — such as *of, the, it,* and forms of the verb *to be* — become more numerous; but when language hugs near earth and life, when it becomes more concrete and emotional, as it is likely to in poetry, plump monosyllabic words and heavy stresses characterize it. Donne starts with a bold command, goes twisting through a logical explanation, and returns to a tone of vigorous assertion. Notice how the stresses are related to this pattern.

As you write, the danger is you will have too few stresses rather than too many. Think of it in terms of maintaining tension or pull on a cord. When you release it, with too many unaccented syllables falling together, there is danger of the line turning to prose. Donne deliberately skirts this danger in his third line; notice how the tongue races over the syllables and the rhythm is blurred. Snap: he tugs the next line tighter than ever with four strong beats, and you are back into poetry again. Strings of unaccented syllables are sometimes dramatically useful, but you can hardly get by with more than Donne uses in that line (an accent will emerge whether you want it or not). And such a passage demands some reassertion of beat; another limp line following Donne's third and the poem might have been irrecoverable.

The first two lines start with reversed first feet — the commonest of all variations of iambic, especially for dramatic, down-beat openings. There is one other substitution of a trochee (DUM da) for an iamb, in that rocky third line. Mid-line trochees have a startling, disruptive effect; usually they occur after a caesura — when they divide the line in two. A similar effect comes from a truncated iamb or monosyllabic foot. These are most common at the beginning of lines, particularly following a feminine ending (unaccented syllable) on the preceding line, when they merely continue the alternating rhythm; after a caesura, a monosyllabic foot can throw a wonderfully strange, breathless emphasis on the caesural pause. ("The fence is gone; gone the furrows, too.")

Spondees and pyrrhics can occur in any position. Anapests rush or lilt; even one extra syllable gives a line a noticeable, sudden fillip (as, later in Donne's sonnet: Thou art SLAVE to FATE, CHANCE, KINGS, and DES per ate MEN). Dactyls (DUM da da), amphibrachs (da DUM da) and other more exotic feet are of little service in iambic verse; they almost invariably dissolve into other units.

Iambs, trochees, anapests, spondees and pyrrhics are, then, the basic colors on your palette, and you will find by experiment the tonal possibilities of their infinite combinations. By following iamb with spondee, or trochee with anapest, you get completely different emotional effects. If you put two of the same kind (other than iambs) together, they run away with the line (which, of course, can be desirable): as when two or three trochees stalk in mournful measure, or a series of anapests bubble or skip through the line. A steady, heavy beat or a tricky, complex meter tends to subvert the sense so that the reader is chanting or trotting along without too much regard for what the poem is saying. Unless you want that effect of incantation, your verse should be a sweet disorder of perpetual variation, coordinated so exactly with what you are saying that the rhythmic reinforcement is felt without being consciously noticed. So used, rhythm is the most useful single tool the poet has for guiding and intensifying his reader's response.

Line Units

where to draw the line

Mary	Mary had a	mar yhAD a (lit)le
had a little lamb	little lamb its	1,AM(bit)s
its fleece	fleece was white as	(flee) cew as w(hit)e
was white	snow and	ass(no)
as snow	everywhere that	w,AND EVE
and everywhere	Mary went her	r, y, W (hER) Et
that Mary went	lamb was sure to	(hA)t
her lamb	go	Mar ywen
was sure		thE,r lambwaSS
to go.		ure
		TOgO

Faced with so many possibilities, we may wonder how the poet struck upon the line arrangement he finally adopted. He may have noticed there were fourteen accents and that the seventh, *snow,* rhymed with the last. Conventionally punctuated, there is a complete sentence ending with the fourth beat and another ending with the seventh. Let us assume he saw the possibility of symmetry, and although he had only a clause ending after the eleventh beat, *went,* he chose to divide there, contrasting the rolling sentence to the two blunt statements which begin the poem. We have, then, as it usually is printed:

> Mary had a little lamb.
> Its fleece was white as snow.
> And everywhere that Mary went
> Her lamb was sure to go.

There is also a chance that the poet may have been influenced in his choice by the conventional ballad stanza which breaks up a couplet of fourteen syllable lines into a quatrain of four, three, four and three beats per line (discussed later in this chapter).

Line units are the most pervasive characteristic of all poetry, and it is not a simple matter in our day for a poet to decide where one line ought to end and the next begin. Some poets employ instinct. They have no fixed principle, but divide when they feel the urge. We have mingling traditions — units determined by number of stresses as in Anglo-Saxon verse and units determined by number of syllables. As explained in the last chapter, the most common practice is to mingle the two, creating accentual-syllabic verse in which the units are metrical feet. Notice that in the nursery rhyme the syllabic count does not quite work out, as the first foot is truncated (it would be more regular if it started, "Oh, Mary . . .") and an extra light syllable occurs in the third line. But there are, of course, a variety of principles which can be used with good effect. The three versions of Mary I gave at the beginning, though written in parody, can be used to illustrate technique which can actually be quite useful.

Notice first of all how important the line divisions are. Each gives a decidedly different emotional tone and effect to the words — because although we read right on, the line units make a momentary impression; we get the impact of the line and then of the sentences and rhetorical units. The first example breaks after significant words so that each line seems to *arrive,* to climb to a minor crest. That is, the lines can be made to emphasize the phrases or thought units or to pull against them.

The second example is based on an opposite principle. The significant words occur at the beginnings of the lines and the last words are all dropped, thrown away, the voice trailing off. Beginnings and endings of lines are the spots for natural emphases, and the endings are usually stronger. By deliberately de-emphasizing them, one gets an interestingly jerky, indifferent tone, a modern slur, shying from emotion and rhetoric.

Apologies to cummings for the third. While it may look silly, actually it is a kind of tribute — for he has taught us so much about the nature of words, punctuation, space, the nature of language, that we cannot use his lessons without seeming to parody him or imitate him too slavishly. Just as much modern painting fragments experience, vision, shape to make us really *see* it, make us aware of color and texture and form, so he fragmented language — and with an illuminating explosion. My version of "Mary" can be used to illustrate some of the possibilities.

Since our perception of punctuation, for example, had become dulled by habit, he put it to new uses. Here, for example, the capitalized letters (as sometimes in cummings) spell out a kind of anagram message: ADAM AND EVE WERE A MESS, TOO. Well, once we begin thinking about Adam and Eve in relation to that lamb and Mary, our minds become open to all sorts of things — from a more sacred Mary and sacred lamb to the bawdier implications of the first line. In cummings one would expect the various words within words, spaces, juxtapositions, interruptions and meldings to have some relevance to the poem's purpose (however difficult that relevance may be to discover). Here, I confess, they are somewhat arbitrary, although you might have fun considering them. Fun is a valuable part of the experience; it would be a great mistake to read cummings deadpan. It would also be a mistake to expect to be able to put all the various innuendoes and side effects of such a poem into a logical paraphrase. The method forces you to see the poem as a *thing,* an art object, no more subject to restatement than would be a statue.

Also, notice, it forces you to see. Poetry is primarily an auditory experience, but since most people come in contact with it on paper, there is ample reason for making it a visual experience as well. Though many poets, old and new, have experimented with its visual possibilities (writing poems like circles or wings or altars or diamonds or mirror images, or including various kinds of anagrams), no one has to the same extent as cummings made the written poem so much a part of its essential being. Many of his poems can be effectively read aloud — he has a magnificent lyric gift; but others cannot be read aloud at all, their meaning is so inextricable from their shape on the page.

Just as speech rhythms play against the standard alternating beat, rhetorical units — phrases, sentences, paragraphs — play against line and stanza units. You get a powerful effect of reinforcement when you make them coincide (with "closed" lines or stanzas, sharp caesuras) and tense straining when you make them conflict (enjambment). Enjambment can speed up the lines, as in Marvell's

> Let us roll all our strength and all
> Our sweetness up into one ball;

Or it can create a number of other effects, such as awkward hesitation (try splitting an infinitive between two lines), humor (as, to end a line with an adjective and start the next line with an unexpected noun), ambiguity (as when the line read as a unit means one thing, but taken with the following line means something quite different), emphasis (forcing you to come down hard on the word that starts the next line) or uneasiness (as when the grammatical function of the words in one line is not clear until you have arrived at the next). It takes advantage, of course, of the instant of hesitation at the end of the line which gives it its definition. Try taking a familiar passage, as I have done with Mary, and dividing it different ways; you will learn much, I think, which you can apply in your own writing.

The values of traditional line patterns can be illustrated very easily in this fashion — if, for example, you destroyed the magnificent cadences of Milton's decasyllabic movement opening *Paradise Lost,* by breaking the lines as Amy Lowell might have done:

> Of Man's First Disobedience,
> And the Fruit of that Forbidden Tree,
> Whose mortal taste brought Death into the World,
> And all our woe,
> With loss of *Eden,*
> Till one greater Man restore us,
> And regain the blissful Seat,
> Sing Heav'nly Muse, . . .

The tension, the swell and drama are gone. The phrases were there anyway, with the punctuation marks. The poet is neglecting a powerful resource if he fails to make his lines do something else, in addition.

The common line lengths in English poetry are from three stresses to six. One or two stress lines have almost a trick effect, as in Donne's

> And find
> What wind
> Serves to advance an honest mind.

A seven stress line (although it used to be popular), divides almost invariably into four and three, and longer lines similarly divide. A three beat line is, particularly if used with rhyme, song-like, making you very much aware of its rhythm and shape. (But it is particularly useful for "accentual" meter, in which the number of unaccented syllables varies drastically while the number of stresses per line remains constant; a longer accentual line than three tends to lose its definition.) Four beat lines are the most common for song (particularly "headless" lines with a truncated first foot: DUM da DUM da DUM da DUM). It also makes a good jogging meter for longer poems (it is sometimes called "dog-trot," particularly when it occurs as tetrameter couplets).

An interesting variation of the standard line lengths comes of overlapping one with another: Eliot's "April is the cruelest month, breeding . . ." is a pentameter line, but with a tetrameter unit superimposed. The parasitic line holds words in a strange suspension and can be used for other effects, too, particularly if combined with rhyme. (E.g., write out a tetrameter poem, such as "To His Coy Mistress" in pentameter lines, letting the rhymes fall where they may; it may suggest to you some use you can make of this as a deliberate device.) Another variation is to interweave standard lines with phrase-determined lines. (Study the line breaks in Arnold's "Dover Beach," which builds up to its pentameter and recedes from it like the waves it describes.)

the use of silence

The marks the poet makes on the page are, for the most part, signals representing sounds. But the poet must also control, so far as he can, the silences between the sounds. Aside from the punctuation marks available to the writer of prose, the poet has at his disposal line-endings, stanza and strophe breaks, and caesuras to measure his reader's pauses.

The basic unit of meaning in poetry, as in prose, is the sentence (phrases, clauses and even words being subparts). The basic formal unit is the line. In the skillful play of the line against the sentence the poet creates and resolves tension to give his writing that third dimension poetry requires.

Although there may be no stop in sense at the end of the poetic line, there is a momentary vocal and visual hesitation — which may be used to set off a phrase, to bring a slightly heavier emphasis upon the word beginning the next line, or to surprise the reader when the thought twists in an unexpected direction:

> A golden net contained her raven hair
> Which broke upon her neck just like a pair
> Of shoes slung by the laces . . .

Hair completes a grammatical unit, hence the line is said to be "closed."

When a grammatical unit thus coincides with a formal unit, the reader has a sense of stability and harmony, and the line end pause is extended. *Pair,* however, needs more words to complete the idea. The line is said to be enjambed. The pause is slighter, as the inertia of the sentence carries the reader forward to complete the thought in the next line. In this case humor is assisted by the enjambment — a pair of what? the reader wonders; and then his eye or voice comes down hard on the undignified resolution of the grammatical suspense.

The rhyme in that illustration also assists the humor by suggesting some finality in the conclusion of the line. Rhymes at the ends of lines are prominent, emphatic, stabilizing: they have a tendency to stop the voice and the sense. Thus some poor readers of poetry come to a full stop whenever they reach the end of a line or a rhyme, often butchering the meaning. Shakespeare illustrated the chaos induced by a poor reader's misunderstanding of the line-end and sentence-end pauses by his punctuation of Quince's prologue to the play of the artisans' in *A Midsummer-Night's Dream:*

> If we offend, it is with our good will.
> That you should think, we come not to offend;
> But with good will. To shew our simple skill,
> That is the true beginning of our end.
> Consider then, we come but in despite.
> We do not come, as minding to content you,
> Our true intent is. All for your delight,
> We are not here. That you should here repent you,
> The Actors are at hand; and by their show,
> You shall know all, that you are like to know.

The pauses available for a poet's use are more various than those at the disposal of the writer of prose. Graded from the slightest pause to the greatest they are:

1. Line-ending within a grammatical unit (e.g., "a pair/ Of shoes")
2. Semi-stop, or comma, within a line
3. Semi-stop, or comma, at line ending
4. Full stop (.?!) within the line
5. Full stop at line ending

The complexity (or variety) is increased by rhyme, which tends to lengthen pauses, especially when it occurs at the end of a line.

Internal rhymes and strong sound echoes tend to slow down the pace of lines by making the notes linger — or to create slight pauses if they occur at the end of grammatical units.

A pause necessitated by the completion of a grammatical unit (usually marked by punctuation) within a line is called a *caesura.* Usually there is one caesura per line, though some lines have no distinct pause at all. In some poetry (e.g., ancient Greek and Latin and Anglo-Saxon), caesuras are used with such strength and regularity that each half-line is almost a line in itself; for illustration I have marked the primary caesuras with a double bar (//):

> Older than English:// how evil emerges
> on a moor in the moonlight,// emotionless, faceless,
> stiff-kneed, arms rigid,// and stalks through the fog field
> until finally its fist falls,// forcing the oaken door
> of whatever Heorot// harbors the gentle folk.

In this imitation of Anglo-Saxon poetry, each half-line has two beats. The first or second beat before the caesura alliterates with the first beat after the caesura. Such poetry was probably chanted by the bards with the rhythmic chords struck on the lyre for each half-line.

Ordinarily, however, in English verse the caesura is used in freely varying patterns of speech rhythms imposed upon the formality of the line unit. "The artistic use of the caesura," says Shipley's *Dictionary of World Literature,* "is one of the surest tests of a writer's skill. In general, the more the composer adjusts his phrasing by normal speech cadences and less by prosodic rule, the richer will be the interlacing pattern." That would imply the more variety the better. Rather, I would say that the caesura — like line endings, rhyme, meter and other elements of poetry — can be used to emphasize regularity, stability, harmony, and order or to create raggedness, tenseness, disorder, and imbalance. Which is the better use depends upon what the poet wants in a given poem.

To illustrate the interworking of these various units and kinds of pauses, I have marked up the opening lines of Browning's "My Last Duchess." Complete sentences (even if they are divided by semicolons or colons) are boxed. Caesuras are marked by double bars. Enjambed lines are marked with arrows; closed lines are followed by an X.

/ | That's my last Duchess //painted on the wall, | X

| Looking as if she were alive.// | I call |₂   →

2 | That piece a wonder,//now:// | Frá Pandolf's hands →

3 | Worked busily a day,// and there she stands. ✗

4 | Will't please you sit and look at her?// | I said   5 →

"Frá Pandolf" by design,// for never read →

Strangers like you// that pictured countenance, ✗

The depth and passion// of its earnest glance, ✗

5 | But to myself they turned// (since none puts by →

The curtain I have drawn for you,// but I)   10 ✗

And seemed as they would ask me,// if they durst, ✗

How such a glance came there;// | so,// not the first →

6 | Are you to turn and ask thus.// | Sir,// 'twas not →

Her husband's presence only,// called that spot →

7 | Of joy into the Duchess' cheek:// | perhaps   15 →

Frá Pandolf chanced to say,// "Her mantle laps →

Over my lady's wrist too much,"// or// "Paint →

8 | Must never hope// to reproduce the faint →

Half-flush that dies along her throat:"// | such stuff →

Was courtesy,// she thought,// and cause enough   20 →

9 | For calling up that spot of joy.// | She had →

A heart — // how shall I say? — // too soon made glad, ✗

10 | Too easily impressed;// she liked whate'er →

11 | She looked on,// and her looks went everywhere. ✗

12 | Sir,// 'twas all one!// | My favor at her breast,   25 ✗

The dropping of the daylight in the West, ✗

The bough of cherries// some officious fool →

13 | Broke in the orchard for her,// the white mule →

She rode with round the terrace — // all and each →

Would draw from her alike// the approving speech,   30 ✗

The first line rolls out to its full length and closes — establishing the line length for the reader's ear. A caesura late in the line, as in the second, tips the reader forward, sends him quickly on to the next line so that the rhyme closing the couplet is hardly noticed. The fourth line, balanced by a central caesura, concluding on a firm rhyme and the end of the sentence, marks the end of a movement of the poem, but in the fifth line the poet wants speed and instability again to fit the conversational tone, so "I said," like "I call" above, propels the reader into the long fifth sentence. The Duke is being very deliberate and careful, however, and so the sentence is broken into distinct units, tending to closed lines. When he reaches the point of his elaborate explanation in line 12, tension increases, so we have a long sequence of rapidly enjambed lines, suppressing the rhyme, pulling hard against the line unit with short sentences and phrases ending emphatically within the lines. A passage such as this builds a strong expectation — even a need — of resolution in a closed line; when it finally comes, in line 22, the key phrase, "too soon made glad," is set up for us by the hesitation, the rhythmic uncertainty of the beginning of the line, and then the four strong beats together, ending a couplet with a rhyme, ending a grammatical unit. The Duke then backs off and tries again, at last spilling out with lyric grace the central clue to the personality of the Duchess:

> . . . She liked whate'er
> She looked on, and her looks went everywhere.

Browning has, by skillful managing of his pauses, made us yearn for the fulfillment of that line: we ride out to its length and conclude couplet and sentence together.

It is commonplace to note about this poem that many readers and listeners finish it without being aware of the rhymes at all. Browning had so successfully tamed the rigidities of the heroic couplet that it seems limber and various as blank verse, and yet the resources of the rhyme and balance are there, even if only perceived subconsciously, to underscore the Duke's formality and calculation — in contrast to the blank verse silver ramblings of his "Andrea del Sarto" or spurting comments of "Fra Lippo Lippi."

Caesuras are sharper, more definite, when they occur at the end of metrical feet ("to say,// 'Her mantle . . .'") than between the syllables of a metrical foot ("Sir,//'twas all one"). If an internal rhyme occurs before a caesura it is more emphatic than if it occurs elsewhere in the line — and, in general, caesuras provide the occasion for other devices associated with line endings. For example, trochees are most common in iambic verse in two positions — at the beginning of a line and after a caesura.

Silence — or pause — is one of the most valuable resources a poet has, and yet it is difficult to control. Readers can put in pauses at will to suit their subjective interpretations — and a poet can imagine pauses which have great significance for him but do not reach the reader unless the poet has succeeded in building them into the verse. Caesura and enjambment are the chief means he has of exercising control over dramatic hesitation and the emphasis of stillness.

free verse

Many beginners start writing verse in rhymed and metrical patterns because that is the kind of verse they are most familiar with. The tune is memorized, and to write a poem one need only supply new words. Some are timid about trying their hand at free verse. Without the reassurance of stanza form, recurring rhyme and regular rhythm, they have no confidence that what they are writing is poetry.

I will not try to decide with them whether the results are poetry or not, but I will provide some suggestions and some ways of looking at free verse which may encourage such writers to overcome their timidity. In the first place, recognize that you are boss. It is your poem. You put what words in what form on the paper you please. There is no mysterious tribunal that decides that a piece of writing is or is not a poem. It is a poem if you call it one. I may choose not to publish it. I may not like it. But I have no right to say it is not a poem.

And it logically follows that there is no "right" way to write free verse: that would be a contradiction in terms. If there were a way it was supposed to be, it wouldn't be free. Can free verse ever rhyme? Who is to say no? (Much does!) Can it be metrical? Of course. (Most of it can be scanned by conventional techniques!) How long should the lines be? (From a single letter — or even a non-letter, a space, a symbol — to a fat paragraph.) To all such questions there is one answer — one that is sometimes difficult to believe and comprehend: there are *no rules*.

Robert Frost disparaged free verse for that reason, saying that it was like playing tennis with the net down. (Nonetheless, Frost wrote some excellent free verse; see, for instance, "The Lovely Shall Be Choosers" or "After Apple-Picking." I would go Frost one better and say it is like playing tennis without a net, a court, rackets, balls or a partner. The player is free, of course, to use any of those familiar elements he wishes. (He is free to do anything.) But he can dispense with one and all, and, if he chooses, still call the game tennis.

Free verse merely points up something that is true about all poetry, but inescapable in this form. Every line of poetry should be interesting in itself — for the *way* it speaks as well as for *what* it says. Rhyme and meter often carry along very dull writing — as does music. (The lyrics of many lovely songs are quite commonplace when read without the music.)

> I went to town to buy some bread
> and met a lady there who said
> my Uncle Jack had just dropped dead
> so I went home with heart of lead
> and plumb forgot to buy the bread.

That is, I hope you'll grant, quite undistinguished writing. But the rhymes and meter do a little to hold up its starchless lines. What happens if we remove meter and rhyme?

> To get some bread I went down town
> where I was told by a lady
> that my Uncle Jack had just died
> and I was so saddened that I went home
> completely forgetting to buy bread.

The first version may pass as conventional verse; but the second will never do as free verse. (Oh, it will *do;* if I call it free verse, you have no grounds for contradicting me. Nonetheless, it is *lousy* free verse.)

For one thing, macabre as it may be, the first version was slightly humorous, but in the second version the humor is gone. It is almost impossible for free verse to be humorous. Ogden Nash carried freedom about as far as it could go in light verse, but imagine how dead his verses would be without their rhymes. I don't think there is much one can do to redeem that poor anecdote as free verse, but I'll make a try in order to illustrate some points:

Town. Bread. I thread the ordinary
street.
Greet a neighbor, her face a twist of grief.
The grief, I find,
is mine.
Uncle Jack. Abruptly dead. I flee
those streets of commonplace, my young
heart grey and numb and huge, my mind
oblivious to need,
to town,
to bread.

This illustrates some of the devices available to you in free verse
which you are likely to forget about if you stick to conventional
forms. Incomplete sentences, grammatical experimentation. Instead
of end rhymes, internal rhymes (street-greet; bread-thread; find-
mine-mind). Stark enjambment (ordinary/street; young/heart).
Dramatic use of short lines (is mine). In short, writing free verse
forces you to exert new pressures on the language, to twist the
lines tighter, to discover new relationships between words, to find
images and diction that will be more evocative, more compelling
in themselves, and to arrange the words on the page so that the
pattern itself will have meaning (as in the echo of the beginning
words at the end).

The example also illustrates some of the dangers implicit in
free verse. The need to make each piece of expression heightened
and intense may result in a poem that is pretentious and mawkish.
One can imagine that last version of the poem being read at
the local meeting of the Poetry Society by a busty matron who
considers herself an actress *manqué*. Reread it, supplying her
gestures, gasps, heavy articulation, perhaps tears. That should point
out what a truly dreadful poem we have here. Any poem can
be spoiled by a bad delivery, but some poetry, especially some
amateur free verse, is more susceptible to such corruption than
other varieties. The first version, with its mechanical, wooden
meter and rhymes, was at least mildly amusing and humble. Blown
up into high drama, the poem becomes what Alexander Pope called
bathetic. There is nothing wrong with the commonplace in itself;
but when it is hurled out with fanfare and purple banners, the
result is bathos.

Let us ask that same matron to read us a poem by Amy Lowell,
to see how that stands up. In many ways Amy was the prototype

member of the Poetry Society, and often her voice is strident, pompous, melodramatic or bathetic. But her talent was authentic and came through even in minor poems such as this:

THE TAXI

When I go away from you
The world beats dead
Like a slackened drum.
I call out for you against the jutted stars
And shout into the ridges of the wind.
Streets coming fast,
One after the other,
Wedge you away from me,
And the lamps of the city prick my eyes
So that I can no longer see your face.
Why should I leave you,
To wound myself upon the sharp edges of the night?

This is close enough to the kind of poem that a beginner in free verse might write that it will be instructive to analyze it closely. The intent of the poem is to convey an overwhelming sense of loneliness upon departure from a lover. The first three lines are almost a poem in themselves — and, indeed, fall only one syllable short of a haiku. Let me add a syllable and arrange them as a haiku to illustrate:

When I go away
from you the world beats dead like
a slackening drum.

I think I like that better; *slackening* contains within it the sense of moving away, of progressive deadness.

The language of those three lines is simple, flat, the rhythm heavy, stark, in keeping with the thought. The next two lines are a dramatic contrast. They are nearly regular iambic pentameter which is appropriate to their heightened rhetoric, their dramatic posturing. *Jutted* and *ridges* introduce the "sharp edges" which unify the remaining lines of the poem. The next five lines relate the poem to the title: we imagine the lady being whisked away in a taxi (horse-drawn, most likely), and the pace is rapid, breathless, the tone comparatively prosaic. If we reconstruct the dramatic experience of parting, she first feels the dead loss; then she cries out in heroic, grandiloquent protest; next she endures the clip-clopping steady reality of the taxi moving farther and farther away from her beloved, tears coming to her eyes as it seems the sharp passing lights of the city blind her to the face she carries in her memory. Finally, in the last two lines, a simple question (unanswerable), and a return to the imagery of lines 4 and 5 — a lonely woman against the night, encountering the unfeeling universe.

This is good free verse because there is a continual modulation of rhythm, diction and imagery to the content of the poem, its thought and changing feeling. When the emotions are tempestuous, the lines swell out and draw on the conventional rhythms of metered poetry. When they are subdued, the lines become clipped, quiet, prosaic. I don't think that busty matron will ruin the poem by throwing herself into it dramatically as she reads; the poem is conceived of as dramatic statement, and its technique supports that form of delivery.

On the other hand, we can see here some of the limitations of Amy Lowell's poetry — and some that characterize much free verse. She uses phrasal line breaks almost exclusively: that is, each line is a separate rhetorical unit, complete in itself. Free verse is more interesting (to me) when it uses different kinds of enjambment and surprise, when the line endings are used to create irony, dramatic hesitation, blurring, change of cadence. And I find the poem lacking in unity: the experience of the first three lines is not tied into the basic imagery of tenderness thrown against sharp edges. Loneliness can make one feel numb; it can make one feel hurt, agonized; and it can make one feel both of these in succession. But a good poem, I believe, at least takes cognizance of the contrast of feelings, provides either some transition or deliberately pits one against the other. In this poem, as in many of Amy Lowell's, the lines seem just spun out one after another, with too little heed for the overall structure and unity of the poem. That artlessness often characterizes the work of poets who are attracted by free verse and fail to recognize that it is harder — not easier — to make art when working without clearly defined, recognizable formal boundaries.

In spite of the difficulties, I recommend that amateur poets try free verse. I believe it will force them to look more closely at their language, imagery, rhythms, structures, to question how each functions and how each element relates to the overall intent of the poem. Regularity dulls the ear and the perception, both of the poet and the reader. Good free verse draws on the harmonies and associations and techniques of traditional verse; and good traditional verse employs many of the devices of surprise, variation and modulation of rhythm and tone which can be learned by writing free verse. Good poets learn to write both ways — and to make their practice in one mode support and deepen their practice in the other.

Like rhythm, rhyme, alliteration, or any other element of poetic technique, line division usually is more effective when it subtly reinforces or expands meaning without calling attention to itself. For this reason the traditional forms, which do *not* ostentatiously challenge the reader, may well enable the content to challenge him more powerfully. This is not to say, however, that you can relax to a familiar tune and write good poetry. I recommend a continual experiment of pushing and pulling against the boundaries which tradition has provided.

blank verse

Pentameter is, of course, the standard line of English poetry — and for good reasons. Its odd number of beats does not divide monotonously in two (as hexameter, for example, tends to do). It has a comfortable relation to our breathing (so much so that I knew one Shakespearean actor who sucked breath like a pump at the end of every line — not recommended!). It is long enough not to obtrude itself on our consciousness — that is, it can be made, when desired, to slip inconspicuously into sentence structure — and yet it is short enough to be heard as a single cadence, to roll out as a thumping, resonant whole. It is capable of almost bewildering variety so that you can read a mile or so of Pope's couplets and think no two were rhythmically identical; or you can read the pentameter of Frost and Dylan Thomas, for example, without the least consciousness that they are using basically the same meter.

More specifically, the grain of verse in English is such that unrhymed iambic pentameter, or blank verse, over the centuries, has been its most distinctive expression, for that is the form poets return to again and again for sustained work, particularly in drama and narrative and longer reflective poems.

I would like to look at the exciting spectacle of a young poet learning the uses of this medium. When Shakespeare was about thirty he already had some ten plays on the boards, had settled into the use of unrhymed iambic pentameter as his standard form (following the example of Marlowe and other Elizabethan playwrights), had over-indulged in rhyme, alliteration, antithesis and other devices to shore up his insecurity in the open form, and, as he gained more confidence, was learning to risk more run-on lines, more metrical variations, more colloquialism and earthy humor in the creation of character. *Romeo and Juliet,* written at that stage of his career, embodies all that he was learning. He had created rich and varied characters in his other plays, but not so many, not so consistently. Suddenly on the stage appear a whole range of fascinatingly different individuals — all speaking iambic pentameter. Let's take a look at how he did it.

After a Euphuistic prologue, lush with alliteration, balance, antithesis and parallelism, the first scene, between servants, swirls on in racy, colloquial prose — following a convention (which Shakespeare was later to modify considerably) that, for the most part, only persons of dignity, delicacy and rank spoke verse. Accordingly, the first line of iambic pentameter is that of Benvolio, the young nobleman who rushes onstage to stop the fight which is breaking out:

> Put up your swords. You know not what you do.

Probably the Christian echo of that simple line is deliberate. Metrical regularity not only establishes Benvolio's even, unpretentious character, but, as it were, announces the harmonic base for verse to follow. Immediately the fiery Tybalt enters. Note how the heavy, dislocated accents of his rough verse — and the pretentiousness of his language — contrast with the humble sincerity of the line above:

> What, art thou drawn among these heartless hinds?
> Turn thee, Benvolio, look upon thy death.

Two old couples next enter, the Capulets and Montagues, parents, respectively, of Juliet and Romeo. As we will learn later, the Capulets are much the more colorful pair — more coarse, irascible and impetuous than the relatively elegant, placid and moderate Montagues. These contrasts are apparent if one looks closely at their very first exchange:

CAP.   What noise is this? Give me my long sword, ho!

LADY CAP.   A crutch, a crutch! Why call you for a sword?

CAP. My sword, I say! Old Montague is come,
And flourishes his blade in spite of me.

MON. Thou villain Capulet! — Hold me not, let me go.

LADY MON. Thou shall not stir one foot to seek a foe.

Capulet's verse is rocky, his language rough. It is not only physically
that Montague is restrained, and the couplet, tying off the little
encounter, is suggestive of the Montagues' disposition to be orderly
and formal.

Romeo is recognizably a Montague by the verse he uses — as
Juliet is recognizably a Capulet. Romeo's first scene is with Benvolio,
and he reveals himself to be a lovesick intellectual, addicted to
closed lines, verbal cleverness, rhetorical agility and aristocratic
formality. Looking on the scene of the street fight he says:

Why then, O brawling love! O loving hate!
O anything, of nothing first create!
O heavy lightness! Serious vanity!
Misshapen chaos of well-seeming forms!
Feather of lead, bright smoke, cold fire, sick health!
Still-waking sleep, that is not what it is!
This love feel I, that feel no love in this.

He loves paradox, oxymorons, strong medial pauses, philosophic
abstraction and metaphors drawn from literary convention, parallelism, rhetoric. He is very nearly a parody of the courtly lover.
Because he is obviously intelligent, sensitive and well-meaning, we
cannot dislike him, but we may find ourselves suppressing an indulgent smile. It will be difficult to take him seriously as a tragic hero.
But as the play progresses, we will watch him assume his manhood — and his blank verse matures accordingly.

The most remarkable creation of character in the play, and the
best evidence that the young playwright had mastered his verse
medium, is the Nurse. Her very first speech establishes her essential
qualities; Lady Montague has asked her where Juliet is, and she
replies:

Now, by my maidenhead at twelve year old,
I bade her come. What, lamb! What, ladybird! —
God forbid! — Where's this girl? What, Juliet!

Almost every phrase is laced with sexuality, humor and a raucous
buoyancy. As casually as less vivid people might say, "As sure as
I'm sitting here right now," she says, in effect, "As sure as I was

a virgin at twelve . . ." Affectionate endearment tumbles over into mild profanity, soft appeal into screeching demand. In her next breath she bets fourteen of her teeth (confessing parenthetically that she has but four) that Juliet is not fourteen years old. Shakespeare knew he was on to a good thing with this woman. He immediately gives her one of the longest speeches in the play, a wild irrelevant ramble on the subject of Juliet's age and birth date:

> Even or odd, of all days in the year,
> Come Lammas Eve at night shall she be fourteen.
> Susan and she — God rest all Christian souls! —
> Were of an age. Well, Susan is with God.
> She was too good for me. — But, as I said,
> On Lammas Eve at night shall she be fourteen.
> That shall she, marry, I remember it well.
> 'Tis since the earthquake now eleven years,
> And she was weaned — I never shall forget it —
> Of all the days of the year, upon that day.
> For I had then laid wormwood to my dug,
> Sitting in the sun under the dovehouse wall;
> My lord and you were then at Mantua. —
> Nay, I do bear a brain. — But, as I said,
> When it did taste the wormwood on the nipple
> Of my dug, and felt it bitter, pretty fool,
> To see it tetchy, and fall out with the dug!

She runs on, with Lady Capulet trying to shut her up, for another twenty-four lines, carried away with one of those bawdy anecdotes of childhood guaranteed to embarrass an adolescent girl who hears herself remembered as a baby. In the lines quoted above we pick up a bushel of information: that the Nurse was a wet nurse, no doubt hired because she was still giving milk and her own daughter had died, that Juliet was weaned at nearly three, that the method of weaning was (as some parents used to break children of sucking their thumbs) to apply a bitter ointment to the breast, that the parents left the baby with the Nurse (and, it turns out, her now dead husband) while they traveled, and even that the play may be imagined to have been set in 1591, eleven years after the earthquake of April, 1580! We become familiar with her scatter-brained free association, her matter-of-fact piety, her innocent pride in the quality of her memory ("Nay, I do bear a brain"), and her lack of squeamishness about the intimate, physical facts of life.

And the poet, to create this verbal flesh and blood, elbows his way around in the constraints of the pentameter line as though he were wearing an old coat. When I bought a ten speed bike — though I had been riding a bike for nearly forty years — I was nervous and uncertain as a bride on this gleaming, intricate machine. The chain clanked and jerked as I awkwardly shifted; I watched my gears and forgot to watch where I was going, weaving dangerously down the street. I couldn't remember the sequence or which lever did what. So it is when a poet begins working in a new form. He's not familiar with the limits and the changes, the possible variations within the bounds of grace, the way of shifting and steering simultaneously.

The problem in blank verse is how to maintain a sense of poetry without the obvious signals of rhyme, stanzas and other devices. This is the insecurity which causes a poet growing used to the form to use heavily poetic-sounding metaphors, alliteration, balanced and closed lines and excessively regular meter. If he gets too prosy, he knows, the sustaining power of the rhythm and line cadence will be lost. For comparison, let me put some of that passage into modern prose:

> Whether it's an even or an odd day I know she'll be fourteen on the night of Lammas Eve. Susan (God rest her!) and she were exactly the same age, but Susan has gone to Heaven. I guess I wasn't good enough for her. But I was talking about her birthday, when she'll be fourteen on the night of Lammas Eve. By the Virgin, I'm sure of that. It's eleven years now since the earthquake, which was the year she was weaned, I remember for certain . . .

Subdued and loosely handled as the meter is in the original, it contains an excitement and verve and strength of expression which prose can hardly approximate.

Virtuosity of a completely different sort is evident in the play's next set-piece, the long "Queen Mab" speech of Mercutio, Romeo's bawdy gentleman friend. Ordinarily Mercutio is jocular, witty and obscene. Suddenly, to make fun of Romeo's serious sense of foreboding, based on a dream, Mercutio streaks off into a lyrical flight which, though as amusing as his usual speech, is also delicately imaginative and minutely beautiful. He begins this way:

> Oh then, I see Queen Mab hath been with you.
> She is the fairies' midwife, and she comes

> In shape no bigger than an agate stone
> On the forefinger of an alderman,
> Drawn with a team of little atomies
> Athwart men's noses as they lie asleep —
> Her waggon spokes made of long spinners' legs;
> The cover, of the wings of grasshoppers;
> Her traces, of the smallest spider's web;
> Her collars, of the moonshine's watery beams;
> Her whip, of cricket's bone; the lash, of film;
> Her waggoner, a small gray-coated gnat
> Not half so big as a round little worm
> Pricked from the lazy finger of a maid.
> Her chariot is an empty hazelnut,
> Made by the joiner squirrel or old grub,
> Time out o' mind the fairies' coachmakers.

Shakespeare was to learn that a speech which is so much like a poem, which stops the play like a vaudeville act to draw attention to a particular patch of language and particular performer, is not good drama. It may work in comedy, which, as an "entertainment," can have some of the qualities of a variety show. But such devices strain our credulity too much to work in a play in which the effect depends upon our identification with the characters as real people. If this speech is compared with that of the Nurse it will be seen to rely upon a series of self-conscious rhetorical and poetical devices which seriously compromise its authenticity as dramatic speech. It is misleading as characterization of Mercutio, who is simultaneously one of the most sparkling and credible human beings in the play.

Friar Laurence is a wise, rational and compassionate man whose efforts at ingenious manipulation of nature prove to be the downfall of the lovers. His first speech, also a set-piece, is in couplets; the rhyme assists the characterization of him as formal, thoughtful and mannered. It begins this way:

> The gray-eyed morn smiles on the frowning night,
> Checkering the eastern clouds with streaks of light.
> And fleckéd darkness like a drunkard reels
> From forth day's path and Titan's fiery wheels.
> Now, ere the sun advance his burning eye,
> The day to cheer and night's dank dew to dry,
> I must upfill this osier cage of ours
> With baleful weeds and precious-juicéd flowers.

Notice the intricate antitheses: morn and night, clouds and light, drunken darkness and Titan sun, weeds and flowers. Romeo's neat paradoxes pointed up irrationality; Friar Laurence's vision of life is one of balance, harmony, reason and moderation — hence his appearance just between the night's wildness and day's heat. (Among its other tasks, this speech serves the purposes of scenery and lighting in modern drama.)

Another example of the strains and uses to which the pentameter line may be put in this explosion of old Capulet's temper when Juliet refuses to marry Paris:

LADY CAP. You are too hot.
CAP.   God's bread! It makes me mad.
        Day, night, hour, tide, time, work, play,
        Alone, in company, still my care hath been
        To have her matched. And having now provided
        A gentleman of noble parentage,
        Of fair demesnes, youthful, and nobly trained,
        Stuffed, as they say, with honorable parts,
        Proportioned as one's thought would wish a man —
        And then to have a wretched puling fool,
        A whining mammet, in her fortune's tender,
        To answer "I'll not wed, I cannot love,
        I am too young, I pray you, pardon me."
        But an you will not wed, I'll pardon you.
        Graze where you will, you shall not house with me.
        Look to't, think on't, I do not use to jest.
        Thursday is near. Lay hand on heart, advise.
        An you be mine, I'll give you to my friend.
        An you be not, hang, beg, starve, die in the streets,
        For, by my soul, I'll ne'er acknowledge thee,
        Nor what is mine shall never do thee good —
        Trust to't, bethink you, I'll not be forsworn.

The words and phrases pile up, stream out, congest again, and swirl forward in a tumultuous clotted stream.

Juliet, his daughter, also has a temper that can flare and an invective that can flow like burning oil. In contrast to Romeo, she tends to be down-to-earth, realistic. When she asks him how he got into her garden he answers with a flight of fancy:

ROMEO With love's light wings did I o'erperch these walls,
        For stony limits cannot hold love out.
        And what love can do, that dares love attempt,

Therefore thy kinsmen are no let to me.
JULIET If they do see thee, they will murder thee.
As must always have been true of young men and women, he
rhapsodizes and she wants to know about the marriage arrangements. (See the further discussion of this scene in Chapter Eleven.)

In comparison with the other speeches I have quoted, Juliet's
incarnation in blank verse is hesitant, girlish, pushing forward
with tentative impulses and withdrawing in blushing confusion. She
has imagination, too, and a throbbing tenderness (and sometimes
passion), but her speeches are simpler than Romeo's, less addicted
to rhetoric and stock phrases from the world's storehouse of love
poetry:

> Thou know'st the mask of night is on my face,
> Else would a maiden blush bepaint my cheek
> For that which thou has heard me speak tonight.
> Fain would I dwell on form, fain, fain deny
> What I have spoke. But farewell compliment!
> Dost thou love me? I know thou wilt say "Aye,"
> And I will take thy word. Yet if thou swear'st,
> Thou mayst prove false. At lovers' perjuries
> They say Jove laughs. O gentle Romeo,
> If thou dost love, pronounce it faithfully.
> Or if thou think'st I am too quickly won,
> I'll frown and be perverse and say thee nay,
> So thou wilt woo; but else, not for the world.
> In truth, fair Montague, I am too fond,
> And therefore thou mayst think my 'havior light.
> But trust me, gentleman, I'll prove more true
> Than those that have more cunning to be strange.

His love is headlong and, as she accuses him, "by the book." Hers
is a continual challenge. As their personalities meld it is intriguing
to watch how his characteristic verse patterns invade her speech
and thought and how he gradually grows up to her simplicity and
realism. When he hears of her supposed death his response is
brief, manly, and hard-nosed:

> Is it e'en so? Then I defy you, stars!
> Thou know'st my lodging. Get me ink and paper,
> And hire post horses. I will hence tonight.

The richness of his imagination, so lightly spent in mere verbal
cleverness at the beginning of the play, serves at the end to give
the poetry a luminous intensity; He speaks to drugged Juliet,

thinking she is dead:

> Death, that hath sucked the honey of thy breath,
> Hath had no power yet upon thy beauty.
> Thou art not conquered; beauty's ensign yet
> Is crimson in thy lips and in thy cheeks,
> And death's pale flag is not advancéd there.
> . . .
> Why art thou yet so fair? Shall I believe
> That unsubstantial death is amorous:
> And that the lean abhorréd monster keeps
> Thee here in dark to be his paramour?

If you will compare that with the first of Romeo's lines which I quoted, you will see much less use of artificial rhetoric and merely decorative metrical devices. The imagery is fanciful, but strong and fresh; it permits us to believe in the depth of his feeling.

Repeatedly my advice to poets hoping to learn craft is to scan Shakespeare. Learn the rudiments of metrics — which you can do in an hour — and then analyze passage after passage of the plays, studying how the rhythms are related to the imagery, the dramatic function of the lines, the characterization of the speaker. I have only given some clues here — some suggestions for further study. If you wrestle with the details of the quoted passages until you are confident you understand what is going on in them and why, you will acquire a repertory of skills which can be adapted to an infinite range of poetic purposes.

native English meter: the traditional ballad

If blank verse is our predominant literary form, the ballad is our predominant folk form. As is true of most primitive art, ballads which survive are likely to be built on a basic structure of astonishing aesthetic strength. A study of one of them, "Frankie and Johnny," will illustrate the enormous complexity involved in line division when accentual and accentual-syllabic meters are rolled together in traditional song. Hundreds of variants of "Frankie and Johnny" (or, as older versions have it, "Frankie and Albert") exist; I give here some of the familiar stanzas. (Some versions run to more than thirty.)

Frankie and Johnny were lovers, O, how that couple could
love.
Swore to be true to each other, true as the stars above.
He was her man, but he done her wrong.

Frankie she was his woman, everybody knows.
She spent one hundred dollars for a suit of Johnny's clothes.
He was her man, but he done her wrong.

Frankie and Johnny went walking, Johnny in his brand
new suit.
"Oh, good Lord," says Frankie, "but don't my Johnny look
cute?"
He was her man, but he done her wrong.

Frankie went down to Memphis. She went on the evening
train.
She paid one hundred dollars for Johnny a watch and chain.
He was her man, but he done her wrong.

Frankie went down to the corner to buy her a bucket of
beer.
She says to the fat bartender, "Has my lovingest man been
here?
He was my man, but he's doing me wrong."

"Ain't going to tell you no story. Ain't going to tell you
no lie.
I seen your man 'bout an hour ago with a girl named
Alice Fry.
If he's your man, he's doing you wrong."

Frankie went back to the hotel; she didn't go there for fun.
Under her long red kimono she toted a forty-four gun.
He was her man, but he done her wrong.

Frankie went down to the hotel, looked in the window so
high.
There she saw her loving Johnny a-loving up Alice Fry.
He was her man, but he done her wrong.

Frankie threw back her kimono; she took out her old
forty-four.
Root-a-toot-toot three times she shot right through that
hotel door.
She shot her man, 'cause he done her wrong.

Johnny grabbed off his Stetson. "O good Lord, Frankie,
don't shoot!"
But Frankie put her finger on the trigger, and the gun went
root-a-toot-toot.
  He was her man, but she shot him down.

"Roll me over easy, roll me over slow,
Roll me over easy, boys, 'cause my wounds are hurting me
so.
  I was her man, but I done her wrong."

First time she shot him he staggered. Second time she
shot him he fell.
Third time she shot him, O Lordy, there was a new man's
face in hell.
  He was her man, but he done her wrong.

Frankie heard a rumbling away down under the ground.
Maybe it was Johnny where she had shot him down.
  He was her man, and she done him wrong.

"Oh, bring on your rubber-tired hearses, bring on your
rubber-tired hacks.
They're taking my Johnny to the burying ground but they'll
never bring him back.
  He was my man, but he done me wrong."

The judge said to the jury, "It's plain as plain can be.
This woman shot her man; it's murder in the second degree.
  He was her man, though he done her wrong."

Now it was not murder in the second degree, it was not
murden in the third.
The woman simply dropped her man, like a hunter drops
a bird.
  He was her man, and he done her wrong.

"Oh, put me in that dungeon. Oh, put me in that cell.
Put me where the northeast wind blows from the south-
east corner of hell.
  I shot my man, 'cause he done me wrong."

Frankie walked up to the scaffold, as calm as a girl could be,
And turning her eyes to heaven she said, "Good Lord,
I'm coming to Thee.
  He was my man, and I done him wrong."

Connoisseurs may miss some of the bawdy details as well as the pearl-handle of the forty-four, "She aimed it at the ceiling, shot a big hole in the floor," or Johnny's dying words, "High-low Jack and the game," but these stanzas will serve as representative. It may seem absurd to analyze in detail lines which vary so from singer to singer; but I think these lines illustrate some of the rhythmical and other variety which the form permits, and I will treat this as though it were a finished poem. "As our American culture advances," Carl Sandburg says in *American Songbag,* "it may be that classes will take up the Frankie songs as seriously as a play by Moliere or a Restoration comedy or the Provençal ballads." The song, in one form or another, long antedates the murder of Allen "Albert" Britt by Frankie Baker in St. Louis in 1899, but there is little doubt that the familiar details of the song we know grew up in connection with that incident. See B. A. Botkin, *Sidewalks of America,* for the pathetic story of how 27 year-old Frankie, of the "sporting circuit actually in self-defense, killed her ginger mack, ten years her junior." The application of a familiar song pattern to a current event reminds us of the days before newspapers when broadside ballads were hawked in the streets of London reporting the news of the day — back when poetry served a practical purpose.

Actually the song is not in what is usually termed ballad form, which consists of quatrains of alternate tetrameter and trimeter, the short lines rhyming. Although a theoretical metrical base can be abstracted from "Frankie and Johnny," it is so irregular, probably so weathered and distorted in years of oral transmission, that the remaining poem is not in metrical but in *accentual* verse — what is sometimes called "native English meter." That is, the lines are determined by accent alone, without much regard to unaccented syllables, as were the lines of *Beowulf,* of many nursery rhymes, and of the poems of Hopkins. The tune most familiar today is probably the "blues" version, a languid, melancholy melody with a mean twist. The variety in the management of the lines permits a singer now to pump with heartfelt simplicity, now to writhe and cry out streaming lines of awkward agony. In its musical mode it has four accents in each of the three lines — a twelve bar tune — as a musical friend explains to me. He writes: "there has never been any trouble in music with extra syllables: if your basic pattern is four quarter notes to the measure, and if extra syllables are needed, just divide up the quarter notes into sixteenths, or triplets, or whatever is required:

```
    1                                   2       3
FRANkie and Johnny were LOVers, O how that couple could
         4
        LOVE

    1                              2         3                    4
SWORE to be true to each Other, TRUE as the stars aBOVE,

                            1       2                       3        4
        he was her MAN . . . ' but he done her WRONG . . . ' . . ."
```

A singer, though, bears down hard on some syllables which do not receive musical stress, and if we are to regard it as a poem, I think we can learn much from the underlying (or "theoretical") pattern, determining the basic structures and the extent of variation possible. The verses I have given above fairly well strain the limits of the possible. Most of the lines have a strongly marked caesura, or pause, in the middle — so strong that we can almost think of each line as two. Three beats fall before the caesura and three after in the stanza proper, two before and two after the caesura in the refrain. The first stanza is the most regular of all; I hear the beats as follows:

FRÁN kie and JÓHN ny were LÓV ers,// Ó, how that
  CÓU ple could LÓVE.

SWÓRE to be TRÚE to each Ó ther,// TRÚE as the STÁRS
  aBÓVE.

HÉ was her MÁN,// but he DÓNE her WRÓNG.

I suggest that for practice you go through the rest of the stanzas underlining the syllables which should be stressed according to this pattern. In some cases you will notice that a choice is possible; e.g., "the WO man sim ply DROPPED her MAN" or "the WO man SIM ply DROPPED her man" — either will work. But the remarkable thing is that this happens so rarely, though there is, as you will see, an enormous variety in the way the accents are distributed. *A mark of success of good accentual poetry is that it controls its emphases exactly and yet does not repeat the same pattern monotonously; it makes you accent the right syllables.* The tune, of course, helps you control the beat.

The off-rhyme of *lovers* and *other* in the first stanza suggests that in some versions there may have been more internal rhymes than have survived. Notice that most of the half-lines are closed, i.e., they end with the completion of a grammatical unit, usually with a mark of punctuation. When, occasionally, one sweeps through without a distinct pause, the effect is striking — as in the swift information of the bartender: "I seen your man 'bout an hour ago with a girl named Alice Fry." The complete six-beat lines are, however, invariably closed and rhymed (sometimes imperfectly). Notice that the norm is to have an unaccented syllable just before the caesura; sometimes there are two or three. At other times there is none at all, and the line takes on a strange intensity, as in the juxaposition of accents across the caesura in the ninth stanza: "SHOT//RIGHT."

Although the surviving poem is accentual, the theoretical metrical idea can be detected. Notice that there are usually two unaccented syllables between accents. We may regard the poem as essentially dactylic. In falling meters, (those written in feet which end with unaccented syllables) it is quite common for the final feet of the lines to be catalectic, i.e., with one or more unaccented syllables missing. For the sake of demonstrating the pattern, I will treat each half-line as a line. I indicate missing syllables with *x*'s, unaccented syllables with *u*'s. Here is the first stanza:

> /uu /uu /ux
> /uu /uu /xx
> /uu /uu /ux
> /uu /ux /xx
>   /uu /uu
>   /ux /xx

In order to account for what actually happens in the composite version I have given, we must allow for these variations: (1) *u*'s may be substituted for *x*'s and vice-versa; (2) one or sometimes two *u*'s may be added at any point, even before the initial beat (a variation called *anacrusis*). We should remember, too, that any extreme variation calls for some reassertion of the norm or variation in the opposite direction — as I will demonstrate.

Let us try that formula on one of the more irregular stanzas, XIV:

> u/uu /uu /ux
> /uu /uu /xx
> u/uu /uuu /uuu
> u/ux /ux /xx (refrain as above)

First we must remember that the song was never written as an accentual poem, nor could we read it that way if we didn't have the tune in mind. Second — good accentual poetry avoids lapsing into meter. We can see terrific strain in the third and fourth lines above, the feet swollen with unaccented syllables. There are a total of five unaccented syllables between the last beat in the third and first in the fourth: "BUR y ing ground but they'll NE ver." You may find a more graceful way to accent the line, but you will still have to account for only three accents in twelve syllables before the caesura: "They're taking my Johnny to the burying ground." It is such a mouthful one is tempted to condemn it as simply a bad line, except that the speed of the first half-line contrasts so deliberately (it seems) with the thumping finality of the second. I call that "variation in the opposite direction" because a passage distorted by more unaccented syllables than the norm is immediately compensated for by one in which there are fewer than the norm. The extreme in condensation would be to drop *all* unaccented syllables between beats (the JUDGE SAID to the JUR y), but this can hardly be done more than once in a half-line.

Try writing a ballad which can be sung to this tune, making a story which is invented or an adaptation of some familiar tale — or, as was "Frankie and Johnny," a rendering of a story from the newspaper or neighborhood gossip. Try a nursery story, such as *Beauty and the Beast,* or a tale from the Bible or a plot from Shakespeare, as he borrowed from histories, romances and other sources:

Macbeth went down to the witches, see what they had to say.
They told him he would win the game, but they didn't say
    how to play.
            Got a crown on his head. Got his head on a spear.

Let us look at the narrative technique and organization of "Frankie and Johnny." The first four stanzas (as I have recorded the poem) tell of Frankie's devotion to Johnny, expressed in hundred dollar units on various shopping expeditions. But we jump — with a neat parallelism — in the fifth stanza to the next episode, a very different shopping trip. The bar scene occupies two stanzas, and we jump again. This episodic treatment is characteristic of ballads. The camera jumps ahead; there is no effort to summarize the intervening events. Such a method maintains vividness and dramatic force. Notice the shifts in tense, the gravitation toward the present tense, bringing us directly on the scene, the quoted dialogue, the close-ups, even of the trigger finger squeezing. Imitators of folk ballads often overlook these techniques and tend to fill in unnecessary transitions, usually with dull material. One must sense that nothing exists in the poem but the hard facts, all the rest worn away in the erosion of oral transmission.

The scenes themselves are apt to be curiously static. Notice that the central incident, the shooting, occupies five stanzas in this version, and often takes many more. There is a dwelling on the material, as though the photographer were taking a variety of shots from different angles. We keep coming back to those three shots through the hotel door. The remainder of the poem is filled with lamentations, the court scene, and execution. In some versions there are scenes at the burial, Frankie looking into the casket, and a scene with the mother of the slain man is fairly common. But in each case, the concentration is on vivid pictures and memorable speeches, with little concern for the passage of time. The reader can fill in the rest imaginatively.

Most important of all are the apparently arbitrary, concrete details. If you have ever told stories to children you know their insistence on the *exact* facts. You had better not say Jack sold a pig for his handful of beans or that the bears ate cereal instead of porridge — though that word is practically unknown now except in the context of the story. Such details take on an almost hallowed significance, providing that element of spookiness which must be near the core of any successful poem. The facts — the trip to Memphis, beer, that long red kimono (which sometimes is sky-blue), the forty-four, the geography covered by hell's winds — the poem lives in such details; the plot itself is not remarkable.

Factuality, too, suggests restraint. See how the fans and combs touch with truth the grief of the ladies in this ancient ballad:

> O lang, lang, may the ladies stand
> Wi' their fans into their hand,
> Or e'er they see Sir Patrick Spens
> Come sailing to the land.
>
> O lang, lang, may the ladies stand
> Wi' their gold kems in their hair,
> Waiting for their ain deir lords,
> For they'll see them na mair.

There is nothing here — or in "Frankie and Johnny" — which is sentimental, excessive or indulgent in tone. Though "Frankie and

Johnny" is more moralistic than most ballads, even its confrontation of Heaven has an integrity and toughness, even a suggestion of saving humor about it. In the way in which the narrator obsessively lingers on the details of the shooting we may detect a crack in the wall of objectivity, but the poem never breaks into overt emotion except through its characters, and even their wails have an essential dignity. "Roll me over easy" is the grim understatement of a hero, nothing of whose life becomes him so much as the leaving of it, and who, though he begs Frankie not to shoot, does not protest the justice of his murder. Notice the repetition of "O good Lord" — her innocent appreciation of the "cute" fellow she has dolled up is brought into contrast with his fear as he sees her aiming. Johnny was something of a dandy, a gigolo, in the early verses, but he rises to some stature in his death. Frankie's kimono marks her trade (as does her going to the bar unescorted); but her love and self-sacrifice for Johnny give her some grasp of dignity and self-respect. Her capacity for jealousy is not only the cause of her ruin but the basis for her redemption. The narrator would describe her act as impersonal, amoral — "like a hunter drops his bird" — but immediately the outcry of a woman with moral awareness breaks the tough crust of narration.

If you are resisting my analysis with the protest that the poem is simple, intuitive and touchingly artless, remember that innumerable ballads disappear — and this one not only survives but must be one of the half-dozen best known songs in America (and not for its music!) The poem is immortal, however it happened to develop into the form in which we hear it now — churned and eroded in the oral stream, it is smooth, irregular and hard as a rock; only the most enduring elements remain, its most resistant, toughest nucleus. We can learn from it much about what sort of poetry abides through time.

As with most poetic devices, line length can be used to reinforce or pull against meaning. The first results in harmony, useful for expressing serenity, confidence, resolution and related emotions. The second results in tension, and for most poems is thus the more useful, as it keeps the poem alive, the reader involved, the meaning radiating. The irregularity of native English meter (e.g., in the Mother Goose rhymes as well as traditional ballads) tugs hard against the regularity of song. Shakespeare's blank verse, as well as that of other poets (Browning is a good example to study), owes much to that native grain, and its irregularities and swift enjambments offset the monotony of a stable form. One might think that free verse would be even more effective in creating tension, but it has the disadvantage of having no norm to work against. Nonetheless it can surprise and enliven, provided the poet doesn't fall into the trap of writing merely phrase-determined lines.

A poet should remember that line lengths, like words, have connotations. Free verse implies an *avante garde,* modernistic attitude. A ballad stanza connotes a folksiness which a poet will have difficulty in overcoming if he doesn't want it present. Short lines imply wit and song. Long ones (i.e., longer than pentameter) imply stateliness and gravity. Again, it is pentameter, above all, which is most neutral, and most flexible for all poetic purposes.

CHAPTER SEVEN

Rhymes

rhyme or reason

An ancient quarrel in the history of poetry is whether or not one should rhyme. Rhymes did not occur in the Greek and Roman classics; they crept into medieval Latin verse and vernacular poetry, coming particularly to be associated with chants and spells, and later with other varieties of poetry. Middle English poetry took up the continental habit, but in the Renaissance and seventeenth century a number of writers — e.g., Jonson, Milton, Temple — inveighed against rhyme as a barbarism. Dryden heroically defended the use of rhyme in heroic plays and then promptly abandoned the practice.

The key term in the dispute, of course, is artificiality. Should art be artificial? Can it be anything else? But should it *seem* artificial — and to what degree? In more or less the same terms the debate still goes on.

Some sophisticated readers of modern poetry respond to rhyme with about the same sort of pained appreciation they use in response to a pun. The grudging recognition of cleverness is accompanied by visceral protest. *Must* you? It is culturally an evil time for rhymes, puns, sleight of hand and card tricks, long jokes, parlor games, stories with morals, and "well-made" plays. In short, there is widespread distrust of, even resentment of, cerebration and artifice. Readers crave the dripping meat of the unconscious, which they take to be more "real" than cleverly balanced equations of reason. Anyone with the wit to rhyme must not, they assume, be in touch with the Springs of Revelation.

On the other hand, aspiring artists persistently rhyme — as much now as ever. When one starts putting words down on paper hoping they will be regarded as poetry, there is a certain security in blatant end rhymes, as there is in capitalizing the first letter of lines. These signals warn a reader that he is not to apply the criteria of gross common sense, such as he might use on prose. They are an unconscious appeal from the poet that his words evoke that uncritical, hushed respect we pay to things like death, Mother, yarmulkes, crucifixes, patriotic bumper stickers, and female disorders. They reassure the poet himself that what he has written down is somehow Art. As people moving into a new apartment urgently hang pictures from the old one before they get their socks sorted, so versifiers scurry to hang a few rhymes on the ends of their lines before they've got their thoughts straight — just to establish a homey atmosphere.

This impasse of taste between poets who fervently jingle and readers whose ears are oversensitive to jangle has little to do with the innate value of rhyme. Rhyme never saved a bad verse nor spoiled a good one. Most of the world's poetry is unrhymed, including most of the best poetry in our own European, Western traditions. But to the popular mind rhyme and poetry are near synonyms, and most short poems are rhymed. Much of this rhyming is, indeed, mechanical and meaningless, yet persistently, irradicably human, like jump-rope jingles. A poet who hopes to reach past the vagaries of current taste and his own insecurities will learn this resource of our language and discover the exact occasions when it can be used with grace and power.

For people without much practice in writing poetry, rhyme is apt to seem a burden, or, rather, a threat, as they feel the search for a rhyme might lead them to say something they didn't intend. (This assumes that any alteration in intention is for the worse; I am often grateful for the new ways rhyme leads me.) You will hear complaints about the intractability of the English language. We do not, certainly, have the wealth of rhymes that the Romance languages have, but it seems to me that our rhymes are correspondingly more interesting and effective. An accomplished poet can say anything in rhyme he can say without it; but, of course, that doesn't answer the question of whether he should.

What do rhymes do? Like rhythm, they may provide a background pattern, create an expectation which the poet may toy with by satisfying or frustrating; he may gratify the reader with a harmony or arrest him with a dissonance. If the rhymes have a "scheme" or recurring pattern, as in couplets, quatrains, the units of a sonnet or in stanzaic structures, they provide an organizing shape which can be integrated carefully with the structure of thought. Internal rhymes (within lines) may occur regularly (making the pattern more intricate) or in unexpected places, drawing attention to a word, developing a cadence, or they may raise a phrase to sharp prominence. At the conclusion of an unrhymed poem a rhyme may have a chordal resonance, making the ending decisive and firm; or if the poem has been rhymed, the absence of rhyme at the end may create a sense of indecisiveness or incompleteness that one may want. Rhymes have a musicality which can be exploited for incantatory or lyric passages. They are useful as hinges, giving the thought of the poem a clear and emphatic turn. And, of course, they can be funny; it is difficult to imagine a comic poem without rhyme.

A true rhyme in English is one in which the sounds of the last stressed syllable and all succeeding sounds are identical *except* for the initial consonant sound of the last stressed syllable. In monosyllabic rhymes, the last syllable is all we consider. *Pig* rhymes with *fig* and *periwig.* In the last word, though the accent on the final syllable is secondary, that is sufficient to make it rhyme. *Tight* does not rhyme with *appetite,* because the initial consonant of the rhyming syllable is the same in both words. The same rule applies in disyllabic and trisyllabic rhymes. *Aversion* rhymes with *dispersion,* but not with *version. Comprehensible* rhymes with *defensible,* but not with *reprehensible* (nor with, say, *irascible,* in which the last stressed syllable — *ra* — does not rhyme with *hen*). Master those few principles. There are many good alternatives to true rhyming, but ignorant approximations are not among them.

Notice that *sounds,* not spelling nor word endings, matter in determining rhyme. In fact, to rhyme words with different spellings and word breaks is more attractive, because subtler, than the opposite. Thus *what* is a more attractive rhyme for *not* than is *shot,* though both are true rhymes. *(Knot* does not rhyme with *not.) Can it* is a better rhyme for *planet* than *Janet* is. *Bough* is a better rhyme for *cow* than is *now,* and so on. The curse of rhyme is expectation; anything a poet can do to surprise or befuddle expectation will improve his rhyming. Some rhymes are almost unusable because they have become hackneyed *(trees-breeze),* or because there are so few rhyme words available *(bush-push)* that one inescapably creates expectation of the other.

Beware of peculiarities of dialect. I am a little uneasy about the example of *what-not* above because in my own dialect these words have slightly different vowel sounds. In Clement Wood's *Rhyming Dictionary* (World Publishing Co.), I see *anger* rhymed with *clangor* — a rhyme I would never use because I pronounce a hard *g* in the first word and not in the second, just as I don't pronounce Long Island *Lon Guiland.* Except in humorous or dialect verse, a poet should avoid drawing attention to regional pronunciations. In some parts of this country *Dinah* rhymes with *finer* because both words end in *r* sounds, in other parts because both end with *ah* sounds, but neither pronunciation is sufficiently neutral to make a good rhyme in serious poetry.

Good serious verse, like ballet, exhibits skill by hiding it. If you want to emphasize or draw attention to rhyme, you put it at the end of lines, the closer the better, at the end of grammatical units; if you want to de-emphasize it, you do the opposite. For example, much of the best rhyming is internal, subtle; if it occurs in end positions, it is often in the middle of a phrase:

> A sick age — or a bad one? Look across
> the weaving river and the valley there,
> beyond that string of trees. See smoke? The air
> is dingy: that's the garbage dump. They toss
> the waste of the city there and burn it. Do
> we say disease or evil clouds our view?

Lines 1, 3, 4 and 5 are enjambed, tucking the rhymes relatively out of sight. These are all end rhymes. Even subtler is to place the rhyming words within lines:

> And then we came about, the boom raking
> the deck like death's own scythe, the sheet snapping
> out like voltage, the sail breaking, straining as a bud
> about to bloom. The slapping sea now broke
> over starboard bow as we leaned in the planing wind.

In that passage invented for illustration, I overdid it a bit, but you can see the play of different rhyme effects in deliberate but subdued echoes: *about-out, raking-breaking, snapping-slapping, straining-planing, boom-bloom, now-bow.*

off rhymes

There are also a variety of off-rhymes (sometimes called slant rhymes, false rhymes, sour rhymes, etc.) These may approximate true rhyme closely or the relation between words may be very tenuous indeed. (Actually alliteration, consonance or any verbal harmony is a kind of rhyme; I am discussing here, though, only end-rhyme or internal rhyme deliberately placed to emphasize rhetoric or structure.) Off-rhymes have a long history, but they have been used increasingly by twentieth century poets. Some argue that the spread of this practice is an attempt to enlarge the limited fund of rhyme in our language, but it seems to me that off-rhyme functions in quite a distinct way from true rhyme. It is not an extension but a very useful alternative.

Off-rhymes (e.g., *heart-heat, red-rod, time-tan, age-jail, courage-engage, lurk-lark, cat-take)* can, obviously, be formed any way the poet chooses: consonant or vowel sounds may be varied, accents contrasted, or sounds even put in reverse relationships. It is a matter of taste, of course, how close the sounds should be. Two sounds which are very similar, but not quite alike, sound unpleasant to my ear, like adjacent notes on the piano (e.g., *bed-beds, ten-tin, kick-licked* — but I don't object to *bed-bad-beads, tin-tent, lick-lacked).* Some of the rhymes of Dylan Thomas, for example, are so distant they are out of my auditory range; so while I don't object to them, I can't appreciate them.

The stanza pattern of the six stanzas of his "Fern Hill," for example, is fairly regular — suggesting that he had a definite rhyme scheme in mind. Here are the final words of each line in each stanza:

1st stanza		2nd		3rd		4th		5th		6th	
boughs	-a-	barns	-a-	hay	-a-	white	-a-	house	-a-	me	-a-
green	-b-	home	-b-	air	-b-	all	-b-	long	-b-	hand	-b-
starry	-c-	only	-c-	watery	-c-	maiden	-c-	over	-c-	rising	-c-
climb	-d-	be	-d-	grass	-d-	again	-d-	ways	-d-	sleep	-d-
eyes	-d-	means	-d-	stars	-d-	day	-d-	hay	-d-	fields	-d-
towns	-a-	calves	-a-	away	-a-	light	-a-	allows	-a-	land	-b-
leaves	-b-	cold	-b-	nightjars	-b-	warm	-b-	songs	-b-	means	-a-
barley	-c-	slowly	-c-	horses	-c-	stable	-c-	golden	-c-	dying	-c-
light	-d-	streams	-d-	dark	-d-	praise	-d-	grace	-d-	sea	-d-

In the sixth stanza, lines six and seven are reversed in position, but otherwise the rhyme scheme appears to be consistent. Most of these rhymes depend on repetition of the accented vowel. Some pairs (e.g., *barns-calves, watery-horses)* have so little relationship that if it were not for the pattern, one would hardly be inclined to associate them, and in some cases rhymes which are not supposed to match according to the scheme are more prominent than those which *are* supposed to match (e.g., *nightjars-stars).* But the astonishing thing is that the poem which appears at first to be nearly rhymeless does, after all, have a discernible rhyme pattern. Even the variation in the sixth stanza is prepared for by the closeness of the *a* and *d* rhymes in other stanzas, so that when he moves *means* closer to *sea* (apparently to reinforce that climax) it seems a natural progression.

Thomas, of course, worked his poems through hundreds of drafts and packed them with much ingenuity which, I'm sure, will never be discovered. One may argue that rhymes strained so far as those in "Fern Hill," like many other of the infinite interrelationships in sound and meaning in his poems, (note, for example, the rhymes between stanzas and, rhyme aside, the relationship in meaning of rhyme words) are too subtle to be perceived in reading or hearing the poem. Why, then, bother?

There are two answers. The remarkable cohesiveness and unity of the poem arise from that dazzling complexity of cross-currents. You don't "see" every curlicue in a figured carpet, every stone in a mosaic, every brush stroke on a canvas; you don't perceive every note in a symphony; but that is not to say that some might as well have been left out. "Fern Hill" first makes the impression of a rich swirl of language; but one becomes conscious of more and more reason, design, in the torrent as one listens. How much? Who is to say? By laborious craftsmanship Thomas has made certain that the most sensitive reader will not be disappointed; echoes will find echoes endlessly. His poem is like a Persian carpet, each hand-tied thread having its necessary function in an elaborate, bewildering design. If the rhymes were "true," however, much of that initial effect of tempestuous, flooding language would be lost.

The second answer pertains to the value such a pattern has for the poet himself. Most poets recognize that one of the values of an arbitrary pattern (no matter what it may be) is that it forces him to greater awareness and control. In one sense a poem is like a problem, a puzzle; or you may think of a poem with a rigid, preconceived form as a box which must be exactly filled to the brim. In other words, your poem makes demands on *you;* you invent it, sure — but at some point in its composition the responsibility begins to shift from you to it, to this incomplete design on the paper. You must honor its rights, of course, for it to be able to make demands of you. But once it does, and once you begin searching back in the corners of your consciousness to find the means to satisfy it, you are very apt to turn up wealth you never thought you owned. The reader may never detect what rules you forced yourself to obey; but he has the benefit of the labor, nonetheless, in a better poem. If you wrote a poem setting yourself the task of making every 17th letter an *h,* it would probably be a better poem than if you accepted no arbitrary discipline.

If you use one off-rhyme in an end rhyme position in a poem, use more than one — lest it appear to be a gaffe. But internal and end-rhymes, true and off-rhymes can be intermingled in a poem, and, in fact, the ideal is to establish a thick enough texture of sound echoes that the reader is no longer waiting for rhymes to click into place in expected patterns:

> And then this dream. I thrashed, my flesh
> stinging from grass and sweat, and my
> chest crushed as though someone would mash
>
> me with the heel of the hand of the world.
> Relief, then: weight off with a rush
> and rising, inflated, stretched, whirled
>
> into air too thin, dangerously lifting,
> exploding, then, the scraps flung, rolled
> and shaping to a mass down drifting,
>
> I settled wetly back to the grass,
> hearing in sleep the birdsongs grieving . . .

This is *terza rima,* the first and third end-rhymes of one stanza creating the rhyme sound for the end of the middle line of the next. But the passage is so rich in internal echoes, the end-rhymes so enjambed, and true and off-rhymes so mixed that the pattern is subdued at the same time that the poetry is resonant with rhyming devices.

Off rhymes, then, can provide, as they do in "Fern Hill," an almost imperceptible but nonetheless cohesive texture. If you want to use them for deliberate dissonance, put them closer together and make the rhythm fall harder on them. Much the same principle applies to true rhymes; if you want them to be (the reverse of good children) heard but not seen, either use them internally or in cnjambed lines, and let them fall farther apart. If you want the artificiality to be noticed, bring them close together, end-stop the lines, and make the beat fall hard. Inversions or other grammatical strains help emphasize the artificiality of the rhyme. The couplets, for example, which end many of Shakespeare's scenes and his sonnets are very often labored, even awkward, and some critics complain of them. I think it likely he wanted you to notice the artificiality, the pirouette.

bad rhymes

Pope gave much misleading advice about writing poetry (advice which he did not always follow) in the "Essay on Criticism," including these familiar lines:

> . . . ring round the same unvaried chimes,
> With sure return of still expected rhymes:
> Wher'er you find "the cooling western breeze,"
> In the next line, it "whispers through the trees:"
> If crystal streams "with pleasing murmurs creep,"
> The reader's threatened (not in vain) with "sleep."

Clever — but it doesn't really explain why some rhymes are hackneyed. The rhymes in our language were fairly well summarized in six pages of older editions of Merriam Webster's *New Collegiate Dictionary,* and of the few listed, about one fourth are, for all practical purposes, unusable in serious poetry (e.g., archaic, technical, foreign or other rare words). More elaborate rhyming dictionaries (such as Wood's) are chiefly valuable for writing humorous verse and lyrics, as they include polysyllabic rhymes. I am no more ashamed of using a rhyming dictionary than I am of using an ordinary dictionary or thesaurus, but the same admonition holds for all three reference works. They may help jog your memory, but they should not (while you are writing) teach you new words. Rare and erudite words almost never work in poetry anyway, but especially should never be used as rhymes. The language of your poem should be as familiar and comfortable as your underwear; use only words that you have had long acquaintance with, whose whole range of nuances you know well. Especially when rhyming, vocabulary plums look more like sore thumbs.

The clichés preceding the rhymes in Pope's passage make the lines painful — not the rhyming words. Poems rhyming *sing* and *spring* are apt to be bad poems, true enough — as are those rhyming *love* and *dove, life,* or *heart* and any other word — but that is because the subjects are outworn which call for these words.

The only "bad" rhyme is a strained one: when it is quite obvious that having gotten *siege* into the poem you had to work in *liege,* although it had little relation to your subject. Hours spent with a rhyming dictionary won't help; you have to recast the line. Similarly, grammatical dislocation for the sake of rhyme is bad — though there seems to have been a higher tolerance of this in other periods. That is, avoid monstrosities such as:

And when the battle was getting hot

He at the advancing enemy shot.

or the inclusion of expletives:

When, wanting to see a picture show

He often to one with his girl did go.

The *did* is a device for getting around the more normal word *went,* which, of course, does not rhyme.

Of any two rhyming words one is bound to be more essential for your poem than the other. (A good trick is to use the less essential one first, so the more essential one will seem "right" as it falls into place.) Your task is to find pairs of which both terms are as relevant and necessary as possible. For that reason, masculine rhymes are generally more useful than feminine ones (the latter being more noticeable), and common endings (like *ain* and *ate)* are more useful than unusual ones like *(ulch* and *ube).*

feminine and comic rhymes

Rhymes with one or more unaccented syllables after the last accent are called feminine; those which end on the accent are called masculine. Disyllabic feminine rhymes have a lightening effect, sometimes ironic, humorous, sometimes song-like. Notice how Eliot undercuts the dignity of Prufrock's vain attempt to dramatize himself — not only with the details of the tea party, but with the little jiggle of feminine rhyme:

Should I, after tea and cakes and ices,

Have the strength to force the moment to its crisis?

Or notice how the feminine rhymes deepen and complicate the tone in this final stanza of E. A. Robinson's "For a Dead Lady":

> The beauty, shattered by the laws
> That have creation in their keeping,
> No longer trembles at applause,
> Or over children that are sleeping;
> And we who delve in beauty's lore
> Know all that we have known before
> Of what inexorable cause
> Makes Time so vicious in his reaping.

The lilt of *keeping* softens it, suggesting the security we have in the strong arms of universal law. *Sleeping* comes, then, as so pleasant an image, so innocent a melody, that we are lulled into thinking of the mother's death as hardly more grim a thing than the repose of her children. *Shattered* in the first line and *vicious* in the last are the only clues we have to the cruel and destructive aspect of death, but those are enough to prepare us for *reaping.* The idea of death as a harvest, as fulfillment, is bitterly denied by the context (the grim reaper bears a sharp scythe). The light song of the feminine ending is similarly denied; and the effect is not, finally, of tragic mask, of straightforward grief, but of a kind of twisting smirk, the man beyond tears struggling against hopelessness and heartache. It is a variety of mockery — without humor but also not without overwhelming compassion. Those lines might easily have been rearranged to conclude with *keep, sleep* and *reap;* it would make for a starker, more dramatic effect — but less effective, and certainly less complex.

On the other hand, trisyllabic rhymes (such as *griminess-sliminess)* are too amusing to use for any other purpose than humor. Humorous poetry inverts all the standards applicable to serious poetry. Usually the rhymes themselves are part of the humor: the rhymes may be funny *because* they violate the principles of good rhyming. Beware, however, of mere sloppiness. Comic rhymes, however awkward, must appear ingenious. Thus to rhyme *acceptable* with *kept a bull* might be funny, but to rhyme that word with *adaptable* or *imperceptible* might seem merely careless or mechanical *(adaptable* has a different sound in its last stressed syllable; *imperceptible* begins its last stressed syllable with the same consonant sound as does *acceptable).* In serious poetry even disyllabic rhymes are suspect (because they draw attention to themselves as merely clever), and rhymes of more than two syllables are *verboten;* but humorous poetry takes naturally to polysyllabic rhymes.

Some devices of comic verse are stamped almost as copyrighted

by skillful, individual poets. For example, it is doubtful that
any poet today could get published a poem which tacks strained
rhymes on the end of long, unmetrical lines, because the technique
was so highly developed by Ogden Nash that any venture in the
same mode will look like an imitation:

> Farewell, farewell, to you old rhinoceros,
> I'll stare at something less prepoceros!

or:

> And that is why I admire a suave prevarication because I
>   prevaricate so awkwardly and gauchely,
> And that is why I can never amount to anything politically
>   or socially.

Though the method was earlier practiced by Gilbert (of Gilbert and
Sullivan):

> He was quite indifferent as to the particular kinds of dresses
> That the clergyman wore at the church where he used to go
>   to pray,
> And whatever he did in the way of relieving a chap's distresses,
> He always did in a nasty, sneaking, underhanded, hole-and-cor-
>   ner sort of way.

W. S. Gilbert and other nineteenth century poets rather exhausted
the humorous mine of stringing together long series of rhyming
polysyllables, intricate refrains and syncopated rhythms. Don Marquis
(creator of Mehitabel the Cat) developed another distinctive style
of humorous verse (and here is the exception that proves the
rule: much of his was unrhymed) which another poet could hardly
imitate without seeming a plagiarist. Dialect verse, as developed by
such earlier poets as James Russell Lowell, Eugene Field, James
Whitcomb Riley, Robert Service and Edgar Guest, is another vein
that has, for the time being, produced its last ore (or o'er). On the
other hand, a mode that might stand a contemporary revival is
Hudibrastic verse, named after the mock-epic *Hudibras,* by the
seventeenth century English poet Samuel Butler. This is a rough
tetrameter which jams incongruous rhymes together like a husband
packing a suitcase:

> For his *Religion* it was fit
> To match his Learning and his Wit:
> 'Twas *Presbyterian* true blew,
> For he was of that stubborn Crew
> Of Errant Saints, whom all men grant
> To be the true Church *Militant:*

Such as do build their Faith upon
The holy Text of *Pike* and *Gun;*
Decide all Controversies by
Infallible *Artillery;*
And prove their Doctrine Orthodox
By Apostolick *Blows* and *Knocks;*
Call Fire and Sword and Desolation,
A *godly-thorough-Reformation,*
Which always must be carry'd on,
And still be doing, never done:
As if Religion were intended
For nothing else but to be mended.

As you read that, you can detect what you should avoid in serious verse. One begins to wait for the rhyme as for the proverbial second shoe; he tolerates or even enjoys a dislocated accent or sour vowel in order to eke out a consonance; and the more syllables that clatter together into place the better. The jokes come spaced as in the patter of a stand-up comedian.

some exercises for review

The way poets use (or do not use) rhymes is a useful litmus paper for detecting incompetence. Untalented novices are generally of one of two types. Some turn to poetry because they think it offers freedom from the prosaic necessities of logic, evidence, restraint, good taste, sound sentence structure, coherency and clear purpose. Poets of this type generally eschew rhyme altogether. They write phrasal free verse, hoping to make it poetic by such devices as one-word lines, liberal use of exclamation points (and little other punctuation), strong (often obscene) diction, obscurity, intimate confession and bombastic abstractions. The other type looks to poetry for elevation, formality, permanence and dignity. The way they cope with their insecurity in writing verse is to imitate the poetry they have read — probably in the sixth grade — most of which was written in England in the nineteenth century. They use archaic and pretentious words, grand generalizations about life and the world, uncertain but insistent meter, and, inevitably, rhyme. If you suspect that you fall into one or the other of those categories, I suggest you try verse of the opposite type. If you don't rhyme,

rhyme. If you rhyme, don't rhyme. It will test you mettle — and teach you something about the verse you are writing.

There is nothing shameful about being a novice, and lack of talent is primarily lack of experience and commitment (especially commitment). The first notion to disabuse yourself of is that poems are going to start springing full-blown from your pen. You will write poems eventually; first you must learn to write poetry. (The difference is that between learning to draw and paint and producing a painting — a finished piece of work worthy of exhibiting in some way.) I will suggest some palette exercises. Try writing a few lines on any subject using rhymes as I indicate just to give yourself a feel for the technique. Then, later, writing poems, you will have a greater array of resources on which to draw.

I.   Closed couplet, with true end rhyme (use pentameter or tetrameter):

> These keys fly up with agitated speed
> Like legs of some inverted centipede.

The lines are closed — i.e., they are complete grammatical units — as is the whole couplet. There is end rhyme because the rhyming words are at the ends of the lines.

Such rhymes are good for poetry characterized by wit and abstraction. The units are sharp, precise; the rhyme serves as a kind of heavy punctuation. The form runs the danger of becoming mechanical, and does not absorb variation gracefully. If you want to emphasize the innate characteristics of such couplets, use balance and antithesis (in the manner of the heroic couplets of Dryden and Pope):

> Pope served no beer to victims — only wine,
> And strangled not with rope, but linen twine,
> To sever heads, yet never bruise the skin,
> And leave on each dead face a grateful grin.

The *v*'s of *served* and *victims,* the internal rhyme of *Pope* and *rope;* the *o*'s of *Pope* and *only,* the rhyme of *sever* and *never* (and similarity in sound to *served)* and the *gr*'s of *grateful* and *grin* are a few of the balances inside these lines besides the obvious antitheses of beer and wine, rope and twine, etc.

II.   Free or blank verse with internal rhyme only. (The first and third lines below are blank verse.)

> In that drift of coral fans, by the ink blue
> caverns, in the lift of chill sea, I slip
> through spans of bony architecture, sink

> to stony roots of mountains, graze
> lazily along a lip of darkness, bubbling past
> creation's rubble on the vast moon floor.

Some of the rhymes are emphasized by their occurrence in parallel structures *(In that drift, in the lift, of bony, to stony)*. Others are suppressed, being tucked into distant or very different structures *(ink blue, through spans, sink)*. Some are true rhymes *(past-vast, slip-lip)*. Others are partial or off rhymes *(bubbling, rubble, graze, lazily, coral, floor)*.

This use of rhyme is better than end rhyme for emotion, description, for verse in which you do not want the continuous flow to be interrupted by closure and a sense of finality. It provides a rich, harmonious sound texture unobtrusively. It permits great flexibility and variation, but runs the danger of becoming merely prosaic. If one works too hard to avoid *that* danger, the verse may become too lush and mannered, too self-consciously poetic.

III. Polysyllabic end rhyme, in ballad quatrains:

> A day is long enough to find
> a night to follow after,
> a lady of the loving kind,
> a morning of low laughter.

Disyllabic rhymes have a lilt which can be comic or ironic and poignant:

> Now in our grassy graveyard where
> we draw our breath and blow it,
> our cheeks are warm, by dark are fair —
> but no one dead can know it.
>
> So lean upon the mound, my dear,
> and part your lips so quaintly,
> and listen to the earth, my dear,
> which throbs not even faintly.
>
> And put your hand upon my chest
> and kiss me now, and wonder
> if loving on the earth were best —
> or hugging nothing under.

That delicate, light effect is almost inescapable, and no one should venture into polysyllabic rhymes unless he is fully aware of it. Trisyllabic rhymes are comic. It is impossible to imagine their being used where any gravity of tone is desired:

> I slapped her hard and saw her cheek
> first flush, then quickly palliate.
> Her little arms flew back as she,
> in tears, moved to retaliate.

or:

> The farmers guarded barns all night all over Pennsylvania
> When rumors spread that Luke was loose with rabid pyromania.

IV.   A stanza pattern using off rhymes as end rhymes:

> Pick up your tempo, courtiers, after the king
> exits — like long-beaked birds you must have seen
> feeding quickly in the sea's withdrawing, then
> scurrying to dry sand when the wave rolls in.

It is, surprisingly, somewhat harder to work with off-rhymes than with true rhymes, for while off-rhymes vastly extend the range of words that can possibly be used, they are harder to think of: you can't turn your brain on automatic pilot or use a rhyming dictionary to churn up suggestions. But they are a rich resource, if well used, creating tonal shadings and subtle nuances with some of the tightness and force of true rhymes without their self-consciousness and conspicuous artificiality.

It is the purpose of the poem which should determine whether and how you will rhyme, not some affectation that you do or do not like rhyme. That sounds as ridiculous to me as a statement that someone does or does not like music: it all depends on what kind and when and what for. And that, surely, is the only answer there will ever be to the problem of whether art should or should not be artificial. It depends entirely upon what you want to do with it. For most purposes rhyme may serve as an unobtrusive and valuable reinforcement of sense. In some cases even the subtlest harmony is out of place. In others a rhyme, artificial, even absurd, can point its knobby finger at a word.

CHAPTER EIGHT

Diction

words, words, words

Number the following list of words from the most poetic to the least poetic:

> advertisement
> extrapolate
> nightingale
> sallow
> lavender
> puissance
> onomatopoeia
> deoxidize
> ere
> ear

Wait! If you are about to toss the book aside in exasperation, you may have talent after all. No word is inherently more poetic than any other. In fact, the notion that some things are poetic (or, worse, poetical) and some are not, is the chief disability of many amateur poets.

When they sit down to write they think not of their experience or ideas, but of what sounds like a poem. What comes out may sound very much like a poem indeed: exactly like the poetry they have read. There will likely be a nightingale, though the poet has never seen or heard one. There will surely be a moon, probably in June. There will be sighs and hearts and flowers. There will not be carburetors, shampoo, grunts or nasturtiums — though violets, moans, sable locks and caskets may occur in a world where people wend instead of walk and languish rather than fag out.

Nothing could be more stultifying to a vibrant sensibility — the kind which, one hopes, is inclined toward poetry — than a view of the art which thus limits it to a rarefied, second-hand segment of language. Today even our poetical poets — those of sunsets, roses and violins — would smile at the poetic diction of Thomas Gray, who thus described the boys of Eton hiking, swimming, catching birds, chasing hoops and playing ball:

> Say, Father Thames, for thou hast seen
>   Full many a sprightly race
> Disporting on thy margent green
>   The paths of pleasure trace,
> Who foremost now delight to cleave
> With pliant arm thy glassy wave?
>   The captive linnet which enthral?
> What idle progeny succeed
> To chase the rolling circle's speed
>   Or urge the flying ball?

But as they smile they may not realize they have borrowed a diction just as phony, stilted and circumscribed, ironically enough from the Romantic poets, such as Wordsworth, who struggled so to defeat eighteenth century elegance and replace such quaint locutions as "glassy wave" for "water" with words spoken by real men.

The idea that some words are more appropriate for poetry than others is as ancient as poetry itself. Originally poetic diction must have been in part a mnemonic device (like rhyme and rhythm), the ritualistic repetition of certain fixed epithets (such as Homer's winedark sea) which stayed easily in the memory. Also, of course, periphrastic terms (such as "fleecy wealth" for "sheep") emphasize particular qualities, often those most valued in a culture. The kennings of Anglo-Saxon poetry (e.g., "whale road" for sea, "life's house" for body) similarly preserved and ritualized values. There were handbooks of kennings which a poet might use in composition — to be sure he got his clichés right. In the seventeenth and eighteenth centuries Neoclassic theories of diction were carefully formulated. Part of the reason for such a perversion of language as that quoted above, from Gray, was a conscious interest in and imitation of Greek and Roman classics. But even more important was the preconception that language of poetry should be neither too rare nor too mean. The concept of decorum, of appropriateness, governed word-choice. It would have been vulgar to say the boys were swimming in the river; it seemed more proper, more decorous, to say they clove with pliant arm the glassy wave. A similar concern for propriety — not in poetry but in everyday life — led Victorian ladies to refer to the limbs of a table because the word *legs* was indecent.

poeticisms

The term is not in the dictionary, which makes it, I suppose, a poeticism. I would define that term as the fancifulization of language with the intent to poetify it. Some poeticisms are neologisms, such as *poeticism, fancifulization, poetify.* More often they are made of standard words — but words which the author has selected because he thinks they sound poetic rather than because he thinks they are the best ones to convey his thought.

Having written that much, I stopped to find an illustration. I reached for the top envelope on a stack of manuscripts submitted to a magazine. The very first poem I encountered was made up of these phrases, and more like them: "misty green," "bright as blood," "instant pulse," "bursts of joy," "scented air," "rapturings," "fiery path," "aurorean rhapsodies," "divine as love." No, the poem does not seem to be parody. Somehow the poet has gotten to the point of sending out manuscripts which look professional without having learned that her work is compounded of phrases and words (and ideas) so egregiously poetified that any one of them would damn her in the eyes of good editors.

Note that poeticisms are not necessarily clichés. It may well be that no human being in the history of the world, except this author, has thought of saying "aurorean rhapsodies" before. Does the context justify those words? It would be difficult to imagine a context which did — but in this case the poet is talking about finches mating, and the phrase refers to the noises the male finch makes while engaged in the act. I don't believe I have ever overheard a finch in this situation, but "aurorean rhapsodies" suggests sounds of almost symphonic majesty — and I somehow doubt the phrase reflects accurate observation.

The Scylla and Charybdis between which the poet must steer are Fashion and Self. He maintains a true course by keeping his eye firmly on his subject. Only this faithfulness to his *matter* can save him. Veer a little leftward, heartward, and he swirls into the maw of mere expressionism; the point of the poem comes to seem the recording of his own idiosyncrasies — or, as he is likely to describe them, his moods, his fleeting impressions, his feelings. He becomes a case study for the reader (if he should have any reader), a blind monster of ego for himself, unable to go anywhere at all, so swathed is he in the mummy-wrap of his own numbing self-awareness.

Veer rightward, headward, and he crashes on the fashionable rocks; he stops writing poetry and writes poeticisms; he loses all sense of personal authenticity and cuts himself to the pattern of what he imagines taste to demand. Such a catastrophe is not, usually, caused by commercialism; poetry is so poorly rewarded commercially that few are guilty of selling out. Pathetically, like over-anxious hostesses, poets who crash on this side generally fail by trying too hard to please. The lady who committed "rapturings" on paper is very likely one who through sheer modesty lacks all conviction. She would sacrifice herself in a moment to do things "right," and the sad fact is that her very willingness to conform is what causes her to be rejected. How can I tell her this? My rejection will make her strive harder to please. Poeticisms breed poeticisms like cancer cells breed cancer cells.

Her efforts are the more pathetic and more obviously misguided because she is conforming to a fashion which is no longer fashionable. I am looking, now, at a poem entitled "Yellow Warblers." Some of the phrases that strike my eye are "first faint dawn," "dreamland still bewildering mine eyes," "beyond my casement," "And lo!," "golden buds," "veil of willows," "clear as drops of dew," "fleck the blue," "sparkling visitants," "isles," "wee," "blithe notes," "lyric dawn," "Eternal joy," "all mortal things," etc. This poem is by Katharine Lee Bates, published in an anthology called *The Second Book of Modern Verse* in 1919. I could well imagine the finch poem in these pages. Both poetesses imagine music in the sex life of the birds they contemplate. Here is how Ms. Bates renders it:

> Foretelling in delicious roundelays
> Their dainty courtships on the dipping sprays,

There is skill there which the manuscript poem lacks. Notice how the *l*'s play through the first line, the neat balance of *dainty* and *dipping,* the *p*'s and *s*'s in the second line. And I find it a little easier to imagine "delicious roundelays" in the flirtation period than

I do "aurorean rhapsodics" at the moment of impact. But in both poems there is a very similar speciousness of diction; both ladies are breaking their backs to be poetic, and, alas, that is something one never succeeds in being by trying to be.

But this is flogging Edgar Guest — may his soul rest in peace. Poesy of the first half of this century ran to this general type: a kind of careless compound of sentimentality and beautification, a cheap veneer on the deep-grained oak of human experience. There is still an incredible amount of such verse going round, as the manuscript I selected by chance illustrates. One of its chief characteristics, true enough, is an uncritical use of language. It is in this verse that one always finds "distant skies" (as opposed to those which are close?), "stately sarabandes" (as opposed to those which are sloppy? jazzy?), and "tremulous hands," (or tremulous anything elses). It is what I call "newspaper verse," perhaps because so many newspaper editors who are willing to run a poem on their editorial pages seem to have had their tastes formed about 1919. It fills religious and inspirational magazines, and those stalwart, corseted little magazines of "traditional" verse, with names like *Spindrift,* and *Leaves of Gold,* and *Orpheus,* which, in all our Midwestern cities, carry on their ceaseless war against the calendar, cushioned by the cultural interests of the local banker's wife.

No, this is not the false coinage we should be alert for today. Though *poeticism* is usually taken to refer to phrases such as "vesper peace, vermillion-hued," the term must be updated to accommodate current fashions, which are just as stupefying as those of 1919. Consider this poem:

> MORNING AFTER
> (for Franz K.)
> Smoke-hooded monks suck
> sockets of marble chill
> to the tune
> of circling doves across
> William's guitar-strung
> nerves:
>
> Oh, Franz,
> in the gullet of Being
> they march! You have
> no exit
> but
> Becoming.

> and I light one more
> and puff until
> maybe dawn maybe
> then this salt
> will ooze off letting
> a guy see clear

I did not at first understand this poem, but, luckily, I was able to ask the author what he had in mind. I will transcribe here portions of his taped comments:

"I'm surprised you don't get it. The monks, of course, are the critics. See, they worship Kafka, but they are eating him up; they're living off him. They're kind of foggy-minded, dull, cold; I was thinking of something like *The Seventh Seal,* these winding processions down into the tombs. That's why the marble. Then the sky, see: the doves. But these critics have been brought up on William Wordsworth. William is such an Anglo-Saxon name, contrasted with Franz, you know, the Middle-eastern Jew, the victim of our civilization. So their ideas of literature are all based on the old stuff like Wordsworth, and they have no idea how strung-up Wordsworth must have been. That's an allusion to Lorca, of course, the guitar, the taut strings across the black hole, like the nervous system, and the mysterious unknown of the personality. But the monks, or critics, think in absolutes, in terms of Being. Gullet, see, is this tomb they are marching in, after him. It's like a Kafka-situation: the winding black caverns, the guy running for his life and finding no exit. That, of course, is an allusion to Sartre's play: it is Hell. They are hounding him out of Hell, as though to save him, but they will destroy him, unless he can be continually Becoming. That's a pun. Attractive — and always evolving, always different from what he just was, slipping out of the hands of the monks which would tie him down to one meaning. The wonder of Kafka's work to me is that though he's dead and buried, in the tomb, see, he is always changing, developing. I had Proteus in there, but decided that was too literary. Well, then, the second stanza is a contrast, all small letters, all tiny and quiet and personal. Here I am literally weeping about how Kafka might just get caught by the critics, strung-up, nailed down, whatever. Explained, you know. And I'm breathing with him, like for a criminal escaping the fuzz. I light up one joint after another, rapt, thinking about how he will surely get away. That's where the dawn comes in. Hope. I finally come to see how he'll make it;

they'll never get him. So with daylight I can clear my eyes of this salt ooze and face the day. What I've really learned is that feeling can never be defeated by intelligence. I'm able to *be* intelligent — that is see clear in the day — because of Kafka's example. I'm not afraid to think because he showed me that thought — even the critics — will never explain life away. That's where the title comes in. After a drunk you suffer a little, but you take a little nip of the hair of the dog and go at it again. Remorse will never really catch up with pleasure. That's what the poem is all about."

He went on to point out how the smoking in the second stanza echoed the "Smoke-hooded" in the first — how both he and the critics have their "thing." They "suck" their chilly rationalism just as he sucks his joint. He also explained the pun on "light," which, he pointed out, plays throughout the poem — images of darkness contrasting with images of light, the irony being that the "enlightened" critics are delving into the guts whereas the gut-oriented speaker is working toward enlightenment.

I asked him questions such as these: How does one suck a socket? How can one imagine a socket as a chill? How can one suck to the tune of anything? How, especially, to the tune of circling doves, which are silent? Are we sucking *across* the nerves? Or did he mean that the nerves are across something else? How can a reader be expected to know that "William" refers to Wordsworth? I had even more questions. He was shocked, indignant, that I should bring such a literal mind to the reading of poetry.

The poeticisms of "modern" verse make those of "newspaper" verse seem serenely logical and fresh. What has happened to a poet such as the author of "Morning After" (and, believe me, there are many) is that he read some Hart Crane and early Dylan Thomas and got the idea it was poetical to wrench and dislocate language, that it was poetical never to say what you mean or to provide a reader with an image he could experience directly and literally. Then he read some William Carlos Williams, Robert Lowell or Louis Simpson and got the idea that it was poetical to write humbly and directly and colloquially. The one thing he never did was ask himself what he wanted to say and what was the most accurate language for conveying this. He was faithful to fashion, albeit to conflicting fashions, rather than to the *matter* of his poem.

If there were degrees in badness, I would say "Morning After" is a much worse poem than the poem about finches. It is worse because its fashionableness *is* more-or-less up to date. Above all, it is worse because it absolutely excluded the reader from knowing what it is all about. It is worse because, however sentimental, a depiction of finches — an experience in the world we all live in — is more humane than a more-or-less random collection of words which has as its intent the shaming of readers. "Morning After" was written to make readers feel foolish for not understanding.

obscurity

How does this poem strike you?

PROCNE

Beneath the crabbéd eglantine
    our hour, our cloudy hour
nor pricket stamps, nor woodcock
    mutters there:
but in clear moon on the bare hill
    and conscious in our bower

Bolts like the hand of fire God's endless melody!

I am no coruscant of yearning
I am no avalanche of time
I am no joint of briar burning
I am not nourishéd of thyme

My song turns on its wing like a swallow

That is one of ten poems which constitute the complete collected works of Edwin R. Roon. I know. I wrote them in less than an hour about fifteen years ago. The other day I was going through some old papers — and I was reminded why. My father-in-law had copied out by hand from an anthology, *Modern Poetry, American and British*. A poem written by Howard Moss in the late forties entitled "Waterfall Blues," consists of five stanzas; these are the first two:

I gnarled me where the spinster tree
Unwound its green hosanna
And built its sorrow leaf by knee,
A lachrymal cabana.

> The selfsame night I cracked my cowl,
> Unwound myself with Anna:
> Speech by speech and howl by howl
> O don't you cry Susanna.

My father-in-law said he had difficulty understanding the poem. As a glittering young Assistant Professor of English, I promptly supplied an explication which was as pretentious, prissy and peremptory as was characteristic of literary criticism of that day and age. I explained that the poem was about the replacement of religious values by secular values, that in losing his virginity (i.e., cracking his cowl) and launching himself on a life of merriment he found that a new sorrow replaced the old. The last stanza pictures him as the Ancient Mariner on a "downtown ferry" with the albatross of sorrow around his neck — recognition (I gather) that Anna will never die:

> But when my halfway laughing gulls
> Despair the death of her,
> Dumb sorrow rides the same old hulls
> With his mad mariner.

I am not sure that my explication — which was full of references to history of civilization, spiritual decay, positivism, psychology and magic — has much to do with what the poem says. Today as I read it I have little understanding or interest in what the poem says. It looks like a playful romp with language — and I would hope that the poet would agree that it is pretty much ingenious nonsense and that the apparent effort of that last stanza to evoke some kind of ironic poignancy is rather fraudulent: the poem has given us very little reason to share any sadness concerning the poet's carnal life.

In my letter to my father-in-law I said:

> Communication is achieved more by association, by juxtaposition, than by statement. Every device of language is used to create an emotional tone appropriate to the ideas. Exotic words *(hosanna, cabana, lachrymal, cowl,* etc.) are used . . . to establish an essentially mysterious atmosphere . . . . The jolting juxtapositions, the provoking images, the dramatic shifts in tone, all make the poem tremendously effective — if you can put up with unintelligibility. I can't. I don't think it's worth the effort.

Hence the work of Edwin R. Roon. I was fed up. I was bitter.

And I probably took secret delight in the opportunity to give imagination and language free rein without the obligation to make sense or adhere to responsible statement.

As I look back over Roon's tattered manuscripts I find, indeed, some gems — as these lines from "Yonder, La Antigua":

The instant singes as a poker thrust
The hour consumes as billow of Lethe
The day extenuates itself in particles of infinite continuity
The year drops like a card from the pack
After the bedtime fables let there be dreams

Usually Roon was not so clear. He chronically attitudinizes ("I am no wolf of petals") and drops learned allusions as one drops names at a cocktail party, as in "Alta Quies, Buccinator":

Ascend, traveller, the blank road.
Abler acrobats have through these nares passed,
the lowly spirochaetes, like Cambyses,
have, in an eyefleck, hewn a homey node.

He was relentlessly visionary and played footsie with all religions:

Echo II: Marhabharatta

Vyasa, compose me in my moment of stillness.
pellucid
the instant
hanging
from the key
stone of
the arch
of the groin
of God
Where no breath disturbs there is no drowning.

Steeped in erudition, intoxicated with verbal refinement, yearning for some vaguely Eastern salvation, he seems to have foreseen, even in the early fifties, the advance of cultural armies of the night. Judging from its Whitmanesque lines I might guess that "Los Ciegos" (The Blind Ones) was a reaction to what was then being called "The West Coast Renaissance," and has subsequently been called the emergence of the beatniks, the hippies, and the youth rebellion:

Armies are gathering on the border.
Dawn rises from the mudflats like a nude and on the silver fields they are marching, their knees in drift of mist

Or as the wind staggers lost across the earth they are hammering
   at the corners of their flapping tents
Or as the night wind carries along its customary whirl of stars
   they are standing by fires before their tents or are intent
   on machinery in the orange interiors
. . .
Their hounds are leaping in the high grass and their trumpets cry
   assembly.
They are armed.

Alas, the barbaric invasion overwhelmed him. The last of Roon's
poems, "Decalogue: All Beat Up," was written to be read at a
beatnik party and clearly shows the influence of such writers as
Ginsberg, Corso and Kerouac, though Roon was never able to
throw off the preciousness of his heritage. Most of this poem is
obscene. These lines suggest the tone:

Kill?
Like, man, fallout gives me asthma.
Like that Korean mud is too cold for a skinny butt like mine.
Like numb me first with Milltown
and a sniff of Gunsmoke and a snort of Old Ike
and a fix in the veins of T. S. Sellout
   (those pinstripes and five stars — in spray-can, roll-on, or
      screw-lid jars)
and maybe I won't notice that thou
are done doing that which thou shalt not.

Roon's work illustrates most of the diseases poetry suffered in
the mid-fifties, and I would like to be able to say that we are cured
from them today. But that is not the case. Perhaps we will never
be. To some extent poetry has always contained an element of
privileged communication among an in-group. In the English Renaissance, for example, what were then called "dark" or obscure lines
were highly valued — for a very explicit reason: they limited the
audience of poetry to an elite, highly (or, rather, narrowly) educated aristocratic group. As literacy spread and vulgar tongues
(i.e., English, Spanish, French, German — as opposed to Latin)
were increasingly used for literary work, hordes of ordinary
people began encroaching on the literary domain. To defend it,
poets used classical allusions, scientific references, polysyllabic
vocabulary, cryptic grammar and other devices to defeat common
understanding. I can remember plowing through a very difficult
poem given me by a student in the fifties. When he explained it,

I said, "Well, if that is what you meant, why didn't you say it?"
He said, "I wouldn't want some football-player-type to understand
it." Not only was he protecting his poem from uncouth readers,
he was giving the couth ones the joy of self-congratulation when
they were able to grasp the references aimed at those who had
the requisite special knowledge.

Repeatedly I receive letters such as one before me which says,
"I have read and enjoyed poetry for nearly half a century. I'll be
quick to admit that my taste runs pretty much to Markham, Bryant,
Scott, Riley, etc., altho I like Dylan Thomas, Shaemus O'Sheel,
and a few modern poets. . . . But honestly, Mr. Jerome, does the
enclosed actually qualify as poetry?" He sent me a long poem by
James Tate, who won the Yale Younger Poets award some years
ago for *The Lost Pilot* and has since published eight other books,
mostly (I gather from the bibliographic descriptions) in limited,
art editions. Tate is a recognized and influential figure in current
poetry, but I can understand my correspondent's bafflement. *Amnesia
People* (the pamphlet-length poem he enclosed) begins:

> Have we not gathered here because
> a machine with thousands of tiny gears
> sucking the air out of the room
> considering Amanda's feverish condition
> the gun fired and the picture-tube exploded
> I found myself polishing my old wing-
> tipped shoes his laconic master
> had gone loco and I'll tell you why.

I read on, but I didn't discover why. A highly applauded book
by W. S. Merwin, *The Lice,* begins with this poem:

THE ANIMALS

> All these years behind windows
> With blind crosses sweeping the tables
>
> And myself tracking over empty ground
> Animals I never saw
>
> I with no voice
>
> Remembering names to invent for them
> Will any come back will one
>
> Saying yes
>
> Saying look carefully yes
> We will meet again

A former student of mine, Phil Fried, who graduated from the Writer's Workshop at the University of Iowa in 1968, sent me copies of his poems published by the *North American Review;* this is one:

NEIGHBOR, RISE

Neighbor, rise with me in twilight;
I speak the rose-blue vanishing,
The waters that dwindle, black.

I know Misfortune looked in, leaning
Upon the sill with potted plants, and I
Was the body of the flies that lingered
Over the stain of honey, buzzed and dipped
Then scattered at random across the fields.

At night I am in my mouths, the dark
Leaves rattling at the throats, and through
The pores of my earth, the winds.

Readers have good reason to be mystified. Whatever these poets are doing, communication with the general public is not high on their scale of values. Edwin R. Roon was no more than the Edgar Guest of this league.

One can enjoy such poetry as one can enjoy abstract painting — responding to texture, color, shape and the general feeling the work conveys without demanding meaning (or representation) in the usual sense. The Moss poem quoted earlier is at least fun to read; the rhythm and rhyme and splashy diction save one from boredom. And the poetry quoted here of Tate, Merwin and Fried has a haunting strangeness about it, churns up resonant images and phrases which, like a ghostly conversation overheard in a dream, sound luminous and profound and just beyond the reach of comprehension. If we demand more coherence than that — i.e., linear, logical statement, paraphrasable content — we will be dismissed as Philistines.

I find myself bemused rather than indignant at the phenomena of art in our time. Brilliant men — and some of the poets I have been quoting are brilliant men — mutter in the streets, ravaged by their vision. These are phenomena of the fissures of decaying empire — rich and aromatic seams of corruption crazing the granite face. Philip Slater's provocative title, *The Pursuit of Loneliness,* expresses his theme that many characteristics of our present culture maximize alienation. Scientists even in the same narrow sub-specialty often cannot communicate with one another, so arcane is their jargon, so abstruse their knowledge. These poets seem, too, in an almost desperate pursuit of loneliness, as though one could sense his own validity only if he pressed himself to such an extreme of sensitivity and individuality and uniqueness that no one could touch him. It is as though there were no escape from the great mechanizing, homogenizing, crushing technocracy except into the recesses of consciousness, the Minoan maze.

Desmond Morris writes:

> Wild animals do not mutilate themselves, masturbate, attack their offspring, develop stomach ulcers, become fetishists, suffer from obesity, form homosexual pair-bonds, or commit murder. Among human city-dwellers, needless to say, all of these things occur . . . The zoo animal in a cage exhibits all these abnormalities that we know so well from our human companions. Clearly, then, the city is not a concrete jungle, it is the human zoo . . .

What is the poetry of the human zoo? It is everywhere in evidence around us. Another reader tells me in a letter:

> Poetry has drifted away from the common man. His education, comprehension, understanding and pleasure is such that he cannot fathom the mysterious, hidden meaning of poetry of today. Poetry is now for the aesthete . . . . It is a pitiful and degenerate state when poets have become so rutty, narrow and small. With all the big things in the world to do, why must people do such little things . . . The great good poetry could do as a medium has become confined by class . . . The life run of our nation, like all past world powers, is setting . . . . And if we are yoked like dumb drawn cattle, where will be the place of chowder head poetry that could have done so much by reaching the multitude to form, propagate and teach the great things that poetry can teach to a great nation.

It may be that the fuse of our empire is burning out, after a short and violent two hundred years, but if poetry ever had any part in sustaining a civilization it was under conditions in which poets could identify with the values and goals of the civilization. If the nature of our own is such as to drive our most talented seers into the back corners of their minds, we cannot expect the kind of poetry which can teach great things to a great nation.

It is true that much contemporary poetry is unintelligible, and the obscurity is in part the result of haughtiness, preciousness and contempt for the common man. It is also true that Philistines will not inspire poets to love them or to communicate with them by crying, "Love me." I think the job of us all, poets and readers alike, is to bring about greater coherency and authenticity and humanity in our civilization. Then we may expect to have these qualities in our poetry as well.

clouds of meaning

Meanwhile, though there are conflicts in echelons of taste, the theory still persists that some words are more poetic than others. It is closely related to conceptions of "pure" poetry — a view which demands that poetry be "beautiful" and usually solemn, usually about "nature" (meaning outdoors), and be characterized by consistency of "moods." All of these concepts — beauty, nature, mood — are limiting and somewhat vaporous. They have been the basis of good poetry, of course; but their continuing popularity is probably owing less to a real interest in poetry than to a natural desire to indulge one's melancholy, demonstrate fine sensibilities, to strike tragic poses and sneer at vulgar flesh and blood. Perhaps the passing of titled aristocracy made it necessary for people who felt themselves refined to distinguish themselves by allegiance to a new aristocracy based on feeling, sensitivity, innate superiority demonstrated not so much by ability to think or do as by susceptibility to what earlier ages called "the vapors." The resulting poetry is, at its driest, that of the limp wrist and lifted brow, but it often goes moist and becomes that of parted lips and dilated vision. Whatever advantages it may have had in the early 19th century, it is poisonous in our times. A distaste for life is poor grounds for creativity.

T. S. Eliot claimed that every age has its poetic diction, language close to, but not identical with contemporary speech. This seems to me to say very little, for written prose is also usually close to, but not identical with contemporary speech. Surely every individual has a characteristic vocabulary just as he has a characteristic grin or walk or dresses in a characteristic way. The compound of all his individual traits is his style; and any severe violation of his own style is almost unthinkable, though not wrong.

There are certainly words I would not use in a poem: like *teosinte* (I don't know what it means) or *mallow* (which strikes me as affected, and too easily poeticized). Humor inevitably broadens the base of vocabularly — and whiie I can imagine using scientific terminology (which is pretty funny) in light verse, I would find it hard to work *saccharofarinaceous* into a serious line, though that word, implying a combination of saccharine and mealy qualities, might be a good one to introduce into poetic criticism.

Any poet, of course, has unconscious preferences and even principles which affect the words he uses or excludes. I would suggest forbidding oneself the use of the dictionary while composing (though it must be used often in revision), to keep the vocabulary range to that of one's ordinary conversation. Rarity, preciousness, can be as offensive in poetry as it is in life. Unless you work with the words of your current, active vocabulary you betray the sense of voice good poetry must have. Moreover, much of the effectiveness of the words of poetry lies in the accurate evocation of their connotations; and you do not find these in the dictionary. If your experience with words out of poems is free and far-ranging you will have an adequate vocabulary to draw on for composition. Just as you are more interested in certain subjects than in others, you will find yourself using certain kinds of words and excluding others — such as dialect, philosophical abstractions, technical terms, or whatever. I do not mean you *should* exclude those categories, but that there are, of course, categories of words which you will automatically exclude from your poetry.

I admire words in Wallace Stevens which I wouldn't dream of using myself and doubt that he ever spoke aloud (which shows the limitation of the "conversational" standard). Robert Sward wrote a fine little poem about an apteryx — lifted from the page of the dictionary into poetry, made poetic by the sheer fact of its poetic employment. Theories of poetic diction become deadly when they pretend to legislate the language which ought and ought not occur in all poetry, when they assume that the adjective *poetic* may somehow be used to snip the blossoms of life from the roots.

Every human activity takes place in its own cloud of language. If you overhear *grease, wrench, jack, lug* you know you are in a garage; but now they are talking about *run, fly, out, bunt* and you know the mechanics under the car are rehashing the ball game — or perhaps you hear *spinner, line, reel, hackle, gut,* and you know the conversation has shifted to the coming weekend's freshwater fishing. None of these clouds of words is poetry; each, however, is a diction. All dictions overlap with such neutral words as *and, is,* or *maybe;* but the languages of sociology, of the kitchen, of the insurance office, of the Scout hike, are each largely distinct. To say that poetry has a proper diction is to imply that one of those clouds (a lonely, little dark one) floats alone compounded of hearts and flowers.

I would rather believe that poetry is what happens when two or more clouds come together. The process may be seen very clearly in Henry Reed's "Naming of Parts."

> Today we have naming of parts. Yesterday
> We had daily cleaning. And tomorrow morning,
> We shall have what to do after firing. But today,
> Today we have naming of parts. Japonica
> Glistens like coral in all of the neighboring gardens,
>   And today we have naming of parts.

That is the first stanza. The first sentence could apply to anything. The second, with *daily cleaning* begins to show us the outlines of the forming cloud. The word *firing* in the third enables us to link cleaning and parts to rifles, a connection which becomes clear in the second stanza. The monotonous tone, the pretentious awkwardness of "We shall have what to do after" suggests a sensibility to us: that of a droning instructor in basic training speaking to a class as though to children. The cloud is established. The next sentence surprises us, though: the repetition of "today,/Today" suggests a reflectiveness we would not have attributed to that meat-headed instructor. Next we hear of japonica glistening, we have a simile, we notice the surrounding gardens. Surely it is not the instructor. We are now in the mind of one of his listeners; we are in another cloud, another sensibility, one with little attention for the rifle in the man's hands, a sensibility capable of dwelling on a moment, of observing, comparing, of seeing the irony of this plodding attention to the mechanics of warfare in the midst of a lush and colorful world of life and beauty. The two clouds met at the end of line three, and there was a flash of lightning. The poetry is not in the diction of either sensibility but in their explosive juncture.

This same pattern continues through the next three stanzas. We begin with the language of stupid concentration on the metallic parts of battle. Then there is juxtaposed the language of an inattentive student growing increasingly bitter, poignant, as he contemplates the discrepancy between this mechanical concentration and the flowering possibilities of life suggested by the natural background. Here is the second stanza:

>   This is the lower sling swivel. And this
>   Is the upper sling swivel, whose use you will see,
>   When you are given your slings. And this is the piling swivel,
>   Which in your case you have not got. The branches
>   Hold in the gardens their silent, eloquent gestures,
>   Which in our case we have not got.

The irony deepens as the instruction thus becomes absurd even in its own terms, aside from its tragic incongruity in the midst of the flowering affirmation of life around them. As the instructor goes on in the third and fourth stanzas unimaginatively describing the bolt and breech and the process of easing the spring by sliding it rapidly backwards and forwards, and the bemused student — with a flicker of appropriate humor — observes the bees "assaulting and fumbling" the "fragile and motionless" flowers; we see nature as reproductive, warm, fertile, eloquent, colorful — and man, proud man, dressed in a little brief authority, bent on analysis, naming of parts, on mechanism and death. In the final stanza the clouds of diction intermingle in a kind of fugue:

>   They call it easing the Spring: it is perfectly easy
>   If you have any strength in your thumb: like the bolt,
>   And the breech, and the cocking-piece, and the point of
>   balance,
>   Which in our case we have not got; and the almond-blossom
>   Silent in all of the gardens and the bees go backwards and
>   forwards,
>   For today we have naming of parts.

One might say the poem means that war is a perversion, that in all of the gardens man will always be, as the first man in the first garden, naming parts and missing the point of life's verdant possibilities. The important aspect of the poem is not what it means but the way that meaning is achieved through juxtaposition of *kinds* of diction.

What is the proper diction of poetry? I think Reed's poem illustrates something essential about all poetry, regardless of the theory that governs its conception: that is, poetry brings one kind of language to bear on another. It applies, in a sense, always the wrong terminology. Unless there is some discord there can be no music. Or, to return to my clouds, so long as you remain in a single kind of diction you remain in a fog.

the visible voice

In Chapter Four I spoke of the "sense of self" to which one responds in a poet's "voice." Your "voice" is in large part what determines your diction — as distinct from that of your subject matter or your poetic theory. Even in an age in which reading is largely silent, poets write less for readers than for listeners. And much bad poetry might be forestalled if poets made the initial effort to *hear* their own poems. Try one of your own by reading it aloud. Does your tongue tangle? Do you hear your syntax thrashing futilely, your sense drowning in a mumble? Can you imagine anyone saying what you say there? And do you know exactly how he should sound?

Notice that I am not referring to melodiousness or sonority or "beautiful" sound, although in some poems, of course, these are appropriate qualities. I am referring to the vigor and supple force of ordinary speech. Some poems should surely sing, but for most it suffices that they speak. A very simple rule (oversimple, as I will explain) can help you make them speak: cut everything you cannot imagine being naturally said.

First apply the rule to grammar and structure. Speech rounds and smooths many of the ornate and awkward constructions which make sense, of a sort, when merely written. You don't speak to the air, or to a page; you speak to a person (even if it is yourself), and for a reason. Your concern is not merely to be understandable but to prevent misunderstanding. Your references are clear, your word order logical and habitual, your sentences have point and direction (or at least in your best speech you strive for these qualities). When composing a poem, though, one is apt to become enamoured of individual words, of descriptive phrases, of artful elaboration, which blur beyond recovery the intention of sentences and clauses. In ordinary speech the immediate word or phrase is disciplined and subordinated by one's awareness of the problem of how to get from here to there.

Naturalness of word order has become increasingly important, almost a fashion (a good one, I think), in twentieth century poetry. As poets have freed themselves from the confines of narrowly construed metrical, line, and stanza forms, they have found less reason to invert and distort word order — so that some of the grammatical gymnastics of a poet as recent as Hardy are likely to appear strangely artificial and "old-fashioned" (as are poetic contractions such as " 'tis" or "e'er" to preserve meter) when used in modern poetry. Meanwhile such poets as William Carlos Williams and Robert Frost have directed our attention to the native grain of American speech and taught us to respect the raw material of our language rather than abandon it in favor of a false and bloodless gentility. It is sound advice, but by no means entirely modern. Before and after Chaucer the best poetry has always been vernacular, colloquial, adhering reverently to the turns of everyday speech. Some poets, of course (Milton and Pope come to mind), transform artificiality to art, although even in their work the sinews are those of conversation. And even when heightening (as artificial elegance used to be called) is appropriate for passages of exceptional dignity, grandeur or eloquence, good poetry may never cut itself loose from, though it may transcend, its vernacular roots.

Apply the rule to diction. Once you could not refer to fish except by some locution — such as "finny tribe"; now you had better say "fish" unless it is clear that you are joking. Any page of the dictionary will show you dozens of words which, if not impossible, are at least very difficult to use in serious poetry. I open at random and see *pediform, pedology, peducle, peise, pelagic, pelerine* — all words I would ordinarily avoid in poetry, not because they are "unpoetic" but because they are not normal to my conversation.

On the same page I see *peignoir,* which Wallace Stevens used evocatively in "Sunday Morning" — but set like a gem in a background of less flashy stuff. Stevens, of course, was addicted to curious words and made them so much a part of his manner that he created a convincing, though artificial, idiom much wider than the range of anyone's normal speech. One would have to class him with Milton and Pope as a supreme artificer, and he would have been delighted with the appellation. But unless such language is an integral part of a poet's style, it is dangerous material for him to touch at all.

But shouldn't one be fresh? Assuredly, but originality is a quality of thought and perception rather than of decoration. Fancy words, far from being fresh, are often the most vulgar of cheap ornaments. The essence of our language is monosyllabic; and if Pope mocked poetry in which ten low words oft creep in one dull line, he was temporarily overlooking the most characteristic and best of English poetry (even his own) which is plain fare, heavily monosyllabic, with its strength in its feeling and wisdom rather than coruscant vocabulary.

Finally, in more general terms, apply the rule to the poem as a whole. I find it useful to imagine nearly every poem as a dramatic speech spoken by some specific person (often myself) to some specific person or audience (again, often myself) on some specific occasion. The poem should imply all three conditions: says who? to whom? and, why? Try reading your own poems as though every one were direct address, with an implied "you." I think you will find that those which come alive, which spring from the page, are those in which the dramatic situation is most clear. Others may wallow and lie flat. Is it because they are words merely, said by no one to no one for no reason?

I said the rule was oversimple, and I must now warn you of its limitations. Conversation is the warmest and liveliest form of communication, but it is also (with most of us) apt to be slovenly, disorganized, repetitious, trite, drab. These are qualities one is not likely to want to emulate in poetry. Moreover, poetry cannot convey the animation of expression and gesture which relieve face-to-face conversation of its more tiresome characteristics. Poetry must, of course, be *better* than conversation — more intense, more accurate, briefer, better expressed — and must compensate for the characteristics of human contact that it cannot approximate. For example, to make a difficult point in conversation one may repeat, restate, illustrate, answer questions. A poem may rely on a single very exact but perhaps dense or even obscure statement to accomplish the same thing. The reader may read again, and, in fact, he may enjoy participating in the poem by contributing a considerable effort to understanding it. Because he is not, ordinarily, limited to a single reading or hearing, he is more willing (and able) to wrestle with complex structures and language. If poetry gave us no more than conversation, I am sure we would all prefer conversation.

Moreover, all I have said here applies only to "serious" poetry. Any rule may be profitably stood on its ear for the sake of a joke. And "serious" poetry is difficult to define, particularly as much of the best poetry of our century (like that of the 17th and 18th centuries) uses a thousand shades of wit, irony, wry archness and self-deflating humor in order to make serious points. John Crowe Ransom, for example, successfully exploited all varieties of artificial, archaic, even deliberately awkward structure and language to create very moving blends of emotion and protesting wit much in the way that a composer may color and extend the emotional range of his music with discord and sour notes. You cannot be simple-minded about anything pertaining to poetry, and any "rule" is implicitly a challenge. Find the occasion, it dares you, when this standard can (or must) be violated.

But the standard of speech is, basically, the requirement that the poem have a voice. Here I think you will find that even those poets I have named as exceptional — Milton, Pope, Stevens, Ransom — fulfill the expectation we have of any good poet. However peculiarly they speak, one *hears* them, one recognizes the resonance of human lungs and throat, the characteristic tones and cadences of human personality.

Read the poem aloud again, now. Can you wrap your tongue comfortably around the language? Is there posing, posturing, showing-off, which you would find offensive in a person and should find no less offensive in a poem? Have you been faithful to your own idiom or that of your imagined speaker? Is the poem's occasion clearly enough implied, and the way this governs tone, cadence, intensity? Is it coherent (unless, of course, you are deliberately portraying incoherency)? Now let someone else read it aloud to you. Have you guided him sufficiently with your phrasing, diction, punctuation, to enable him to approximate the intended tone of voice? If the poem satisfies all these requirements there is some chance you may have achieved the miracle any successful poem must achieve: mere words strung together on a page have disappeared and instead of seeing, you are suddenly hearing a distinct human voice.

CHAPTER NINE

Sound Values

the isness of the art

Unless you see that poetry cannot be translated your instincts are wrong for poetry. Can paintings or symphonies or statues be translated? The question makes no sense in regard to the other arts.

But art in language frustrates and tempts us. We can look at a statue and think our thoughts and experience our reaction in Chinese or Italian. The words of a poem, though, permit very little reaction to people who do not understand the language from which they come. The temptation is to find other words in other languages to paraphrase. It is possible to put those new words in a form that suggests the form of the original. The resulting poem may be very gratifying, even better than the original, but it is not to be confused with the poem itself. Art is distinguished by *isness*. "A poem should not mean/ But be." For a work of art, like an organism, cannot be duplicated.

Poetry, of course, if you are lucky, can be printed. Your typescript is a set of instructions to the printer indicating, even to the commas and spelling, how the work should appear. Its isness, then, is not a particular object, like a statue, but a set of instructions, like a musical score. Change one word and it is a different poem. Sometimes improved, but different.

Because thought is that aspect of a poem which *can* be paraphrased, we may say the isness of the poem, its flesh, its color, its texture, resides above all in its sound. Sound is sometimes disregarded as though it were some incidental adornment *added to* the essential poem, but to consider the poem without its dimension of sound is like studying a black and white reproduction of a painting. You can tell what it's *about,* but you can't know what it *is.*

On the other hand, those who do not disregard sound often suffer misconceptions about how it works and attribute to it too much of the wrong kind of significance. Most language is prose, and in prose, of course, meaning is primary. (Prose can often be paraphrased without loss of its essential values.) Some people, naturally, regard poetic elements as decoration, as some sugar sweetening of a prose pill of meaning. And for them, the poet's preoccupation with words, sounds, rhythms, artful phrasing, figures, images, is apt to seem faintly corrupt, like the eloquence of lovers, which often disguises an ulterior aim.

The problem is complicated, in our world of advertising and diplomacy, by the fact that language *is* often adorned to make it more palatable; and the common man's distrust of eloquence is well-justified. He trusts, curiously, what is badly said, out of a kind of habitual cynicism, believing that what a man expresses clumsily and inarticulately he must surely mean. Clever, resounding, lovely, even precise expression seems insincere or dishonest.

You can talk about the climate, but you can't do anything about it except adjust. Knowing that excessive alliteration, for example, recalls the sweet nothings of Swinburne, that neat phrases recall soap slogans, that sonority recalls Fourth of July oratory, the poet has to be subtle. Roughening sounds is often as important a process as smoothing them. (Modern art often seems that of coating the sugar with pill.) But above all, the poet must remember that for him sound values are inherent in the meaning, not something separable and alterable at will. He cannot, and be a poet, produce the same proteins in seven delicious flavors.

There is no such thing as a synonym. *Dog, hund, chien* and *perro* all may point to the same four-legged phenomenon — as might *mutt, cur, pup, canine, flea-bag,* and *man's best friend.* But poetry is not mere finger-pointing and diagrams. For you, as a poet, words have shape, color, texture; they have life, and living things are not interchangeable. A poet does not, as is sometimes believed, manipulate sound by finding a word, among several alternatives, which happens to contain the consonants and vowels desired.

Poetry is not that easy. You do not seek merely to make sense, but to make inevitable sense. This is more than a rightness of logic; it is a rightness of everything. In a given poem, of course, there may be only one or two words which fall into place with that thrilling sense of inevitability. But you strive for that success and never permit yourself to rest with the idea that one word will do for another merely because it sounds better.

Much nonsense has been written about the correspondence of sound and sense. As it usually goes, the critic finds plosives, gutturals, fricatives, or something else, echoing exactly the subject matter of the poem. An example from Pope:

> See! from the brake the whirring Pheasant springs,
> And mounts exulting on triumphant wings;
> Short is his joy; he feels the fiery wound,
> Flutters in blood, and panting beats the ground.

Notice, the critic will say, the fricative and liquid sounds — *s's, f's, r's, w's,* climaxed with the *l* in *exulting* — as the pheasant arises. Blended in, then, are the nasals — *n's, m's,* and *ng's* of humming flight. When the bird is hit by a bullet, a harder series of fricatives occurs in the initial sounds of *feels, fiery* and *flutters,* mixing with low vowels and gutturals as he flops, defeated, on the forest floor, particularly in the dead, heavy sounds of *blood* and *ground.*

Or, if the critic were hostile, he might argue that when we should be given flight we are given heavy plosive sounds — *br* and *spr* — gutturals, *like k* and *x,* low vowels as in *from, mounts, whirring,* and *triumphant,* and a stuttering succession of *t's* in the second line. When the bird should be falling, the sounds rise with fricatives and higher, lighter, more forward sounds (e.g., *fiery* — a word that soars upward) and death is rendered with another nervous succession of *t's* in the last line.

The illusion is that of program music. You read that the composer hoped to convey a gurgling stream, and, sure enough, it gurgles. But had you not read the program you might have imagined skimming swallows or taxis on Fifth Avenue. In poetry, the meaning of the words is the program. *Flat* sounds flat and *round* sounds round because you know what the words mean and adjust your voice accordingly. *Ugly* sounds ugly, doesn't it? But *snugly,* veritably the same sounds, seems cozier. You hit plosives hard in words suggesting violence and soften them in words suggesting, for instance, peace. *Dog* does not sound a bit more like a dog than *chien.* There is little or no innate emotional effect of sounds isolated from meaning.

There are, curiously, various sound clusters which in our lan-

guage seem to be associated with a particular emotional effect
— like the *sn* of *sneer, snipe, snort, snare, snaggle, sneak,* and
other words with an unpleasant, sharp significance (but not *snow),*
or the *fl* of words like *flicker, flight, fling, flee, flutter,* which seem
to have in common a sense of lightness and swiftness (but not
flood). Other words, of course, are clearly and intentionally
onomatopoetic — *buzz, snap, bang, tweet.* Rhythm, too, can be
used to produce sound effects, like the galloping of a horse; but
these are tricks, and, overused, become showy and cheap and
not very profound. *Cockadoodle doo* in Spanish is *ki ki ri ki,* which
tells us less about the high vowel sounds of Spanish cocks than
the limitations of onomatopoeia.

A Chinese man once said *cellar-door* is the most beautiful
word in the English language. Tennyson spent much poetic energy
trying to avoid the sound of *s.* Such stories reflect the persistent
belief that some sounds of human speech are more innately beautiful
than other sounds; and like the belief that specific sounds arouse
specific emotions or sense impressions, it is largely nonsense. It
gives rise to a search for melodiousness and harmony in sounds —
an analogy with music; but a dangerous analogy because it relies on
a false, limited understanding of music.

In both poetry and music there are elements of concord, agreement, harmony, order, and those of contrast, discord, and disorder. When we think in a simpleminded way of music, it is the
first group of elements which comes to mind, those which are
cohesive, resonant. But if you listen to a good piece of music, you
will notice that the moments of greatest resonance or harmony
are carefully placed, climactic. The texture — all the body and
excitement — is composed of contrast and irregularity; otherwise
the music would be a great bore, like a succession of tonic chords.
It is much the same in poetry. Browning is, in the real sense of
the word, a more musical poet than Spenser. His rugged rhythms,
his discords, his consonant clusters, frustrate the heart's desire for
solid resonance, and when his occasional harmonies and soft
passages occur they are all the more welcome, meaningful and
effective. Some poets are so preoccupied with the narrower sense
of musicality that they compose only in one mode — that of the
lullaby.

Music is not sounds, but sound relationships; relationships
govern the effect of poetry as well. The sounds of poetry are
embodied in words, and it is always *meaning* which makes a word

sound pleasing or displeasing. Without altering the sounds we can convert one of Shakespeare's most beautiful, musical song lines into something which "sounds" quite hideous:

Oh what is love? 'Tis snot hereafter.

Some sound combinations, of course, are awkward; some softer, easier, more mellifluous. But of the innumerable interrelationships of the elements of poetry, that between meaning and sound is far more important than that between sound and sound.

In discussing these various misconceptions I may seem to have removed any need of talking about sounds at all; but, in fact, an "ear" for poetry is chiefly the ear for sounds, and while a writer can do very little to develop this instinct, it is immediately apparent when a writer without an ear (witness Stephen Crane, Edgar Lee Masters) attempts poetry. I dislike giving credit to mysterious talents, but in this case I must admit I know no rules. You can't listen to a line and say it shouldn't have a *p* in it, or that its excellence arises from the juxtaposition of open vowels with *f's*. Almost all such judgments — and they are frequently made — are impressionistic and fallible.

Yet there *is* a cohesion and rightness about the succession of sounds in good verse. I can best describe how it comes about with another musical analogy. An excellent, experienced pianist can usually improvise interminably: just playing, he says — following chord with chord, melodic unit or phrase with phrase, never exactly repeating music he knows, never inserting a familiar tune, never boring us with hackneyed cadences — but giving us, all the while, something that sounds convincingly like music. He may not be a composer. But he has developed an ear. He knows, having struck one chord, the whole range and variety of chords which can follow, which are interesting, and his fingers avoid instinctively the sounds which may *not* follow. To prove this, listen to the improvisations of an inexpert pianist; he will quickly be driven to playing recognizable snatches, or to monotony, or to awkward transitions which just don't sound like music. I don't mean dissonance, for dissonance can be artful and convincing, and though it is harder to improvise dissonantly than harmoniously (the harmonious chords are the easiest learned, and it is sometimes harder to avoid them than to hit them), it is possible to play near cacaphony and still obey the inner logic of the developing, unfolding music.

Similarly, the poet, even when feeling out the phrases he will come to reject, seldom violates the inner logic of his language.

Mostly, of course, this is a matter of syntax. The poem flows along the current of its grammar, and a poet must have enough varieties of structure, as well as of sound, at his command to regulate that flow exactly, either to ripple limpidly, cascade grandly, snarl and twist tortuously in the rocky rapids of tension, or issue in quiet amplitude in long lagoons of greater profundity.

The role of sound is to assist. Meaning draws attention to sound. "Brief as noon," or "out in the broad noon," give different sound values to the same word; we see *brief* and our mouth tightens as we say *noon; out* and *broad* warn us, force us to extend *noon* to include all outdoors. My phrase above, "long lagoons," draws out the same *oon* sound its liquid length, echoes the long *u's* of *issue* and *amplitude* (altered afterwards in *profundity*.) This is not, notice, to say that *oon* sounds like the still depths, or that the phrase is melodious. Nor, of course, did I plan all these relationships as I wrote the sentence. The ear takes advantage of what happens to have passed; and as he selects for what will come, the poet repeats, echoes, contrasts, modulates, to provide a texture which supports the emphases of meaning and the pace of the grammar.

This texture of sound relationships, more than any other single element, creates the isness of the poem. Because of its inherent fluidity and relativity, it is the element most difficult to reduce to principles — and, consequently, the most difficult to learn. Reading good poetry aloud and listening to the sounds is the best way to build up a repertory (like that of the pianist) from which you can improvise. It is a process of accumulating possibilities, storing them in the deeper levels of habit, so that you can play by ear effortlessly, avoiding the obvious, the monotonous, the showy, yet articulating neatly the appropriate resonance to give body and color to your thought and feeling.

the dancer and the dance

> O body swayed to music, O brightening glance,
> How can we know the dancer from the dance?
> > W. B. Yeats, "Among School Children"

Composing poetry is done with the whole body. If you have a sense of muscular involvement as you write, your reader is likely to share it as he reads. If *he* does not have a sense of muscular involvement, the poem, for lack of that dimension, will remain flat on the page.

Test this: watch how successful lines prove themselves in gesture, posture, voice, tone, especially in constriction and release of throat and mouth muscles.

> Like as the waves make towards the pebbled shore
> So do our minutes hasten to their end;
> Each changing place with that which goes before,
> In sequent toil all forwards do contend.

Read the lines, experimentally, with exaggeration, letting everything happen to you which can, letting your arm and hand curve forward in the broad sweep of the first line, piling up on those three wide accents in the middle, folding on the pebbled shore, then, with fresh breath, so do (and how round the mouth, how little the minutes!) our instants roll, tumble and hiss. Waves, as we know, are rotating particles, and we tighten and turn with the third and fourth lines, the very syllables becoming little distinct entities confused. The churning and boiling process and then destruction are created for us not only by the sounds but by grammar, structure, the very movement of the line. We have experienced a wave swelling to its crest and crumbling as it piles in on the strand.

That motion continues through the rest of the sonnet (Shakespeare, 60), though the imagery changes:

> Nativity, once in the main of light
> Crawls to maturity, wherewith being crown'd,
> Crooked eclipses 'gainst his glory fight,
> And Time that gave doth now his gift confound.

Notice the contrast between the fast little syllables of *Nativity* and the ample ease of *once, main, light;* then the poem bunches again with *maturity;* and breadth, the stasis before the wave collapses, comes at the end ("wherewith being crown'd"). The next line is all crunching and folding, and the eighth — the summary of the octave — wells out again in the slow, full syllables, stasis being achieved by the uncertain balance of paradox.

The waves of the first quatrain are elaborated in the second to terms of climbing, growth, light, debility, darkness, destruction. We simultaneously get notions of a child crawling to a height, standing an erect moment, and moving off in crippled old age, of a sun reaching a zenith and being eclipsed, even of Christ being crowned with what turns out to be thorns, and, always, the idea of the sea (*the main*) crushing its dignity on the shore (*confound* means, etymologically, to pour together). In all these there is that common physical sensation of slow ponderous rising, a still, serene moment, and rapid confusion and demolition.

The sestet changes images and manner:

> Time doth transfix the flourish set on youth
> And delves the parallels in beauty's brow,
> Feeds on the rarities of nature's truth,
> And nothing stands but for his scythe to mow:
> And yet to times in hope my verse shall stand
> Praising thy worth, despite his cruel hand.

But the motion of rising and falling continues. That paradox in line eight, capped by the *f's* in *gift confound,* sets up a series of balances. Notice how the hinge of the poem is carefully marked by repetition, not only of sounds but of words *(Time doth)*. "Transfix the flourish" is a moment of crest (*transfix* suggests not only impaling but fixing, stabilizing), and after it the delving line runs its rutting course with liquid swiftness. We come up full-chested to a climax at the next line ending, the full glory of "nature's truth" (note the echo of *nativity* and *maturity* in *rarity*), only to slide back to nothing, sliced down by the whispering scythe. The first line of the couplet marches with steady beat and firm, fat syllables, brings us to a moment of hesitant stasis ("Praising thy worth,") — and inevitably topples us as the cruel hand cuts; for though the poem claims to say that art makes a permanent stay against time, it is only to "times in hope" that it pretends, and we are left with a stronger impression of destructive power than of endurance in the face of it. If you have felt the poem, in arms, fingers, breathing, throat, the march of that couplet, its rocking, balanced moment, and its spitting, cutting dissolution, these muscular elements have told you a meaning the literal sense seems, unsteadily, to deny. Art is more eternal than most things, but not eternal enough.

Actually, there is no language for describing this muscular response that poetry demands — of the poet in composition and of the reader in receiving the message. To speak of it is very much like trying to describe a painting or a symphony. It is too concrete, too much a matter of immediate experience. A good poem is not mere communication of meaning, but communication of a total response.

The practical consequence may seem a bit silly at first. That is, it helps to wave your arms when writing poetry. Get up from your machine or manuscript and walk around, assume postures, orate, *act* the poem — the whole thing and line by line. Every line must have a shape; if you have a line for which you don't feel the inevitable gesture and tone, perhaps it is broken wrong or incomplete. It is better doing this acting privately, as a composer working with his sheet beside the piano might play back for himself the themes or effects he has written. All this helps. Public performance (after the poem is finished) might intimidate you, but in your shyest littlest voice some shape of intention should come through. There are poets for whom actual acting might be unnecessary, and you may be able to leave the practice after awhile, imagining all response without going through the motions. But, believe me, it helps most of us. Go get one of your poems and act it for yourself. I predict (unless the poem stands perfect) you will find yourself changing phrases, line breaks, words. Listen to the poem. You may not have heard it before.

"Heard" is not quite what I mean; "received," which I used earlier, is closer. It may seem absurd that you could have written a poem without having received it; but I have often asked beginning poets to read their poems to me, poems I felt were unsuccessful, and have seen them shrug halfway through, giving it up. No comment necessary. It was as though they had written a score, then as an afterthought, tried to perform it and found it impossible, dull, affected, or embarrassingly awkward.

This is not merely a matter of rhythm or of sound manipulation, of harmony or discord; it is a matter of voice-stance, of posture, in which ideas and sounds and tones and gestures are inseparable when the poem works; when it does not, one element works against the other until the whole texture frazzles. It is no accident that Shakespeare was an actor before he was a playwright, a playwright before a poet (in importance if not in sequence). His poetry could never be merely words on a page.

You may be complaining that you have no acting talent. More's the pity. You do not need, of course, the talent to go on a stage; but you should be able to act in the privacy of your study. There are some poets who destroy their poetry by reading it aloud; but this is not merely a comment on their theatrical ineptitude. It relates directly to weaknesses in their work which (regardless of its other virtues) limit it to secondary importance. They haven't the personal capacity, apparently, really to control voice-stance, or reception, on the page or in the flesh. One can do a better job with his poems than he does, but not much. Some degree of acting talent is as essential to a poet as his sense of rhythm, his ear for sound, or his conceptual intelligence.

Theatrical aptitude in the usual sense, of course, is not the question. Emily Dickinson was, for example, able to convey a universe in the vocal range from a frightened whisper to a New England "humph." Some poets seem always to trace their words with their lips silently on the ear. Frost never raised his voice above a dry crackle.

> Cold as a spring as yet so near its source,
> Too lofty and original to rage.
> (We know the valley streams that when aroused
> Will leave their tatters hung on barb and thorn.)

Variety, however, though within a limited range, is essential, and so is a tension deeper than pronunciation, that tightens the stomach muscles with waiting, that makes the shoulders flex with arrested motion.

And the eyes at times should start with tears. The very containment of gesture makes for this effect, the very futility of words and inadequacy of physical action. John Crowe Ransom was one of the subtlest at working tears from my eyes. Read "Blue Girls" alone, aloud, with the love you might give to a poem of your own. Stand up. Let your hips sway to the progress of the girls across the grass, watch the dry, evaluative antiquated words fall dusty and useless before their dewy presence, feel the simple certainty "of what will come to pass" and the triviality of present chattering, yet its bright appeal, the throat-catching brevity of the short lines at ends of stanzas, and then the utter directness and inevitability and tragedy of the last horrible stanza. Perform this poem, and learn how to perform.

BLUE GIRLS

> Twirling your blue skirts, traveling the sward
> Under the towers of your seminary,
> Go listen to your teachers old and contrary
> Without believing a word.

Tie the white fillets then about your lustrous hair
And think no more of what will come to pass
Than bluebirds that go walking on the grass
And chattering on the air.

Practice your beauty, blue girls, before it fail;
And I will cry with my loud lips and publish
Beauty which all our power shall never establish,
It is so frail.

For I could tell you a story which is true:
I know a lady with a terrible tongue,
Blear eyes fallen from blue,
All her perfections tarnished — and yet it is not long
Since she was lovelier than any of you.

he who has an ear

Regular meter and rhyme are props which can make almost any
passage assume some semblance of poetry. This is not to say that
meter and rhyme are bad devices to use, but only that they obscure
more than they reveal whether a poet truly has an ear. For that
reason, I would like to illustrate with a passage of free verse, the
first stanza of James Dickey's "The Beholders":

Far away under us, they are mowing on the green steps
Of the valley, taking long, unending swings
Among the ripe wheat.
It is something about them growing,
Growing smaller, that makes us look up and see
That what has come over them is a storm.

I deliberately chose a very unornamented, rather prosy passage made
up of two rather ordinarily constructed sentences. Here are none of
the poetic devices such as metaphor, striking imagery, experimental
sentence structure (let alone conventional meter and rhyme) to give
the language a boost into the realms of poetry. Line divisions, of
course, are used — and used well — especially to emphasize the surprise that "growing" leads to "growing smaller," so that we imagine
first a process of enlargement (suggestive of the covering shadow of
the storm) before one of diminishment as it becomes more difficult
to make out the figures of the reapers. The enjambment of the first

two lines creates a delicate hesitation that both emphasizes the strong syllables at the ends of those lines and sweeps us on into the lines that follow. Similarly, "see" at the end of the fifth line holds us for a moment of wonder before we discover the explanation for what is happening.

Line endings, of course, are a major device available to poetry, as distinguished formally from prose. But it is to the internal management of sounds within the lines that I would like to draw your attention. Let me try to rewrite those lines unpoetically to illustrate. I will retain the words at the ends of the lines so that the breaks will be a constant factor:

At some distance beneath us, people mow the verdant steps
Of terraces using lengthy, continuous swings
In the midst of the mature wheat.
In some respects they appear to be growing,
Growing more minute, which causes us to raise our eyes to see
What is descending on them: a storm.

Though I dislike the subjectivism of the word *poetic,* it has some uses; and it seems evident to me that the passage I have written above is less poetic than Dickey's. Can we point to specific characteristics which make the difference?

First of all, my passage uses more syllables — 70 to Dickey's 59. At the same time, my passage has only two more stresses than Dickey's (as I count the stresses: Dickey's lines have, respectively, 7, 5, 3, 3, 5, and 5; mine have 7, 5, 3, 4, 8, and 4). It is generally true that the ratio of stresses to syllables is higher in poetry than in prose. Poetry seems relatively more intense, emphatic; to achieve this effect it uses relatively more monosyllabic words, fewer unstressed "business" words such as *the, of, by.* English poetry tends to an Anglo-Saxon rather than a Latinate vocabulary (e.g., *ripe* rather than *mature).* Its idioms are likely to be simpler, more informal *(e.g., that makes us* rather than *which causes us).* The simplicity of Dickey's language has a suggestiveness, a mysterious quality which disappears as more complex (and sometimes more precise) words are substituted. For example, "Far away under us" can mean a great deal more than "At some distance beneath us": it has a spectral vagueness about it which makes the poetry more resonant. "It is something about them" similarly evokes a sense of strangeness which is lost when the language takes on a more formal quality, "In some respects."

The busy, fast syllables of my version lose the music of Dickey's

lines. A test of musicality might be an effort to chant the lines.
You can sing "Far away under us, they . . ." (helped, in this case,
by that suppressed rhyme of *way* and *they*), but you would have a
hard time chanting "At some distance beneath us, people . . . ."
A poet is likely to get a sound combination or rhythmic unit going
and to repeat it — like the several words ending in *ing* in Dickey's
passage. The sound of *n* drones through his lines. The repeated
word, *growing,* is anticipated by the rhyming word, *mowing.* The
double stress, *green steps,* is echoed in the similarly stressed *ripe
wheat.* A poet does not necessarily think about or plan such effects:
if he has an ear, he intuitively reaches for the sounds and rhythms
which harmonize and relate. I doubt that Dickey noticed the
variations on the long *e* sound in words in key positions: *green,
swings, wheat, growing, see.* But the note is sustained so clearly
that we feel the letdown in the last line, which does not use it.

From what I have said above one might extract a series of
rules to help him distinguish the poetic from the unpoetic, but it
would be a mistake to take them too narrowly. Consider these
versions of roughly the same idea:

> The dread risk of a second's yielding
> That years of caution cannot undo
> By this only we have lasted
> Which finds no place in our life's story
> Or in keepsakes webbed by the kindly spider
> Or under seals torn by the thin lawyer
> In our void rooms.

Another poet might write:

> The awful daring of a moment's surrender
> Which an age of prudence can never retract
> By this, and this only, we have existed
> Which is not to be found in our obituaries
> Or in memories draped by the beneficient spider
> Or under seals broken by the lean solicitor
> In our empty rooms.

The first version has many fewer syllables, many more words of
Anglo-Saxon derivation. It is simpler, more idiomatic, less formal,
less precise, more strongly stressed. Like Anglo-Saxon poetry, the
first passage tends to fall into half-lines, each with two strong
beats:

> The *dread risk* / of a *sec*ond's *yield*ing
> That *years* of *cau*tion / can*not* un*do*

The second passage is in a diffuse iambic pentameter, hardly scannable:

The aw| ful dar| ing of| a mo| ment's sur ren| der
Which an age| of pru| dence can| ne ver| re tract|

Much more evident in the first than in the second passage are sound links, such as alliterative combinations (e.g., *caution cannot, keepsakes . . . kindly*). In my view, the first version (which I wrote) is not bad poetry, chiefly because it retains the powerful thought and imagery of the second, which is the original, by T. S. Eliot in "The Waste Land." But there will certainly be no question to anyone who has an ear for poetry that the second is far superior.

In Eliot, the Latinate, formal diction has a function, creating an atmosphere of decadence, a medium for dry thought. The music of his lines is more intricate and delicate, as befits the subject, than the slugging rhythms of the first version. (Note how the falling rhythm of *memories* is echoed by *beneficient,* the gentle interplay between *surrender* and *prudence,* the hissing of *this, and this only, we have existed).* The almost legalistic, philosophical, somewhat ironic tone is a ghostly preparation for the grim, dignified images of death at the end of the passage.

If these examples serve, it may be seen why an ear for poetry is so difficult to cultivate. It must accommodate an infinite range of tonalities and purposes, and yet make judgments. The sheer variety of poetry which is considered to be excellent by discerning readers and critics is bewildering to the amateur; he is sometimes tempted to believe that in such an anarchy of taste, anything goes. In one sense he is right. Some contexts justify almost any imaginable choice of words, rhythmic techniques and combinations of sound. Still, whether we recognize it or not, some poetry is evidently better than other poetry, and the differences in quality cannot be explained entirely by the vision, sincerity, or profundity of the poet. A reader or poet has to be attuned to the whole range of possible expressions of human meaning, the whole range of possible linguistic forms which might express that, and to make sensitive, sometimes instantaneous, therefore intuitive, choices as he sees form relate to content.

Impossible? Of course. There will always be differences of judgment and taste, always alternative strategies, and the "intuition" I speak of is neither wholly intuitive nor wholly accurate, even in the best poets. As for a means of learning, the only thing I can suggest is that you attune yourself as carefully as possible to as wide a range as possible of excellent poetry. A poet who can hear only one kind of music — e.g., that of Milton or Pope or Tennyson or cummings or Ginsberg — will inescapably sound derivative when he composes his own work. To counterbalance the derivative effect you have to fill your ears with rich variety; and your own music then will be a blend as original as your own vision which, too, is shaped by the way others see.

CHAPTER TEN

Imagery and Symbolism

doublevision and doubletalk

Among the several human disabilities which qualify a person to be a poet is doublevision. This is not like the doublevision of a drunk, which makes for too many clocks on the wall, multiplying reality like a jammed machine; nor is it like the blurred vision of the myopic which distorts a bush into a bear. It is a faculty for seeing a thing at once precisely for itself and at the same time as part of a larger phenomenon, or an endless chain of phenomena, to envisage a white whale in such a way that it is inseparable from evil, goodness, nature, obsession, and a whole echo-chamber of such abstractions; it seems to prove, in fact, that these abstractions are inseparable from one another. Thus you, the poet, see one thing, put it into your poem, and expect the world to know you meant not that, or not that only, but something else, or everything . . . until the eyes dazzle with seeing. The critic, then, comes along and calls this process symbolism.

Symbolism, resulting from doublevision, is a variety of doubletalk — not stuttering incoherency or deliberate obfuscation of meaning, but the habit of meaning something other than what one is literally saying. Poets may recognize that this is what other poets are doing, but they rarely admit that it is what they do themselves — producing such amusing denials as when Dylan Thomas violently objected that Edith Sitwell misunderstood one of his denser poems because she refused to read it literally. Just try reading Thomas literally:

Abaddon in the hang-nail cracked from Adam,
And, from his fork, a dog among the fairies,
The atlas-eater with a jaw for news,
Bit out the mandrake with to-morrow's scream.

And Frost, perhaps a hundred times a year, insisted that "Stopping by Woods on a Snowy Evening" has nothing to do with the death-wish. I think what he meant (I assume he did not mean what he said) is that the death-wish and many other things are so essentially linked to the experience he explicitly describes that it is a waste of time to isolate it triumphantly and say, "he means *this.*"

The whole significance of doublevision lies in that commitment to what the words literally say. The poet has searched for the "best" way of saying what he means and has put it down because he sincerely believes it *does* say what he means — everything he *means,* which, of course, is a great deal more than he says. That larger significance, though, is so intimately linked to what is on the paper that he thinks we are blind or obstinate if we introduce other words, other concepts, to "explain" what he regards as right before our eyes. When he reads other poets he may find himself interpreting — like a critic, or any ordinary reader — because it is almost as hard to share another person's doublevision as to share his dreams.

There is a kind of hallucination about the very best poetry to which one has to find a key. Such poetry includes the keys. For a simple example, consider that utilitarian horse in "Stopping by Woods on a Snowy Evening." He thinks it queer the speaker should stop out there on a road, knowing, with horse sense, that a road is to go on, especially in a snow storm. If we pause to think, we sense the parallel with the absent owner of the woods, whose house is in the village. The narrator seems to be relieved to think that the owner will not see him stopping by the woods. Why? To look at them is no transgression. But the owner, like the horse, is apt to be of a utilitarian disposition, and also likely to think it queer to see a man stop to watch woods fill up. The narrator seems uneasy about — perhaps even a little ashamed of — a private, irrational, aesthetic moment which is so inexplicable in utilitarian terms. So we have a symbol: the horse, of course, but the horse includes the owner, and the two "stand for" much more — all that opposes, disapproves of, or is incapable of understanding a man's need for such a moment. Now the surprise: the narrator himself adopts that point of view at the end of the poem, and reluctantly surrenders to the utilitarian values.

He has miles to go before he sleeps, and we are reminded of other oppositions in other Frost poems, almost all of them contrasting the humane, loving, irrational, useless, fun values with those of use, need, duty, and reason. It is the old heart-head dichotomy (or heart-feet):

> The heart is still aching to seek,
>   But the feet question "Whither?"
> Ah, when to the heart of man
>   Was it ever less than a treason
> To go with the drift of things,
>   To yield with a grace to reason,
> And bow and accept the end
>   Of a love or a season?

Treason to yield with a grace, but it becomes clear in poem after poem (as in "Stopping by Woods") that when love and need (or avocation and vocation) conflict, need wins out:

> And where the two exist in twain
> Theirs was the better right — agreed.

"Theirs" here refers to the need of two tramps who want to do for pay the woodchopping he is doing for pleasure. He goes on:

> But yield who will to their separation,
> My object in life is to unite
> My avocation and my vocation
> As my two eyes make one in sight.
> Only where love and need are one,
> And the work is play for mortal stakes,
> Is the deed ever really done
> For Heaven and the future's sakes.

Love and need are united, of course, in the "vocation" of the poet, or of any artist, or of old Baptiste's carving of axe-helves, or, one might go on, in social effort which is impelled not only by principle but affection (or brotherhood).

This tension pervades Frost's poetry and causes him to see symbols of this basic conflict everywhere and to direct *our* vision to the same symbols. For doublevision implies specifically that the poet sees the situation clearly and at the same time sees *into* it, in his private fashion, so that as he talks about it he means both the situation and its significance. In a sense it is doubletalk to say *horse* and mean *need,* but we cannot translate that way. That little horse that thinks it queer to stop on the snowy road is, first of all, himself, and, afterwards, part of the complex which includes a whole range of values opposed to aesthetic moments. And if the poet had to choose between the horse's point of view and his tug of heart to remain watching, he would side with the horse, though with reluctance and without grace.

I spend so much time on that horse because it works in just the way symbols should operate; it is a much simpler and more domestic example of the way Melville's white whale operates as a continually reverberating, resonating and expanding center of meaning. Symbols are, however, used in other ways, some of which I would like to describe.

The simplest use of symbols, of course, is allegory in which A = B in simple equivalence and the apparent narrative is of much less interest to poet or reader, both of whom are concerned with the interplay of abstractions which the symbols stand for. A parable is somewhat richer, less ingenious, less elaborate, but more concrete, more fully created. The prodigal son almost takes on some personality. Both of these, like jokes, are oriented to situation. "A man wanted to sell his cow, and . . ." we are off, any man, any cow, at any fair; the meaning, obviously, is in the application to many other situations. Proverbs and homilies are similarly rudimentary poetry. And if you find readers who object to the fact that poetry doesn't mean what it says, remind them that they accept easily that a rolling stone gathers no moss, knowing that the thought has nothing to do with either stones or moss. It is a bad poem incidentally, because stones do not roll long enough that their growing of moss becomes a question; nor is a stone with moss inherently preferable to one without it; and — learn this: poetry ought to make sense in what it literally says, even though that is not what the poet means.

The difference between these more abstract uses of symbolism and what Frost does is that between a hypothesis and laboratory demonstration. Rather than saying that under given conditions a given thing ought to occur, Frost says as convincingly as possible (though he may be making it all up), that under precisely these conditions precisely this occurred. If the conditions are not sufficiently controlled, or if the measurements are ignorantly misread, nothing can be inferred. If, on the other hand, it is a good poem, a statement of the hypothesis is unnecessary; the proof is beyond need of the guess. One definition of a successful symbol might be that it is a definitive circumstance of an important truth.

There have always been symbols, but they have only recently come to be named, looked-for, and, worst of all, put into poems deliberately — which makes for the doubletalk without the necessary doublevision. Or, more simply, it makes for insincerity. Freud and Jung inadvertently have much to do with turning poetry into a variety of double-crostics. Freud teaches us about one kind of symbol: the disguise. Because our conscious minds do not find it comfortable to deal with all the burps coming up from the nether regions, we have developed a mechanism for converting contraband notions into innocent appearances for the sake of smuggling. The literary use of this discovery has often been exactly the reverse: to fill a poem with innocent objects to which the poet has (by reading his dream book backwards like a witch's prayer) attached hidden meanings. Far from a strategy for dealing with life, such symbols become a kind of tragic playing around with our confusion. Far from a necessary but sick backing-off from truth, they become substitutes for truth. Far from a personal bureau of censorship, they become sophisticated *double-entendres* which, like jokes, poke a lewd elbow in our ribs whenever a glove or purse or fork or pistol or fish is mentioned.

At times the symbols pile up like the montage of an erotic dream:

>A candle in the thighs
>Warms youth and seed and burns the seeds of age;
>Where no seed stirs,
>The fruit of man unwrinkles in the stars,
>Bright as a fig;
>Where no wax is, the candle shows its hairs.

This stanza (from Dylan Thomas' "Light Breaks Where No Sun Shines") is one of several which tell us repetitively that life is generated in secret places and overcomes death. It is a powerful, beautiful poem; and I do not object to its sexuality or even its puzzle-like doubletalk. Puzzles are fun. But the use of Freudian symbols in this way is a dead-end. It is like allegory, in which the code exists, the message exists, and there are no tremors beyond identifying A with B. Well, that is unfair. Thomas gets two or three significances out of his symbols (e.g., a candle serves as a symbol not only in shape but in having fire at the end, heat and light, and light is the basic symbol for life in the poem, etc.) But the process stops there. You end with a reading that is so cross-hatched with lines relating one thing to another that somehow all you are left with is the system, the truism, and a voice like blue thunder.

Jung caught the literary imagination with another concept of symbolism — the archetype — which seems to make for a bit more depth in literary application, but is put to hack use just as was Freud's discovery. He set off the great Snark hunt: myths, archetypes, unconscious memories, racial reservoirs, all were plumbed to find how people said what they always knew. This concept is similar to that of disguise, only without the implication that truth is indecent and must be repressed. Consider Ulysses as Tennyson thought of him, as Joyce did, as Peter Viereck sees the archetype emerging in the wartime "Kilroy Was Here." A note to the poem tells us that the scrawled slogan (made popular by soldiers in World War II) indicated an "unfaked epic spirit . . . implying that nothing was too adventurous or remote." Here is the first stanza:

> Also Ulysses once — that other war
> (Is it because we find his scrawl
> Today on every privy door
> That we forget his ancient role?)
> Also was here — he did it for the wages —
> When a Cathay-drunk Genoese set sail.
> Whenever "longen folk to goon on pilgrimages,"
> Kilroy is there;
>   he tells the Miller's Tale.

It is a simple, witty poem, nor is it in the least obscure, although in these few lines we have, as trophies of the Snark hunt, Kilroy, Ulysses, Columbus and Chaucer. The mythic significance is proved, too — even to modern readers who don't know the *Odyssey* from Oz. It comes not from a mythic mind, but from a mind that has read books about myths (and other things). A minimal experience (not included, though I wish he had put it in!) in which the poet is sitting contemplating the Kilroy inscription, is expanded almost mechanically into significance. It is not doublevision, but vision footnoted. Richard Wilbur once wrote with refreshing frankness, "one does not, merely by referring to the dying god or what not, evoke a legitimate emotional response."

Good poets must be, I think, instinctively anti-literary in the sense that they recognize that though there's a lot of good stuff in books, it's not theirs. I find myself (as editor) almost automatically rejecting poems commenting on paintings, giving monologues of historical or fictional figures, or reinterpreting myths, because these have become literary exercises. Symbolism is something that happens, not something you do, and for a doubletalk license you have to prove doublevision. Without that license, however, it is almost impossible to write poetry. I would put it almost as an axiom that it is not poetry if it means just what it says.

shadows of heaven

For this reason Aristotle said metaphor is the soul of poetry — and the very statement is a complex metaphor. Metaphor is to poetry as the soul is to man, and the word *soul* is a complex concept, too, usually apprehended through other metaphors such as spirit, ghost or angel. We rarely know what *is,* and we approximate by figurative language. Everyone thinks in metaphor (and simile, which I mean to be included in the more general term) to a great extent in ordinary life. But it is the poet's business to do so; though in the process of composition, the less self-conscious he is about it, the better.

First, he has to believe, to *know,* that metaphor is a means of apprehending truth. It is not a way of making prose statements pretty. I will return to this notion later, but let it suffice for now that it is simply impossible for metaphor to beautify or illustrate statements which can otherwise be made in prose. Willy-nilly, metaphor alters the very nature of the statement. Metaphor is a linguistic mode as essential to discourse as any other; it is a means of saying what cannot otherwise be said at all.

Important truths are not to be apprehended directly, as Milton's Raphael explains to Adam:

> . . . and what surmounts the reach
> Of human sense I shall delineate so,
> By likening spiritual to corporal forms,
> As may express them best, though what if Earth
> Be but the shadow of Heaven, and things therein
> Each to other like, more than on earth is thought?

He is worrying how to explain war in Heaven to mortals incapable of conceiving of angelic reality except in comparison to things of this world — nay, of Eden, which is more limited still. But whether or not poetry is concerned with angels, it is likely to be working at truths beyond sensible apprehension and yet must cope with them in sensible terms.

At night all cows are black. Meaning is perceived only through contrast and comparison. We always understand one thing in terms of another, and when we figure forth the unknown in terms of the known, one referent of the metaphor is available to the senses, the other only to the mind. A less theological explanation of the metaphor than that given by Raphael may be found in science. Any figuration of reality is likely to be called a model. Material is itself a model which makes certain relationships comprehensible. We do not know what the atom may be, and it makes no sense to the senses to express it purely in terms of formulae. A model, then, is posited — a metaphor — in which particles move in orbit about a nucleus like planets around the sun. The solar system is, in turn, a model — as described (for example) by the astronomer Hermann Bondi:

> The model of Copernicus, which put the sun at the
> center and supposed the planets to go in circles around it,
> was simpler and hence superior to the model of Ptolemy,
> in which the earth occupied the central position.

He doesn't seem to know or care where those supposed planets actually may go in relation to the alleged earth and hypothetical sun; the choice between models is purely in terms of their utility.

Poets, too, resort to fictions to make their perceptions knowable. Most common language is metaphorical. The word *metaphor* is a metaphor, meaning transfer or the act of carrying over or beyond. As metaphors become stale (metaphor) or lose their vividness (metaphor), writers use them with increasing indifference and begin asking readers to keep their shoulders to the wheel and nose to the grindstone with a stiff upper-lip so they can keep their ear to the ground and their eye on the ball. Well, no — the trouble with those clichés is that they are not stale enough, and are ridiculous in combination because we are still aware of some faint imaginative pulse in language on its way to the grave.

But one can hardly avoid mixing metaphors, the language is so full of them. And the metaphoric texture of some poetry, like that of Shakespeare or Keats, is so thick, the poets think so completely in a metaphoric mode, that hardly a word occurs that has not some figurative overtone (and if the mixed metaphor "figurative overtone" bothers you, it would not have bothered Shakespeare). Macbeth says:

> I have no spur
> To prick the sides of my intent, but only
> Vaulting ambition, which o'erleaps itself
> And falls on the other.

Unsort it if you can. Intention is like a horse. Motivation is like a spur which goads intention on. The only such spur Macbeth has is ambition, which (now switching from spur to rider) leaps over its horse (itself?) and falls on the opposite side. The more one thinks about it, the more comic and confusing it becomes, though it occurs in a serious context and offers no difficulty in dramatic communication. Similarly, when Cleopatra complains to Antony that she is neglected, she loses track of her own sentence and interrupts herself:

> Oh, my oblivion is a very Antony,
> And I am all forgotten.

It makes no sense at all when you reduce it to reason: my forgetfulness is like Antony himself (the archetype of forgetfulness), and forgets me totally. But if her forgetfulness forgets her, is she not thereby remembered? It is too much for logic, though no one doubts a moment what she means.

To look for reason or pattern in Shakespeare is to miss the point entirely. True, certain related images recur, related strands of thought keep coming to the surface as sinews of a cable wind down to the core and out again and through. These threads enlarge the total meaning of poems or plays (as the references to animals in *King Lear* or to disease and decay in *Hamlet).* But we must not imagine his planting them; he had no other way to think about the subjects he was considering. The metaphors recur because there is no better way to apprehend what is most importantly true.

Can you learn to delight in this description of the weeping eyes of Saint Mary Magdalene, imagined as following Christ?

> And now where'er He strays
> Among the Galilean mountains,
> Or more welcome ways,
>   He's followed by two faithful fountains,
> Two walking baths, two weeping motions,
> Portable and compendious oceans.

"Motions" may refer to glove puppets.

How are we to take such a string of metaphors? Surely the seventeenth century poet, Richard Crashaw, in effusive, innocent

praise, elaborated his adoration for the Saint's magnificent tears
without thought of how baths related to puppets or ambulatory
oceans. I would not claim that this is a successful passage; the
whole poem is rather funny. But the sheer exuberance is moving
even as it is silly, perhaps *because* it is silly, as we are convinced
that no critical faculty whatsoever constrained the fertile fancy.
Such excess may not tell us much about tears (which, in the course of
the poem, flow not down but up to Heaven, become part of the
Milky Way, a wine for heavenly cherubs who drink it for breakfast and burp delightfully all the day long), but it does convey the
quality of ecstatic devotion in a way we wiser and more tasteful
poets might envy.

No case can be made for such metaphors on the grounds of
intensification or interrelation or extension of meaning; the more
one thinks about them the worse they get. But somehow the whole
crazy thing is imperishable. It is this habit of metaphoric thinking
that creates poetry — an organic, verdant expression capable of
carrying itself over the objections of the reasonable mind by naked
vitality.

Of course the "reasonable mind" itself is a kind of fiction. If
we look to the heart of reason (and it has one), we find it just as
desperately metaphorical. Here are Pope's Sylphs in *The Rape of
the Lock:*

> Transparent forms, too fine for mortal sight,
> Their fluid bodies half dissolved in light,
> Loose to the wind their airy garments flow,
> Thin glitt'ring textures of the filmy dew,
> Dipped in the richest tincture of the skies,
> Where light disports in ever-mingling dyes,
> While ev'ry beam new transient colors flings,
> Colors that change whene'er they wave their wings.

We need not ask what happens when a fluid dissolves or how in-
visibility glitters; to be poets (or read them) we have to learn, like
the queen beyond the looking glass, to believe a half-dozen impossible things before breakfast. Such exercise also helps one
deal with relativity and quantum theory.

Contradiction is the soul of metaphor, if we may go Aristotle
one better. Inevitably it asserts an untruth to assert truth. Some
metaphors are more harmonious than others: "I love you like fine
wine," is a more harmonious metaphor than "I love you as a pig

loves mud," or Donne's comment on souls in love, referring to a draftsman's instrument:

> If they be two, they are two so
> As stiff twin compasses are two:

In relatively classical periods more harmonious, more easily acceptable metaphors are sought; in less classical periods the search is for bizarre, incongruous relationships which may be tensely insisted upon, to assert relationship in spite of appearances. But there is no point in your trying to put yourself in a school; concentrate upon perceiving deeply, without logical bounds, and let your metaphors take the form they will. If your mind is whole your poem will somehow be whole, though you (like Donne) get geometric compasses, gold foil, cosmology, geology and religion side by side. Let your mind range widely and digest everything.

Digestion is the opposite of collection — and here we come back to metaphor as decoration. Poets have been known to keep little notebooks of cute comparisons, little plastic blossoms with which to garnish their work. And, in fact, critical theory in certain periods of literature has supported this practice, regarding the prose sense of poetry as separable from its imaginative elaboration, illustration or beautification. But it doesn't work. The model affects the thought; the metaphor becomes the statement, whether that is what the scientist or poet intends or not. Nothing so quickly undercuts commitment and meaning as ingenuity. The wit of Donne was part of his vision; the wit of Cleveland was manufactured because he thought that was what poetry was supposed to be — and produced such horrors as this, on the occasion of the drowning of an educated friend:

> Some have affirmed that what on earth we find,
> The sea can parallel in shape and kind.
> Books, arts, and tongues were wanting, but in thee
> Neptune hath got an university.

Absurd? I agree, and yet there is a fine line in poetry between absurdities which extend thought and those which merely leave the poet with pie on his face.

varieties of logic

Just as mathematicians have advanced by consciously setting aside the axioms of Euclid, so poets, particularly in the twentieth century, have attempted to open up new areas of meaning by deliberate, almost systematic, contradiction of the very bases of metaphor traditionally accepted. When we say March came in like a lion and left like a lamb, we are making a fairly easily apprehended and translatable comparison between the characteristics of the weather and those of animals. But, the poet might ask, can I make an *untranslatable* statement, with its own grammar, its own logic, to say something about March which ordinary comparisons cannot say. Well, switch to April:

> April is the cruelest month, breeding
> Lilacs out of the dead land, mixing
> Memory and desire, stirring
> Dull roots with spring rain.

This is fairly translatable, but notice that the metaphor has become diffuse. Eliot compares April to a being which tortures the earth with breeding, mixing, stirring. The life force works cruelly on inert material. The axioms — such as the desirability of life, the preferability of spring rain to dull roots — are deliberately turned inside-out. We have a point of view, a new language, a new system of values established quickly by metaphor. Eliot's hope, of course, is that he will not only communicate in a more condensed and efficient way than ordinary language would permit, but that this diffuse, startling metaphor will say something true and important about April in a world committed to death, which other, more traditional comparisons could not say at all.

Deliberate dislocation of sense is not entirely a modern invention. When Andrew Marvell in the seventeenth century wrote of "Annihilating all that's made/ To a green thought in a green shade," he was reaching for a metaphysical reality which could not be apprehended by ordinary logic. He demands that we sense what a green thought in a green shade is, and his poem, "The Garden," pushes us up to the brink and leaves the imaginative leap to our own courage and sensibility. It is a fairly easy leap because the texture of the poem is woven of more traditional comparisons. The poem guides us to the paradox of the One and the many, associates the One with nature, invites us to imagine the sweet rendering of individuality into green generality, then, with that sensuous image of the green thought, impels us over the edge of sense into absorption in Idea.

Here the texture was logic, but that very texture may become innovation piled on innovation in a dizzying fashion. Emily Dickinson provides an excellent introduction to this characteristic of poetry. Attempting to convey the metaphysical quality of love (or friendship) in "The Soul Selects Her Own Society," she says:

I've known her from an ample nation
Choose one;
Then close the valves of her attention
Like stone.

Did she have in mind a barnacle? a tomb? Though the image of the valve might be mechanical, my guess is that she meant something organic (like the valves of the heart). The point, though, is that she does not want us to have a specific or vivid image. The vividness comes from the sharp juxtaposition of different kinds of ideas — of valves with attention, of attention with stone. The passive waiting, the blank inalterable shutting, the inanimate, impenetrable surface, the process of literal *incorporation* — these qualities of love that so mingle sensitive selection, organic processes, and eternal solidity are what the new logic of her language hopes to comprehend.

When she speaks of "zero at the bone," or an ocean "Too silver for a seam," or "doom's electric moccasin," or "the weight/ Of cathedral tunes," she forces us not so much to see the qualities of one thing in another (like those of a lion in March) as to make new qualities existing in neither term of the metaphor.

The brain in just the weight of God,
For, lift them, pound for pound,
And they will differ, if they do,
As syllable from sound.

This is reminiscent of Donne's bitter:

Just such disparitie
As is twixt Aire and Angells puritie,
'Twixt women's love, and men's will ever bee.

It similarly yearns to articulate the reality sense and logic fail to reach. It will take a poet to tell us what an atom would be like if we could experience one.

I will stay with Dickinson a moment to illustrate some of the typical dislocations which cause so much trouble with more recent poets. In "I Heard a Fly Buzz When I Died," (discussed more fully in Chapter Eighteen) the fly which is not only a fly but the very idea of mortality hums away in the distance while the last business of life is done and the mourners-to-be are gathered around the bed for the final moment:

                                              — and then it was
There interposed a fly,

With blue, uncertain, stumbling buzz
Between the light and me;
And then the windows failed, and then
I could not see to see.

"Interposed," a buzzing sort of word, sets up several varieties of relativity. First, of course, it comes between "the light" and the dying person, as a small dark object, close, obstructs vision. The light may refer, as well, to "the king," mentioned earlier — death or God. But the fly also interposes itself between the speaker and "the eyes around" and human affairs, and the room begins to tilt off into oblivion. It is the windows which fail — a simple dislocation like that of a dock moving away. The fly itself is perceived as a sound, but a *blue* sound, a *stumbling* sound. This rendering of one sense in terms of another, here of the aural in terms of the visual and kinesthetic, becomes increasingly common in the twentieth century. Finally, of course, the poem ends with a complex play on the word *see*: most simply, "I could not see my way clear to — or manage — to see," but the suggestion is of levels of experience, of one cliff falling off behind the next, as the little fly blocks off all light and all is annihilated to a blue thought in a blue shade.

Another common type of dislocation in metaphor is more simply linguistic: deriving ultimately from the pun, which is, essentially, a kind of metaphor. When Hopkins writes, "Though worlds of wanwood leafmeal lie," he sounds a little like Joyce, who, in turn, sounds rather like "Jabberwocky." The wan wood is waning, its leaves lying piecemeal, a meal for the earth. Freud, dream language and subconscious malapropisms and other kinds of idiomatic melding, have made such poetic devices popular in their suggestiveness of subconscious reality. Hopkins provides many examples: "He father's-forth whose beauty is past change," "manmarks treadmire toil there/ Footfretted in it," etc. And simpler puns abound in modern poetry, jolting one always to readiness for multiple communication in a world where a single cable bears a million simultaneous messages. When Thomas writes of "Abaddon in the hangnail cracked from Adam" we must think not only of the angel of the bottomless pit, from *Revelations,* but "a bad 'un," and possibly of "abandon," or even of "abdomen," to carry out the birth image, of Christ as the hangnail, who hung by nails, and of several varieties of cracks.

It gets to be a bit too much. Good poets outgrow it, as Thomas did. The best of our surrealistic poets was Hart Crane, who never lost his sense of melody and visual beauty, carrying a reader willingly over much obscurity. I wanted to quote all of "Voyages," but, instead, will send you to it as a kind of apotheosis of complex metaphor — with its "Adagios of islands" in the Caribbean, "In these poinsettia meadows of her tides," and "The seal's wide spindrift gaze toward paradise." There is a swirl of meaning, a consummate interchanging, which carries one, uncomprehending, untranslating, off the brink.

A much more logical poem is this one by e. e. cummings:

> anyone lived in a pretty how town
> (with up so floating many bells down)
> spring summer autumn winter
> he sang his didn't he danced his did.
>
> Women and men (both little and small)
> cared for anyone not at all
> they sowed their isn't they reaped their same
> sun moon stars rain
>
> children guessed (but only a few
> and down they forgot as up they grew
> autumn winter spring summer)
> that noone loved him more by more
>
> when by now and tree by leaf
> she laughed his joy she cried his grief
> bird by snow and stir by still
> anyone's any was all to her
>
> someones married their everyones
> laughed their cryings and did their dance
> (sleep wake hope and then) they
> said their nevers they slept their dream
>
> stars rain sun moon
> (and only the snow can begin to explain
> how children are apt to forget to remember
> with up so floating many bells down)

one day anyone died i guess
(and noone stooped to kiss his face)
busy folk buried them side by side
little by little and was by was

all by all and deep by deep
and more by more they dream their sleep
noone and anyone earth by april
wish by spirit and if by yes.

Women and men (both dong and ding)
summer autumn winter spring
reaped their sowing and went their came
sun moon stars rain

I think this is a good poem for poets to learn from because the varieties of metaphorical dislocation are so neat and clear. What kind of town did Anyone live in? Reverse a cliché, "How pretty!" and you have the first clue: it is a town in which beauty is reduced to prettiness and eloquence to clichés. That kind of wrenching of the idiom of the streets is one of cummings' favorite devices.

But a how town is also a near cousin of a cow town, so we know something more about its location and cultural climate. In a how town, also, one would expect the emphasis to be on how rather than why or what, on means, on process; it is a practical town. Anyone, who (we learn) is an individual, a non-conformist, one who — in typical cummingsesque fashion — accentuates the positive and eliminates the negative, lived there. He married noone, then died, and she was buried beside him by the someones (that fellow with the shoestore on the corner: he's *someone)* and everyones, and the affirmation of anyone and noone, even as corpses, sustained the mechanical deaths (one cannot call them lives) of the rest of the village.

It is a narrative poem that makes its own language as it goes along. cummings repeats each unconventional word-usage at least once, in a different context, so that the poem may be decoded. The characteristic metaphors are like those I have described in Dickinson, Hopkins and others: animation of abstractions, incongruous juxtapositions, puns, word-associations, transfer of senses. He also employs a kind of mathematical device: *by* is used as a term of mutiplication (in the sense of breeding as well as mathematics), so that a logical relationship is forced on concepts which are not commutable, e.g., "earth by april," "bird by snow." Earth exists by, or alongside, April. It is multiplied by April to the new product. Also it is answered by April; April is the response to the dust to which we return.

The image of the bells in the second line remains for me untranslatable. The town is surely sprinkled with spires, and this religion (stanza six) distracts people from important truths. The bells also suggest the cyclical, mechanical nature of experience in this town, where people (both dong and ding, Yin and Yang) perform rituals without comprehension or animation. But the line "(with up so floating many bells down)" is, above all these interpretations, an exquisite image for bells, with the movement — up, floating, down — sound and idiom overlaid.

The inversions and repetitions are the most obvious grammatical principles of this language. While the people of the town do their dance, or perform art mechanically, anyone dances his did, or performs his duties artfully — or, better, with spirit, gusto. While the people sleep their dreams, noone and anyone, dead, dream their sleep, or infuse even the sleep of death with spirit and imagination. They answer all possibilities (if) with affirmation (yes), whereas the people of the town reap the sameness they have planted, persist in monotonous routine given meaning only by the occasional occurrence of an anyone, understood only imperfectly now and again by children, able to live spontaneously, sympathetically and creatively. For all its lyrical incantatory quality, it is a superlogical construction, a metalanguage, extending language in a useful way.

stoned thinking

Some insight into the sources of figurative language and symbolism in our minds is provided by recent scientific study of the neglected resources of the right hemisphere of our brains. For example, a young doctor, graduate of Harvard Medical School, through his study of the effects of drugs upon the mind, has provided a formulation which may help poets understand the nature of poetic thought and learn ways of opening their minds to this capacity. Andrew Weil, in *The Natural Mind: A New Way of Looking at Drugs and the Higher Consciousness,* uses the term "stoned thinking" to apply to creative and integrative thought patterns, a term derived from the jargon of the drug culture — but this is misleading, as is the book's focus on the drug problem. As he argues, drugs may, indeed, trigger stoned thinking, but all of us naturally engage in this mode of thinking without using drugs. In fact, drugs deceive us about the source of stoned thinking (i.e., the experience comes from our minds, not from the drugs), and are likely to have other undesirable effects upon us physiologically. As all the great religions of the world, especially those of the East, have taught, the higher consciousness is available to all, and best achieved without the stimulus of drugs.

Weil calls the ordinary waking state of consciousness "straight thinking," a mode of thought so highly valued in our culture that most people tend to regard it alone as valid perception of logic and truth, especially in science and government. Straight thinking, he says, has certain distinct characteristics, "always present in some degree":

1. A tendency to know things through the intellect rather than through some other faculty of the mind;
2. A tendency to be attached to the senses and through them to external reality;
3. A tendency to pay attention to outward forms rather than to inner contents and thus to lapse into materialism;
4. A tendency to perceive differences rather than similarities between phenomena;
5. A tendency to negative thinking, pessimism, and despair.

Straight thinking is ego-centered, in large part a means of reinforcing the armor we all carry in our heads to protect us from the outside world — in some cases insulating us so completely from that world that, with impeccable logic, we become, in fact, mad. The phenomenon is much like that of a wheel in a rut, digging itself in deeper the more desperately it spins to get out.

Before looking at the alternative mode, stoned thinking, which seems to me to be the essential mode of poetry, I will note briefly some examples Weil gives of straight thinking carried to extremes. (1.) The use of insecticides to control insects. Straight thinking leads one to try to make things which cause trouble go away by exercise of force. What insecticides do — as we have rapidly learned since the introduction of DDT into the world, is accelerate the evolution of species which are not susceptible to such poisons. An endlessly escalating war is undertaken, calling for ever more powerful chemicals and ever stronger species to resist them. Instead of learning how to live with insects, people try to obliterate them, but the recuperative and reactive powers of nature are too great, and humankind is the loser. (2.) The use of antibiotics — exactly the same pattern. This method of fighting infection produces ever more virulent strains of microbiotic life — to the point that the danger from hospital infections becomes in many cases greater than the danger of diseases patients bring into them. Weil weighs and finds wanting the allopathic model in medicine and psychiatry — virtually the only model recognized by approved American practitioners — according to which illness is treated by counteracting its symptoms. Powerful methods are devised for wiping out symptoms in both body and mind, but since they do not affect the psychic roots of illness, often only lead to new symptoms and greater degeneration. (3.) A final example of straight thinking is the use of political action as a means of producing social change. As in the case of insects, bacteria, or mental disorder, force and repression generally only produce stronger, different, or more subtle counter-effects. The recent war in Vietnam is a case study of the effectiveness of straight thinking in solving world problems.

To find out what stoned thinking is all about, you need only open any anthology of good poetry at random — as I just did, hitting upon the opening lines of William Blake's "Auguries of Innocence":

> To see a World in a Grain of Sand,
> And a Heaven in a Wild Flower,
> Hold Infinity in the palm of your hand,
> And Eternity in an hour.

The similarity between what Blake is saying and reports of LSD trips indicates why Weil chooses the term "stoned" to describe this mode of thought. But you don't need acid to achieve it. All of us experience it daily (or nightly) in our dreams, our daydreaming, especially in the twilight regions between sleep and waking when the mind gambols on the fields of imagination freely — before we slap it into its straight jacket, often using for this purpose strong drugs such as caffeine and nicotine. Weil believes we would be healthier, happier and more sane if we learned to dwell longer in those ranges of consciousness where we perceive the world in a grain of sand or Heaven in a flower.

Stoned thinking has such characteristics as these:

(1.) Reliance on intuition as well as intellection;

(2.) Acceptance of the ambivalent nature of things;

(3.) Experience of infinity in its positive aspect.

These characteristics can be illustrated from the poem by Blake. The first, intuition, is the recognition of connections obscure to the straight mind. As Weil says:

> Intuitive flashes are transient, spontaneous altered states of consciousness consisting of particular sensory experiences or thoughts coupled with strong emotional reactions. But — and this is the distinguishing feature — the intellect cannot explain the association; there is no logical reason for the feelings we get on meeting certain persons, places, things, or ideas.

In "Auguries of Innocence," Blake has many couplets such as this one:

> The wanton Boy that kills the Fly
> Shall feel the Spider's enmity.

If we try to reconstruct the experience that led to such a couplet, we may imagine the poet feeling an inexplicable sense of revulsion as he sees an act of random cruelty. Why should he care if a boy kills a fly? Is it mere sentiment — an exaggerated, misplaced identification with the life of the fly? As a human being, isn't it more likely that he will identify with the boy's search for amusement than with the imagined suffering of a pest?

Look again. His reaction was not sentiment, but an intuitive flash, a recognition of a relationship not easily perceived by logic. Note that it *can* be perceived by logic, once the relationship has been revealed by intuition. Ecologists are bombarding us with just such relationships these days: the wanton killing of a fly does indeed disturb the balance of an ecosystem, and in one way or another the life dependent upon the life of the fly will have its vengeance in time upon the agent of the disruption. Both the boy and the spider would kill the fly — one for fun, one for food. The primal power of the latter motive will eventually have its effect: the more aggressive spiders have to be to find their dinner, the more likely are they to encounter — with destructive effects for both — the human population which has made their ordinary diet scarce. But spelled out this way, the relationship begins to seem absurdly tenuous; the straight mind reassures us that there is small likelihood that any particular spider will bite any particular boy for killing any particular fly, and this is true. But such logic should not blind us to the accuracy of the intuitive insight — that one cannot forever go about unbalancing ecosystems with impunity.

Essentially the intuitive flash reveals an important general principle from which particular truths can be deduced. The poet senses that all life in interrelated, even in what seem minor and scattered phenomena. The insight comes powerfully, emotionally to him, not as a logical conclusion, but as a sensation of almost magical awareness, a tenet of faith. This is exactly the way in which most scientific discoveries occur — not merely as the result of the slow accumulation of data, but as intuitive recognition of how things fit together, how data are to be interpreted. The scientist, on the basis of such intuitions, makes a prediction or hypothesis which can be interpreted experimentally. The poet makes, as Blake did, a prophecy; the boy "Shall feel" the enmity of the spider. His observations of immediate experience then fall into place within the intuitively perceived framework. "Auguries of Innocence" is a kind of ecological vision filled with at least symbolically accurate perceptions of subtle but significant relationships:

> Each outcry of the hunted Hare
> A fibre from the Brain does tear.

We cannot hunt without dulling our sensibilities to the signals warning us of our own implication in all death. Do it enough, and it is as though a faculty, a fibre in the Brain, were torn from us. (Don't object that rabbits are silent: I used to work in a laboratory in which we took blood samples from rabbits' hearts with hypodermic needles, and anyone who has heard the piercing, metallic scream of a rabbit in pain can never again be insensitive to their desperate voices.)

The second characteristic of stoned thinking Weil mentions is the acceptance of ambivalence, the recognition that reality is composed of opposites, of Yin and Yang. As Weil says:

> Modern physicists have pursued this paradoxical dualism into the subatomic world, where they find that entities like electrons and photons can exist either as waves or particles, energy or matter.
>
> The problem is not that things have this ambivalent nature, but that our ordinary consciousness cannot accept it. Stoned consciousness, however, is perfectly capable of substituting a both/and formation for the either/or of the ego.

I have mentioned that Blake saves himself from mere sentiment by his intuition of the necessities, the general principles, of nature.

The spider, indeed, eats the fly — and that, too, is as it should be. Even more startlingly:

> The Lamb misus'd breeds Public Strife
> And yet forgives the Butcher's knife.

While I doubt that lambs under the knife experience anything we could rightly call forgiveness, I also doubt they experience resentment. Whether or not a lamb to be eaten faces death with equanimity, it is clear that nature can absorb its own necessities. In Blake's vision, it is the conflict of human artifice with nature that forbodes evil:

> A dog starv'd at his Master's Gate
> Predicts the ruin of the State.

Nature will prevail — and the gates and states we erect upon it will in time disintegrate.

Straight thinking produces conceptions of right and wrong as antitheses of one another, rather than complements. Stoned thinking accepts their coexistence as natural and good:

> A Truth that's told with bad intent
> Beats all the Lies you can invent.
> It is right it should be so;
> Man was made for Joy and Woe;
> And when this we rightly know,
> Thro' the World we safely go,
> Joy and Woe are woven fine,
> A Clothing for the soul divine.
> Under every grief and pine
> Runs a joy with silken twine.
>   . . .
> The Child's Toys and the Old Man's Reasons
> Are the Fruits of the Two seasons.

And, in words taken from Blake for a beautiful folk song:

> Every Night and every Morn
> Some to Misery are Born.
> Every Morn and every Night
> Some are Born to Sweet Delight.
> Some are Born to Sweet Delight,
> Some are Born to endless Night.

Poetry discovers tragedy in affirmation, affirmation in tragedy, and enfolds both in a comprehensive vision of reality in which stoned passivity, the detachment of the Yogi, reflects the cosmic inclusion of all contradictions and conflicts in transcendent reality, far beyond the range of straight thinking's tunnel vision.

The third characteristic of stoned thinking is "Experience of infinity in its positive aspect." Most of us can remember the fascination bordering on terror with which we first encountered the phenomenon of infinite regression — as in the old Morton's salt label in which a little girl carries a box of salt with a picture of a little girl carrying an identical box of salt with a picture of an identical little girl carrying an identical box, each more and more minute, beyond the reach of the eye, teasing the imagination out of thought. Some remember it sitting in barber chairs, seeing the image of themselves receding into the facing mirrors. Perhaps the most ancient and archetypal experience of awe known to humankind is our slowly encroaching realization of infinity as we gaze at the stars, contemplate the ceaseless, repetitive variety of waves crushing themselves on the shore, or stare hypnotized into a flickering fire. Our telescopes and microscopes take us not to the edge, but to the recognition of edgelessness, and even our conception of a finite universe merely teases us with the mystery of what, then, lies beyond.

Blake knows you can "Hold Infinity in the palm of your hand," and discover "Eternity in an hour." Indeed, to live at peace with awareness of infinity is perhaps the basic poetic experience. Weil speaks of the phenomenon he calls "positive paranoia." In straight thinking (which can be heightened as well as diminished by drugs, depending upon the mind set and environment of the user), paranoia is the perception of patterns in external reality that seem to be inimical to the self. Once one begins seeing or imagining a threat, each new experience confirms the last, until reality seems a vast conspiracy to destroy the perceiver. The more elaborate the pattern becomes, the more easily new components fit into it, because the very complexity of the design allows for the inclusion of any conceivable new piece of evidence. The communist scares that sweep our nation from time to time are examples of societal paranoia, and the ingenuity of those caught in their grip is phenomenal as even a President Eisenhower is interpreted as a new and sinister emergence of the Red Menace. Some religions are equally clever in discovering the Devil in the most innocent-seeming appearances.

A more sane interpretation of the infinitely connected pattern of our surroundings is that of stoned thinking: to see it as a conspiracy for our benefit. As Weil says:

Mystics of all centuries have experienced the entire phenomenal world as a radially symmetrical pattern, its center coinciding with the center of focused consciousness. But they have interpreted the experience positively, if not with ineffable joy. Mystical experience is the mirror image of negative paranoia.

Upon such experience is the ecological vision of Blake based. He sees himself and mankind as a part of an encompassing and coherent benign intent. In that context, perversion or madness is the failure to see and believe, to see intuitively the infinite relationships, the harmonious ambivalence of Yin and Yang, the endless bounty of creation in all its self-mirroring aspects. Evil is the result of such blindness as is called clear sight by those trammeled hopelessly in straight thinking.

CHAPTER ELEVEN

Tone

on decoding humor

That jokes are not always funny is only one indication of the difficulty of interpreting literature. I would like here to discuss some specific instances of complex tone, beginning with some in which the complexity arises from the coloring of serious passages by humor. I think awareness of or communication of tone is the central problem in reading or writing literature and that failure to recognize humor is perhaps the commonest error in mistaking tone — whether it appears in a reader's failure to understand or a writer's failure to control.

By *tone* I mean implicit emotional coloring, such as is rendered in spoken communication by intonation. I discover a flat tire and say, "Oh, splendid!" A hearer has not received the message unless he incorporates an understanding of my tone of voice, my exasperated sarcasm, in his interpretation of my speech. He should have some perception of what it means for me so to address an ironic comment to the universe at large, of this strategy for reconciling myself to a dirty trick of chance by showing superiority to it in a willingness to joke, however bitterly. The message is all this: not the words or even the words in context alone, but comprehension of total meaning — even though I might not understand that meaning myself, or might not have thought it out.

Tone of voice is difficult enough to interpret. You may say, "I love you," in such a way as to convey hate, anger, tenderness, lust, thousands of subtle variations and mixtures of emotions which are not simple to begin with. Your intonation can convey exactly the coloring you wish instantaneously and accurately, provided your audience is willing and able to receive your meaning. In writing, the problem is incomparably *more* complex. I think the only way we understand tone in writing at all is by imitating the spoken language imaginatively, by approximating silently in our throats the voice stance we feel is appropriate. To do this our feelings must be unbelievably sensitive to context, to the author, to his age, to the finest distinctions of language. (I wonder whether the "bad" habit of reading with the lips might not contribute to a more sensitive comprehension of tone; at any rate, I recommend reading poetry very slowly — hardly more quickly than one reads aloud — as the mind is unable to accommodate itself to complex and shifting tones without waiting for an almost muscular response imitating the appropriate intonation.)

By *humor* I mean whatever appeals to our disposition to smile. We may *not* smile when so disposed, for other appeals may at any moment be stronger. And our smiles, if they occur, may reflect no happiness or pleasure. (In fact, the opposite is more likely. Humor tends to be critical, and in moments of greatest serenity or most intense pleasure, smiling is less probable than tears.) When we are sharply aware of a disproportion, an absurdity, a critical inadequacy, an unexpected accuracy, a surprising coincidence, a nerve twitches somewhere and tugs our lip-corners. A man sputtering with rage does not mean to be funny, but an author who presents him to us may mean humor as an element in the message. A woman screaming with grief for what turns out to be the wrong corpse may experience no amusement, but an author imagining or writing about such circumstances may hope to convey to a reader some recognition of universal incongruity, to evoke the twitch of a smile among other emotional responses demanded by the grotesque antics of our cosmos.

I once read Swift's *A Modest Proposal* to a university freshman class. This is the essay in which Swift proposes that the Irish solve their economic difficulties by eating their most overproduced commodity: their babies. In the ensuing twenty-minute discussion, some students doubted that the plan would work for Ireland; some were mildly outraged but felt that allowances had to be made for the level of eighteenth century civilization. Finally one quiet fellow raised his hand and asked cautiously, "Is he *kidding?*" This is the primordial spark of literary sensitivity. I can imagine a multiple choice test giving clear alternatives: "Swift was (1) serious; (2) kidding; (3) confused; (4) a thirteenth century translator of the Bible; and (5) none of the above." I would feel fairly confident that there was a right answer and that some literary talent was required in order to arrive at it. But the brighter students would ask, rightly, "What do you mean, kidding?" and "How do we *know* what he intended?" and "Mightn't he have been serious and kidding at the same time?" Even if one can correctly label the essay as satire, has he really felt the compassion which enabled Swift to write in such cold blood, the despairing, almost tearful vision of the horror of poverty which prompted Swift to perpetrate the very amusing horror of recipes for roasting and boiling babies, evoking the ravaging laughter (except from freshmen) which lies beyond sympathetic tears?

Even with these complexities, the case is too simple. Shakespeare is a master of tone, of voice-stance, controlling every last reverberation and overtone of feeling with astonishing sureness. His greatest lines are frequently those which appear to be the simplest, and their greatness lies in the way they define a human situation, often torn by the most complex circumstances and feelings, exactly and clearly. In Hamlet's closet scene with Gertrude, for example, we have a crescendo of infinitely strained emotions. Having shortly before been convinced by the play-within-the-play of Claudius' guilt, having just decided against killing Claudius at prayer, having, in his mother's bedroom, stabbed Polonius behind the arras, thinking he was the king, Hamlet, so inordinately agitated, has the delicate duty of making his mother understand her own crime in marrying a villain. Polonius, the wrong man, is disregarded as a swatted fly, and the scene sweeps ahead in the urgency of its central problem. With the portraits, Hamlet evokes the images of his father murdered and the present king, speaking daggers to the queen until she can endure no more. But suddenly the ghost of the elder Hamlet appears to Hamlet, although invisible to his mother. Hamlet breaks off the conversation with the queen and seems to be talking in distraction to nothing at all. After reminding his son of his "almost blunted purpose," the ghost notices Gertrude, gaping at her son's apparent madness, and tells Hamlet to speak to her.

Now Hamlet is bewilderingly ready of tongue, acute in analysis, always on top of the action, knowing everyone and even himself too well. But what is he to say to Gertrude? He loves her and hates her too much, has been too disillusioned by her marriage, is too frightened (after all, a ghost is a ghost!) and awed by the spectre before him, too disturbed by the events of the past few minutes, the conversation of the past few seconds, to say anything at all. He says, ridiculously, rightly, "How is it with you, Lady?" It is one of Shakespeare's greatest, most courageous lines.

Its courage and greatness are in the way it skirts the comic. If anything were a shade wrong about the line, the audience, tense beyond endurance, might well break into laughter. But the ineffectuality, the comic helplessness and double-taking matter-of-factness of the line deepens and defines the complex of unlikely, devastating events focusing in this scene. It is ludicrous — on reflection, by light of day. But as it is experienced, absurdity is horror: the terrible insanity of circumstance, of clashing emotions.

Consider some of the emotional factors I have not mentioned. Gertrude has just been brought to a violent confrontation of her own guilt but now is experiencing relief mixed with sorrow as she escapes into the notion that Hamlet's accusations can be disregarded because of his obvious madness — that all her guilt is one of his morbid delusions. Hamlet has had a moment of ecstasy and certainty when Claudius showed his guilt at the play; but this has been followed by two serious frustrations: he could not kill Claudius praying, and when he thinks he *has* killed Claudius, it turns out to be meddling, tiresome Polonius, who seems always to be there botching things. Now he has risen to a new height of clarity and resolution as he has eloquently convinced the queen of her guilt, not for murdering Hamlet senior but for marrying such an unworthy man as Claudius. Just then the ghost reminds him that this is all beside the point — which is, after all, revenge. Correction of his mother is, like stabbing Polonius, a frustrating, distracting (no matter how self-satisfying) waste of energy on a side issue. At this moment he is reminded that he must be polite, as it were, and, certainly, as the affairs of life go on heedless of our personal agony or grief, he *must* speak to her. The ridiculous situation and ridiculous line interrupt the action only as a genius can — daring our laughter, showing us for an instant the whole tangle of the action and emotional forces by slicing it with trivia. My contention is that to receive the message one must instantaneously see (or feel) all this — not in words but in, perhaps, a tremor.

Similar cases occur often enough in Shakespeare to assure us he is aware of the dramatic effectiveness of inarticulateness. Othello, finally convinced by Iago, mutters incoherently and falls into a trance. Lear, in the height of his rage, sputters at his daughters with emotion beyond words:

> I will have such revenges on you both
> That all the world shall — I will do such things —
> What they are, yet I know not, but they shall be
> The terrors of the earth.

In the beautifully placid Sonnet 73 we have a suggestion of the same effect:

> That time of year thou mayest in me behold
> When yellow leaves, or none, or few, do hang
> Upon those boughs

Yellowness suggests perhaps too pretty an autumn, a golden age. The speaker wants the pathos of age to be felt and so corrects himself grimly, "or none." But absolute barrenness is perhaps *too* grim, like imagining oneself as a skeleton. So he corrects himself again: "or few," and goes on, but (as though inadvertently) he has left us with a final suggestion of withered brown leaves clinging to the sapless bough — an image more horrible, more pathetic than that of a bough cleanly bare. The hesitation, the awkward feeling for the word and giving it up, defines the tone.

In Sonnet 129 in which he rages against his own fleshly desires, he says that lust "Is perjured, murderous, bloody, full of blame," rising in intensity to the blasphemous "bloody" and then sinking to the relatively weak and general "full of blame." In case we doubt that this is what he meant, we might look at the very next line, "Savage, extreme, rude, cruel, not to trust," in which "Savage" and "cruel" are the strongest condemnations, but the line ends in the weakest phrase of both lines, "not to trust." Later in the sonnet he does it again. He says a lusting person is

> Mad in pursuit, and in possession so,
> Had, having, and in quest to have, extreme,

in which the word *extreme,* repeated from earlier in the poem, is like Lear's inarticulate curse. What it is, I know not, but it is the terror of the earth.

Complexity of tone is one of the great attractions of the popular metaphysical poets of the seventeenth century. How are we to take it when Herbert, in deepest devotion, imagines God as a prostitute luring him to love, when Donne, in a prayerful poem, keeps returning to a serious but painfully corny pun on his own name —

> When thou hast done, thou hast not done,
> For I have more.

Crashaw, whom I quoted in Chapter Ten, is one of the most

shocking of 17th century poets in this respect. For example, his devotional poem, "On the Bleeding Wounds of our Crucified Lord," is a tortuously witty chain of hyperboles pertaining to flowing blood.

> Jesu, no more! It is full tide
> From thy hands and from thy feet,
> From thy head, and from thy side,
> All thy *Purple Rivers* meet.

He says Christ's feet swim in his own flood, the gift of his hand is its own blood, his side, like the Nile, is flooding and thereby fruitful, the weeping of his head makes the weeping of his eyes unnecessary:

> Water'd by the showres they bring,
> The thornes that thy blest browes encloses
> (A cruell and a costly spring)
> Conceive proud hopes of proving Roses.
>
> Not a haire but payes his River
> To the *Red Sea* of thy blood,
> Their little channels can deliver
> Something to the general flood.

And on and on. One may, of course, dodge the question by saying simply that it is a terrible poem. But I think it is not; in its own way it is beautiful and moving. And its own way is to employ humor as Shakespeare employed it in the closet scene, to intensify and sharpen tragic feeling. It is as though the poet were to say, "Laugh if you dare, but this is the blood of God I am talking about — a transcendent paradox in itself. Would naturalism, would good taste be sufficient to convey its magnitude?" The pathetic inadequacy of words, concepts, imagination to deal with Christ's bleeding is part of the poem's effect.

Universally, modern readers smile or groan at Dryden's youthful gaucherie in his elegy on Lord Hastings, who died of smallpox. Dryden is imitating the metaphysicals (an influence he was soon to reject entirely) and goes all the way, speaking of the pustules:

> Each little Pimple had a Tear in it,
> To wail the fault its rising did commit:

Our groans may reflect our insensitivity to tone. Perhaps Dryden also saw these lines as ridiculous. He might justify them by saying that ridiculousness is essentially part of the experience: the horrid ugliness of death, of disease, so ironically and heartbreakingly in contrast to our tender feelings about the person mourned. Put an edge of bitterness in your voice, as you do when you read Marvell's celebrated couplet:

> The Grave's a fine and private place,
> But none, I think, do there embrace,

and the lines take on a macabre dignity.

An even greater challenge to perceptiveness of tone is one of Dryden's richest, most mature lyrics, a poem with the unpromising title (and perhaps deliberate humor?) "To the Pious Memory of the Accomplisht Young Lady Mrs. Anne Killigrew, Excellent in the Two Sister-Arts of Poesie, and Painting: An Ode." A mediocre poetess, daughter of a friend of Dryden's, Anne Killigrew was not important in herself. Her early death is mourned in the most extravagant and fanciful of terms: her "Pre-existing Soul" rolled "through all the Mighty Poets . . . Who Greek or Latine laurels wore,/ And was that Sappho last, which once it was before." A swarm of bees left honey on the lips of Plato at his birth, but the heavenly spirits didn't have time at Anne's birth to arrange such a miracle, although it would have been appropriate. They were too busy celebrating the holiday! She wrote love poetry, this child far too innocent to have loved. Dryden pokes the kindest sort of fun at her passion; her love poems remind him of the hot little god Cupid bathing in the cold stream of Diana's chastity. Unsatisfied with her complete control of poetry (writes the Poet Laureate), she sneaked into the neighboring province of painting and captured that, too. The dear one *did* try her hand at everything.

Unless we imagine that Dryden was simply too foolish to know what he was doing, we must try to discover the tone in which such remarks are appropriate. A kind of humor, again, modifies the quite sincere grief. The gentle tone of coddling and even gentle mockery, completely without contempt, which one uses in speaking of a lovely but perhaps overserious child, is something like what Dryden must have meant. Combine with this a certain pleasure and release in extravagance for its own sake, for the ingenious elaborations of fancy, for civility carried beyond reason, for pomp — a quality much in disrepute in our time and culture — for ceremony. The chief thing Dryden saw in Anne Killigrew's passing was the instant of innocence soon to be lost in a sophisticated, "lubrique" age. We who are wiser are more defiled. His own sophistication, which produces the poem, strains in appreciation of simple purity; a kind of amusement pervades and clarifies the poignancy of regret and grief. To appreciate his tone, we must be alert to his amusement, just as we must to the value he placed upon ingenuity, ceremony, learning, tenderness — in short, to the full range of interpenetrating and rapidly shifting voice postures needed to express complex feeling. Unless we hear *how* he says it, we do not know what he is saying.

Milton is frequently regarded as humorless, but the more I read him the more I think it is readers who are humorless, as well as presumptuous in thinking Milton did not know when he was funny. When we read of the wars in heaven, of angels in armor tearing up the landscape by the roots,

> So hills amid the air encounter hills
> Hurled to and fro with jaculation dire,

we should smile, I think, but not in superiority. In what dream of egotism do we imagine that Milton did not smile too, as he must have smiled in discussing the sexual habits and digestive processes of angels, in depicting a smug bourgeois Adam and dissatisfied housewife Eve, in toying with the nudity of our parents — which, of course, meant nothing, or something, or little, in the way of titillation? Our mistake is in associating humor with levity. The existentialists have emphasized the prevalence of absurdity in our most tragic affairs, but most of us turn on solemnity, humor, piety, grief, love, respect, contempt, delight, as though they were wired sequentially in our sensibility and could not burn in interesting combinations. As poets we must be emotionally more versatile.

To illustrate the difference reception of tone makes in understanding a whole work, consider Donne's popular Sonnet 10:

> Death be not proud, though some have called thee
> Mighty and dreadfull, for, thou art not soe,
> For, those, whom thou think'st, thou dost overthrow,
> Die not, poore death, nor yet canst thou kill mee.
> From rest and sleepe, which but thy pictures bee,
> Much pleasure, then from thee, much more must flow,
> And soonest our best men with thee doe goe,
> Rest of their bones, and soules deliverie.
> Thou art slave to Fate, Chance, kings, and desperate men,
> And dost with poyson, warre, and sicknesse dwell,
> And poppie, or charmes can make us sleepe as well,
> And better than thy stroake; why swell'st thou then?
> One short sleepe past, wee wake eternally,
> And death shall be no more; death, thou shalt die.

The opening lines and closing lines have a heroic ring that induces many readers to think of the poem as a courageous confrontation of the void, much like that of Henley's "Invictus." Henley is out of style; Donne is in — and those who would in another age beat their chests to Henley's tune now beat it to Donne's — out of time, I think, because they ignore the shifts and complexities of tone occurring between the beginning quatrain and the couplet.

Death demonstrably *is* mighty and dreadful, as Donne well knew, however we might whistle in the dark to avoid that recognition. The sonnet is one of frantic grasping at logical straws to palliate an inevitable conclusion quite the opposite of the surface meaning of the final, firm, "death, thou shalt die." The first quatrain asserts a faith that those who die actually have eternal life. If death were a person and that person took pride in overthrowing men, he would be ironically mistaken, for men rise again. The poet says, like the little fox, "You can't catch me!" Had he stopped there, we might take this as a not unusual testament of the immortality of the soul.

The next two lines introduce a familiar conceit; death is but the image of rest and sleep; if rest and sleep, the "pictures," bring much pleasure, surely the original will bring much more. Compare with the logic-chopping lines from Donne's poem, "Woman's Constancy" (discussed in Chapter Sixteen):

> Or, as true deaths, true maryages untie,
> So lovers contracts, images of those
> Binde but till sleep, deaths image, them unloose?

Donne knows and we know that whatever superficial resemblances there may be between death and sleep, sleep is not an imitation of death, and the pleasure sleep brings is simply irrelevant. By reminding us of the fanciful conceits of love poems, of other sonnets, of his own poetic past, he is tipping us off to the real significance of this licensed exaggeration: I am proclaiming, he says, what I would *like* to believe, but it exceeds my confidence.

The next two lines seem to support the idea of death's pleasantness: "And soonest our best men with thee doe goe,/ Rest of their bones, and soules deliverie." But why do the best men die soonest? Because they throw themselves forward in battle, sacrifice themselves in some way? One cannot reflect without irony that the reward for virtue is an early death, and the interrupting line, "Rest of their bones, and soules deliverie" sounds like a prayer over the corpse, a tone of mourning which would be entirely inappropriate if we really believed death were a rest and a delivery.

Death is pleasant? He goes on to say that it is the agent of "Fate, Chance, kings and desperate men,/ And dost with poyson, warre, and sicknesse dwell." Of course, the ostensible reason for these lines is to diminish death's importance by association, by saying you are no good because you work for a bad master and come from a bad environment. But for these very reasons, death might be *more* mighty and dreadful (as might any criminal) — and the notion that death might be a source of pleasure is forgotten. Logic is forgotten; for although the word "slave" suggests that death is weak, we find that it is the slave of mighty and dreadful powers, and if we had one moment of consolation thinking of death as a peaceful slumber, it is remarkable that the actual examples Donne selects are horrible: poison first, suggesting the cramps and writhings of stage deaths at Machiavellian hands; then war's slaughter; then the putridness of disease. Pleasure, indeed!

But he goes back in the next lines to the theme of sleep: "And poppie, or charmes can make us sleepe as well,/ And better than thy stroake"; but now it is the sleep of drugs, the spells of witchcraft, which are, ironically, "better" than death's stroke. "Stroake" is a strong and sinister word, ending the argument, as it were, for the remainder of line 12 and the couplet take us back to the beginning thought.

The joke, bitter as it may be, is not far below the surface. If one were to say, "Why, death is nothing to fear; it's pleasant, just like sleep, and must be some kind of reward, since it gets the best men earliest (poor fellows); and besides, it has an unsavory background associated with all kinds of horrors, and all that; and besides, once it's over, *it's over*," we would see more easily the half-kidding, the half-desperate tone, given increased irony by the noble fanfare with which it is introduced and ended. As such, the poem seems to me much more important, much more moving, than it would be if it pretended that death really *were* nothing to worry about, which is patent sentimental nonsense. Of course, too, as I have described it, the poem has more effect as religious persuasion than would be self-reliant-courage-in-the-face-of-fire Henleyesque refusal to face facts. It throws the reader (if not into desperation) onto the bosom of the church. Death which *is* mighty and dreadful requires that we find some consolation.

dramatic complexity

A common statement about poetry is that it "expresses a mood." Tone and mood are related, of course, but like a lightning bolt and a cloud. Tone is alive; it accompanies statement, colors it, clarifies it. But mood absorbs statement, or holds it in suspension. Nothing happens, nothing is said; an emotional state is preserved for its own sake. There are beauties in mood — particularly in music — but mood hangs in the air, and one can become very weary of hanging in the air too long. When emotion becomes the object of statement rather than a means of statement, emphasis must be on sustaining it at the expense of the quick shifts of tone which catch delicate reverberations of thought and feeling.

The skills that reading or writing calls for are flexibility, responsiveness, a capacity for receiving the whole experience — sense, emotion, thought — all together, each element modifying and defining the other. "Go not too near a house of rose," says Emily Dickinson, and we might apply this injunction to writing poetry: "The depredation of a breeze/ Or inundation of a dew/ Alarm its walls away." The measuring instrument distorts the measurement. "In insecurity to lie," Dickinson says, "Is Joy's insuring quality." If we apply that to writing, we see that our understanding must be dynamic rather than static, compounded more of wisdom than of knowledge; it must settle on the stream like a leaf to know its most delicate currents.

Dickinson is telling us the difference between a real rose and a wax one. The failure of most poets occurs before they ever set pen to paper: they do not grasp life and experience with sufficient complexity; they are unwilling to entertain a vision of manifold and contradictory truth. A great work of art is like a cavern of endless echoes. Its mystery and profundity and resonance arise from the sense it conveys of inexhaustibility. We stand back in awe because our capacity to explain, describe or contain is overwhelmed.

This can be illustrated by returning to *Romeo and Juliet,* now to examine the balcony scene (Act II, scene ii). As a mood piece — young lovers in spring moonlight, chaste in act, effusive in imagination — it is a paradigm of triteness. That image, gleaned from innumerable amateur performances, bears little relationship to the poetry of the scene itself — which is as foolish as it is beautiful, as earthy as it is lofty, as humorous as it is passionately earnest. It leaves us with a heightened sense of the full reality of adolescent love — complete with all shades of idealism, adoration, clownishness, evasion, insecurity and glandular urgency. In a mere 190 lines of poetry, perhaps five minutes of stage action, a world is created rich in philosophy and insight, peopled by two very individual lovers who are simultaneously themselves and universal symbols of the human predicament.

Romeo has been presented, in the first act of the play, as a comic stereotype of the slave of love. While his elders and companions are involved in the serious adult business of quarreling and negotiating, Romeo is mooning about the stage enamored of some Rosaline who hardly knows he exists. He has crashed a party with his friends, however, and there set eye upon Juliet. Rosaline is instantaneously forgotten as Cupid's arrow strikes his heart — and he is off on new poetic raptures over a new face which he saw across a crowded room. He manages to get close enough to deliver a speech so studied and ornate that Juliet critically notes that he loves by the book. After the party his male friends drunkenly and lewdly call for him, thinking him still enraptured of Rosaline. But Romeo hides from them inside the Capulet garden. Hearing the obscene taunts of Mercutio, he dismisses them: "He jests at scars that never felt a wound." Only a man who has never been wounded by love can make fun of it. With that line Romeo clears the air of our cynical responses: it is true that the capacity for love is a quality superior to the capacity for making crude fun of it.

Just then he sees Juliet at her window. "But, soft! What light through yonder window breaks?/ It is the east, and Juliet is the sun!" We are off then on a familiar Petrarchan conceit — i.e., an exaggerated, elaborate comparison idealizing the beloved in the manner of Petrarch. The sun (Juliet) is attended by the pale, envious moon. Diana, the goddess of the moon, represents chastity. Wittily (and unheard by Juliet) he advises her to cast off the "vestal livery" — in other words, to surrender her virginity. For all the ornate language, it is quite clear what he has in mind.

Suddenly his imagination plummets from the heady heights to present reality:

> It is my lady, oh, it is my love!
> Oh, that she knew she were!
> She speaks, yet she says nothing. What of that?
> Her eye discourses, I will answer it.

What Juliet actually says to the night is irrelevant except insofar as it provides Romeo with the pad to launch into another orbit of conceit. He imagines that a couple of stars have asked Juliet's eyes to take their place in heaven for awhile. One fantasy is heaped upon another: if her eyes were to shine in heaven, they would wake the birds, who would think it dawn — so bright are Juliet's eyes. The notion that optical candlepower was a measure of spiritual intensity came from Petrarch, too. It is as though the young lover standing in the dark, observing his sweetheart unaware, were ecstatically reviewing his undergraduate education.

Suddenly, though, he sees Juliet lean her cheek upon her hand, and again his mind plummets to sensuality:

> Oh, that I were a glove upon that hand,
> That I might touch that cheek!

That is more like it: a considerably more honest and direct approach to female beauty than imagining her eyes gadding about the universe, waking birds. Juliet emits an eloquent sigh: "Aye me!" And Romeo, with that stimulus, streams off on another few lines of outrageously exaggerated metaphor. When Juliet again speaks to the night we discover that her mind is not on poetry at all, though it is on Romeo. She is worrying about the practical obstacles to marriage — for the families are feuding, and the fact that he is a Montague and she a Capulet is as insurmountable a barrier as if he were white and she were black for many American families:

> O Romeo, Romeo, wherefore art thou Romeo?
> Deny thy father and refuse they name,
> Or, if thou wilt not, be but sworn my love
> And I'll no longer be a Capulet.

An adolescent is both endearing and foolish for refusing to accept the "reality" defined by elders. Juliet muses rebelliously, idealistically:

> What's Montague? It is nor hand, nor foot,
> Nor arm, nor face, nor any other part
> Belonging to a man. Oh, be some other name!
> What's in a name? That which we call a rose
> By any other name would smell as sweet.
> So Romeo would, were he not Romeo called
> . . .   Romeo, doff thy name,
> And for thy name, which is no part of thee,
> Take all myself.

We hear in Juliet the same capacity for wit and imagination as Romeo has demonstrated, but in Juliet it is more focused and practical, a rumination on the hard facts. At the same time it is touchingly naive. "What's in a name?" What's the difference of skin color? A difference in religious faith? Nothing — and everything. A whole emerging tragedy results from the implacable differences the world finds in such quibbles. A word is an "airy nothing," yet it kills.

Juliet does not yet know that Romeo is down there listening. But when she offers her 98 pounds of bouncing teenager to the night, Romeo can no longer contain himself: "I take thee at thy word." (Note the building irony: What's in a name? Nothing. Yet he takes her at her *word.*) Juliet doesn't recognize him in the dark — and he claims he cannot identify himself by name, since she disapproves of his name: "Had I it written, I would tear the word." This childish response again underlines the absurdity and gravity of the problem. Imagine the intransigent feud being settled by writing a name on a piece of paper and tearing it!

Each of the lovers' speeches delineates the difference in their characters. At each instigation, Romeo leaps away in swirls of imagination, whereas Juliet keeps her mind steadily on their practical circumstances. If Romeo is in her garden, he is in mortal danger. How did he get there? How can he escape notice? But the foolhardy young hero continues cockily to spread his Petrarchan feathers:

JUL: How cam'st thou hither, tell me, and wherefore?
The orchard walls are high and hard to climb,
And the place death, considering who thou art,
If any of my kinsmen find thee here.

ROM: With love's light wings did I o'erperch these walls,
For stony limits cannot hold love out.
And what love can do, that dares love attempt,
Therefore thy kinsmen are no let to me.

JUL: If they do see thee, they will murder thee.

ROM: Alack, there lies more peril in thine eye
Than twenty of their swords. Look thou but sweet,
And I am proof against their enmity.

JUL: I would not for the world they saw thee here.

ROM: I have night's cloak to hide me from their eyes,
And but thou love me, let them find me here.
My life were better ended by their hate
Than death prorogued, wanting of thy love.

JUL: By whose direction found'st thou out this place?

ROM: By love, that first did prompt me to inquire . . .

And so on. No straight answers. In Romeo's book love is a contest of rhetoric, but Juliet is very concrete in her preoccupations, very frightened, and very young. She is embarrassed to have been over-

heard declaring her love to the night. A proper girl waits to be
wooed, and denies her own feelings as long as possible to an
importunate swain. But she has been caught, as it were, with her
feelings hanging out, and there is no point now in denying them:

> Fain would I dwell on form, fain, fain deny
> What I have spoke. But farewell compliment!
> Dost thou love me? I know thou wilt say "Aye,"
> And I will take thy word.

What, though, is in a word? She knows the perjuries of lovers —
and yet has no alternative but to trust him. She is a little girl
whose sophisticated cover has been blown:

> Or if thou think'st I am too quickly won,
> I'll frown and be perverse and say thee nay,
> So thou wilt woo; but else, not for the world.
> In truth, fair Montague, I am too fond,
> And therefore thou mayst think my 'havior light.
> But trust me, gentleman, I'll prove more true
> Than those that have more cunning to be strange.

On cue Romeo launches into a flowery oath, swearing by the
moon, but she cuts off his rhetoric:

> Oh, swear not by the moon, th' inconstant moon,
> That monthly changes in her circled orb,
> Lest that thy love prove likewise variable.

Romeo is comically nonplussed: "What shall I swear by?" And
she wants to dispose of all further poeticizing:

> Well, do not swear. Although I joy in thee,
> I have no joy of this contract tonight.
> It is too rash, too unadvised, too sudden,
> Too like the lightning, which doth cease to be
> Ere one can say "It lightens." Sweet, good night!

Like any lover with his foot in the door, he is reluctant to
leave unsatisfied; he wants at least a vow. She points out that
she gave hers before he asked it.

> JUL: And yet I would it were to give again.
> ROM: Wouldst thou withdraw it? For what purpose, love?
> JUL: But to be frank, and give it thee again.
> And yet I wish but for the thing I have.
> My bounty is as boundless as the sea,
> My love as deep; the more I give to thee,
> The more I have, for both are infinite.

Her own flights of fancy, as imaginative as his, seem less learned, less studied, less conventional. One hears the tones of earnest struggling for a way of expressing transcendent feeling — not the formulae of transcendence recited by one more in love with love than with a specific person. The nurse calls within, and Juliet leaves a minute, asking Romeo to wait. When she comes back, it is for the very practical purpose of arranging marriage. In spite of the feud and the danger, she is resolved to take the necessary steps to consummation — if his intent is serious.

But we should not get the impression that Juliet is merely a hard-headed girl bent on the security of marriage. She, too, is carried away by the night and the romance, by her irrepressible affection. Even as she thinks up practical details to postpone his departure, she is able to laugh at her own excess of fondness:

JUL: I have forgot why I did call thee back.
ROM: Let me stand here till thou remember it.
JUL: I shall forget, to have thee still stand there,
      Remembering how I love thy company.
ROM: And I'll still stay, to have thee still forget,
      Forgetting any other home but this.
JUL: 'Tis almost morning. I would have thee gone,
      And yet no farther than a wanton's bird,
      Who lets it hop a little from her hand,
      Like a poor prisoner in his twisted gyves,
      And with a silk thread plucks it back again,
      So loving-jealous of his liberty.
ROM: I would I were thy bird.
JUL: Sweet, so would I.
      Yet I should kill thee with much cherishing.
      Good night, good night! Parting is such sweet sorrow
      That I shall say good night till it be morrow.

"Sweet sorrow" and, indeed, even "good night" contain the rich paradox of tone in the scene and the play. We know as surely as Juliet does that their love is "too rash, too unadvised, too sudden," that it is doomed to tragedy because passion and love have over-whelmed realism and practicality, that it is the night which is good — and the hot, brash day brings in another kind of passion, the contentiousness and anger which will defeat this night's sweet intent.

It is that ambiguity which makes the scene powerful — not unalloyed romance. We love Romeo more, not less, because he is cocky and wordy and impetuous and even a bit hypocritical as he wraps his sexuality in poetic satin. We love Juliet more, not less, because she is wavering, pointedly practical, frankly lustful, frankly scared. Pure and simple lovers, perfect in their idealism, could be made of plastic; but Romeo and Juliet are very much creatures of flesh. It is not idealized love which interests us and evokes our commitment, but spirit incarnate in very recognizable human beings.

As the play progesses Romeo grows in dignity and manhood. He even becomes more practical — enough so to kill a declared enemy and finally, himself. He becomes, as it were, soiled by traffic in the world, growing and diminishing at the same time. But in the death scene at the end of the play we have no doubts that a mature man rather than a boy has sacrificed himself for his love. Juliet grows too — developing a capacity for evasiveness and conceit, even a ferocity as she learns the shallowness of her parents and her closest ally, the nurse. She achieves womanhood — not without the loss of some of the innocence and simple candor she shows in the balcony scene. If the deaths at the end were of children, the play would be merely pathetic. But it is tragic because the vision of life it contains is sufficiently mixed, complex, ironic, and resonant to convince us that it is not merely two people who are dying. What we are forced to confront is the impossibility of purity and transcendent love in the given world.

It takes more courage (as well as more wisdom) than most poets have to accept and deal with the mixed bag of reality, to incorporate humor and inconsistency and vanity in their conceptions of beauty and the ideal. To write love poetry, for instance, which claims absolute perfection of the people involved and their feelings is to remain on the Petrarchan level from which Romeo had to descend to discover a real woman and his own manhood. It might be literary, but it will never be literature.

wit and tragedy

One might say that the tragic stature of *Romeo and Juliet* arises precisely from the play of wit over the sweetness of romantic love, a lemon spice that brings out the succulence of the fruit, that enables even a pair of adolescent sweethearts to achieve dignity. The same phenomenon occurs on a smaller scale in a short lyric written in the year of my birth, 1927. John Crowe Ransom must have faced, as does any poet, the propositions that (1) the great themes of love and death have been trodden bare; and (2) poetic vision is always paradoxical. As I reread his "The Equilibrists" this black December morning, wind racketing the windows, the second of those propositions seems to renew the first as the steamy sap of spring will arise from winter snow.

Equilibrists (accent on the second syllable) means something like tightrope walkers: an equilibrist is "one who balances himself in unnatural positions and hazardous movements." Ransom is writing about the plight of lovers who are sensually attracted to one another, but separated by an idea: honor. It is, indeed, a balancing act, a state of abnormal suspension. By using an archaic title, with connotations of the circus, Ransom seems to be taking their tragedy not quite seriously, and, indeed, much of the poem seems to make fun of them. It starts:

> Full of her long white arms and milky skin
> He had a thousand times remembered sin.
> Alone in the press of people traveled he,
> Minding her jacinth, and myrrh, and ivory.

Each stanza is made up of two heroic couplets, often, as in the second above, with strained rhymes. In a sense, the poem is a series of jokes, of punch lines. It is absurd for a man in the midst of making love to be thinking about sin. It is equally absurd for him, away from his mistress, to be thinking of her in terms of adoration suggesting the worship of the Magi. The writing is deliberately awkward and archaic: the inversion, "traveled he"; the quaint word "Minding." The "press of people" suggests a modern crowded street, through it threading this old-fashioned lover "minding" the symbolic, oriental wealth of his sweetheart's body.

These devices are used again and again as the poem goes on:

> Mouth he remembered: the quaint orifice
> From which came heat that flamed upon the kiss,
> Till cold words came down spiral from the head.
> Grey doves from the officious tower illsped.

The members of the local poetry club would probably rip such writing to shreds. "Quaint" is insulting, "orifice" rather grossly scientific for a loved one's lips. The meter of the last line quoted limps and hobbles like the labor of an amateur:

Grey doves| from the| of fi| cious tow| er ill sped.|

Nonetheless, the image of words — symbolizing thoughts, abstractions — as doves spiraling down from the "'officious tower" of the mind to quench the heat of sensuality is a powerful one. After another stanza in which her body begs for his touch, this image is repeated more sharply:

> Eyes talking: Never mind the cruel words,
> Embrace my flowers, but not embrace the swords.
> But what they said, the doves came straightway flying
> And unsaid: Honor, Honor, they came crying.

> Importunate her doves. Too pure, too wise,
> Clambering on his shoulder, saying, Arise,
> Leave me now, and never let us meet,
> Eternal distance now command thy feet.

With these words deliberately evoking the corny melodrama of high romance, the poem ends its first movement. It has depicted a lover yearning for a woman, a woman yearning for a man, has carried them into embrace, then separated them with a moral consideration that prevents consummation. The poet has not spoken in his own voice, but we have been aware of an intelligence, an outside observer wryly studying their little drama. We suspect already that his attitude is amused and condescending. How do we know that? Through the language he uses to describe them — the archaic words, the apparently clumsy versification, the mock-heroic imagery.

The sixth stanza swings away from the lovers themselves into contemplation:

> Predicament indeed, which thus discovers
> Honor among thieves, Honor between lovers.
> O such a little word is Honor, they feel!
> But the grey word is between them cold as steel.

The word *predicament* seems to belittle their emotional plight. Imagine it applied to King Lear's discovery of his daughters' betrayal. The next line seems to equate thievery and love — with intellectual aptness. Thieves do, indeed, invent their own code, as do lovers: the human tendency, apparently, is to create abstractions that restrain us from pursuit of the purely practical, purely animal. Us? Indeed, as the poem moves into reflection, the problem the lovers are facing becomes more general, involving, as we will see, this very objective and somewhat disdainful poet himself.

He enters the poem frankly in his own person in the seventh stanza:

> At length I saw these lovers fully were come
> Into their torture of equilibrium;
> Dreadfully had forsworn each other, and yet
> They were bound each to each, and they did not forget.

The alexandrine, or six foot line, that concludes the stanza, plods with unshakable emphasis. As that stanza defines their problem abstractly, the next does lyrically, with cosmic imagery:

> And rigid as two painful stars, and twirled,
> About the clustered night their prison world,
> They burned with fierce love always to come near,
> But Honor beat them back and kept them clear.

Though still drawn from the classical repertory of love imagery, the placement of the lovers in the stars, the "clustered night," the "prison world" attributes to them a loftiness and dignity which had been undercut in the previous stanzas. Apparently the poet takes them somewhat more seriously than he has let on — and himself less seriously:

> Ah, the strict lovers, they are ruined now!
> I cried in anger. But with puddled brow
> Devising for those gibbeted and brave
> Came I descanting: Man, what would you have?

One can believe his sympathy. It is almost as though he were a child playing with dolls, but becoming so involved in the game, so carried away by imagination, he is pained by the drama he has projected them into. Or as though he were God watching the mess humanity makes of its possibilities. At the same time he is aware of his own posturing and deflates it. His brow is "puddled" like packed mud. From his unavailing position as an observer he can only "devise" and "'descant" while those he writes of are hung from a gibbet, suspended for public scorn, and are, in all the richness of the word, "brave," both courageous and flamboyant. They are committed, while the poet can only look on, make fun perhaps, but finally (ironically) *honor* them in their hopeless engagement. When he asks, "Man, what would you have?" he addresses humanity at large. The plight of the lovers is ours and his own.

> For spin your period out, and draw your breath,
> A kinder saeculum begins with Death.
> Would you ascend to Heaven and bodiless dwell?
> Or take your bodies honorless to Hell?

> In Heaven you have heard no marriage is,
> No white flesh tinder to your lecheries,
> Your male and female tissue sweetly shaped
> Sublimed away, and furious blood escaped.
>
> Great lovers lie in Hell, the stubborn ones
> Infatuate of the flesh upon the bones;
> Stuprate, they rend each other when they kiss,
> The pieces kiss again, no end to this.

The irony directed at the lovers has been gentle, indulgent; but that he directs at the cosmos is embittered. A kinder saeculum (i.e., age or era) begins with Death, indeed! At that point, it seems, a choice must be made — between a pale, sexless, cold afterlife with sweet flesh "sublimed away" and the blood of our passions gone, and a Hell of senseless sensuality, the horror of being bound to endless, tearing passion.

To find *saeculum* you have to go to a Latin dictionary. To find *stuprate* you have to go to a dictionary of early English, such as Shipley's, which defines it as "given to rape, adultery, whoredom," from the medieval word *stupre,* meaning "violation of a woman." Some readers will ask whether it is fair for a poet to demand such scholarship of them — to which the only answer is, there are no rules. He takes a risk of losing readers or, at least, losing their comprehension by such diction. And I am not sure that enough is gained in precision or suggestiveness to warrant that risk. But for me, these words do not diminish the value of the poem, and his use of them is consistent with the stylistic device we have seen throughout, the deliberate use of the archaic. This was also a favorite device of Spenser, Milton and Whitman, though they did not generally use rare words with the ironic overtones that characterize Ransom's work.

But to return to the meaning of the poem, the choices of Heaven or Hell seem equally grim, not only to the lovers, but, clearly, to the poet. By now his identification with them is complete. They can make no choice; they are doomed to stable orbit, satellites of one another:

> But still I watched them spinning, orbited nice.
> Their flames were not more radiant than their ice.
> I dug in the quiet earth and wrought the tomb
> And made these lines to memorize their doom: —

EPITAPH

Equilibrists lie here; stranger, tread light;
Close, but untouching in each other's sight;
Mouldered the lips and ashy the tall skull,
Let them lie perilous and beautiful.

Their flames come from their bodies, as the "ice" from their ideas. Their honor, in other words, is seen as equally radiant with their flesh. The situation seemed absurd at the beginning of the poem — absurd desire, absurd restraint. By the end, however, it is truly heroic.

And it is amazing that Ransom is able to achieve that tonality without shifting his style. That word "nice" has an archaic flavor, meaning exact, scrupulous, as well as wanton, silly, pleasant: see the range of meanings in the dictionary. *Memorize* is an archaic usage; we would say memorialize, or commemorate. Notice how the irony is tempered by phrases of honest feeling: *quiet earth, Mouldered the lips, ashy the tall skull.* The last two phrases encompass the mind-body conflict, and both lips and skull are submitted to their distinctive forms of decay. *Perilous* seems to be double-edged, referring both to the hazard of their equilibrium, i.e., the hazard to themselves, and that of their challenge to the world. Rarely can a poet find a way to end a poem with that soggiest of noble words: *beautiful.* But Ransom gets away with it here, because his feelings have been so chained in by wit that when he does finally express himself in untempered praise we can believe him.

Nothing could be more commonplace, especially in the poetry of the world, than the themes, the "message" of this poem, which says that there is an irreconcilable conflict between human desires and human ideals, that capitulation to either is undesirable, that the human condition — appropriately in quiet earth rather than in the clustered sky — is that of painful equilibrium between these contending forces. Immortal themes are worn threadbare for good reasons: their truth. Paths are always worn along the easiest and nearest ways.

But the "message" itself is paradoxical, and the style that enlivens it in this poem is interwoven with paradox as by a tapestry's golden thread. It is the play of wit, of a willingness to see and accept the amusing, absurd, the awkward, all as a part of experiencing the tragic, which enables the poet to go so near the flaming center of his poem. Triteness in a poem does not result from familiarity of the subject matter but from an uncritical gushiness in the style, the emotion leaning all one way, the response too simple for the multi-faceted character of the experience. For some readers' taste, Ransom overdoes his indulgence in baroque diction: the poem comes out all knobby and twisty with irrepressible reaching for the strange, antique and quaint. This is, however, all background for solid, harmonic tones. For me it is a style perilous and beautiful, orbiting nice.

Wit is essential for tragedy, and most tragic figures are sharp-tongued and quick of mind. If a person is too quickly and easily engulfed by emotion, his suffering is merely pathetic. Those who bite back effusive responses and slice through waves of sentiment impress us with their stature and define human problems of heroic dimensions. The same can be said for lyric poets. Their song is more moving if we know they can smile.

counterstatement

> Dare we for Gabriel have scorn,
> So wasted in his noble war
> Against the Universe? Forlorn,
> He does his very life abhor!

There are several reasons why this is not so good as the first stanza of "Miniver Cheevy," which, remember, goes:

> Miniver Cheevy, child of scorn,
> Grew lean while he assailed the seasons;
> He wept that he was ever born,
> And he had reasons.

But the chief reason, I believe, is that the ditty I composed goes all one way; it is poetry of statement. True, there are poetic and stylistic embellishments; it uses the resources of language and rhythm in a way that mathematical formulae do not. But these — rhythm, dignified inversions, rhetorical stance, alliteration, resonant rhyme, elevated diction — all *support* what the poem is saying. We may grin *at* the verse, but we are hardly inclined to grin with it. You are apt to think you are superior to the poet, that you see more, are more critical of posturing and false emotion, of cliché and merely decorative elaboration. Once a reader so begins to measure a poet's mind, the poet has lost him. He has lost control of tone.

E. A. Robinson is stating exactly the same thing about Miniver as I am saying about Gabriel, but all the while he is sending us signals behind Miniver's back; we stay on his side, against his unsuspecting subject. Here, of course, his purpose is satirical; but in other poems we are aware of similar signals, directly from the poet to the reader, which qualify, modify, ridicule, expand the meaning of, undercut, or plainly deny the literal statment of the poem. The poem says one thing, but we are simultaneously aware that the poet is saying another. A comprehensive term for this phenomenon of communication apart from direct statement is *counterstatement*.

Often when I am reading unsuccessful poetry (of which I read a good deal), my reaction is a kind of helpless sigh which means, "This poet is merely *saying* it." I sense the lack of counterstatement. The poet is simply telling me something — and I may be interested, I may be bored, I may agree or disagree, but nothing is happening on the page, nothing is happening to me. Poetry can survive moments of statement, but not whole stanzas, hardly whole lines. The term "poetry of statement" has been used to describe the work of poets such as Dryden, even Tennyson, but this is merely a mark of insensitivity on the part of the reader who fails to see more than one thing going on at a time. There is nothing wrong with statement, but unless there is simultaneously a counterstatement, the poem falls flat.

Flat, in fact, is a good word for it. The function of counterstatement is to establish dimensions. A world of two-dimensions would be a diagram, a picture. A work of art has to take its place in a real world, of more than two dimensions, a poem must have more than two dimensions to exist as art. Another way of putting that is to say a poem must get up off the page. A poem is a dramatic statement, which is to say it is deliberately composed for performance. It is an event, but unlike an event in nature, we know it was created; our experience must include a sense of the creator's intention.

If you overhear a heated quarrel, say, in a restaurant, you may be interested, embarrassed, amused; you may regard the event as dramatic in the sense that it is exciting, astonishing, moving, but you know it is not drama. In a theater you might see the same restaurant on-stage, with two people arguing, saying the same lines quarreling people might use in a restaurant off-stage. This *is* drama, though, because the event on stage, you realize, is deliberately arranged for you; you try to understand what the people are saying, what the event means to them, but a large part of your mind goes to seeking other meanings in the lines, for you are seeking the intention of the playwright: why did he select this event for me to see? why did he make them say these things? what does he mean? what is he saying to me? It is this dimension that distinguishes art from nature.

But one of the unwritten rules of drama is that the author cannot stop the action and tell you what he means. When he attempts to — as when a character moves to the front of the stage and comments on the action — you interpret *that,* too. You recognize that this deliberate violation of the dramatic illusion is part of the art, and you still do not have the kind of direct communication you would have if, for instance, the author jumped up from his seat in the audience and gave you an unpremeditated analysis. Coming back to the poem, now, this rule means that the poem must *seem* to be all statement, to be unselfconsciously performing, as an actor reciting his lines. The poet may, though, plant significant words in those lines, manage the rhythm in a particular way, arrange rhymes, manipulate syntax, so that the poem will imply things it appears not to mean to say. Unless that happens, unless there are two distinct lines of communication (true, sometimes coinciding) which I would call statement and counterstatement, the work remains flat, neutrally natural, remains on the page.

Perhaps the simplest illustration of counterstatement is connotation. As you know, a word points to, denotes, an X, which we call its literal meaning. But it has an emotional, suggested meaning as well, or several such meanings, which are called connotations. Girl, dame, wench, dish, doll, honey, all might be used to denote the same featherless biped; but, in most contexts, denotation is less important than attitude, implied emotional stance or tone. One might say Miniver Cheevy's life was a disaster because he could not reconcile himself to reality, or that it was a flop because he lived in a dream-world. Only in a very narrow sense do the statements mean the same thing. Words do not, of course, have fixed and agreed-upon connotations. *Please* appears to have pleasing connotations, but a mother calling her child for the sixth time to *please* come to dinner can make the word downright frightening. Here, tone of voice creates counterstatement.

All this is fairly obvious, but I would like to discuss how some of the more technical elements of poetry also contribute to counterstatement. Images, for example, are the poet's commonest means for saying something other than what he is saying. Emily Dickinson's "Go not too near a house of rose" surprises us as the terms of the image tug against one another. A house is one sort of thing, a rose another, and the discord resulting from thinking of one in terms of the other is what brings the line to life. When Miniver assails the seasons we are asked to see a man attacking an abstraction in the manner a soldier might attack a fortification; we imagine Miniver drawing his sword on the weather. A refusal to accept the immutable conditions of our life may be valiant, even tragic; but the image, with its alliteration, its whistling vapidity, reduces the action to the ridiculous. Similarly, weeping occurs in serious contexts — but after *child* has occurred in the stanza, followed by an image of absurd futility, *wept* gives an image of immature blubbering, and the excessive word *ever* in the line pushes it over from sentiment to bathos. This line, the third, is a cliché — as is the fourth; but a cliché used knowingly with a wink at the reader is able to carry weight as counterstatement. The clichés in my version of the stanza are hideous because they seem to be used straight-forwardly; speaking nonsense is no offense, only speaking nonsense and meaning it is.

I had to change the name; Miniver is bad enough (i.e., satirical enough), but Cheevy, with its *v* alliteration, makes what might be quaint inevitably silly. (Compare with the very different emotional attitudes Robinson wants to form with Richard Cory.) The alliteration of *ch* in the second half-line is amusing, too. The half-lines, witty, ingenious, balanced, lighten our response, for wit comes from the quicker, more critical aspects of intelligence, as opposed to our capacity for profundity, deep emotion, gravity. Moreover, the first half-line has a falling rhythm. The line is, of course, normal iambic tetrameter with a reversed, or trochaic, first foot: /u u/ u/ u/ — but the caesura alters it, so that it actually reads /uu /u - /u/. Little syllables, short, tight, close-mouthed little vowels, all lighten. Compare the relative speed of *Miniver* with my metrically parallel *Dare we for*.

Falling rhythms, and, particularly, feminine endings invariably give concluding cadences a little fillip, robbing them of some of their dignity. I changed all feminine endings to masculine, full syllables. That fillip does not always have comic effect. Robinson (like Housman, De la Mare, Hardy and others) was particularly clever in using feminine rhymes for ironic twists in which the flavor of melody or lightness was deliberately contrasted with grave statement (simply another variety of counterstatement), achieving a bittersweet bite thereby.

"Miniver Cheevy" owes much of its complex tonal effect (which I will come to in a moment) to this use of feminine rhyme. First, though, notice the two-foot fourth line, "And he had reasons." This surprise, the failure to fulfill expectation, has possibilities of amusement and of shock. A poet may break off in mid-line in excess of

emotion or with the abruptness of wit; the mouth shuts and the
eyebrows rise. Certainly it is mockery that dominates in the first
stanza. We hear that he had reasons, then, in a doubletake, reflect
that perhaps his reasons were ridiculous; or the poet himself might
have reasons, different reasons, for wishing that Miniver had never
been born. Regularly, Robinson uses that short line to provide an
imbalance, to trip us, to pause for two beats while the implications
sink in. Notice the contrast (sixth stanza) between the flowing richness of "the medieval grace" and the short countermotion of "Of iron
clothing," the final line.

Statement, then, establishes a man who yearns for the past and
is miserable in the present. Counterstatement establishes our attitude
toward that man, ridicule. The poem says what Miniver is; the poet,
by counterstatement, laughs at him for being so. The next-to-last
stanza brings this development to a climax:

> Miniver scorned the gold he sought,
>   But sore annoyed was he without it;
> Miniver thought, and thought, and thought
>   And thought about it.

In addition to everything else, we find that Miniver is a hypocrite,
but so ineffective that he hasn't even the ability to bring his hypocrisy
into action. The comic devices — repetition of his name, archaic
diction, two-word feminine rhymes, and, of course, the piled up
thoughts — all heap on ridicule.

But aren't we beginning to get weary of the poet's detestation of
Miniver? Okay, I react at the fourth *thought* — do you prefer that he
go out and grab gold like the rest of us? I find myself looking for
arguments in Miniver's defense. Well, he scorns gold, likes Romance
and Art, detests the commonplace; at least he isn't as Philistine as the
other inhabitants of Tilbury Town, the imaginary setting of Robinson's collection of poems. I put up with Hamlet's endless thinking
and incapacity for action; in fact, I find it admirable. I am, in short,
beginning to react against the poet's flashed signals; I want to make
up my own mind.

Ah, but Robinson knows how to exploit that very reaction and
turn it to the uses of counterstatement, now to counter his own
counterstatement. The last stanza begins, as did the first, with the
whole name, two half-lines; reminded of that first stanza we experience a kind of sigh, summing up, looking back — well, what about
this figure of fun?

Miniver Cheevy, born too late,
  Scratched his head and kept on thinking;
Miniver coughed, and called it fate,
  And kept on drinking.

Surely the idea has occurred to us by now that if Miniver doesn't fit
into the world it might be partly the world's fault, or, at least, the
world's loss. No one would make Miniver a hero; he is a pathetic
little fellow, but it is the pathos which is new to this stanza. Except
for "Grew lean" in the first stanza, we have not seen him as a
physical being. Here, though, he is scratching his head, coughing,
drinking; heretofore his action has been purely mental, even his
dancing, his assailing, his sighing, dreaming, mourning, loving, curs-
ing. Now he *does* something: scratches, coughs and drinks. Not
much, but enough to make us aware of flesh and blood and suffering.
We may detest Miniver, as Robinson has directed us to do; but the
poet has also moved us to some compassion, taking advantage even
of our rejection of satire as insufficient to deal with the man; we have
found some values in his archaic life and have learned to pity the
creature wasting with his alcoholic hack. Here the final rhyme has
something of that bittersweet effect I was discussing; and the chopped-
off final line moves from humor to something nearer resignation.

"Miniver Cheevy" is a rather simple poem. By insisting on a
third dimension I am not asking for complexity, except in the way
any round, whole object is complex by virtue of its innate ability to
stand up and occupy space. Two artistic principles are involved. For
the poem to stand alone, the poet must cut himself off from it, which
means establishing a separate, larger point of view (within which the
work of art is comprehended); and he must establish that the poem is
design, that is, designed, planned, executed with intention, which
means alerting the reader to that point of view, external to the object
itself.

More practically, you, the poet, have a great number of resources
at your command as soon as you begin putting words on paper.
Unless you use them, they use themselves, possibly to defeat what
you are trying to do. I go again to a dramatic analogy. A director
has his expanse of space to employ. If he ignores the empty reaches,
they speak for themselves and belittle the scene he is bringing to
performance. A poem *has* rhythm, whether you control it or not.
Words *have* connotations, and patterns have implications. Use of
such resources, the possibilities language has for meaning beyond
statement, is the specific area in which you operate as a poet. Lan-

guage, perforce, *says;* but it approaches poetry as it employs more and more of these powers of counterstatement. This is not a device, not decoration; it is the specific element which converts a piece of writing into a piece of art.

CHAPTER TWELVE

Statement

the pain of amputation

A test of my contention that poetry must mean something more than it says is to examine recognized poetry that veers very near to pure statement, even to propaganda. Like other intellectuals, poets, of course, have opinions and beliefs and naturally use the poetic medium to convey these. There is a fashionable distinction, which takes a number of forms, between poetry and writing which attempts to speculate, inform or persuade. An ironic crux in regard to this distinction occurred when a distinguished panel of poet-judges awarded the Bollingen Prize in 1949 to Ezra Pound for his *Pisan Cantos,* making it explicit they were honoring the "poetry" and ignoring the Fascist content. It was an incidental insult to Pound, who quite deliberately and intently wrote for political persuasion. It was as though a drowning man were screaming for help and a music critic complimented him on his voice. One cannot legitimately separate form and content in evaluating (and understanding) poetry. But it is true that a poet's obsession with his message may cause his art to be ineffective. And his concern with getting his message across may, after all, be hopeless, for it is a good question whether poetry makes things happen in the world.

The question is, how much counterstatement (as defined and illustrated in the last chapter) persists through the statement of poetic essays or diatribes. Robinson Jeffers is an example of a poet whose commitment to art was inextricable from his commitment to ideas and attitudes and causes. He often used poetry to persuade. And it is instructive that Jeffers, who died in 1962, had achieved much earlier than that date the essential oblivion he had sought with all his fitful flame of life.

Literary taste has confirmed that he did not belong in the ranks

of Pound, Eliot, cummings, Stevens and Frost. Incorrigibly he refused to adapt himself to acceptable fashions (as Frost refused). He
insisted on his message of inhumanism — and the message was as
unpalatable as his style. His rejection of Mandarin aestheticism was
quite explicit:

> It seemed to me that Mallarmé and his followers, re-
> nouncing intelligibility in order to concentrate the music
> of poetry, had turned off the road into a narrowing lane.
> Their successors could only make further renunciations;
> ideas had gone, now meter had gone, imagery would have
> to go; then, recognizable emotions would have to go;
> perhaps at last even words might have to go or give up
> their meaning and nothing be left but musical syllables.
> Every advance required the elimination of some aspect
> of reality, and what could it profit me to know the direc-
> tion of modern poetry if I did not like the direction? It
> was too much like putting out your eyes to cultivate the
> sense of hearing, or cutting off the right hand to develop
> the left. These austerities were not for me; originality by
> amputation was too painful for me.

And critics typically have treated him with condescension or have
ignored him altogether (e.g., he does not appear even in the index of
Roy Harvey Pearce's fat book, *The Continuity of American Poetry).*
Babette Deutsch, in *Poetry in Our Time,* says:

> In his effort to retrieve vigor and substance for poetry,
> Jeffers has sought, as he confessed, "to attempt the ex-
> pression of philosophic and scientific ideas in verse."
> Unhappily his work bears witness to the truth of Mal-
> larme's observation that poems are made of words, for
> his tend to be overwhelmed by ideas.

I have been asking myself, "What were we overlooking? What
did we fail to hear?" I remember my excitement as a college student
first reading "Roan Stallion," hearing the majestic cynicism of "Shine,
Perishing Republic," the noble, restrained passion of "Hurt Hawks."
I will examine one of his typical lyrics, published in 1937, to see
whether counterstatement emerges from the statement. "The Purse-
Seine" begins this way:

> Our sardine fishermen work at night in the dark of the
>   moon; daylight or moonlight
> They could not tell where to spread the net, unable to
>   see the phosphorescence of the shoals of fish.

I suppose one can say that information dominates aesthetic effect here: one learns something about sardine fishing. *Phosphorescence* stands out as a scientifically exact word; elsewhere Jeffers used words such as "the slow oxidation of carbohydrates and amino-acids" unblushingly, so intent was he on saying what he meant rather than sacrificing intelligibility to some theory of poetry. The language remains matter-of-fact, very direct, until there is need of imagery to convey the mysterious sense of a gleaming shoal:

> They work northward from Monterey, coasting Santa
> Cruz; off New Year's Point or off Pigeon Point
> The look-out man will see some lakes of milk-color light
> on the sea's night-purple; he points, and the helmsman
> Turns the dark prow, the motorboat circles the gleaming
> shoal and drifts out her seine-net. They close the circle
> And purse the bottom of the net, then with great labor
> haul it in.

The ten stress lines flow nearly to prose; the words are ordinary until they assume a dim luminescence as the fish appear. He continues:

> I cannot tell you
> How beautiful the scene is, and a little terrible, then,

And I can imagine a thousand English composition teachers circling "beautiful" and "terrible," writing in the margin "Show, don't tell." Robert Frost once said each poet should have a card which would be punched each time he used the word *beautiful* in a poem, allowing him only ten punches in a life-time. Frost claimed his own card would still be intact. Again and again we tell writers that if they want us to have the sense of beauty and terror they must create these feelings, not merely name them. But *beautiful* is one of Jeffers' favorite words, occurring in poem after poem with an almost holy significance — almost always, as here, linked to terror. His tolerance of life's agony, meanness and futility is rooted in his awe for the beauty of the universe and its frightening necessity; it is his love and fear of God.

In terms of the cadence of the poem, that line about beauty and terror provides a hushed pause between the prosaic exposition of the first verse paragraph and the wild panic of the description to come:

> when the crowded fish
> Know they are caught, and wildly beat from one wall to the
> other of their closing destiny the phosphorescent

Water to a pool of flame, each beautiful slender body
    sheeted with flame, like a live rocket
A comet's tail wake of clear yellow flame; while outside
    the narrowing
Floats and cordage of the net great sea-lions come up to
    watch, sighing in the dark; the vast walls of night
Stand erect to the stars.

I suppose the confusion of the scene itself justifies some blurring of
grammar and imagery, but I find the sentence shape here, as I often
do in Jeffers' poetry, unnecessarily awkward. The fish "beat . . . the
phosphorescent/ Water to a pool of flame," but look at the phrases
I have dropped out and how they interrupt the flow. One could make
a case that the sentence structure reflects the panic of the fish as they
become aware of the closing walls of net, but the explanation seems
strained. Does the word *destiny* seem inflated? Perhaps, but I can
understand why Jeffers wanted to push our minds away from the
literal scene to prepare us for the latter part of the poem, which, as
we will see, contemplates nothing less than the fate of our civilization.

I find blurring again in "a live rocket/ A comet's tail wake." In
the first place it seems rather grandiose to think of an individual
sardine as either a rocket or a comet; moreover, the two terms fight
each other — the rocket image is too much like the comet image,
and I cannot see the significance in the use of both. Notice the same
kind of blurring in "tail wake." Which does he want us to think of:
the tail or the wake? the tail as a wake? *Flame* is used three times
in succession — for the pool, for the sheets of light around each fish,
and for the tail or the wake. Is this failure of invention on the poet's
part, or an artistic means for creating the seething, glowing mass?

Contrast that blurred passage with the clear lines preceding and
following: the precise and fearful image of "narrowing/ Floats and
cordage of the net"; the way we hear that steamy, ambiguous sigh of
the sea-lions, thinking for a moment that perhaps it is compassion for
the trapped sardines, then, no, that it is regret that they must miss
all that captured dinner, then realizing the simple accuracy of the
word *sighing* to describe the noise of great hungry animals breathing,
without a trace of human emotions of compassion or regret. That
thought leads us to the "vast walls of night" and the magnificently
impassive universe, indifferent to the plight of the seined sardines.

Then the poem swings massively from the scene on the black sea
to Jeffers' real intent:

Lately I was looking from a
night mountain-top
On a wide city, the colored splendor, galaxies of light:
how could I help but recall the seine-net
Gathering the luminous fish? I cannot tell you how beautiful the city appeared, and a little terrible.
I thought, We have geared the machines and locked all
together into interdependence; we have built the
great cities; now
There is no escape. We have gathered vast populations
incapable of free survival, insulated
From the strong earth, each person in himself helpless,
on all dependent. The circle is closed, and the net
Is being hauled in. They hardly feel the cords drawing,
yet they shine already. The inevitable mass-disasters
Will not come in our time nor in our children's, but we
and our children
Must watch the net draw narrower, government take all
powers — or revolution, and the new government
Take more than all, add to kept bodies kept souls — or
anarchy, the mass-disasters.
These things are Progress;
Do you marvel our verse is troubled or frowning, while
it keeps its reason? Or it lets go, lets the mood flow
In the manner of the recent young men into mere hysteria,
splintered gleams, crackled laughter. But they
are quite wrong.
There is no reason for amazement: surely one always
knew that cultures decay, and life's end is death.

Here, of course, is what Babette Deutsch complained of. Abstractions such as *interdependence, populations, survival, inevitable mass-
disasters, government, Progress, anarchy* require us to think and not
to feel. Such language is associated with essays, editorials, speeches.
Where is the dimension of counterstatement? The statement, or idea
of the poem, should inhere in the material; when the art is working
well, the statement need not be explicit at all.

Or so I have argued. I can imagine myself asking Jeffers to end
his poem with "the luminous fish." Let the silence at the end of the
poem be full of the unstated significance of the analogy the poem
has drawn between the trapped sardines and the galactic city. The
rest, I would say, is merely a lecture. You must have confidence in

your poem to contain its meaning, not run along after with an explanation.

And, as Horatio says, I do in part believe it. And yet I must confess that the real impact of the poem came for me in this second half, particularly in the passage from "We have gathered . . ." to "the net/ Is being hauled in." Part of my reaction, frankly, is what I take to be the uncanny accuracy of the prophecy. In 1937 the urban problem was far from the brink of catastrophe, but now that is exactly where we are — and the three equally unwelcome alternatives Jeffers specifies (dehumanizing governmental regulation, or a revolution resulting in an even more tyrannous regime, or anarchy and mass-disasters) seem a remarkably comprehensive list of the possibilities. I have seen the panic and the seething, radiant churning, the slender, beautiful bodies grown electric in final terror.

Why not put the idea into an essay? One might answer: because he chose not to, and what difference does it make? With the burden of this message, how much patience should we have with questions of whether the writing is art, whether it is a poem? But I believe one can as easily answer that the elements of poetic form strengthen the impact of the statement — those suspended enjambments followed by grim completions ("now/ There is no escape"), the surging rhythms, the adroit weaving of the sardine imagery into the abstractions, the majectic movement of the lines.

In a larger sense I believe we can justify calling this composition a poem rather than a mere exposition of ideas because it is a structure of tensions. Poems, like geodesic domes, maintain their shape and stasis by a complex of forces pulling against one another. Here the key terms are "beautiful" and "terrible." The imagery of night fishing is essentially beautiful, the terror creeping in only as we identify with the sardines. The second part of the poem pulls against the first — both in its abstract language, its discursiveness, and in its insistence upon pushing terror to the full. Another kind of tension is that between the external phenomena — sardines or people (whom the poet calls *they)* — and the poet. If the poem were merely a discussion of fish and civilization, with the poet standing pristinely apart, it would, indeed, be merely a lecture. But the poet is first awed by the beauty and terror, and, finally, implicated in it. There is an astonishing shift of tone in the last verse paragraph: an archness, simplicity, and a struggle against panic, a tension between "reason" and letting go. There is a confession of the poem's own oppressive grimnesss and its occasional blurring into hysteria. At the very end the poet attempts to extricate himself from the "recent young men" who are "quite wrong," and the last line is overly haughty as well as bathetic and trite. If it is saved at all, as poetry, that is because we recognize how desperately the poet needs to remind *himself*, indeed lecture himself to find some stable point of reference in the midst of exploding chaos and the limits closing in.

I said before that the beauty and terror were Jeffers' love and fear of God. This poem is, like much of Jeffers' work, ultimately, strangely religious. The only way an individual can transcend his capture in the inevitably tragic human condition is by identifying himself in some way with the overarching System which causes it, as the sardine might calm his despair if he could identify with the fishermen. As Jeffers uses "end" in the last line he means not only conclusion but purpose. He is attempting to summon from himself — not completely successfully — a sense of worship of the inescapable power of nature's necessity. As the sardines are individually weakened and doomed by the very interdependency which enables them to survive, so are all the processes and systems within nature sustained and defeated by their limits, all contained within and governed by the unfathomable needs of nature itself. Resignation of self to that all-powerful and grandly neutral reality is a supremely religious quest — emphasized more strongly in Eastern than in Western religions, but present in all.

The drama of the poem, then, is in the poet's struggle to reconcile himself to that necessity which, he sees, will destroy him. The calm, objective, prosaic beginning holds necessity off at arm's length. In the second verse paragraph the poet begins to admit his involvement, and emotion begins to swirl. In the third he retires to a mountain-top and is again able to maintain some serenity as he dwells on the appalling destiny of other men. But when he speaks of "our time" and "our children's" we feel the encroachment of reality on the poet himself, and the last verse paragraph is a struggle to fight off — by sarcasm, hauteur, self-conscious composure — the "mere hysteria, splintered gleams, crackled laughter" which wrack the individual who cannot transcend his own identity.

I cannot claim the poem completely satisfies me. Like Babette Deutsch, I have been educated in an aesthetic which Jeffers consciously rejected, and it is difficult for me to accept his poem on his own terms. Often the writing seems lazy, repetitive, emptily rhetorical or pompous. But though Jeffers' seriousness is somewhat deadly, it is also urgent; like the Ancient Mariner, he grips me and makes me unwillingly listen. What I take to be aesthetic faults in his work are almost always direct consequences of that urgency. His style implies, "I will say this as well as I can, but please don't dwell on the how at the expense of the what; it is *what* I am saying which matters." That attitude may not suit the sensibilities of literary critics, but it may be, after all, the most humane approach to the use of language one can take.

how to stop a war

Carl Rogers once said that everyone likes to learn, but nobody likes to be taught. A good poet, like a good teacher, has to be sensitive to this normal aversion to didacticism. In another sense all good poetry teaches or preaches: it embodies values, and in doing so necessarily implies something about how people should live their lives. But the key word in that last sentence is *embodies.* It is the body that makes the poem: the substance of experience, the facts of life, the images, the drama. A good poem does not preach values so much as it demonstrates them. If a poem is well-written the "moral" or meaning can remain unstated as pure counterstatement — a ghostly presence in the poem like spirit in the body, unseen but dominating.

　　Here is a poem by e. e. cummings which dangerously skirts preachiness:

> plato told
>
> him:he couldn't
> believe it(jesus
>
> told him; he
> wouldn't believe
> it)lao
>
> tsze
> certainly told
> him,and general
> (yes

mam)
sherman;
and even
(believe it
or

not)you
told him:i told
him;we told him
(he didn't believe it,no

sir)it took
a nipponized bit of
the old sixth

avenue
el;in the top of his head:to tell

him

The "lesson" is never stated, yet it is felt powerfully throughout the poem. Exactly *what* wisdom of the ages was taught by Plato, Jesus, Lao Tsze, General Sherman, you and I is never made explicit. From the reference to Sherman we may gather that the unstated moral is that war is hell, since that is the only piece of wisdom widely associated with that general. Some readers may not know that scrap iron from the junked elevated tracks in New York was sold to the Japanese shortly before World War II, but that might easily be deduced from the poem. The message comes through like shrapnel to the skull: war is a bad thing.

I say the poem "dangerously skirts" preachiness, but some readers may feel it doesn't skirt it successfully, so apparent is the moral. The poem is almost devoid of imagery. (We are not even given that "nipponized bit" of iron vividly enough to see or experience it.) The poem is compounded of allusions and abstractions. If it works as a poem (I think it does), this is largely because of the dramatic presentation, the hesitations of the stanza breaks, the accelerating pace as statements are run into one another, the inevitable, enclosing, grim, understated note of conclusion. It is a good poem to read aloud, so carefully has cummings worked out the notation for performance. And even though the "him" of the poem is not really characterized, he assumes a certain common humanity. We can identify with the hard-headed clunk. He is like all of us, who continue in one way or another, to let wars go on. We can pity him.

Compare that with an anti-war poem I read in manuscript:

WHY DO WE DO IT?

Our mothers, when we were but kids,
  Kept saying not to fight,
But like the tough guys on the block,
  We did — and thought it right.

The Bible said to turn our cheek,
  Our teachers said, "Be kind,"
But when our pride or feelings hurt,
  That teaching left our mind.

And now our government calls up
  Our youth and sends them out
To other people's homelands, saying
  To fight another bout.

Our honor is at stake, you know.
  Our rights must be defended.
Is it any wonder, then,
  That war has never ended?

I doubt that many readers find this poem as moving as that of cummings, though it says substantially the same thing. As I look over the poem for reasons why it is ineffective, I might point out a few awkward spots in the meter. I find the rhyming mechanical, the language commonplace. But I also know of very good poems with mechanical rhymes and commonplace language. There is no way I could tell this poet to revise his work to make it better except to tell him to start again, not with this poem, but with his basic conception of poetry.

When I read "Why Do We Do It?" I do not hear the voice of a person. The poet talks about what "we" heard and did and thought, and I am not sure that I want to be included in that "we." As it happens, that alternating tetrameter-trimeter quatrain, rhymed abcb, is a standard hymn as well as ballad stanza, and I am inescapably reminded of church and the moralism of elders. I find the language, like the form, trite: I find it hard to believe that the poet deeply thought or cared about his subject. He seems willing to go along with conventional attitudes and practices in his poetry, so I am not really surprised by his apparent willingness to go along with a war he thinks is wrong. I don't think he sees war as tragic or ghastly: he sees it merely as naughty — something mothers and the Bible and teachers disapprove of. In fact, there is almost a joking, cynical quality about the last stanza which I find offensive, in view of the seriousness of the question it raises. Like the excuse for bad behavior, "Boys will be boys," the poem seems to shrug and accept the fact that men will be men, governments will be governments.

In other words, even as argument the poem is unconvincing to me; and I believe that is a reflection of a conception of poetry which is similarly weak. A poem has to earn the right to its generalizations, in my view. How does it do that? Basically by making something happen on the page, creating an experience, rather than summarizing abstractly what the experience means. For example, the experiences referred to in the poem are probably real. He probably did fight as a child, along with the tough boys on the block — against his mother's teaching. What went on in his head? What were his emotions? How did he feel about his mother and her teaching? How did he feel about the Bible? Where did he encounter the Bible? What associations did he have with the Bible? What tug-of-war went on between the realm of "teaching," from the Bible, his mother and others, and the realm of the street and the playground? How were his models of manhood formed? Which boys did he admire? Which did he fear? Was it to prove himself that he fought? To protect himself? To show off? Was there some strong, intuitively pugnacious drive in him, or was his fighting really another variety of conformity — going along with the crowd? And how does he feel about "government"? How does he experience it? Has he himself been drafted to fight? Does he have friends who have gone to war? How does he feel about the "other people's homelands"? Has he seen them? Can he imagine them? Has he truly grieved for the dead? Has he weighed this cost against "rights" which must be "defended"? Are rights really threatened by the people with whom we are at war?

I wouldn't, of course, expect the poem to answer all those questions, but they suggest ways of getting into the experience of the poem, of stirring up authentic and moving images, of understanding the complexity of the issues. If his experience and thought were more profound, the poem would be better, even if it used no more than an image or two from the churning complex.

In asking for "seriousness," I am not asking for excessive gravity or dramatic effusion. The poem by cummings is almost light in tone, witty, and its power arises from its understatement. But even good comic verse takes life, issues, and experience seriously enough to arrive at profound insights, however flippantly they may be expressed. Nor is that ballad stanza form beyond redemption: Emily Dickinson used it regularly in poems which breathe across a century with continual freshness, and poets such as Housman and Robinson and Auden have used it with great power. But the poem is all talk. It tells instead of showing.

I tried using the basic form and ideas of "Why Do We Do It?" to write a poem which follows the advice I have given here:

THE BURDEN

"Stay out of trouble," Mother said,
    by lamplight, darning socks.
In alley dusk my sweating palms
    searched for the right-sized rocks.

The lady in my Sunday School
    said, "Win by being meek."
Out on the street I never saw
    a man who turned his cheek.

I came of age. They stripped me down.
    I was not blind nor deaf,
but feared, in skinny nakedness,
    I would be classed 4F.

In olive drab, "So long!" I waved
    to Mother and my books,
and followed Dad, with bayonet,
    to civilize the gooks.

So far as I am concerned that is the end of the poem. But I am going to add one more stanza to demonstrate, I hope, how the poem would be weakened if I tacked on a "moral," as so many poets are tempted to do. What happens when the poem moves from experience to preachiness?

It will go on; we will not learn,
    so long as this is true:
boys hear what books and women say,
    do what they see men do.

I hope your nausea will have an effect on what you write in the future.

In the anti-war poetry of Denise Levertov we can see the struggle between statement and counterstatement vividly dramatized. During the Viet Nam war many poets felt that it was more important to influence the policies of the government and the attitudes of the public than to devote themselves to excellence in art. But what political impact can poetry have on specific issues? Shelley called poets "the unacknowledged legislators of the world," suggesting a powerful secret influence on history. On the other hand, Auden — something of an activist and propagandist himself — wrote in his elegy for W. B. Yeats:

> . . . mad Ireland hurt you into poetry.
> Now Ireland has her madness and her weather still,
> For poetry makes nothing happen: it survives
> In the valley of its saying where executives
> Would never want to tamper; it flows south
> From ranches of isolation and the busy griefs,
> Raw towns that we believe and die in; it survives,
> A way of happening, a mouth.

Personal suffering, expression, *isness* of poetry — Auden stressed these qualities partly because of the genteel tradition of modern aestheticism, partly because in praising Yeats he had to be very careful to separate himself from Yeats' political ideas. But even a river flowing placidly south from ranches of isolation of human spirit has its effect on the landscape. Were Yeats and Auden not, in some sense, legislators of our future?

Most would agree that beyond (and by means of) its personal expression, poetry exerts some broad, humanizing effect on culture. In some general way, for example, Dryden's masterpiece, "Absalom and Achitophel," is reputed to have had considerable political impact, mustering support for Charles II and taming the witch hunt hysteria of the so-called "Popish Plot." Hood's "Song of the Shirt" may have helped bring about women and children's labor laws in Victorian England. I cannot think offhand of another instance in which a poem has had specific social consequences attributed to it — such as novels have sometimes had (e.g., Upton Sinclair's *The Jungle,* which helped give rise to the Pure Food and Drug Act, or Herman Melville's *White Jacket,* which helped bring about the abolition of flogging as a punishment on naval vessels.)

Yet poets keep trying. Like other human beings, we are consumed by what we perceive to be the necessities of our times, and if these are compelling enough, we will use art — or even sacrifice art — in the service of other values. At some point of social crisis, business as usual becomes immoral. Many poets felt so strongly about our involvement in Viet Nam that it was no longer sufficient to praise life or to condemn war and brutality in general terms. At such times the question is always raised as to whether "art" becomes "propaganda." I respect the motivation which causes a poet to become indifferent to that question: the poet says, in effect, I don't care what you call it — I write what I must. But I believe the question is a useful one, nonetheless, and that it can be resolved by recognizing that ultimately the best propaganda *is* the best art. Aesthetics, like engineering, can be a means of determining and shaping strong and enduring design. Denise Levertov, in "Life at War" *(The Sorrow Dance,* New Directions, 1967), illustrates beautifully some of the strengths — and some of the weaknesses — of poetry aimed to influence attitudes on specific issues.

The poem begins, "The disasters numb within us/ caught in the chest," describing, not for herself only, but for all of us, the very internal, private, lumpish feeling of anguish beyond bitterness. Suddenly, dramatically, the specific theme is introduced: "The same war"

> continues.
> We have breathed the grits of it in, all our lives,
> our lungs are pocked with it,
> the mucous membrane of our dreams
> coated with it, the imagination
> filmed over with the gray filth of it:

The "it" seems to refer to the war, but that colon projects us forward to another referent — our "knowledge":

> the knowledge that humankind,
>
> delicate Man, whose flesh
> responds to a caress, whose eyes
> are flowers that perceive the stars,
>
> whose music excels the music of birds,
> whose laughter matches the laughter of dogs,
> whose understanding manifests designs
> fairer than the spider's most intricate web,

That grand sentence, with its mounting rhetoric, is not complete yet, but I want to interrupt it a moment to bring attention to its parts. It begins in the mood Hamlet suffered, acedia, in which he found life "weary, stale, flat, and unprofitable." The sentence then rises to a kind of Renaissance awareness of man's capacity for good (like Hamlet's praise of man: "how infinite in faculty? in form and moving how express and admirable?"), then plummets to a vision of human corruption:

> still turns without surprise, with mere regret
> to the scheduled breaking open of breasts whose milk
> runs out over the entrails of still-alive babies,
> transformation of witnessing eyes to pulp-fragments,
> implosion of skinned penises into carcass-gulleys.

We are out of *Hamlet* and into *Guernica*. Notice the fine irony of the first line of that last quotation, the cool exactness of "scheduled," all preparing for the unleashing of the purple passage which concludes the sentence. Poetry has never done very well at providing horror footage. I was reminded of a passage from the seventeenth century dramatist, Thomas Otway, in *Venice Preserved:*

> . . . Save the poor, tender lives
> Of all those little infants which the swords
> Of murderers are whetting for this moment.
> Think thou already hear'st their dying screams,
> Think that thou seest their sad, distracted mothers
> Kneeling before thy feet, and begging pity,
> With torn, dishevelled hair and streaming eyes,
> Their naked, mangled breasts besmeared with blood,
> And even the milk with which their fondled babes
> Softly they hushed, dropping in anguish from 'em.

Wading in the carnage of modern warfare on civilian populations, one can hardly be expected to find adequate language to describe what he sees. In his effort to do so he is likely to stumble into the maudlin, the merely macabre, or the ludicrous (which is how I would describe that obscure image of imploded "skinned penises"). And yet Ms. Levertov would fail her theme if she did not attempt to face relentlessly the object of her repugnance.

"Life at War" goes on to contrast the idealism of our language (which "imagines *mercy,/ lovingkindness"),* our vision of man's sacred nature, with our capacity for callousness: "burned human flesh/ is smelling in Viet Nam as I write." Our knowledge of our dual nature clogs our throat like "husky phlegm" as we speak:

> nothing we do has the quickness, the sureness,
> the deep intelligence living at peace would have.

That conclusion puzzles me. Is "living at peace" possible for the human nature represented in the poem? Art generally strives to grasp what is enduringly true of human life — and the most powerful quality of this poem, for me, is its meditation upon the tragic paradox of human potential contrasted ("without surprise, with mere regret") with human actuality. After that knowledge, what forgiveness? Viet Nam seems a mere instance, a bloody patch in the corner of the mural. The vision is one which makes actual policy arrangements such as the tormented cease-fire — seem petty and irrelevant.

I do not mean that as criticism of the poem. Contemplating Ms. Levertov's effort to focus her great power on this issue, an effort with which I deeply sympathize, I am forced to wonder whether the activist impulse is not somehow doomed by poetry's glimpse of the eternal — as the lover is frozen on the Grecian Urn ("never, never canst thou kiss,/ Though winning near the goal.") I share her urge to create a poetry very near journalism, illustrated even more clearly by her long poem, "An Interim," in the November, 1968, issue of *Poetry*. Again the lyric strength of the poem is its exploration of how it feels to be a member of a warring nation:

> While the war drags on, always worse,
> the soul dwindles sometimes to an ant
> rapid upon a cracked surface;
>
> lightly, grimly, incessantly
> it skims the unfathomed clefts where despair
> seethes hot and black.

Seething despair may be a bit overdramatic for an ant's view of a cracked surface, but the interminable, pitiful race of nerve is a feeling most sensitive citizens can identify with, as they can with the mucuous film and lumpishness described in "Life at War."

Again she contrasts language's grand potential ("coral island/ accrued from human comprehensions") with its erosion in war — to the point that a military officer can say "It became necessary/ to destroy the town to save it." She and her husband had fled to Puerto Rico to "repossess" themselves, to regain contact with nature's elemental sanity and proportion — but the news intrudes:

> *Today is the 65th day since de Courcy Squire, war-resister,*
> *began her fast in jail. She is 18.*

Throughout the poem, prose rattles its teletype of the world's fact:
. . . arrested with 86 others Dec. 7. Her crime:
sitting down in front of a police wagon
momentarily preventing her friends from being
hauled to prison. Municipal Judge Heitzler
handed out 30-day suspended sentences to several others
accused of the same offense, but condemned
Miss Squire to 8 months in jail and fined her
$650. She had said in court 'I don't think there should be
roles like judge and defendant'.
The poet remembers peace — peace in childhood by the sea: "Peace
could be/ that grandeur, that dwelling/ in majestic presence, at-
tuned/ to the great pulse." But in Puerto Rico in the peace of the
rustling palms, "where the heat flickers its lizard tongue," the dream
intrudes, as do thoughts of de Courcy in prison. We learn from an
interpolated letter (apparently quite literal) that the "interim" of
the poem is that in which her husband Mitch is awaiting trial — and
that it will come as a kind of relief, "a satisfaction of the need to
confront the warmakers and, in the process, do something to wake
up the by-standers."

She resents the sympathy friends extend to them because it
is unaccompanied by outrage, and mocks her comforters in a jingle:

'The sympathy of mild good folk,
a kind of latex from their leaves;
our inconvenience draws it out.

The white of egg without the yolk,
it soothes their conscience and relieves
the irritations of their doubt.

She contrasts their sympathy with the conviction of "the great savage
saints of outrage" who incinerated themselves:
their bodies rush upon the air in flames,
sparks fly, fragments of charred rag
spin in the whirlwind, a vacuum
where there used to be this monk or that,
Norman Morrison, Alice Hertz.
She herself could never do that — and she remembers the less
violent means of protest of A. J. Muste, Dennis Riodon, Bob Gilliam
("Names on a list, whose faces I do not recall," as Eberhart wrote
of his fellow soldiers in World War II). Many are "alive and free
in the jails," having given language breath again by speaking the

truth of their conscience: "true testimony of love and resistance."
(Notice the pamphlet language, as though the poetess doffed her
poetry in her search for purity.) But the flaming martyrs are
necessary too: "Brands that flare to show us/ the dark we are in,/
to keep us moving in it."

Finally she returns to their need of this interim by the sea,
"the unwearying source — / but not to forget./ Not to forget
but to remember better." She closes with another quotation from
de Courcy Squire: *"I have a medical problem that can be cured/ only
by freedom."* The poem has been a survey of the varieties of spiritual
disease induced by the war — and the variety of responses of spirit
struggling to regain its health.

Is that the intent of the poem — or is it another effort "to wake
up the by-standers"? It seems very much like a letter to a friend —
one who is already awake — a pastiche of clippings, snapshots of
island life, and poignant reflections on personal and public events.
Like journalism, it is a record, albeit a rather private record, of how
it was to be alive and to care in 1968, to be ashamed of one's
country, grieved and enraged by the indifference of one's fellow
citizens, to be in melancholy search for a sense of what peace
was like, in search for authenticity of word and deed. Its power
is in its absolute credibility — and the documentation of quotations,
names, letters, news, helps establish that. I doubt that it awakened
anyone not already awake, or that it will mean much twenty years
from now, but it may have served the purpose a thoughtful
letter from a sensitive friend serves, to pull us together, to enable
us to check out on another's pulse how it is.

It is a valuable human document in that respect. I looked, for
comparison, to Yeats' "Easter 1916," which is similarly laced with
personal references and allusions to now-forgotten events and people.
I am moved by that poem to reflection, to fellow-feeling for the
poet; I am grateful to be able to glimpse his diary, to know out
of what sources his greater poetry emerged, to relish certain splendid
lines and passages which seem to rise above the fabric of report.
It survives "In the valley of its saying." But I don't believe that
poem — or others — made things happen.

I am afraid that poet-activists must always work under a pall
of despair, a sense that the tragic needs of the species invalidates all
their efforts at reform and change. Yeats found that in time of
revolution "A terrible beauty is born," and the spectre of a de
Courcy Squire, the hungry flame burning low in her cell, evokes

simultaneously our admiration, our love, and our despondency, for her very martyrdom was not only futile in stopping a warring nation but may itself have been one of those crimes against the self, against life, which seems to be so deeply rooted in our patterns of need — a terrible beauty, indeed. I recognize in myself that dual nature: one voice cries out that surely something can be done, that it is better to do anything than nothing; and another tells me that the most I can do is bear witness to our doom.

If the best propaganda is the best art, it may be that which accepts the limitations of immediate change, which recognizes that human nature may, indeed, be altered in the long view only by repeated testimony to the magnificence of human potential and repeated grief for our addiction to self-destruction. In some sense the poet should be as heartsick for the Peloponnesian War as for that in Viet Nam, for the endless madness of nations, the brief lustre of Pyrrhic victories. If propaganda, or art, becomes too immersed in the moment, too hopeful of instant salvation, too embittered by the day's defeat, it is liable to become sentimental or strident or banal or clichéd. Yeats sadly watched the woman he loved surrender her beauty and power to politics:

> That woman's days were spent
> In ignorant good-will,
> Her nights in argument
> Until her voice grew shrill.

However righteous her cause, the quality of her efforts was undermined by the short-view of passionate encounter. She became a windbag. And her example helped Yeats to pull back himself, to lace his statement with counterstatement, and to remain a poet.

the philosophical impulse

Political issues tempt one to a greater stridency than philosophical questions, but these, too, lure a poet into realms of abstraction and generalization in which lines of verse run the danger of becoming mere statement. Many poets are, in part, frustrated philosophers, and there is a long battle within them to suppress a tendency to launch from the concrete pad of immediate experience into the stratosphere of thought. Nothing kills a poem faster, in most cases, than giving in to this temptation. In other eras readers seem to have been willing to sit still for versified essays, but modern readers are highly resistant to didacticism (or teaching) in poetry — and you can be sure that modern editors will be swift to protect them from poets inclined to lecture.

Nonetheless, some of the finest moments in poetry are exactly what any teacher of writing will tell poets to avoid: generalizations, reflections. A great poem somehow earns the right to preach a little. Typically the philosophic or instructive passage comes as a kind of climax after a thorough grounding in immediate experience. Yeats became a master at getting his abstractions in, seducing the reader into his study with juicy gobbets of reality in order to lift him into subliminal reflection. For example, his "Among School Children" begins anecdotally: "I walk through the long schoolroom questioning." His casual, daily experience as a school inspector establishes the experiential base. From there he drifts off in the second stanza into memory — of an old woman who was once young as the children in the schoolroom — and that moves him into elegaic meditation upon aging, upon the heartrending discrepancy between the ideal and the actual, upon the hopes of the old that shape the heads of the young, upon the inevitable disappointment when the human embodiment of the mother's dream ages and falls short of perfection, as an infant brought painfully into the world becomes a scarecrow of an old man. We may be grateful that no helpful editor struck off the final stanza of the poem, which leaves school children, memories of old loves, and even thoughts on aging far behind to resolve abstractly the tension between the ideal and the actual:

> Labour is blossoming or dancing where
> The body is not bruised to pleasure soul,
> Nor beauty born out of its own despair,
> Nor blear-eyed wisdom out of midnight oil.
> O chestnut tree, great-rooted blossomer,
> Are you the leaf, the blossom or the bole?
> O body swayed to music, O brightening glance,
> How can we know the dancer from the dance?

Objections to didacticism are strongest when the teaching is moralistic. Yeats often ends his abstract passages with questions, as here, to take the edge off what might otherwise be a lecturing tone. Consider how different the stanza above would be if it ended: "We cannot know the dancer from the dance," or if, before, he had said:

The chestnut tree, great-rooted blossomer,
Combines the leaf, the blossom and the bole.

It is the mystery and paradox, the counterstatement, the poet wishes to draw our attention to, not a conclusion, though a strong conclusion is implied.

John Ciardi included in his first collection, *As If* (1955), an essay in verse which powerfully and successfully defied the fashion against didactic poetry. The very title, "Thoughts On Looking Into a Thicket," with that ominous, dreary word, *thoughts,* staring us in the face, is one most teachers of writing, including Ciardi, would probably advise a poet against. Worse yet — in terms of the fashion — the dramatic setting of the poem is not, after all, one of looking into a thicket. It is set in the library. The poet is apparently reading a naturalist's description of a creature the poet has not himself seen:

> . . . a spider, *phrynarachne d.,*
> to whom a million or a billion years
> in the humorless long gut of all the wood
> have taught the art of mimicking a bird turd.

There is a deliberate, almost arrogant, anti-poeticism in the use of the Latin name and the crude language. And if that is not sufficient to jar the reader out of his preconceptions about what is proper in poetry, Ciardi goes on to give us a whole stanza of raw prose, cut up into pentameter lines — a quotation right out of the book:

> "It is on a leaf," writes Crompton, "that she weaves
> an irregular round blotch, and, at the bottom,
> a separate blob in faithful imitation
> of the more liquid portion. She then squats
> herself in the center, and (being unevenly marked
> in black and white), supplies with her own body
> the missing last perfection, *i.e.,* the darker
> more solid central portion of the excreta."

This is an example of what, in the fifties and sixties, was often called "found" poetry. Whole anthologies appeared made up of prose quotations arranged in poetic lines — as one brings a piece of driftwood into the home and displays it on the coffee table as an art object.

Though the experiential base of the poem is academic, drawn from books, it is also exceedingly (perhaps to some readers even embarrassingly) concrete. A sojourn among such details invites a gasp of relief in generalization. It is as though the poet himself rolled his eyes up from the page to exclaim, as the next stanza soars away:

> Must I defend my prayers? I dream the world
> at ease in its long miracle. I ponder the egg,
> like a pin head in silk spit, invisibly stored
> with the billion years of its learning. Have angels
> more art than this? I read the rooty palm
> of God for the great scarred Life Line. If you
> will be more proper than real, that is your
> death. I think life will do anything for a living.

If any reader were squeamish about the hunting techniques of *phyrnarachne d.,* he is answered by the poet's reflection. How can we, how can the poet himself "be more proper than real" in the face of nature's testimony?

How does the poem overcome the reader's prejudice against the pure statement of abstract lecturing? Imagery helps: "like a pin head in silk spit," "the rooty palm of God." At times abstract language, imaginatively used, takes on the quality of imagery: "I dream the world/ at ease in its long miracle." One almost sees the poet dreaming the world, sees that world stretched out comfortably on the endless bed of miraculous life. But the final two sentences are frankly didactic, sustained by their pungency, their epigrammatic brevity, their breathtaking accuracy. Contrasted with the congested prose of Crompton, which is, indeed, academic and more proper than real, the poet's refreshing simplification and candor breathe life into language that word-by-word is undistinguished and general.

The poem swings between the abstract and concrete continually. The next stanza begins:

> And that hungers are all one. So Forbes reports
> that seeing a butterfly once poised . . .

and carries us on through scientific observation and detail, including the poet's own witnessing of a mantis "eating a grub while being himself eaten/ by a copper beetle." Then we swing back to generality:

> So I believe the world
>
> in its own act and accomplishment. I think
> what feeds is food.

A trick has been turned. In most poems we are attracted to the fleshy details of experience, and general statements seem dry and dull by comparison. But in this poem our noses are so firmly rubbed in the scientific particulars that we welcome the clear air of philosophy. Or of dream: the poet imagines a mosaic "for a Church of the First Passion" in which a chain of fish, each eating the next, crosses an ochre sea:

> Thus an emblem
> of our indivisible three natures in one:
> the food, the feeder, and the condition of being
> in the perpetual waver of the sea.

Though the image has a mordant quality, it is also one of celebration: "I believe the world to praise it." The fact of death is chained indivisibly to the miracle of life:

> if there is an inch or the underside of an inch
> for a life to grow on, a life will grow there;
>
> if there are kisses, flies will lay their eggs
> in the spent sleep of lovers; if there is time,
> it will be long enough. And through all time,
> the hand that strokes my darling slips to bone
> like peeling off a glove; my body eats me
> under the nose of God and Father and Mother.
> I speak from thickets and from nebulae:
> till their damnation feed them, all men starve.

That concluding stanza is the most consistently lyrical and imagistic in the poem. There are, in effect, three levels of language in the poem: factual detail, generality, and metaphorical imagery. The language of the first level is, of course, imagery also, in that it presents vivid sense data to the imagination. But imagery of the third level is metaphor — or near it. Flies may actually lay their eggs "in the spent sleep of lovers," but the statement is better understood metaphorically than literally, as a specific illustration of the earlier generalization that life will grow anywhere. Flesh does not literally peel from the hand like a glove as it strokes "my darling," but metaphorically this image illustrates the unbreakable link between fertility and death. My body metaphorically eats me under the metaphorical nose of God and Father and Mother. One might postulate three levels of reality in the poem: the facts of life, generalizations made on the basis of these, and imaginative embodiments of the generalizations in concrete images.

The last two lines move from the elegaic to the prophetic. There is a kind of pun on the word *from*. The poet speaks *on the basis of* observations of thickets and of nebulae. At the same time, he assumes the stance of the universe itself, speaking its all-encompassing revelation. "Damnation" is a theological word, of course, used here to refer not only to the physical fact of death but to our attitudes toward it — not only of defeat, but of shame. To celebrate life means to accept death, and to accept life's relentless and sometimes tawdry devices. We eat our own filth. We live on our own decay. And to live in a larger sense, not of mere survival, but of joy and liberation, requires not only acceptance of gross reality but celebration of it: "I believe the world to praise it."

The poem, in total only seven stanzas of eight lines each, condenses a great deal of biological information and meditation upon it, as well as lyrical expansion of its "thoughts." One of John Ciardi's greatest strengths is as a personal essayist. It would be a loss to civilization if he could not find a poetic medium for this vein of his personality and mind — in terse, brief, frankly didactic and abstract meditation on whatever strikes his fancy in personal experience, whether it be reading a book on insects or answering a rude hostess at a cocktail party. But he can and does so express himself in poetry, in spite of fashion.

Few can do it as well — which may account for the fashion. If any reader takes this as a license for moralizing or lecturing in verse, he had better take note of the high tension poetic talent which lifts this essay into poetic realms. Without, especially, the lyricism and metaphor of the final stanza, even the excellent abstractions and fascinating facts of the preceding stanzas would be lifeless.

I would not advise beginning poets to try it. I would still predict that a poem with a title such as "Thoughts on . . ." would be a disaster. Nor are many of us able to get away with incorporating long quotations from biology books in our verse — not because we haven't the reputation to carry our name past obstacles to editors' attention, but because we are incapable of floating such concrete in sustaining conceptions and poetic imagination. Above all, few of us have enough to say to engage readers with our "Thoughts," let alone the power to condense them into lines such as "life will do anything for a living."

CHAPTER THIRTEEN

Life and Art

experience and significance

One usually begins to write with an *idea,* a *feeling* or an *experience.* Of these three, the last is the most workable for a beginning poet.

An idea is likely to produce a poem which is too abstract, moralistic or vague. If you do try to write a poem expressing a general idea, you should emphasize very strongly the formal elements of the poem — especially meter and rhyme — in order that the statement not sink to flat prose.

For example, suppose that it is your idea that though wars may be undertaken for noble, morally justifiable ideals, in practice they become mere primitive slaughter in which a pretense to justice is a rationalization used to sanctify the satisfaction of bestial drives. I have just given a prose statement of the idea: the language is Latinate, stale; the rhythms are loose, casual; there is no imagery, no figurative language; above all, the statement has no pattern; my concern in writing it simply was to say clearly what I meant, so I did not attempt to *shape* the statement itself. If I were to turn it into verse, I would try to condense, sharpen, and provide some thrust of imagination plus some controlling pattern:

The sword of Justice tarnishes in use,
Crusader's cause becoming brute's excuse.

The most common urge to write a poem comes not from abstract ideas such as that, however, but from feeling: an amorphous emotional state which one is compelled to cope with by rendering it into imaginative language. Thus the poem itself is therapeutic; it fulfills the emotional need of the poet. If I feel uncontrollably gay or melancholy, it may seem a means of bringing myself back into some coherent relationship with the world to find verbal equivalents for my emotions; nor is it usually enough to write, simply, "I feel sad," or "I am happy," or "I am angry." At such times we yearn for precision to counteract the wild tempest of feeling — and since our words to describe emotions, even our clinical words such as *hostile* or *depressed* or *manic,* are at best vague, we are likely to seek greater exactness by comparing the inner state to something outside us. Thus the poetry originating in feeling will probably be *figurative.* Pattern, wit, humor, sharpness — the qualities one seeks in poetry of ideas — will probably be less important than color, tone, image.

For example, suppose that in a blue mood you recognize a certain pleasure in the exquisite torture of your feelings, but you yearn for an end — even a violent and painful end — of your intolerable melancholy. You might write:

> Oh, unknown cellist drawing
> ingenious variations in low tones
> from my hollow heart,
>
> have you a scimitar
> to bow my strings with a slow stroke
> and let them snap to silence?

Such unrelieved romanticism is out-of-favor these days, just as is the neoclassicism of the couplet on war. These stanzas seem too self-indulgently sentimental. Note that the suggestion of patterning (stanzas of three lines with three, four, and then three beats respectively, alliteration, the parallelism of "low tones" and "slow stroke," etc.) is suppressed, as compared to the emphatic rhyme and rhythm of the war couplet. The lines are mostly enjambed as opposed to the grammatically closed lines of the couplet. The aim is to suggest a swirl of feeling and disorder; one does not want to distract the reader from the imagery and the feeling with poetic devices which suggest cerebration, cleverness and control. Yet there must *be* subtle control, for the poem is, after all, subtly aiming to contain and define the mood.

Ideas and feelings themselves arise from *experience* — and both of these poems might be improved if they actually included the experience (real or imaginary) which gave rise to them. I will add a stanza to each to illustrate:

> Can I deny my own triumphant glee
> Popping a slant-eyed sniper from a tree?

> The sword of Justice tarnishes in use,
> Crusader's cause becoming brute's excuse.

and:

> I watch at the window where
> last week I saw those blonde braids
> transect the truck's path.

> Oh, unknown cellist drawing
> ingenious variations in low tones
> from my hollow heart,

> have you a scimitar
> to bow my strings with a slow stroke
> and let them snap to silence?

It seems to me that the poems gain force by being rooted in experience.

Of course, ideas and feelings *must* be rooted in experience (again — real or imagined), whether or not the poem reveals those roots. We might say that every poem has two parts — its experience and the significance of that experience. But either of these may be unexpressed. Looking back at the two little examples above, note that the first stanza of each could stand alone as a poem. In the first case we would be left to figure out for ourselves the general implications of the fact that a soldier may get a certain pleasure from killing. In the second example, made aware of tragic cause of feeling, we may be left to imagine just *how* the speaker feels. As I gave the poems originally, the reader was left to imagine what experience led to the general conclusion about war and what heartache led to the delectation and desire for an end to melancholy. It seems to me that if one of the two elements, experience or significance, is to be suppressed in the poem, it is better to suppress the significance. Readers would rather have significance understated than overstated: they dislike being preached at or being asked to wallow in subjectivity.

Thus the poet's first job is to isolate *an* experience from experience in general: to recognize a *unit* in life which has some implicit meaning or emotional impact. Such a unit might be as large and complex as the Fall of Man, which prompted *Paradise Lost,* or as slight and fleeting as the dropping of a lotus petal on a pond — the sort of experience which has prompted untold thousands of haikus. A poet may not — for various reasons — want to use his own, literal experience. Such reticence is the chief reason that many amateur poets attempt to give the abstract meaning or describe the emotional state without recounting the experience at all. Rather than leave it out (and thereby, in my judgment, weaken the poem), he might seek to find an equivalent, fictional experience. For example, he might write in another voice than his own: this is called using a *persona*.

Suppose you are a fellow who has been stringing a girl along with flattery and talk of love simply to exploit her sexually. When she is with you she makes a great point of talking about not wanting to be tied down, of making fun of girls who are desperately hunting for husbands. Then you find out, perhaps from girls who work with her at the office, that she has been telling some of her friends that the two of you are engaged. At first you are resentful, thinking that she is hypocritically trying to trap you. Then you realize — perhaps it comes at some specific moment, as when she is nervously rotating her coffee cup in the drugstore — that she *knows* she is being used, that she doesn't expect anything else but exploitation from you, but that she is so desperate for affection and esteem that she will pretend to believe you love her and pretend to her friends that you have committed yourself to her. Depressed by this recognition, you haven't the heart to exploit her further — and yet do not know whether it is kinder to her to go along with the game or to bring it to an end.

Out of that morass of experience it might be possible to draw a short story or a dozen poems. But where to take hold of it? And how to write about such intimate matters without being paralyzed by natural reserve? If you get too far from the experience itself, the poem (or story) may become too vague or subjective, yet if you try to represent it exactly as matters stand you will find yourself bogged down in circumstantial detail on the one hand and embarrassment on the other (coupled with decent respect for the girl's private feelings!)

First you might consider separating yourself from the story by adopting a *persona* — a friend of the girl, or an invented mother, or the girl herself. You badly need a symbol — some concrete act or thing — which will embody and provide a focus for much of the story's meaning. Let us suppose — for the sake of the poem — that the girl has purchased an engagement ring which she does not wear in your presence, but wears at home (let's leave the office out). Her motive is, at least in part, to make her behavior more comprehensible to her mother, who, let us say, is a foreigner — thus separated by language and custom from the mores of America.

In concocting an illustration for this purpose, I decided to use an easygoing iambic pentameter with plenty of variation (chiefly anapests) to maintain a conversational style. Free verse demands too much emotional intensity for the quiet, hard-thinking poem I wanted, and lines shorter than pentameter call attention to themselves, tend toward sing-song, especially if rhymed. I wanted occasional rhymes because the girl (I am using her as a *persona*) is thinking in a clear, bitter way which calls for a suggestion of control and neatly completed statements. I wrote this example in quatrains (four-line stanzas) and then re-divided it into five-line stanzas so that it would flow without quite so much emphasis upon the rhymed stops. (Besides, I am attracted by the way a four-line rhyme pattern revolves through the five-line stanza in a twenty-line poem — and that's the length it turned out to be.) Also, to offset the regularity of the pattern I "roughened up" the first draft, introducing more variation in meter and more abrupt stops, starts and enjambments:

DINNER DATE

Eyes catch. I saw you stare at the pink crease
on my left ring finger. I saw you wonder. Yes,
Lothario, I've been lying. Expert as
you are, you'll ferret out the truth, or guess.
Behind the practiced softness of your eyes

(like candlelight on silver) gleams your smile.
Those eyes (as does this phony gypsy's fiddle)
persuade me in a passionate, high style
that you are not amused as you imagine
that scene at the jeweler's — comic pantomime —

the ingénue whispering over the counter
as she buys herself a diamond ring on time.
Nor do you let me see you mock the Wop
old lady, who by this means was deceived,
who wept old country tears for her daughter's ways

until she saw the ring and was relieved.
But all your art cannot disguise your panic:
knowing our terms, now, can we play the same?
Do not deprive me of *your* lies, Lothario.
They say in time one learns to love this game.

To the degree that the poem works, the idea and emotion are contained in the experience itself. Since the poet does not speak out in his own voice, the poem has some of the objectivity of drama.

Were the poem your own I hope you would be able to criticize it. It seems to me rather too crowded with circumstantial detail: perhaps it needs to be longer, or the basic situation needs to be simplified. The conversational idiom carries it often into cliché and flatness; it needs more figuration, more imaginative surge. Go through and mark all the dull "business" words — i.e., those demanded by grammar and sense but of no intrinsic interest, the *of*'s, *the*'s, *and*'s, *you*'s, etc., and you will see by this measure that too few words have the pulse of life in them. Once you see what portions of your poems are devoted to experience and what portion to the significance of that experience, you will have some basis for deciding where you want your line breaks, the appropriateness of meter or rhythmical organization, the kind of diction, imagery and figurative language you wish to use.

Perhaps the principal matter of choice is whether (and how) artificiality of expression is to be used and where it is to be played down for the sake of "natural" appearance. Regularity of meter, rhyme, closed lines, symmetrical stanzas, alliteration and strikingly imaginative figures of speech all bring attention to artifice — and there are very good reasons for emphasizing artifice in many poems. Looser rhymes, enjambment, colloquial ease, asymmetrical divisions and other devices imply spontaneity, the emotional at the expense of the rational and orderly. And there are plenty of good reasons for wanting those effects in poems, too.

from thing to thought

All we have to go on is experience. If we find "tongues in trees, books in the running brooks,/ Sermons in stones, and good in every thing," like Jaques in the Forest of Arden, it is after all a fairly widespread human need to interpret experience and, moreover, to state our generalizations about it in such a way that they will explain or illuminate other experiences for other people.

Science and poetry are co-workers in this area, but with important differences. The point in science is to arrive at generalizations, formulae, which state abstractedly and exactly the principles which account for an enormous variety of individual experiences, to discover a fixed, often a quantitative relationship — as between energy (all energy) and mass (all mass), regardless of whether an atom of uranium or the vitality of Junior on the baseball diamond is in question.

In two important ways that kind of generalization is unsatisfying. The first is that it seems somehow to leave out the very life it summarizes. Poems ordinarily work at the opposite end of the abstraction ladder — saying that under precisely these conditions precisely this occurred (it may be fiction, but nonetheless resembles a report of a laboratory experiment) — but what it all *means,* the generalization which would be the scientific result, is frequently left unstated. The poet wouldn't go so far as to say that everyone passing snowy woods would (or should) stop, would experience a mysterious temptation to linger too long, and finally accept again the world of duty, obligation and practicality, but *one* evening, anyway, *he* did, and here's exactly how it was . . .

The second way that scientific generalization is apt to be unsatisfying is implied by the first. The formula tells us what is, but not what we ought to do about it or with it. Even though "Stopping by Woods on a Snowy Evening" has no moral attached, there is an ethical weighing going on, a choice made, which is part of the *fact* of the reported experience but, in addition, suggests an oughtness, a value. It is ultimately better to accept the demands of life than to surrender forever to the aesthetic still moment, though momentary surrenders are important too. One *should* stop to watch the woods fill up with snow, and then he should go on. The poem doesn't *say* that, but it relates the experience in such a way that the problem and the choice seem inevitable and applicable to other situations.

Ultimately there may be no distinction between knowledge and ethics; once we clearly and sensitively know what life is and what the consequences of our choices are likely to be, our decisions may be automatic. It hardly seems a matter of ethics to decide not to stick your hand in a fire. If all questions of choice had such clear consequences, ethical ambiguity might disappear. But we keep overlooking factors. One function of the concreteness of poetry, its constant preoccupation with the immediate individual, the particular, the *thing,* is to draw our attention to elements of experience which wisdom must take into account. To the extent that it does that, it is ethical, which, notice, is not to say it should contain morals or slogans or mottoes, which, like formulae, may seem empty of experience. Once we lose the warmth of the panting breath of life, we are likely to have left poetry for science.

These two basic elements of poetry, the thing and the thought, are inseparable. Much of your effort as a poet is to capture life whole, its exact quality and curve and weight and texture, to hold it, save it in words. The other (more scientific) effort is to organize it, point it toward something, so that abstractions can be made. This anonymous lyric has persisted almost as long as there has been English:

> Westron winde, when will thou blow,
> The smalle raine downe can raine?
> Crist, if my love wer in my armis,
> And I in my bed againe.

What are the reasons for its endurance? First, of course, we might say that it is a cry of loneliness, and the universality of our desire, when out in bad weather, to be home in bed with our mates in our arms, is sufficient to guarantee the popularity of the poem. But that, of course, is not true; the sentence in which I paraphrased the poem will not endure through the remaining time English is spoken. Nor is a cry, or groan, or sigh a work of art. Try it; groan with heartfelt loneliness and desire, listen to it on a tape recorder, and compare your noise with the poem.

Well, the poem alliterates — rather remarkably. All those *w*'s, *l*'s and *n*'s, and that careful interweaving of sounds help further to capture the quality of the yearning, its liquid resonant sigh. Its rhyme, with *raine* repeated, is particularly strong, the conclusion rounded and final. The rhythm is powerful, particularly the pounding spondees of the first and second lines. Those in the first line give a fearful insistence to the question. In the second line the beats seem to imitate the rain as they fall distinctly. After the next exclamation, *Crist,* the meter hurries with little syllables so that the accented words — *love, armis, I, bed, againe* — seem spaced, deliberate. And the poem sings, a combination of all the elements just discussed — so that the naked feeling is given the dignity and reserve of a haunting melodiousness.

All this discussion relates to the way in which the poem delicately incorporates its experience, the element I have called *thing.* But it still does not account for the impact of the poem, and we should look on to thought. First though, let us be clear about what we are looking for. We do not expect a moral, such as that sailors should not sail too far offshore in early spring, or if one prays to Christ for his girl he will get her. We do not expect some philosophical observation on the nature of love, or its relation to changing weather. Nor do we expect meteorological information pertaining to low-pressure fronts, western wind, and drizzle.

All such ideas are in a distant way relevant to the meaning of the poem, but they are *not* its meaning, any more than was my paraphrase.

Draw a large equilateral triangle, upsidedown, its base on top and fulcrum on the bottom. That is the *shape* of the experience of this poem. It begins with widespread arms and lifted face, appealing to the elements — as broadly universal and impersonal as possible. The second line narrows the experience from wind to rain, from vague to specific. But we are still talking about the weather. The next ejaculation is not to a force of nature but to a specific God, a man's god, and the sentence form has changed from a question to an interjection, a subjunctive, imagining a particular resolution; we go from *love* to *my armis* to *bed* in steady steps of increasing concreteness.

It is that *shape,* that bearing down on the particular, which seems to me comparable to a scientific formula. It is the shape of an experience which you can imitate physically by flinging your arms out, your head back, then, symmetrically, smoothly, sweeping your arms in, as in an embrace, pulling your head forward, until you are all tucked in. The same shape might contain any variety of particular experiences. (Note, by the way, how the ballad stanza line lengths of 4 and 3, 4 and 3 beats reinforce that narrowing of focus.)

We might turn the poem inside out:

Wer I in my bed againe,
My love in my armis entwined,
The smalle raine downe might raine,
And blow, blow, Westron winde!

It seems a bit weak by comparison, but *that* shape, too, the movement from the personal, intimate, particular, to the wide sweep of the vague and general, might well serve as a formula for a poem, the shape of a different kind of experience.

Both the concrete and abstract, specific and general, must always be present in the poem. I have been discussing so far the poem's need of a shape — a beginning, a procedure, a resolution — with some general applicability to experience. But shape is only one example of that relationship between the concrete and abstract. You may see the relationship in every element of the poem — diction, imagery, sounds, tone. Manage these elements so that you are always saying (and letting your reader know you are saying) more (not less) than meets the eye. It is this quality of suggestiveness, of the hard, clear image with its edges blurring off to generality, which makes the difference between the simple greatness of "Westron winde" and the commonplace.

A very simple illustration is in W. C. Williams', "The Red Wheelbarrow." I'll give it without the first stanza:

> a red wheel
> barrow
>
> glazed with rain
> water
>
> beside the white
> chickens

Okay, but there's nothing there. It's a "pretty picture" which contains perhaps a germ of imagination in the word *glazed,* a startling economy, and a rigid organization. Add the first stanza, now:

> so much depends
> upon

and you still haven't much, but at least it is a poem. The thing has thought. True, the "thought" is no more than an insistence upon a significance which is unexplained, but that touch of suggestiveness makes the difference between just writing and poetry. (Not, I'm afraid, poetry which will endure like "Westron winde.")

A final illustration, a longer passage, will illustrate the way poetry characteristically moves from abstract to concrete and back again. This is the secret of Frost's "Mowing." In the octave he questions what his scythe whispers as he works — perhaps something about the heat, or the silence — and asserts that it cannot be about imaginary rewards, for:

> Anything more than the truth would have seemed too weak
> To the earnest love that laid the swale in rows,
> Not without feeble-pointed spikes of flowers
> (Pale orchises), and scared a bright green snake.
> The fact is the sweetest dream that labor knows.
> My long scythe whispered and left the hay to make.

After the generalizations of the first quoted line the poem pulls in quickly, back to fact, the swale and its minutely-described (and named!) flowers and a quick glimpse of a snake. Through all this the breath runs out as detail follows detail in the long sentence winding earthward. Take a breath. Another generalization — a restatement of the last one, or, better, a corollary. Then back to fact; but note the last word, *make,* which is suggestive again, pushing off into generality, as the word takes our mind back to the "earnest love" and implies that the sweetness of the dream of labor is in its fertility, its productiveness. The fact is richly potent. The thing bears seed of thought.

In theme as well as manner this passage illustrates that both fact and generalization are aspects of truth — provided the generalization is based firmly on experience, or fact — and is not some "dream of the gift of idle hours,/ Or easy gold at the hand of fay or elf." It is characteristic of Frost — and of the best poets always — to nudge the fact into larger meaning, but without losing that vital sense of what it is, in itself, as he pushes it to find what it may imply.

born dead

But if you suppress experience and concentrate on feeling and idea, you may get the kind of results achieved by a middle-aged man whom I heard read his poems, unconsciously illustrating a principle we might call *born dead.* He preceded each poem with an anecdote or, typically, a piece of information, often from the New York *Times,* giving us background which made the poem more easily intelligible. The poems themselves, when they came, were usually short, intense, well-written — but born dead. The anecdotal and informational material was always fascinating, but the rhythm of the performance was like that of a radio show in which the patter of the DJ engages the attention and the records he plays are relaxing interludes of less immediate interest.

I am not objecting to the pattern of his performance, but I think we can learn something about writing poetry from this effect. Poetry ought to be at least as interesting, engaging and intelligible as prose. Somehow what is good about anecdote and information needs to be incorporated in the poetry itself, so that it can hold us without so much ad lib propping. I know from hearing many readings and giving them myself that an hour of unrelieved poetry is difficult for an audience to take. Simply for the sake of change of pace it is helpful if a poet chats a little between his poems. But the chatting should not undermine the impact of the poems. More importantly, we should not write the kind of poems which can be so undermined.

In trying to figure out what was wrong I was at first inclined to say that the poet should have been more involved in the poems. They seemed like art objects held at arm's length, turned over in the light, like curios from some other culture and other time, small artifacts which derived their interest from the explanations of the museum guide.

The element of self seemed almost removed from the poems — and it is true that one way of achieving a greater sense of involvement would be to bring the poet more directly into the poem. We could tell by the way he read that he was passionately involved, yet he seemed rarely to use the pronoun *I*. One of the appeals of much poetry is the sense of self-revelation. If you look through an index of first lines you will find that a very large number of poems from any period begin with *I* or contain a reference to self in the first few words. That tactic is used often for good reason: it is perennially effective.

But we would not like a theory of poetry requiring all poems to be self-expression. Artists are sufficiently notorious for their egocentricity anyway. Some poets bare their chests until we grow sick of seeing skin, but this poet was unnecessarily shy or modest. Our first and last material as artists is ourselves, though we may fictionalize and disguise and strain to objectify. I doubt that we would want to be poets at all if we did not have some inclination toward self-exposure; we derive a little secret kick by revealing what others usually hide. If we become aware of that impulse, we may sharply repress it in embarrassment. But, as Freud taught us, such snakes beneath the skin do not stay repressed: they simply find another, often more grotesque, way to surface. If we acknowledge these dynamics in ourselves, we can live with them and use them and yet not slobber over our readers with the necessities of our own egos.

One way of doing that is to dramatize, to treat self as a character in a play. That character, as I create him, may resemble me in every detail, and yet he remains in some sense an *other*. Though I may feel what he feels now, as I write, I know that by the time the poem is finished or published I will be quite different, and he will be frozen in time. As you read this sonnet, ask "Will the real Michael Drayton please stand up?"

> Since ther's no helpe, Come let us kisse and part,
> Nay, I have done: You get no more of Me,
> And I am glad, yea glad withall my heart,

That thus so cleanly, I my selfe can free,
Shake hands for ever, Cancell all our Vowes,
And when We meet at any time againe,
Be it not seene in either of our Browes,
That we one jot of former Love reteyne;
Now at the last gaspe, of Loves latest Breath,
When his Pulse fayling, Passion speechlesse lies,
When Faith is kneeling by his bed of Death,
And Innocence is closing up his Eyes,
    Now if thou would'st, when all have given him over,
    From Death to Life, thou might'st him yet recover.

The opening is immediate and dramatic — yet we know it is fiction. The poet could not be right there with his mistress, breaking off their affair, while writing the poem. Between the first and second lines we are asked to imagine some expression of emotion on the lady's face to provoke that "Nay." The language is that of direct speech, with conversational emphases: "glad, yea glad withall my heart." We can see the scene, as on a stage — and yet we can believe that the feeling is authentic, that the poet, at least at some time, was profoundly relieved to cut off an affair abruptly, even cruelly, and to free himself from love's bondage.

This dramatic speech continues through the second quatrain as he instructs the lady on how to behave. Note that first he asked for a parting kiss, and now he asks for the less tempting gesture of a handshake, but there is (in spite of what he says) a lingering desire to touch — preparing the reader subtly for the twist at the end of the poem.

The sestet is one sentence, divided into the distinct parts of the third quatrain and final couplet. Though the quatrain is still addressed to the mistress, it turns away from dramatic exchange to paint an allegorical picture in which abstractions are personified in a static scene. We see Love or Passion stretched on a deathbed, with Faith kneeling beside him and Innocence leaning over him to close his eyes. Snap. The picture seems fixed and final, but the sentence leaks back into action with the repetition of "Now" and the return of attention to the lady, who alone has the power to revive the dying figure.

Does Drayton want the love to be ended or continued? In the poem he clearly emerges as still yearning, but even there we can witness his divided mind. And this tells us nothing, really, about the real Michael Drayton. After all, the poem *is* an art object, rounded and complete in itself and separable from the poet's ego. But this kind of poem has a distinct advantage over those the poet was reading to us. It is not, finally, *about* something: it *is* something. It contains its own reality. I cannot imagine what patter would enrich or add to it. It is not a comment on something external to itself. If there is any dead portion it is that static third quatrain — but even this functions dramatically in the poem, giving us a pause, a moment of suspension, before the final reversal.

Let me illustrate by showing you how the poet at the reading might have done it (though this is an unfair parody, to make my point). He might have introduced the poem with this comment:

At one point in my youth I was hopelessly in love with a young lady who vowed that she loved me in return and would love me always, but who maintained a personal distance and coolness which were very frustrating to me. My ardor demanded more intimacy and physical expression than she was willing to engage in. Love to her seemed to mean primarily constancy — but that seemed to me like constant suspended animation, and I was too eager and passionate to endure that. Our conflict was, I thought, irreconcilable, and so I finally told her as much, saying that we should part good friends, no hard feelings and all that, but we should simply stop seeing each other. As I spoke I could feel a wild surge in my heart of freedom, for I had too long been enslaved and frustrated. But I noticed that at the very same moment that I was declaring my independence, I was hoping that my strong words might prompt her, after all, to give in. Simultaneously I wanted freedom and continued bondage. My bidding her goodbye was subconsciously a tactic to bring her to me. As I walked home I became aware of this paradox in myself, and it occurred to me that what was at work was very much like the balance of centrifugal and centripetal forces which maintain the earth in orbit around the sun. If the centrifugal force were stronger, and the earth flew off in a straight line, streaking across the universe, it might collide with something, or, anyway, it would surely lose the warmth which gave it life. The pull of gravity which kept it on course was, ironically, that which enabled it to continue. I sat on a bench awhile, contemplating the heavenly bodies in their eternal motion and stasis, and then went in and wrote this poem:

SUN LOVER

At last the fling off through
the spatial night, the chill
and endless vector, free
of sun pull, curving whirl
of centric love, forever
without consummation!

Song of the earth, its outward
straight course ever bent,
its constant veering, never
arriving, never leaving,
bound in a spin, straining
heart's invisible chain.

Earth still reveres its source,
sensing gravity
balancing liberty
with a dream of joy and rest
in sun's consuming flame,
on death's refulgent breast!

Such a poem is a meditation, an idea. The drama and personal
involvement are buried beneath the containing metaphor. The poet
is attempting to tell about something rather than to make it happen
on the page. To understand its poignancy one must absolutely
have the preceding patter. With it we know what the poet suffered,
what the drama of his life contained, what tensions tormented him.
Without the explanation, however, we have an abstraction, a universal irony. And a reader is not likely to care very much or
become involved.

expression and communication

As one starts to read a poem he asks, Who is speaking? To whom?
Why? and he might ask, When is this going on? Where is it taking
place? Perhaps he will glance at the name of the poet: Lavinia Pottle.
Hmm. Never heard of her. Never heard of *her*. Hmm. By a woman.
Will that make any difference in his reading of the poem? Can,
or should, he assume that the speaker in the poem is female? Is it

really Lavinia Pottle speaking? Or has she adopted a *persona*, a mask, but a feminine mask? Is there an *I* in the poem at all?

Let us suppose that this poem (which I have invented for the fictitious Lavinia) is what the reader finds:

BENDING ALL ONE WAY

In snowy still the tree defrocked
Bends all one way: the winds that were
Taught all that weather ever meant
And shaped her random, limber branches.

Somewhere the saplings are taking chances
Stirred by your breath to a green blur.
Stiffly one leans the way you went,
Exposed in winter light — and shocked.

The poem seems to be talking impersonally about a tree — but the pronouns *her, your* and *you* tip us off that people are involved. We suspect that the *one* is Lavinia herself, and that the poem is addressed to a specific breezy individual. For the sake of decency, we may be willing to assume that Lavinia may be merely imagining how an abandoned girl might feel, that she may have adopted the *persona* of such a girl, but part of the poem's attraction is the tantalizing possibility that it is, in fact, confession — and revenge.

If so, why was the poem written, and why should we, who are not personally involved, care to read it? Expression and communication are the twin engines of poetry; sometimes one and sometimes the other dominates. Part of Lavinia's drive may have been simply to express herself — and the metaphors we use for such a drive are revealingly excretory: to get it off one's chest, to get it out of one's system. The emotion is felt as poisonous, corrupting within. If it can somehow be externalized, pressed out (as *express* implies), one will be relieved and able to restore balance in oneself. Curses and wails delivered to the heavens when one hurts oneself seem to serve the same function. The impulse is simply to get the pain *out*. For example, the very title of Allen Ginsberg's *Howl* suggests the poem will be, as it is, a pouring forth of anguish so great that ordered thought and statement are impossible. To the extent that expression dominates communication, the poem is likely to be loose in form and obscure in content. When a person in the next room hurts himself and makes the air blue with self-expression, we can detect very easily that something is bothering him, but we may have to go look in order to find out what. Suppose that Lavinia had been more expressionistic. Her poem might have taken this form:

WIND-STRIPPED

Oh ache and the dry numbing, twigs
        immobile, my cry congealed!
(and hate too in the roots deeply
potent, in the grip of hard earth
like a memory of fire
        under crust of winter field!)

Yes, brittle in this chill,
        but yet I remember
that sunny green languishing, the summer plying
        where the wind vanished
to a warm breath
without name . . . .

as emptily I reach and lean southward
        where the wind vanished
            and the beguiling sun . . .
I am silent in vacant air, and the bark
stiff, sensing
the deep burn and viscous strength
        of longing hardened,
            the bitter flow,
        the resurging shame . . .

This is a step removed from uninhibited outpouring. Lavinia seems to have had enough composure to stick to the insistent central metaphor of the tree, and to have rounded her expression with an occasional rhyme. But if we ask her why the lines are divided and spaced as they are, whether the sap represents hate or love, whether the poem is about one man, or several, or a more general condition, her answers are likely to be, "This was the way I *wanted* it; this is the way I *felt*." The authority for the poem lies in her own feelings entirely — and considerations of form or consistency or adequate communication are by and large irrelevant.

The appeal of expressionism to a reader is that of participating in another's life vicariously. The poem appears to be a document; it is like a candid snapshot, which may lack art, but which draws our interest because it seems real, unrehearsed; we catch the subject, which, in this case is the poet, with his (or her) defenses down. We share in the intimacy of private experience — and perhaps take some pleasure in our ability to interpret actually more than the poet intended to reveal. For example, in the last poem of Lavinia's, there is an ambiguous or perhaps confused treatment of hatred and longing, both associated with the fluid of returning life, dormant in the winter tree. Ah ha! we say to ourselves — believing that Lavinia herself may be only half aware of the fact that her resentment of her departed lover may be inseparable from an inevitable lust for him.

An artful poet may write expressionistic poetry if he is aware of the rather clandestine nature of its attractiveness. He must seem, whether he is or not, willing to put himself on the line. As Pirandello might have said, he must know how to play the sincerity game. He must bring himself to utter all that he can bring himself to utter, and the remaining mystery, or obscurity, must seem fiercely repressed, yet hinted. The more personal the poem seems to you as an individual, the better. For example, in "Among School Children," W. B. Yeats says, "I dream of a Ledean body," and the knowing reader delights in saying, "Ah! That means Maude Gonne, the woman he loved early and fruitlessly, and often associated with Helen of Troy, who was born of Leda as a result of the rape of Zeus in the form of a swan." Yeats deliberately dropped such hints in his poems, inviting us to speculate on the facts of his personal life. Suppose that, years hence, someone writes the biography of Lavinia Pottle and discovers that she had an affair with one George Windson in the summer of 1966, and that George moved from Peoria to Memphis that fall. Ah ha! The words *southward, wind* and *sun* take on a meaning that extends beyond the general symbolism they seemed at first to contain. We recognize that the urge to express is inevitably crossed by an instinct to hide and protect oneself from the consequences of too frank exposure. When we break the code we feel we have somehow laid our hand on the poet's flesh — and it is this experience, rather than art, we are after. Art, in fact, seems a barrier, a forgivable but frustrating deception, like Salome's last veil, between the reader and the final truth he desires to know.

By now I have told you so much about Lavinia that this poem will not be puzzling — but you can see how it is compounded of little suggestions which would strike home for one particular reader if he should see it (he will not), but which seem carelessly disguised from the general reader:

TO ONE WHO WENT SOUTH FOR THE WINTER

My silence now speaks no less nor more
than did those last leaves you took and spun
in the Fall.

George, you passed through lightly
as a stripping wind, and your laugh as you stood in the Greyhound
Terminal of Peoria was hollow as November,
and as killing. I saw eyes dazed by visions of Southern
tender boughs and new leaves.

Should you wonder
(you will not), no, you did not father any
embryo but a faintly bitter trace
in the sluggish sap congealed beneath the Plains;
and if you looked back (you did not) you would
have seen from the fogged window only branches
stretching after, vacant, bare, as though
arrested in love, skeletal in a snowy field.

Ah, but how the sap gnaws in the stiff roots
and even twigs retain in suspended grace
some memory of tossing in summer gusts!

Here the focus seems hard on the particular experience of two people. What might be the universal element of the poem — its depiction of a rejected lover anywhere and association of the lover's numbed emotions with a winter tree — seems to arise, as it were, accidentally out of the need to record the facts of personal life. Though the poem is in a rough pentameter — actually more carefully ordered than "Wind-stripped" — it seems submerged in prose. The art of its form, like the universality of its meaning, seems inchoate, like the beauty of some piece of driftwood, like nature surprised.

Lavinia seems to be a very romantic girl, and all these poems, in one degree or another, are more preoccupied with expression than with communication. In the first she archly, shyly, indirectly, reveals herself — but we know, and she wants us to know, she is there. In the second she more frankly gives vent to her emotions but takes some pains to hide what they are all about. The third is the boldest; she exhibits a rather candid willingness to use her life as her material, hardly bothering to comb and button before appearing on the street. Perhaps appropriately for such an indiscreet poetess as we have watched Lavinia become, she puts less emphasis, in the third, on her suffering than she does on her yearning. I think she even hopes George will come back next spring.

A completely different kind of poem results if communication, rather than expression, is emphasized. If the poet regards his poem not as some kind of emotional excretion but as a product designed to perform some specific function in the lives of others, his own personality will be suppressed in the interest of form and general meaning. It will never (and should never) be suppressed completely. Think of a handmade piece of furniture, say a rocking chair. What we admire about it is the way personal idiosyncrasy of the craftsman has been overcome: the arms and legs are of equal length, hewn to a pattern; the bows of the rockers are evenly curved. In a way, its virtue is in the way it resembles other rocking chairs. Nonetheless we appreciate a subtle personal touch in the design — perhaps in the arch of the back, the knobs used as simple decoration — and the traces of chisel marks which survive the sanding.

Lavinia preferred to assert her identity rather than to try to transcend it. Even in the first poem, "Bending All One Way," she teased us to seek out the identity of that "one," implying that there is more to the story than she has quite said, that she has a secret she cannot bring herself to share. We cannot avoid, after all, being what we are, and we have no other material available. But a poet who seeks to transcend his identity will dissociate himself from immediate experience, to release it into universality and art.

If Lavinia shared this ideal, she might have come up with something like this song. (Note that the use of the personal pronoun has little to do with the matter. Here the *I* is clearly not Lavinia, but anyone.)

THE WINTER WAITING

Forlorn the branch of winter
As it starkly grieves
The passing of the summer wind
Through careless leaves.

And by the window watching,
   I reach out still
With rigid arms for one who crossed
   That southern hill.

The leaden sky, the sheeted fields,
   The frosted pane . . .
Oh, that I cared, or did not care
   For leaves again!

Poets can achieve externality, objectivity, by deliberately turning experience into fiction. Lavinia, made wise by whatever personal disasters, might project what she wants to say into the life of an invented heroine:

AS CHILL FOLLOWS FEVER

All Winter Sally stared and stared
   At the naked tree outside
In season of paralysis —
   And Sally never cried

And never told her mother or
   Various maiden aunts
How she remembered Summer, and
   The green boughs' windy dance.

In both these poems there is more regularity of form, less use of arbitrary, idiosyncratic detail. The marks of the making are more thoroughly sanded away. In "The Winter Waiting" a sense of melody sweeps us along so that we are less aware of the author as a person than we are in the three earlier poems. In "As Chill Follows Fever," the jog of rhythm and play of wit have a similar effect of making us look at the poem rather than through it to the poet. As the artificiality of the poem becomes more apparent, we are less concerned with the sincerity and factuality of its content.

   Both of the last two examples have a lightness and simplicity which may diminish their impact for some readers. We might give Lavinia one more chance, lettering her try a poem with more narrative substance, more probing toward generality. As she has become willing to surrender her individuality, let her play a male role:

THE RENDEZVOUS

The January trees seem upside down,
networks of roots all dead in the air. I rattle
through them pursuing quotation marks of rabbits,
cracking the painless twigs. The forest arches
above me like the ribcage of the world.

And there it is: the place of love, a drift
in the winter light. In August it was deep shade.
That long bulge like a sleeping Eskimo
is the log where we had our lunch. But she
left with the leaves, the birds, the sun, retired
with Dis to warm Antilles. I scuff the bark.

Well, life, they say, continues all year long
as a dull burn in the depths. I stamp my feet
and puff ahead in the still air, snapping
the dry bolt, squinting for cottontail's white flight
on white. They say the surge of sap in Spring
burdens each trunk with leaves and a new thin ring.

There are many characteristics here of the expressionistic poem.
A very specific experience is implied, and one might wonder how
close it was to the facts of the author's life (if he didn't know it was
Lavinia). But if you compare this one with "To One Who Went
South for the Winter," you will see that it has much less emphasis
on the emotions of the speaker, much less insistence that you understand personal peculiarities. The rendezvous itself is a generalized,
classical experience compared to the affair and departure in Peoria;
the love experience seems only an instance, though the central one, in
achieving the poem's larger intent. The spectacle of the fleshless
woods, the search for the elusive, jogging tail, the intrusion of thin
light into love's bower, the myth of Proserpina, the biological cycle,
the ambiguous burden of life contrasted with the trackless freedom
of the winter hunt — all these elements, among others, must be
contemplated in relation to one another in order to understand the
poem, a process which takes us a long way from understanding
Lavinia.

At various periods — and among various personalities — poetry
of one or another of these types is favored. Clearly the expressionistic
poems communicate, and the communicative ones express; the difference is one of degree — and of the poet's intent. Are you attempting

to get something of yourself out onto the page — or are you using yourself as material in an effort to make a product, an *other,* which can survive independent of any identification with your actual life? Once you have some clarity about your own ends, it is possible to discover the basic poetic devices which may achieve them.

CHAPTER FOURTEEN

The Whole Poem

starting in the middle

Pick up some standard anthology and study awhile the index of first lines. In fact, it is interesting to study just the first words. Most numerous, of course, are the poems beginning with *the,* but a close second are those beginning with *I* or *my* (or an occasional *methought*).

I is one of the most informative words in the language. *I* tells us someone is making a personal statement. It locates us, prepares us to listen, and you may be fairly sure it will appear in nearly every poem you read, usually in the first line. Until the speaker is identified, the words are words on the wind; too many, and one stops listening.

Similarly each word, each unit of sense, establishes something and brings the reader into comprehension and sympathy with the grey blur he holds before him. In fact you might consider that your problem as a poet (or as a writer, for that matter) is to convert that grey blur of print into an experience for your reader, to involve him in the poem, to make him forget that the print is print, the words are words, because something is happening to his sensibility. You have no right to assume he will follow you. You have to lead him. You have no right to assume his patience. He will be patient only if you have convinced him something important is going on; you *earn* the reader's patience by interesting him, and a grey blur is not inherently interesting. By good fortune he has read your first word. Is it such a word that will lead him on to read the second?

The reader begins with the title, such as that of W. H. Auden's "September 1, 1939," a specific date of an autumn month of a tragic year. The poem, then, begins with "I sit" and we are oriented. The verb is present tense. The speaker, on the date in the title, is going to tell me exactly what he is doing. He's sitting down, so I had better make myself comfortable too and expect a rather long poem. But *sit* is a relaxing sort of word, suggesting a low emotional pitch, as it were, and suggests the speaker will continue, as he began in the title, being very factual, specific, detailed. We don't expect high rhetoric or much passion from a man who begins by telling us he sits. Consider how different are the connotations of these other beginnings (taken at random from a first-line-index): "I am," "I caught," "I envy," "I heard," "I know," "I looked," "I love," etc. Each takes off in a different direction.

The entire first line is, "I sit in one of the dives," which may seem undistinguished enough, but prepares us perfectly for the fairly long poem to follow, draws us in. *Dives,* current American slang, tells us a great deal about the speaker. Here is a guy we know, a man of the streets, willing to use informal language, sitting in some bar, any bar (although the next, "On Fifty-second Street," locates it fairly exactly), probably alone, brooding, perhaps melancholy this September afternoon (the third line tells us he is "Uncertain and afraid,") and the title helps us guess he is not preoccupied with his own private problems (no need to give a date for heartache) but with public, world affairs (as lines five and six confirm: "As the clever hopes expire/ Of a low dishonest decade.") That simple first line has prepared us to listen to the gloomy consideration of world events on the eve of the war as revealed in the thought of an ordinary fellow in a Manhattan bar.

In other poems, of course, there is no point in conveying so much specific information. Setting may not matter, nor time, but, clearly, you should be establishing *something* word by word, very efficiently, and it is helpful to look back and consider just what information each unit of thought conveys.

Another common beginning is an exclamation. Look in that index under *Ah, O* and *Oh, Lo* and *Alas,* and for phrases with exclamation points — all very obvious attempts to convince the reader that something significant is going on, arousing natural curiosity for any moment of alarm or passion. This device, of course, is overused. An *Oh* is hard to live up to, and if the reader feels that the poet is crying wolf with insufficient cause, he is very apt to lose sympathy quickly. To go to journalism for an analogy, it is sometimes said that the perfect lead is " 'Damn,' said the Duchess, as she lit her cigar." I have never heard the end of that story, and it epitomizes the danger of the gimmick when used in poetry. Yes, as a reader, I want to be aroused — but with sufficient cause, not false alarms. Poetry has accumulated in its history much phony emotion to live down, and I find myself much readier to listen to the quiet fellow in the dive than to the dazzle-eyed howler baring his chest. Some readers, it is true (mostly teenagers of all ages), come to the poem disposed to emote. But I think it safer to assume a kind of skepticism and toughness in the reader. Engage his mind first, his emotions afterwards. Convince him you are self-contained, and your excitement, when it comes, will have more meaning.

Direct address, commands, questions or statements to a specific, often named person are among the most effective of openings. I began this chapter with a command, hoping not that you would actually drop the book and run for an anthology, but that you would be curious enough about why I should command you that you would keep reading. It is another gimmick, of course — THIS MEANS YOU — but has a certain legitimacy in poety because a poem is essentially dramatic statement, like a speech in a play, and the command assumes someone is talking to someone. Look at one of your own poems and ask, "Who says this to whom, and why?" If the answers are inherent in the poem, preferably established in the first line or so, a reader is much more likely to keep reading than if the words swirl along without any recognizable dramatic intention. After "Come live with me, and be my love" who can stop reading? Although we have no intention of obeying the poet's command (he is dead), we have the salacious interest, at least, of reading someone else's mail or overhearing a conversation on the party line. Something very interesting is going on.

More importantly, we are immediately oriented to the situation, and beauty or emotion or profundity may be absorbed once we know, essentially, the purpose of the message. The poems I quit reading halfway through are those which fail to satisfy me in this respect. I don't demand clarity, for obscurity, difficulty, and even, sometimes, vagueness have valid and valuable functions in some poems; but unless I have some general notion of who is speaking, whom he is addressing, and on what occasion — or why — I simply shrug and pass on to see if some other grey blur will come to life for me. Ideally, one should not read a poem but *have* it, like an experience, and I cannot have it if it is so tightly sealed I can't tell what it is for.

Dylan Thomas' magnificent "A Refusal to Mourn the Death, by Fire, of a Child in London," needs its cumbersome title precisely because the poem's *raison d'etre* emerges slowly. Nevertheless he uses an effective opening. The first line is, "Never until the mankind making," and it is nine lines later that we take a breath with "Shall I . . ." and crash in three lines to the end of that first sentence, all, I might add, with considerable obscurity in between. There is a good lesson for us here. *Something* has to be clear and to create anticipation in order for us to go on with a difficult poem. In this poem it is the very homely title which orients us and the sentence structure which keeps us going. That "never until" requires resolution, and we sweep breathlessly through the intervening clauses until we find the "shall I" which the opening has led us to expect. A perfectly clear, though elaborate, sentence structure is a strong frame on which to hang your thoughts. Look at the parallelism of Thomas' "The Force That Through the Green Fuse Drives the Flower." We tolerate the difficulties because they fall into place in a very clear and simple pattern. Obscurity is the easy part. The problem is to frame it so that the reader will be fascinated enough to wrestle.

The classic type of the breathless sentence structure is what we might call the *When as* opening, the epic simile. The first words warn us that a comparison is coming up. We then go through a simile that may be extended for many lines, sometimes half the poem, before we find out what the poet is really talking about — the *So does* clause which brings the circling figure back to earth. Look in your first-line index under *LIKE, AS,* and the various combined forms such as *even as* and *how like.* Here is a short example, by George Peele:

> When as the Rie reach to the chin,
> And chopcherrie chopcherrie ripe within,
> Strawberries swimming in the creame,
> And schoole boyes playing in the streame:
> Then O, then O, then O my true love said,
> Till that time come againe,
> Shee could not live a maid.

Four delightful lines of springtime, a singing line of further delay, the "Till" line reminding us of the sentence structure, then only in the last line do we find out what the poem was about; spring figures beautifully both as the stimulant of present passion and the hopelessly distant fairyland my true love does not care to wait for. Here there is no comparison, though "when as" suggests there will be — but true epic similes are followed by passages ingeniously and elaborately comparing the real topic to what might have seemed a quite dissimilar image, giving the poem an exciting, interlaced design in which you go one direction for awhile, then turn and cover the same ground turning each detail upside down.

Proffering a clever or lovely figure of speech is like proffering a plum. Of course there are readers who don't like plums, and subjects which don't admit of beauty, although the shock of ugliness discovered by twentieth-century poets becomes as tiresome in time as the saccharine they reacted against, and, like *oh*'s and *ah*'s, a shock, difficult to maintain after the first line, runs the danger of leading inevitably to anticlimax.

That, above all, implies that beginnings cannot be thought of separately from the poem. It is easier to begin than to go or arrive. Many unsuccessful poems spend the author's one good idea in the first line. It is very clear, reading them, that he hopes to blind us with a flourish to the fact that he hasn't, actually, much to say. There is much false coinage in poetry, sound not backed up by sense, ingenuity not backed up by profundity, much stabbing without penetration. If you *do* have a subject, something to say, my advice would be to think of how it can be cast in dramatic terms (or, in other words, put into the mouth of a speaker in a specific situation), then start, not at the beginning but in the middle, with a first line (or lines) clearly establishing a time and a place and a situation. There are, as I have said, other ways, sometimes good ways, to get into your subject, but it will emerge most naturally and forcefully, usually, if it seems to be life overheard, something going on. Get a reader to believe and he will listen. Even more than a writer of murder mysteries, it behooves the poet to write a poem a reader cannot put down. Here are beginnings of some poems I cannot put down — with brief comments to indicate why I think they work. (You can find the poems, if you don't know them, with your first-line index.)

> See, they return; ah, see the tentative
> Movements, and the slow feet,

Command, mystery, "tentative" line ending and the spondee, "slow feet," sound sinister.

> Here I am, an old man in a dry month,
> Being read to by a boy, waiting for rain.

Spondees, again, settling the first line, helpless passivity and expectation — and an intriguingly concrete situation.

> There came a wind like a bugle;
> It quivered through the grass,

That blast of the first line is immediately undercut by "quivered" in the second.

> I met a traveller from an antique land
> Who said: Two vast and trunkless legs of stone

The parable-like quality of the incident derives largely from the vagueness, "an antique land," a nameless "traveller," and the great stony simplicity and mystery of the "vast" legs.

> Dear Cloe, how blubber'd is that pretty Face?
> Thy Cheek all on Fire, and Thy Hair all uncurl'd:

The word "blubber'd" makes this, of course, with its promise of humor, colloquial ease and intimacy. The swift, light anapests pull us in before we know it.

> They flee from me, that sometyme did me seke
> With naked fote stalkyng within my chambre.

"Naked" is always an engaging word. Note the verbs, "flee," "seke," "stalkyng," and the promise of action. The first line, light, mysterious, fleeting, is brought down hard and close by the heavier sounds of concreteness of "naked fote stalkyng."

> Hearke, now every thing is still —
> The Schritch-Owle, and the whistler shrill,

The first line is obviously an attention-getter, but my excitement rises with the screeching and shrillness of the second, when the silence become eerie.

> Here take my Picture, though I bid farewell,
> Thine, in my heart, where my soule dwels, shall dwell.

Drama, action, people, situation, then what Frost calls "twists of thought," the puzzle and paradox of the stop-and-go second line.

> I struck the board, and cry'd, No more.
> I will abroad.

Almost too much action, decisiveness. A hard beginning to follow without letdown, but this poem manages.

> I saw Eternity the other night
> Like a great *Ring* of pure and endless light.

The simple, matter-of-fact tone contrasts startlingly with the grandeur of the image. Note the limpid movement, the distinctness of the beats.

> "Far enough down is China," somebody said.
> "Dig deep enough and you might see the sky."

The familiarity of this childhood experience is, I suppose, the first thing to draw one into this poem, which promises (and beautifully provides) a resolution to the problem of the earth's roundness. The comfortable, unpretentious diction and cadence help, too, and the paradox of "deep" and "sky."

These great beginnings have in common a power to place us instantly in the midst of life. Something is going on. We forget we are reading a poem.

man bites dog

It is easier to discuss beginnings than the ways of going on from a good start for, of course, each poem demands its own development, and generalization is bound to be meaningless. I will follow through one eminently successful poem attempting to show *how* it demands its own development and how the poet meets those demands.

It has, assuredly, a startling beginning:

> A sudden blow: the great wings beating still
> Above the staggering girl, her thighs caressed
> By the dark webs, her nape caught in his bill
> He holds her helpless breast upon his breast.

What is going on here? Just what the poem says — a girl is being raped by a bird. That, surely, is bigger news than that of man biting dog. The title, "Leda and the Swan," has warned us, of course, that Yeats has taken a classical subject, the strange encounter between the maid and Zeus in the form of a swan; but, even so, that sudden blow strikes hard, to the point that there is danger the rest of the poem may diminish in impact.

This is the poet's first problem: to measure up to his opening. A reader is likely to summon his skepticism and demand that the poet have sufficient cause for so assaulting his taste and credulity, or he will be dismissed as a cheap trickster. How does Yeats satisfy that demand?

Moved by one of the many sensuous Renaissance paintings of the rape, he begins graphically. Except for the word *helpless* this first quatrain is entirely visual. The action, as we come upon it, is underway — as it has to be in a painting. The tense (of the main verb, *holds)* is present. Except for the beating of those great wings and the staggering of the girl, nothing is moving; the principals are posed, transfixed in their furious engagement. The poet offsets the outrageousness of his subject by treating it in tableau.

This quatrain, a single sentence, is a little poem in itself, progressing from the particles of movement to the clench, the breast to breast conclusion. Everything underscores the finality of that last word. For example, consider the rhythm. The poem is a sonnet, and these lines are quite conventional iambic pentamcter; but, as we know, that does not mean there are necessarily many iambs. I would scan it like this:

a SUD\ den BLOW:\ the GREAT\ WINGS BEAT\ ing STILL\
a BOVE\ the STAG\ ger ing GIRL,\ her THIGHS\ ca RESSED\
by the\ DARK WEBS,\ her NAPE\ CAUGHT in\ his BILL\
he HOLDS\ her HELP\ less BREAST\ u PON\ his BREAST.\

Most noticeable, of course, is the way the accents, all heavy ones, pile up: GREAT WINGS BEAT, DARK WEBS, NAPE CAUGHT. All the words are of one or two syllables except one, *staggering* — a dactyl in itself (though, of course, it doesn't figure as such in the scansion), it literally staggers in the context of so many hard, firm beats. That word and *helpless* are all we need to contrast the weakness of the girl to the male surge of the plumed god. Notice that the fourth line is the most regular; here, for a moment, the struggle is resolved, violence gives way to the easy pumping of domination.

Consider rhyme. The enjambment of the first line makes *still,* an unemphatic adverb, slip by without much notice. The voice comes to rest a little more lingeringly on *caressed;* but, again, the line is enjambed and not until the third line does a grammatical unit coincide with the prosodic unit of the line, letting us rest on *bill,* the first rhyme — and, incidentally, a more brutal word than *wings* and *webs* in forcing us to see the animal nature of the attacker. But, of course, we are still in suspension, for the sentence has yet neither subject nor verb. The main clause corresponds exactly to the last line, that effortless, simple (without punctuation) statement, *he holds,* he masters; and *breast,* repeated in the line, is the resonant rhyme concluding foot, line, sentence and rhyme pattern. It is a full stop.

Consider consonance. The dominant sounds of the quatrain are *p's* and *b's: blow, beating, above, by, webs, nape, bill, helpless, upon, breast;* but this pattern of plosives is interwoven with one of sibilants, the *s's in: sudden, wings, still, staggering, thighs, caressed, webs, his, holds, helpless* and *breast*. Three words occur in both lists, and of these *breast*, repeated, is, of course, most important, bringing the alliterative design to its proper conclusion. (A third string of sounds is the breathless emphasis demanded by initial *h's: her, his, he, holds, helpless* and repetitions of these words; since both subject and verb of the sentence begin with this sound it is given a hard prominence, and perhaps requires that the word *his* in lines 3 and 4 should receive emphasis, making these lines end in spondees rather than iambs.)

And consider meaning. Yeat's fascination with the encounter is with the paradox of incarnation, the presence of divinity in fleshly form. In this quatrain the mystery of God is suggested only by the words *great* and *dark*. It is only after reading the rest of the poem that we can appreciate the religious significance of that fourth line in which the helpless human girl, like a nun marrying Christ, is not only dominated by but receives strength from total submission to the love and power of divinity as these qualities ambiguously emerge from that pulsing, steady fourth line.

At this point, of course, we do not know that. It is not only a graphic first quatrain, but an objective one. *Great* and *dark* and *helpless,* the most subjective words used, all are ambiguous; they may be taken as statements of fact — but also suggest spiritual qualities or a subjectively perceived state which expands the meaning. Watch that technique later in the poem. But for the most part, and, certainly, at the first reading, the quatrain is concrete, the excitement is sheerly that of witnessing an astonishing event. And its significance only begins to accumulate later.

That statement suggests the answer to the next question: how can the poem go on after such a definite and resounding conclusion as the fourth line provides? We are ready for reflection. What, we wonder, does it all mean? That question is the most disturbing challenge of the poem. In the second quatrain the author switches to questions. Notice how the poet, still keeping the image of the actual rape before our eyes, moves our mind away from concrete observation to thought:

> How can those terrified vague fingers push
> The feathered glory from her loosening thighs?
> And how can body, laid in that white rush,
> But feel the strange heart beating where it lies?

There is an increase of phrases referring to the attributes of godhead: *feathered glory, white rush, strange heart* — two of which, like *great wings* and *dark webs* above are spondaic, and all of which, like the suggestive words in the first quatrain, both describe rather literally what is before our eyes and imply something beyond. But the phrases are more difficult to visualize. The focus is blurring; the "terrified vague fingers" are not seen clearly, as they push an even vaguer "white rush" — like angels flushed, more dazzling than clear.

The quatrain is almost a still moment; nothing has happened beyond the action of the first quatrain. We imagine the hopeless struggle of a Mary resisting a more violent annunciation, the blinding rustle of the feathered glory, the nude body of the girl enclosed in those feathers, now lying, now aware of another mysterious heart lying upon her. The metrical devices of the first quatrain are repeated here, almost in reverse order as the action diminishes. The thighs are LOO sen ing, another dactyl like STAG ger ing, but now the submissive, slackening rhythm suggests the moment of release when pleasure begins to be mixed with terror at the inevitable penetration of God; in place of the blow and the GREAT WINGS BEAT ing, we conclude the quatrain with the surrendered body aware of the STRANGE HEART BEAT ing, returning us with that word *beating* to the first line.

Again, after such a conclusion, after such neat rounding, how can the poem go on? These eight lines — four depicting, four expanding the significance of the rape — have dealt so conclusively with the subject that another word might seem superfluous. Had Yeats stopped there he would, again, have had a poem. A good poet could appreciate the triumph of those lines and the daring required to go on. But Yeats had to go on because he had not yet asked the question the subject demands of him. He has asked two questions — how can mere human resist the rape of God, and how can we, experiencing that rape, avoid awareness of its mystical nature? But what does it *mean?* What *of* it? He has, in short, not yet justified shocking us with the vision of macabre violence with which he arrested us in the first line.

The sestet of the sonnet begins with perhaps the most vivid and unsettling phrase ever written to describe the moment of union: "A shudder in the loins," capturing the involuntary tremor of the depths, the absolute mixture of horror and pleasure which creates all things. After this close look at the most tender and terrible of all phenomena, the camera backs off to take in not only the world, not only history, but the future. He prepares us for a final question encompassing all human experience:

A shudder in the loins engenders there
The broken wall, the burning roof and tower
And Agamemnon dead.

                    Being so caught up,
So mastered by the brute blood of the air,
Did she put on his knowledge with his power
Before the indifferent beak could let her drop?

One of the results of the rape of Leda was Helen who, in turn, with her beauty of more than human origin, embroiled mankind in the long disaster of the Trojan War, the broken wall, the thousand ships and burning towers of Ilium, the tangle of family tragedies which included the assassination of Agamemnon by his wife's plotting. But if that war was a disaster, it was also the inspiration of some of the world's greatest poetry. In three phrases Yeats jots references to the whole grandeur and catastrophe of human affairs. The violation of Leda was like that of a pond by a stone, with splash, movement, color and concentric ripples of diminishing force.   ,

Thus all creativity. Thus all interference of the divine in mundane order. For every Christ we lose ten thousand crusaders and yet, except for these explosions of divinity, what would our lives mean? Indeed, what do our lives mean *with* them?

And there, exactly, is the question to which the poem tends. Yes, Leda, caught up and mastered by the brute blood of the air, was impregnated with power, for the beauty of Helen moved ships if not mountains. God shares from time to time, in his brute incarnations, his devastating strength:

The Holy Ghost shall come upon thee, and the power
of the Highest shall overshadow thee; therefore also
that holy thing which shall be born of thee shall be
called the Son of God.

But power without wisdom is that of a tribe of monkeys with a submachine-gun. The question is, to what extent does God impart his knowledge when he meddles? We find ourselves with bombs, but little notion of why or wherefore.

My last paragraph is sophomoric. The typical sophomoric poem begins and ends with *why?* and asks with continually refreshed wonder what life is all about. Nothing, in a sense, is easier to ask than why life? why death? why beauty? why destruction? But no one would accuse Yeats of being sophomoric. He has shown us how to ask such questions.

In this sestet we have first the magnificent phrase describing the orgasm, the three phrases alluding to the Trojan War (and to Marlowe's lines on Helen, which, expanding the reference, remind us that war is not merely hell but that God's intervention creates a cultural upheaval of good and bad beyond human comprehension; Yeats is driving us into the corner where Job burned). A midline break, then, and the camera moves back from Leda in her compromised position, mastered by the brute blood of the air, a paradox suggestive of the whole range of Christian paradoxes — the three in one, the life through death, the conquest through submission, purification through sacrifice — blood of the air, the life force materializing in carnate form. And then the question.

We began getting quaint language reminiscent of the King James Version with "where it lies," and now, with "put on" we are more forcibly reminded of religious experience requiring physical vestment (as we are asked to believe *on* Christ, a more intimate preposition than *in)*. But we are left with the sense that the power of the Highest (as described in the verse above, from *Luke)* is merely monstrous without the wisdom and goodness of the Highest. Human history does seem to erupt into creative periods of frightening magnitude as though, whether literally or not, an incarnate god has worked his violent desire on our quiet clay. The high comedy of Troy, the long surcease of Christianity, the glory that was Greece and grandeur that was Rome have occurred like brilliant explosions of impersonal force, with no clear direction, their manifest good no more dazzling than their manifest bad. As the sophomore asks, why?

The last line culminates the rape, returning to the close camera of objective naturalism. The word *in DIF fer ent* contains the third dactyl of the poem; the girl was staggering, her thighs then loosening, and now it is Zeus himself, weakened, like a human lover rolling away for rest, who so listlessly lets her drop. That word, *indifferent,* goes far toward answering the final question. God has taken us as in lust, and, lust spent, lets fall the used object; He appears here as a planter, a tiller of soil, not a reaper or husbander, as unconcerned with the consequences of His seed. Power is a genetic trait; wisdom or knowledge is not.

We are not going to write poems like "Leda and the Swan," but we can learn much from its technique. The first lesson is negative: unless one is tackling first principles, as Yeats is here, he cannot afford to drop bombs like the opening of this poem. The impact of the poem should be in perfect proportion to its idea — or, better understatement than brassy noise signifying nothing. Secondly, we must learn to create the experience. Although this is a rather philosophical poem, its major effect is to rape us, or carry us so vividly through the rape that we ache with its actuality. The philosophy is contained entirely in the suggestiveness of a few phrases referring to this deity incarnate in a swan (phrases which serve a literal, descriptive function as well as implying something about the attributes of God) and in one line, the next to last, which carefully uses two abstract words, *knowledge* and *power,* in a question. A third lesson is that phrases, rather than words or sentences, are the chief units of poetic meaning; it is the phrases like "by the dark webs" (rich word, *webs),* "a shudder in the loins," and "brute blood of the air" which stay in the mind and make the poem imperishable. A fourth lesson is the power of simple diction: it is precisely because of the chunky one and two syllable words that the polysyllables, when they occur, have such disturbing effect, and even these — *staggering, terrified, loosening, Agamemnon* and *indifferent* — are common, easy words, and the one familiar allusion is better than a cluster to bring to our minds the whole Trojan War. A fifth lesson is the value of controlling rhetoric or sentence shape. There are two statements in this poem and three questions. Study the function of each and you will see the careful, logical progression that carries us on, thinking, through the bright spectacle of the rape itself. A sixth is the effectiveness of some of the very simple metrical devices — chiefly, here, the use of spondees, or double accents, with thudding force, played off against the wobbling polysyllables mentioned above.

Finally I would point to what is sometimes called imagination but which I prefer to call courage: the ability and willingness of the poet to see in his subject its fullest significance, however shocking or unsettling, and to treat it so that such implications are clear and unmistakable.

false starts and new beginnings

Yeats is a hard act to follow, but I would like now to apply some of these principles to writing a poem from scratch. The emotional material is commonplace — something anyone can identify with. Imagine — or remember — some painful separation. You quit a job, got divorced, parted from a dear friend, one of your children moved away from home, or someone near you died. Though the parting itself was long-resisted and devastating when it came, on the morning after you wake up with a strange, heady joy you can't quite understand. Your conscience twinges. Why should you feel so happy? It is not the glee of victory. You don't blame the person, job, or whatever. But you are buoyed up by an un-accountable and somewhat disturbing sense of liberation.

For various reasons, you might not want to write a poem about the actual circumstances of your experience. At this point of deci-sion some poets are lured into abstraction, often because they are uncomfortable about revealing on the page what they are actually feeling and what events of their lives they are responding to. I don't think I would be guilty of the following lines, but I can imagine a poet starting this way:

BEREFT

Attachment is support, we know, and lean
on one another, fearing the severing pain,
unable, as we contemplate our lives
without familiar ties, to see how clean . . . .

No, no, no. Strike it all out. It sounds like an essay *about* the subject, not a presentation of living experience. One can feel in the rambling circumlocution and generalization a fear of getting into the poem — as though one were trying to learn to play an electric guitar, but were afraid of getting shocked.

If you are uneasy about dealing with facts, make something up — but it must be concrete, vital, and sufficiently dramatic to engage you (and, through you, the reader) at a gut level. Let us imagine an infirm mother and adult son living together, growing increasingly dependent upon one another. She can't get along without him — she thinks — for the practical necessities of life. But he has taken to drinking and carousing, bringing home strange men at late hours, disturbing the house. She fears that he is on a self-destructive path and that their attachment to one another may be part of the cause — but she is also afraid that if he had no stable home to come to, if he were out on the streets, with an apartment or rented room somewhere, he might get into even more serious difficulties. She is afraid for him, afraid for herself, but finally she loses her temper and orders him to get out and not come back. After an explosive scene he slams out into the night. The old woman is left shuddering in tears, is awake through the night fearful, feeling guilty and resentful, worried, self-pitying, broken. In the morning she goes out to the garden to stake up the tomato plants she has been asking her son to stake up for weeks. By now the stalks are no longer limber, heavy with leaves, set in their crooked ways, and in danger of breaking as she lifts them and ties them to the stakes. But she finds herself humming like a girl, feeling like a girl as she stretches and straightens her bent back in the June sun. Such things happen, and if there is any stuff in the old woman, this might be the stuff of poetry.

The opposite problem of getting bogged down in abstractions is that of getting bogged down in details. The story I summarized in the last paragraph might provide material for a novel. One wants to know more about the characters, their history, what brought them to this situation, exactly what scenes brought the mother to her outburst, and on and on. To make a poem instead of a novel out of it, you have to find what elements of the story have sufficient universality to be presented briefly, pungently, but with sufficient detail to anchor thoughts and emotion in real experience. This isn't easy. Let's take a stab at it, though.

STAKING TOMATOES

> I think I am again a girl in Iowa,
> my young arms itching in this nettling fuzz,
> my hands squeamish of the green worms . . .
> > > > I was
> tender beneath my long dress, sweet in my bonnet.
>
> My knuckles now are knobbed and freckled, my ankles
> thick; I ache, and, aching, sing.
> > > > > Last night
> I sent my son away. It had all gone rotten.
> For years I have been dying inside that house,
> shades drawn against the sun, mustering just
> the gumption to get soup upon the table
> when he came home . . . .

Enough. We can't get there from here. I can imagine where this poem would go, flashing back and forth between three scenes in time — the speaker's girlhood and time of innocence, the long, deteriorating relationship with her son, and her mixed feelings on this present morning, ending with a surge of strength as, relieved from her debilitating entanglement with her son, she recaptures some of the strength and optimism of youth. But there is just too much to explain. Stories of comparable complexity have been told in verse — e.g., in the dramatic monologues of Browning, the narratives of Frost. It would take a couple of hundred lines — and the beginning above is not promising. The approach doesn't feel right to me; and, besides, what I want is a shorter poem, a lyric, focusing on that uncanny experience of elation and pain that followed the separation — not on the whole complex story.

I get up, pace, drink coffee. One way of getting the condensation I want would be through an image, an analogy. I try to imagine examples of new life surging in weakened things — a leg out of a cast, painfully bearing weight for the first time in weeks; a throat with a tumor removed; a bent sapling straightening as it is unencumbered; sun breaking through clouds. I go back to my last false start. Could the experience of staking up the tomatoes itself serve as that analogy? The trick would be to make that image bear most of the emotional weight of the woman's feelings. It is almost impossible to talk about such feelings directly, but if one can visualize and identify with the process in an external object, that may convey fully enough what is going on inside. I try again:

TOMATO VINES

I should (*he* should) have staked them weeks ago.
Now weak but stiff, they cling to the earth like old
women with crooked joints. (My freckled knuckles
know.)

      I lift them gingerly, untangling
tendrils, wincing as string cuts the tenuous
stalks. Behind me down the row they droop
from the stakes, exposed in new air. I know.

We were rotting together, each feeding the other's
rot and clinging, mother and son like wife
and man, shades drawn. For years I wheezed about
that house with hardly gumption to serve the soup
when he came home, drunken and racketing, bringing
men he picked up on the street. I said
get out. All night I shuddered and cowered, limp
with guilt. My son.

June dew and sun will freshen
these vines. I know, straightening, feeling the flow
of long-blocked juice. Sever and pull and tie,
and grimace twists to grin. A girl again,
I feel mind fill with sap and wicked joy.

This poem has quite literally emerged as I have written about it in the steps I have described. I did not share with you some of the formal considerations which also concerned me. The drafts and the final version are blank verse, or unrhymed iambic pentameter. It firmed up as I went along. I was continually aware of trying to pack a great deal of material — much of it information — into a very short space, and if I succeeded, every word counts, conveying simultaneously feeling, information, and characterization of the speaker. I tried to make her sound like a rather strong woman, who might subtly dominate a weak son, perpetuating his dependence upon her, but also a woman capable of decisive action. I was very conscious of packing the lines with hard sounds — *k's,* hard *g's.* I used a number of buried, internal rhymes *(know-row-know-flow,* for example). The *"he* should" in the first line is a kind of teaser, preparing the reader for later expansion of the domestic situation.

Writing such a poem, I find myself getting further and further inside the character who is speaking, just as I do with each character when I am writing a play. I rather like the old girl, her final brave insistence on living her own life, of breaking up the mutually parasitic relationship, even though it leaves her feeling (deliciously) wicked. In this process I get some distance from the original impetus of the poem. In fact I recently went through an experience of agonizing but ultimately creative separation (from a group of friends). I broke off the relationship somewhat harshly, emotionally, in a way I am not proud of, but which seemed necessary — and the most honest way — at the time. The poem is a means of coping with my own mixed feelings, not justifying them, not even sorting them out, but understanding my sense of relief and new energy, albeit crosshatched with a sense of wickedness. My experience helps me understand the old woman I invented, and she, in turn, helps me understand myself.

revision and re-vision

Finally, I would like to trace the process of building and rebuilding a poem with samples from the work of a poet who, I believe, has some talent. He sent me this poem:

THE MYSTERY OF DEATH

My neighbor's daughter, only six,
has a soft heart, even for a child . . .
and often, after children are abed,
we laugh together at her innocence.

The time was Autumn, azure skies
backing the golden hills, when, I was told,
mother and daughter scuffed through copper shards
in mood of gaiety. "Why are the leaves
not always scarlet thus?" asked little Peggy,
lisping, tilting her shock of auburn curls.
Her mother, in the offhand way adults
will use a word of terror, having grown
accustomed as undertakers must
to stages between breath and dust,
said simply, "They're dying. It is death which does
inflame them with these hues of splendor —
wild yellow, pumpkin orange, winey red and tawny brown."
"Dying?" whispered Peggy in her rustling voice.
"As Peregrine, my puppy, died last year?"
"But, darling," the mother smiled, "leaves all
spin to the earth each year. We call it Fall."

But words could not stem the seeping youthful tears.
That night we laughed about it, over beers.

Dear Gerry (I wrote him), pardon my saying so, but this has almost every fault known to poetry. The title is corny. The subject is sentimental. The writing is full of clichés. The form is sloppy. And the whole thing is either off the point — or pointless. Are you writing about the heartlessness of adults? If so, why spend so much time talking about the scene in the woods? What *is* your point?

And thusly my correspondent did reply: Dear Jud, please be more specific. I think it is *you* who is/are heartless. Signed, Gerard.

So I was more specific. First, there are three, possibly four characters here: neighbor, his wife (unless neighbor means the mother), the child, the speaker. It is cluttered with people. What are the relationships between them all? Why put the experience at such remove? "Soft heart" is a cliché. "Abed" is a poeticism. Lines 1, 5, 13, 14 and 20 are tetrameter; 17 is heptameter; the rest are pentameter — so consistently that the variations stand out, yet there seems to be no organic reason for them. "Azure skies," "golden hills," "mood of gaiety," and "auburn curls," to name a few, are clichés. "Shards" — suggesting sharp slivers — is simply a bad image for leaves. Scarlet is about the only shade of red I cannot easily associate with autumn leaves. Scarlet-gold-copper all work against one another, and that mélange of colors in line 17 is simply confusing rather than vivid. It is almost impossible to get away with four adjective-noun combinations in a row, anyway, and these are particularly bad ones because "pumpkin" and "winey" are built from nouns whereas "wild" and "tawny" are not: the ideas behind the adjectives are not sufficiently parallel. In general, lay off the adjectives; for example, need you tell us Peggy is "little" after you have told us she is six? And need it be "only" six? Are the tears "youthful"? Can one stem a seep? Isn't a "word of terror" a bit melodramatic for "dying"? The speeches of both mother and daughter are laughable. If Peggy says things like "Why are the leaves not always scarlet thus?" she belongs in a wax museum. You take up four-and-a-half lines to prepare us for the simple way mother says three lines of ornate, complex language. What is the *does* doing in "death which does inflame them"? Expletives have been used by poets in the past to fill out meter or set up rhymes (e.g., to substitute *inflames* for *inflame),* but it was never a good practice, and it certainly has no justification in as loosely metered a poem as this one. Note how the flame image is disregarded in the color listing which follows. "Hues of splendor" is an appalling poeticism. I don't know how one whispers in a rustling voice, but this is an example of your obsession with describing everything you mention, especially with adjectives. Select! Get a firm idea of what your poem is about and stick to it. The puppy line, I hope you can see by now, is impossible sentimentalism. (You'll have us laughing at your poem, over beers!) The three couplets in the poem suggest you are capable of some tightness of form, though the one about the undertakers is simply macabre (and amusing) in the context because it so laboriously overstates the phenomenon of the mother's casual use of the word "dying." Besides, it is bad grammar, faulty parallelism: "must" what? "having grown"? Syntax demands *must grow.*

The couplet at the end of the second verse paragraph is a little jarring, tying a tetrameter to a pentameter line without any apparent formal or thematic reason. The final couplet nearly works, but "could not stem" is a difficult anapest to swallow rhythmically, and, as I mentioned, the diction seems inexact.

Dear Jud, wrote Gerry, you are a hidebound academic stick-in-the-mud, but you did make one or two good points. I wrote the poem as I felt it, but this compromised version may be more satisfying to your conventional taste:

PEGGY'S GRIEF

In Autumn's swirl of gold a child is standing,
A sprig of Spring perplexed by the fact of age.
Do seasons come to this: a gilded fling,
A gaudy spinning through the cabarets
Before a rasping death, trod underfoot,
A flaking dryness, merely mulch for soil?

She thinks she weeps in sympathy, and we
Are struck that youth so tenderly can care.
We know her heart will toughen with the years,
Accept the seasons, though with secret rue,
Knowing that as her golden age approaches,
Fall leaves prefigure death for me and you.

I told him, Gerry, this is a lot better, but still a dreadful poem. At least you have an organized idea now; the poem has some shape and movement; the pentameter is under better control; the first stanza sets up a scene and a problem, and the second, symmetrically, responds to it; there are fewer clichés and poeticisms. But do yourself a favor, and don't send this out to editors. Listen, Gerry, have you ever tried the piano?

You can't get away with those vague innuendos, Jud, he told me. If there is anything imperfect about that poem I'd like you please to point it out to me.

Well, I said, I don't know what you expect from a stick which is academic and in the mud and bound with a hide, but here are some things which occur to me. The title is better than the last, but flat, unexciting — and my personal response to the name "Peggy" is that you are trying to make me see her as cute, cuddly. (Apologies to all the Peggy's in the world.) I see that you have unified the color imagery, playing on our secondary associations with "gilded," as meaning painted, cheaply beautified and with "golden age" as a kind of geriatric euphemism for decrepitude. But it is difficult for me to think of autumn leaves as gilded. You ask me, for three-and-a-half lines to see autumn as a kind of superannuated flapper, rouge on her sunken cheeks, giddily making the rounds of the bars, then, I gather, hacking her life away (with tuberculosis?) in some lonely room, abused and disregarded. The image is melodramatic, but with some difficulty I can swallow it. Further, however, you are asking me to accept that this is how Peggy sees autumn — and there my credibility snaps. Do you see this problem in the point of view of the first stanza? I find it hard to imagine a sprig being perplexed — and doubt that perplexity is what you mean. Your title mentions grief; your second stanza says she weeps and she will later have "secret rue." "Perplexed" seems the wrong word for the tone you want. "Gilded" and "gaudy" repeat the same idea. Note how often you expect me to regard verbal ideas or abstractions as concrete nouns. She stands in a what? A swirl. What is gilded? A fling. What is gaudy? Spinning. What is rasping? Death. What is flaking? Dryness. Language can, of course, be used this way — sometimes effectively; but aren't you overdoing it? Read the first stanza aloud. Can you come up to that first question mark gracefully? Isn't there too much statement after the colon for us to remember that the sentence started as a question? "Mulch" suggests moist rotting, not "flaking dryness." So much for the first stanza.

Who are "we" in the second stanza? And what have "we" to do with "me and you"? (Incidentally, these pronouns are usually in the reverse order; it looks as though you are straining for the rhyme.) The "we" sounds royal — or editorial — and this is symptomatic of the preachy tone of the second stanza. It says to me, stand back, here comes a generalization about life. She *thinks* her tears are sympathetic? Aren't they? You set up a problem the poem does not resolve. "Struck" is a mighty vague response, is it not? If we are so smart as we seem in the last four lines, I don't know why we should be so astonished in the first two. I'm afraid that "secret rue" is painfully artificial; "rue" just isn't used any more, and nothing about the poem makes an archaism appropriate. And I think your idea went askew at the very end. My guess is that you were thinking that her tears are a kind of conscious grief for herself; that she senses, though she doesn't yet understand it, that fall leaves prefigure death for *her*. If that was your point, you let your desire for a rhyme at the end betray you.

Dear Jud, you are absolutely destroying a person's creativity. If I have to be self-conscious about everything I write I will never be able to express myself. You can pick apart anything, even *Hamlet,* but can you do as well? The critical mind is a kind of disease creeping through the swamp looking for dirty pictures out of sheer jealousy. But just to show you that I can, if I wish, meet your puny criteria with the back of my hand, I send you this perfect version of the poem for your appreciation and acceptance.

MARGARET IN AN AUTUMN WOOD

This little girl now sobs and grieves
That Autumn woods must lose their leaves.
To her young heart each leaf appears
Worthy of her concern and tears.
As she matures she will care less
That trees must annually undress.
She will accept without a sigh
That trees grow barren, all leaves die.
When she weeps then she will know why.
Now she cannot know sorrow's cause:
That mortal life is bound by laws.
We do not say so, yet we know
In heart and soul — our flesh must go.
Death is our human destiny.
She weeps for leaves, for she can see
In their fate what her own will be.

Dear Gerard, I am sorry that this manuscript does not meet our editorial needs at present but thank you for submitting it. Sincerely.

Jud, you crook, you can't get out of it that way. What's wrong with that poem? I ask you! If editors are all as petty as you, genius will perish from the earth.

Dear Gerry, Sorry. I *was* dodging, but wondered whether there were any point in trying to say anything further. The poem is now better, much better, than in the preceding version. It is at least competent. I like your submitting to the rigor of the tetrameter couplets. (One line, "Now she cannot know sorrow's cause" is lumpy; you need either to vary the meter more or to iron this line out.) You got rid of "me and you," I am glad to see — but kept that vague, editorial "we," and it still contributes to a preachy tone.

"Sobs and grieves" is somewhat redundant — and anticlimactic. The whole poem is somehow stilted:

> To her young heart each leaf appears
> Worthy of her concern and tears.

My response is, "Ridiculous!" And your explanation will be that it is meant to be ridiculous, that of course it seems ridiculous to an adult that a child might cry about falling leaves. But the sedate language into which you put this observation makes *you* seem ridiculous, not the child. Lines like "mortal life is bound by laws" seem unbearably pompous; the idea is appropriate for poetry, but you have to find some way to make it seem fresh, concrete, tested on the pulse. The whole poem is sort of anonymous, removed. I don't hear any voice. I am not made to care. You haven't *involved* me. I don't know what to tell you except to say go out and be born again. Go out and have a tragic love affair. There isn't any commitment here — hence no intensity. I sense that you don't care about what you are saying; therefore, *I* don't care. It is like a photograph of a fire. It doesn't move; it doesn't burn.

That correspondence was several years ago, and I did not hear from Gerard until recently, when he wrote, Jud, you were right, at least about the love affair. I had three — two while I was in the merchant marine, one since, while I was weather-observing on Mt. Washington. One result was a fine baby girl, whom I named Margaret in fond memory of the girl in the poem. Speaking of that, I took another crack at it the other day, and would like your opinion:

SPRING AND FALL

to a young child

> Márgaret, are you grieving
> Over Goldengrove unleaving?
> Leáves, like the things of man, you
> With your fresh thoughts care for, can you?
> Áh! as the heart grows older
> It will come to such sights colder
> By and by, nor spare a sigh
> Though worlds of wanwood leafmeal lie;
> And yet you will weep and know why.
> Now no matter, child, the name:
> Sórrow's springs are the same.

Nor mouth had, no nor mind, expressed
What heart heard of, ghost guessed:
It is the blight man was born for,
It is Margaret you mourn for.

Well, gee, Gerry, I wrote, I think maybe you've really got a poem there; I'd be happy to use it in a magazine. I like that jazzed-up tetrameter, though it seems straining (or cheating?) a bit to have to put accent marks in to make sure we get the beat. I'm glad you pulled it into direct address: this is the sort of thing I meant when I said that you must *involve* the reader. The difficulty of the wrenched expressions does that, too. Surely no one ever talked to a child this way — but the unusual language makes that implicit: we know this is not actually spoken, but is a highly condensed, intense expression of thought — of what the speaker would labor to help the child understand, although he knows that he cannot succeed. The strange rhythm, (syncopated, would you say? "What HEART HEARD of, GHOST GUESSED,") also has the effect of removing any trace of sentimentality or pomposity. Congratulations.

It was a few weeks later when he replied, saying, Well, Jud, I figured that if it were good enough for you, maybe it was good enough for a high-paying slick, so sent it to *Knickerbocker Weekly*. Here's the note they sent:

Dear Mr. Hopkins:

Thank you for the opportunity to read this curious poem, but I'm afraid the tortured syntax, barbarous neologisms, affected diacritical markings, clumsy meter and strained rhymes make it unsuitable for publication. I find the situation of a child weeping over leaves falling incredible in the first place, your conclusion about the "blight man was born for" rather too grandiose in the second, and the expression altogether too unnatural throughout. I suggest you acquaint yourself with the poetry we are currently publishing before submitting again.

Sincerely,
William Carlos Criley
Poetry Editor

I tell you, Jud, I'm thinking of giving up poetry and joining a Jesuit monastery. Your buddy, Gerard.

CHAPTER FIFTEEN

Poetry and the Market

One of the frustrations I suffered when I began to submit poetry for publication was that I had very little information about the process of editorial selection. Literature was mostly in anthologies — as though by heavenly judgment. Thin books of new poetry came to me for review through some anonymous process I did not understand. The acknowledgment pages of these volumes indicated the array of magazines in which most of the collected poems had appeared. I puzzled through the magazines: why were these poems chosen, and by whom?

In some respects, as I came to know the process more intimately I understood even less. Nolan Miller and I edited a collection, several numbers of which were published in paperback, called *New Campus Writing,* and I began to see pounds and pounds of fiction and poetry in manuscript. For many years I was poetry editor of the *Antioch Review,* and I have served as poetry editor and advisor for several other magazines and publishers. I am still mystified by why poets submit what they do and by many of the selections I see in print.

But the experience has been very useful to me in sharpening my own judgment about poems — and, I think, in learning to write better poems. If you will, with my help, imagine what it is like to select from the mountains of manuscripts the very few poems which a magazine can publish. I think it will give you a fresh perspective on your own poetry. Little is said in print about the editorial process because editors may be ashamed of the superficial and arbitrary judgments forced upon them by circumstances. I make no defense. But it helps me to have some insight into what my own poems face when they go out on the mails.

As I have said earlier, what poetry magazines publish is not necessarily that which history will judge to be the best. On the one hand there is an operational need of getting poetry into print — and that process is inescapably subject to the distortions of reputation, fashion, politics, readership interest and available space in publications. On the other hand, all these factors are likely to be distractions from writing and publishing the best poetry possible. Becoming a poet in the most profound and culturally relevant sense of that word requires one finally to transcend such categories as professional, tradesman and amateur. But there is no way to get there except to have your work found by posterity in a trunk or to face the realities of the publishing world.

I would not want to sound too cynical about this. All of us from time to time blame the inequities of the system, the fallibility and superficiality of editors, the crassness of the public and other interpretations of social reality in order to explain our personal failures. But I think Shakespeare was a better playwright for having been a commercial playwright. He got in there and found out what would go over and did it — and the buffeting of circumstances probably strengthened his work. For one thing, however abstruse and subtle and profound his plays may be, they are preeminently performable, even today. Their essence gets across to untutored crowds through history and around the world. The discipline that gave them that quality was probably in large part a willingness to adapt his vision to the live audiences and actors and specific theaters and laws and social conditions of his time and place. There is a snobbish attitude toward art prevalent now which regards that as prostitution — and, indeed, Shakespeare must have had something of the same feeling, believing that his real literary reputation would rest on his narrative poems and sonnets. Ben Jonson, his contemporary, was mocked for calling his published plays "Works," as one might sneer today at the publication of soap opera scripts or collected deodorant ads. But commercialism does not necessarily destroy the quality of art, and it may improve it in some respects.

Of course "commercialism" in regard to poetry is a rather ludicrous concept, since so little money is involved. Some of the "better" publications in which one's poetry may appear pay nothing at all, and most pay very little. But there is a very alluring commerce in prestige which can be just as corrupting as commerce in money — and may have less value than popular sales in exercising a demanding discipline on the poet. In a time when the poets regarded as the greatest are both unpopular and obscure, and literary reputation is more a matter of ecclesiastical blessing from the literary establishment than one of sales, the meaning of commercialism in poetry is very strange indeed.

how it looks from here

At one point during the fifteen years I was poetry editor of the *Antioch Review* I was moved to write the following:

I put this sheet in the typewriter in a vengeful mood. For the past few minutes I have been nervously scratching at the flap of a return envelope sent me with a batch of poems from Florida. It was gummed shut. There lay the pristine envelope, all self-addressed and stamped — and here the batch of poems to go inside it. After clawing and finally ripping, I stuffed the poems in and pasted it all up with cellophane tape. The green slip I included contains nothing of my annoyance. I try to be patient: the air is humid in Florida. Perhaps the poet works in a beach hut, unprotected from the damp spray. Perhaps he has a child, or monkey, who licks envelopes behind his back. Perhaps he has pasted it shut out of an over-zealous sense of tidiness.

But I have an urge to tell the world — to confess how petty an editor can sometimes be. Surely poets spend enough effort trying to butter me up with unnecessary covering letters. Perhaps some would like to butter me up by sending me a manuscript I could read easily and return painlessly.

One takes on the job as editor because he knows it is important, valuable, and because it is, after all, exciting to feel the nation's poetic pulse this way, to discover unexpected talent and to read the new work, good and bad, of poets who have already established some reputation. One takes it on because, after all, one likes reading poetry, enjoys the challenge of distinguishing the successful from the unsuccessful. Some editors will not read poetry at all, let alone judge it; someone reasonably experienced and knowledgeable must serve this purpose if magazines are to use poetry, and I would hate to see them discontinue publishing it.

Most quarterlies and little magazines are largely volunteer efforts, their staffs have an overload of teaching and other duties competing for time with their editorial work, and the latter is totally uncompensated for except in what joy and wisdom may accrue. Daily half-a-dozen envelopes of poetry arrive, each containing from one to over twenty poems. Of these less than one per cent can be used in the magazine, and less than ten per cent is likely to be seriously considered. The accumulation begins to be formidable. I don't read the incoming new work because I haven't caught up with the old. This may go on for a couple of weeks, until I simply drop everything else for a day or so and clean the stables.

Before I start I know that it is unlikely that I will accept any for publication. Our inventory at the *Review* already runs a year ahead of the current issue. If we include as many as half-a-dozen poems in each issue of the quarterly, that means I can accept an average of one poem every two weeks — but I am already far ahead of schedule. Perhaps I should have been more stringent in the past; but I know now that a poem which forces its way through to acceptance must have enormous power. It will have to be, in some sense, irresistible. That is one thing submitting poets should recognize: an editor is not likely to be looking for evidence of talent. Rather he is looking for finished poems which perform themselves on the page, which engage him, fascinate or move him on one reading and which stand up and prove additionally rewarding as they are reread and reread.

After eliminating at a glance some nine-tenths of them, those which are speckled with clichés, poeticisms, pedantries and platitudes, are illiterate, or show no control of the medium, I settle down to the hard job of reading the remaining tenth. On top of the first packet is a sonnet with this first line: "You who sang *St. James' Infirmary*," a direct address which pulls me into the poem. By the second line I am discouraged by "with empathetic heart," and find in later lines much trite or undistinguished phrasing. The octave is a kind of profile of a difficult, cynical young man; the sestet, with an awkward grammatical shift, tells of the speaker's choice of flowers — presumably for the young man's funeral. Another grammatical ineptitude: "I go to choose/ Your flowers, who rebelliously regrets . . ." She rejects "red roses," because she imagines him laughing at her, and decides to "send chrysanthemums instead." It is not clear why he might not laugh at chrysanthemums. Overall, not much point and flawed presentation. The best of the five poems included is another sonnet about children desperately building sand castles before the waves wash them under, until, "Relieved, they scream with joy at their defeat." There is an interesting twist, and the sonnet form is handled neatly — a publishable poem, but not exciting enough in language, idea or form to warrant a place in our crowded inventory.

The next packet attracted me because of the plain language, the unpretentious realism of its four poems. Of them I liked best one about an "iceberg of a stone" imbedded in a field which the poet has to go round with his plow. The stone assumes an aura of strangeness, passively sinister, "unmoved/ as prejudice, a cold shape/ from the dark ocean." The poem is adequate — but that is not enough for me to include it. It is too nearly mere description: the flash of significance in the last lines quoted is insufficient to give the poem real impact.

Often a submission, such as the next I am looking at, is garnished with delicious phrases. A girl lies "brooding . . . like a log full of bees." Another "lisps like a thick cello string." There is "a crust-colored cat with jungfrau eyes." In a rented room is a "liver-wurst rug." Moreover, there are images which linger in the mind, even when the phrasing is not ingenious: a girl goes to tend a whistling teakettle on "soft feet in the dark." Another poem creates a haunting image of a girl, in early morning, sitting by blowing burlap curtains, "practicing the cello/ in a pink sack, barefoot . . . bracing her brown lover between her knees." I have confidence that a poet with this much talent is, or will soon be, publishing in the good magazines. None of the poems here quite worked as a whole for me: at times the clever phrasing seemed laid on too thickly; at other times I did not feel the poem had a sufficient *raison d'etre*. Each seemed an exercise by a gifted poet who had great resources to bring to bear when a significant idea or theme comes.

Lest I sound too absolute in my judgments, I want to assure you that the same poems submitted elsewhere may just click with an editor. Editorial judgments are at least as chancy and subjective as the choices poets themselves make in deciding what to write about and how to do it. Often what seems obscure to one reader has immediate clarity and force for another.

The next packet of seven short poems causes me to read and reread, wondering what I am missing. I have immediate respect for the poet, but cannot figure out, usually, what she is getting at. I am not sure whether she is being over-ingenious, subtle, or whether her perceptions have betrayed her into the merely bizarre when she writes of a leaf stumbling from a "drunken branch" and feuding "with murmuring shadows/ of my steps." This seems a rather melodramatic rendering of falling leaves — and I can't tell why she treats them this way. Why are the farm girl's thighs "bug-stuffed"? "Hunched as a muffled/ River," I read, and wonder how hunched a muffled river can be. Pebbles are "holstered in shriveled footsteps," and though I can understand the image, it seems strained for no good reason. The best of the poems is about an orchard "Seen always from a distance —" and the apples:

> each careless, form within
> unknowing form
>
> relaxed amid the eagerness
> of leaves.

There is sufficient profundity and grace in that observation to make me think there are dimensions of the other poems I cannot see.

Next I find three poems from a poet I have used frequently — and who has published widely elsewhere. I decided against the first, about James Dickey's transformation of his football appetites into poetry, partly because I don't think the *Antioch Review* is the place for in-jokes among poets. The literary syndrome is tightly enough enclosed as it is; moreover the poem's strength is more in the critical accuracy of its statement than in its own artistry. The next, a brief narrative about ballet dancers, has some amusing moments, but not enough of these or of fresh insights to justify its twenty-seven lines. The best of the lot is an epigrammatic comment on cruelty, comparing the "circle of cruelty" (his children's cruelty to animals and one another, which evokes his cruelty to them) to a fox "chewing his own leg off," the circle clamping "around the bloody valves." Finally comes a whimsy of "found poetry" in the shape of a Christmas tree. These are by-products of an excellent poet, but I think we would be doing neither him nor us a favor by printing them. Unpublished writers are likely to think that the first breakthrough eases the path of later acceptances, but I have sent back packets from Mark Van Doren, James Farrell, Peter Viereck, John Barth and other well-known writers and poets without an acceptance — and give equal attention to poets I have never heard of.

In fact, when I have an indication that a poet is young or just starting, I am likely to pause over his work and, if I can think of anything useful, make a brief comment. In the next group of four

poems from a college student I am most struck by a poem about
what must have been his first experience voting in a national election:

Should I have begun the revolution now,
and walked out of the booth naked?
Should my private ballot be exposed?

There is, probably, material for a poem in this response, the futility
felt by a young voter — but the poem becomes too strident and
banal for my taste. Other poems in the group seem, in contrast, too
arty and precious. I see evidence of ability which needs lots of
developing.

The best group of poems I have encountered today comes from
a poet whom I encouraged to resubmit after I turned down another
submission. A narrative poem running two full pages tells in simple
but engaging language the story of a couple of boys fishing under
a bridge in muddy water, going upstream and finding a clear pool
where large carp, "big as dogs," sleep in the depths. The boys try
worms, corn, grasshoppers, chicken guts, but cannot get the giant
fish to bite. They end by throwing sticks, then stones, then boulders
into the pool, muddying the water so that they cannot see whether
the fish were ever disturbed. The blank verse moves easily with
occasional flashes of metaphor and humor, and I considered the
poem long before deciding it was a little too prosy and lacking
in point to justify my taking it. He includes a humorous suite about
a professor wrestling with his sexual temptations, a student inducing
"fancies"

of a virgin continent waiting to be explored,
jungles sultry, squirming, where the great worm is
royal, rolling expanses of resources,
gold! Epiphany of epidermis!

Again I am tempted — and it is only memory of the great stock of
poems on hand which persuades me to return the batch with an
encouraging note.

That takes care of seven batches — and I see fifteen still on
the desk, an average of five poems in each. One, two, three, drop
on the rejection stack without comment. I pause over a very good
poet who is just a bit too flat and too long-winded. For example,
he gives us this image for forgetfulness:

. . . a sense of loss
going always on and on
like the cramping seizure
of a missing arm

I was impressed by that, at the bottom of the page, and disappointed
to find on the next page that he couldn't let go of it:

> or leg, or the emptiness
> left behind when a tooth
> is pulled . . .

And on and on. Scattershot. Get the one image you can trust and
let it do the work alone.

Here is a poet from the Watts Workshop who clearly has talent,
powerful themes and a tough, convincing directness. The poem I am
most attracted to is wildly imaginative in praise of the old, neon
whore-mother, the City — and I would like to use it, but it seems
to me flawed. For example, it describes people gathering

> like live pubic hairs round the moon-pocked towers
> for who can see faces?

"Live" is surely the wrong word, for he is not contrasting them
with dead hairs. And the logic of the second line is unclear: they
are like hairs because their faces cannot be seen. Later they flee
the dawn:

> The relentless light pursues
> through red-lipped streets like wounds!

At first I thought the light pursued like wounds, then realized the
streets must be like wounds. That image seems to fight "red-lipped,"
and, besides, I don't know what it means to pursue something
through a wound.

I prefer those honest errors of impassioned vision and speech,
however, to the polysyllabic pedantry and strain of something like
this, from another batch:

> But does Change, or the Changeless, present an illusion?
> One can hold that Parmenides suffered delusion,
> Not sensing the true metaphysical crux
> In the surge of the great Heraclitean flux.

Pope and Dryden and Lucretius handled philosophical abstractions
wittily in verse — but if we look back to them we see how clumsy
and dull this modern effort is as it tries to do the same.

Four batches cannot be returned because they were not sent
with return envelopes, self-addressed and stamped.

And that clears the desk!

I have quoted from the best work I have found — and you
may judge whether in your opinion I have been too harsh. One
or two came close to acceptance, and several other poets are clearly
publishable, though the work they submitted this time seemed to

me not entirely successful. Sometime when you are in the library, I suggest you look at the poetry published by any magazine in the course of a year or two, seeing how many poems you might want to include in an anthology, or which you would predict would be included in anthologies fifty years from now.

the mail bag

Some time after the preceding appeared, I wrote again about my function as an editor, particularly about correspondence, some of which concerned my confessions above.

Letters received from readers during the past month or so are sorted on my desk in four piles. The biggest of the stacks I call the GIMME letters. Typically these begin, "Dear Sir, I enjoyed your article . . ." and, in the second sentence come round to the real business of the letter, telling me the autobiography of the corres-pondent, how many people have enjoyed his or her poetry, and requesting my criticism of the enclosed bundle.

Some are abrupt — with no letter at all, just poems, or letters that skip that initial curtsey of compliment. For example I have one here which comes in an envelope marked "Personal Private Confidential." It begins:

> Please forgive this intrusion on your time. Since high school I have been interested in making writing my career. Poetry is my favorite type of reading and writing. Because you are a successful poet, I turn to you for your assistance and valuable opinion.

It goes on for a full page of autobiography and concludes with a request that I read the enclosed poems and give my "truthful opinion of the same . . . P.S. Will you please return my poetry along with your criticism and inspiration, if any. Thanks." There is, of course, no return envelope. Here are some lines from one of the enclosed poems:

> Floated there I onward
> Upon a leaf in the breeze,
> Fresh air and blossoms I feed upon,

And so on. Clearly anyone who would send such stuff through the mails has never read or understood anything I have ever written about poetry. She got my name out of some Poetic Phone Book.

I do not criticize poetry sent me by readers — either for fun or money. The way to get professional judgment of your work is to submit it to magazines which publish poetry and the judgment you will probably receive will be a rejection slip. Sorry. I wish the world were full of professional poets who had time and inclination to comment on the work of those, like my correspondent, who need criticism. But it is not.

What can you do then, Miss Blank? The first thing you can do is read some poetry. As a minimum, read your way, thoughtfully and carefully, through some standard anthology. Oscar Williams will do for a start: *Immortal Poems of the English Language,* an inexpensive pocket book. Then move on to some of the anthologies of contemporary poetry, such as *New Poets of England and America,* Meridian (more expensive because living poets get royalties). Subscribe to *Poetry.* Read the poetry in *Atlantic, Harper's, The New Yorker* and other magazines. Think about what you read, learn from it, and then try writing. How do you become an architect? Do you sit down and sketch a house, then mail it off to a professional requesting free criticism?

Most of the GIMME letters are simply pathetic, often nearly illiterate: "I used today topicals as subjects controversials etc hoping to interest the reader." Often they are accompanied by privately printed books or pamphlets, which, I am assured, have had enthusiastic reception among the poet's friends. Here is one sent me by a vanity publisher, for review, with a letter telling me "the bookstand sales are exceeding our expectations" and that the poet, with "his network feature 'The Poet's Corner'" has "kept an interest in poetry alive for many years." I will quote one complete poem:

BIRD OF PARADISE

From life's Elysian fields
Fair symbol of
The Promised Land.

You don't really want my opinion of that, do you?

The next pile I call the AGM's (psychological jargon for "attention-getting mechanisms"). Often these contain little verses addressed to me, illustrated by this excerpt:

Am I really very awful?
Do my friends just humor me?

> Should I really ought to stop it?
> Am I only wasting time?
> Is it only wishful thinking
> That makes my thoughts all rhyme?
>   . . .
> Mr. Jerome, I ask you
> Is there hope for folks like me
> Who like their prose in story form
> And a verse for poetry?

The AGM usually takes off from some point raised in an article and uses it as a device to bring attention to the correspondent. "Your last paragraph . . . indicates you relish narrative poetry . . . a lot of other people also do for they have bought 10,253 separate copies of some I have written and hired printed." A pamphlet is enclosed, beginning:

> Operating a service station,
>   May resemble a bed of roses,
> To those whose observation
>   Goes no farther than their noses.

This is clearly lyric; I was unable to find any narrative poetry in the pamphlet, so I assume the writer simply wants to seize any available handle to draw attention to himself.

Here is a letter with a title:

On Greater Perspective

The Editor —

> In response to the article . . . concerning the Avant-Garde and the future of Poetry, much more viewpoint on these things is required . . .

The letter quickly leaves poetry behind and moves into a general essay on the writer's views of "Liberal Democracy," "Love of Country," and other topics.

Another frequent AGM is to couple a legitimate inquiry with a "sample" inviting attention. One lady sends a rejection slip from a magazine apparently called *the other side of silence,* with the crudely inked message: "Try *The National Review* or *American Opinion* — they go for this saccharine-sweet psuedo-patriotism. As far as we're concerned, it sucks." Our correspondent asks — reasonably enough — "what you consider good taste in rejection slips, and what is pure bad manners?" But she adds, "I don't expect an answer, really — I just wanted to say *I* consider it in poor taste (if it matters at all what I think). I also enclose the poem so you can see if it's as bad as it was called." Certainly the rejection slip is both stupid and ill-mannered: there is, indeed, nothing saccharine-sweet in the poem, or, so far as I can tell, any patriotism, pseudo or otherwise. But unsolicited manuscripts are likely to get some unsolicited responses. You take your chances about being insulted if you launch yourself, or attempt to launch yourself, into public print. Would a printed, polite rejection slip have helped her become a better poet? Probably it would have been no more useful than this rejection. But the poem itself is so sloppy and incomprehensible that I should think the poetess would have little reason to talk about the kettle's bad taste.

The liveliest of my four piles is the one I call BRICKBATS. Often I learn from these negative reactions. Sometimes the criticism is stinging but valid:

> As for Mr. Jerome's condemnation of the economic power behind this "hippie idea," may I remind him that it's his generation that is responsible for the sickening commercialization of the teenage fads. If his generation were as quick to adopt the liberal and idealistic philosophy of the young people as they are to adopt the superficial outer-garments . . ., we would all be living in a more pleasant world.

My comments on the trials of a poetry editor brought a torrent of blistering edification. One correspondent regarded it as my obituary announcing "the passing of Judson Jerome from the ranks of 'poetry lovers.' " Another wrote at length about the trials of poets in dealing with editors who demand stamped, self-addressed envelopes, and sometimes don't include the zip code in their correspondence, requiring this beleagured woman to "contact the local postal authority to get it." She justly points out that editors are not consistent in their demands:

> Some want only 3 submissions at a mailing, and those once every three months, others insist on five (in a letter sized envelope) while another editor may demand six or more, but in a flat, unfolded, clasp envelope. Some scream if you don't include a cardboard backing and paperclips to hold the ms together, and others scream even louder if you do! There are editors who write nasty little notes about NOT showing this courtesy for

the convenience of the editor and those (Mr. Judson Jerome) who wonder why you included that extra piece of junk . . . . Yet what would all those little journals do if no one sent them any mss? They can't exist without the poet any more than the poet can get recognition without the existence of little mags.

Still another reader comments in verse:

WHAT DOES HE WANT?

He only wants butter and sticky goo
On the things that he can eat or chew:
He only wants stamps outdated and rare,
So lick'em and stick'em, he won't care!
He only gets peeved, just once in a while,
When mail stacks up in a gigantic pile:
He only wants poems chic and refined,
That's the reason I didn't send him mine.

For which I couldn't be more grateful.

Not exactly brickbats are those truly informative and useful letters which catch my errors and correct misapprehensions. For example, I wondered why some return envelopes came with the stamps paper-clipped to them rather than pasted on. A couple of readers sent me to the horse's mouth, *Writer's Market,* which says:

A return envelope with typed name and address label — and return postage clipped (not stuck!) to it — and inserted with manuscript.

An editor explained why: in large offices, the return postage is separated for independent use, and all outgoing mail is metered. Ho hum! I'd still rather writers do their own stamp-licking.

My fourth stack, which I call KUDOS, is, I am happy to say, nearly as tall as any of the other three. While the brief notes saying "Cheers!" are very valuable feed-back, I especially appreciate those letters which launch into real discussion (whether they agree with me or not) of the subject matter of my columns. One says:

I wouldn't cavalierly dismiss the cover letter listing previous publications. If the poet writes that he has published here and there before I'd definitely want to see his stuff. Previous publication means, not much, but something. Another editor's sensitivity and regard. Which could be a good check on your own. Anyway, I think you should rehabilitate the cover letter that leaves off the drool but lists credits.

I think the point is well-taken, and I should learn to suppress my prejudice against what seems to be bragging, or what seems to be the implication that if all these other people have accepted the poet, I would have a lot of gall to reject him. I must admit that when a cover letter lists credits from magazines I respect, I do look more closely to see what I am missing. On the other hand, I get a special joy from picking up unpublished writers, from having the opportunity to give them their first boost. Whether you should enclose a cover letter listing your credits is at least an open question.

I have here a letter of several pages from a writer with a quarter-century of experience — disturbed, as I am, by the possible use of the hip-cult, the emergence of a sickening alliance between the far-right and the far-left, and the state of literature with anti-intellectualism in the saddle. She expresses relief that the New Critical stone is being rolled away from the door, feeling that writers of a liberal bent were in a stranglehold during the forties and fifties, but she believes it is again becoming possible for them to speak out.

Another suggests that I do a column on poetry of the space age — and included several pages of an essay comparing Donne's relation to the science of his time with the modern poet's plight, and his need for reflecting the sensibility and preoccupation of today's science. Another suggests I do a piece on limericks — but since he includes a page of his own, and news of the publication of a book of his limericks, I am not sure whether I should classify the letter as a suggestion or an AGM.

There is no question that my views on poetry have been shaped by the continual influx of ideas and reactions I receive in the mail. I am not looking for congratulations (though I certainly don't object to them!), but for the indications that readers are intelligently involved with the state of poetry and their own participation in the craft.

how to read a rejection slip

Chances are you have collected a few rejection slips from *POETRY,* crested with Pegasus done in squirming lines, tucking his chin back and glancing down with a disapproving, almond eye. Or perhaps you had an illegible note of encouragement. Or perhaps an acceptance; in that case you were asked for a photograph which is now filed alongside the faces of almost all the other American (and many foreign) poets of any worth who have been writing during the last half-century. (I am proud to have mine there, a blur somewhere with Jarrell, Jeffers and Justice.)

Perhaps you submitted to *POETRY* because you knew it made a special effort to introduce new poets as well as continuing to print work of those who are well-known. It has more consistently and more successfully printed the best available poetry than any other magazine in the English-speaking world. If you have sent them work you were making a bid to be included in the ranks; nothing so much as that first acceptance from *POETRY* is apt to make one think, "Ah, now I am a poet."

Some years ago I asked Henry Rago, the editor, if he had some advice for contributors which I might pass on. He was kind enough to answer at length. I would like to quote and discuss what he says — not only because *POETRY* is of special interest to any learning poet but because his remarks are a good guide to any magazine which publishes what we might call "quality" poetry.

That term itself presents the first difficulty, and I am tempted to define it as Louis Armstrong defined jazz, something to the effect that if you got to ask, man, you'll never know. Rago pleads that contributors study the magazine, "a good rule for sending anything out, verse or prose, but it seems especially important for verse, because there is so much ambiguity about the kind of writing that word can be used to designate." Let's face it, the editors of *Woman's Day* and *POETRY* are looking for different things. Little moral quatrains such as might appear boxed in slick magazines will not appear in *POETRY*, nor will sonnets that celebrate the first crocus, such as might greet spring on the editorial pages of midwestern dailies; nor will that consideration of youth's prospects which had an honored place in your school annual; nor will poems which quote an amusing news item and then make a wry, rhymed comment; nor will religious or propaganda verse in which clichés are regimented in rhyming ranks, in which poetry is subservient to the Cause. The world has more of an appetite for all these things than it has for quality poetry. Very well, feed it, but spare that slender nose of Pegasus such offerings; refusal is painful both for him and you. "We get a full basket of manuscripts each day," Mr. Rago says, "that simply would not be sent to us if the authors really took a good look into the magazine."

This is not to imply, however, that the diet of Pegasus is

specialized, or that by gauging your victim carefully you can learn his weaknesses. "If," Mr. Rago encourages me, "all you accomplished was the negative result of discouraging the mechanical mailing around of poor verse, or convincing people really interested in markets or slants that there is no point in trifling with poetry, you would be doing a valuable thing both for editors of magazines like *POETRY* and for the good, honest people themselves who keep wasting all those stamps and all that time." Here, you see, is the difficulty: it is not a matter of changing a word or line or even writing another poem to please; the trouble with a great body of poetry uselessly submitted lies far back in the personality and the attitudes of the poets, and it is not something they can easily alter. "Nor should he try us if the writing of poetry doesn't seem to him a serious occupation either at the center of his life or very near it. To put this on a low level, but in terms clear enough to eliminate hundreds and hundreds of poems a year if only the advice were followed, I'd say that anyone who regards the writing of poetry as his hobby, and uses that word for it, shouldn't send poems to *POETRY,* though he might very well sell some of his work else-where." He may sell it, I might add, at ten or twenty times the line-rate — so he needn't feel abused. *POETRY,* like most university quarterlies, like the "little" magazines, is a subsidized publication, supported by wealthy donors. There is no possibility that you and *POETRY* will make one another rich — so if your motives are mercenary, don't bother. If they are those of an innocent amateur, don't bother. Like any other "fine art," poetry demands pro-fessional devotion and ability, yet offers almost none of the re-wards that accrue in the non-artistic professions.

We have just taken care of about half of the daily mail. Most of you who read this book, however, know what poetry is and write well enough, at least, to reach the next level of considera-tion. "As for the work that gives us reason to look twice," Mr. Rago writes, "it is some kind of life in the writing that makes us pause — I mean by 'life' not the loud assertion of it but something in the writing that has its own vibration on the page — although the poem might not be completely realized, or other voices might be for the while mixed in with the poet's own, or there might be just a good moment in the poem and the rest not really 'written' but settled for, in a compromise of either feeling or style (the cliché, in either case, that gives up the effort of communicating, of meaning *anything),* or the poem might overreach itself and lose the reader, or . . .," and one shrugs helplessly; it is impossible to summarize all the reasons a poem can fail, although he touched some important ones.

Once Mr. Rago said to me, about the work of a friend, "He doesn't know how to finish a poem," and it is the unfinished, the incompletely realized poem which is perhaps most exasperating to an editor. For, believe it or not, he *wants* to find good work. The poetry editor, unlike other editors, can be of very little help at this point because he can't do your work for you. Even if he can point to a weakness he can do little in the way of correcting it; his positive suggestions are bound to be vague. It is your idea, your poem, and its execution must be of a piece with its conception.

How do you know if a poem is "finished"? No formula can answer that question in its most important aspect: that is, whether the poem completely and fully embodies its idea. But I can suggest some helpful checks. First, regard the poem as though it were a cablegram. Go through it crossing out all the words which are not essential to meaning — the dead words, the articles and prepositions and pronouns and merely decorative adjectives, the uninteresting words. Some of these have to go back in, of course, for your poem to be idiomatically smooth; but if you find you have more than two or three dead words to a line, probably the poem or passages of it need to be recast, the phrasing condensed, a new word selected to replace an uneconomical phrase. Do you know what the poem's intention is? (Surprisingly, it is quite possible *not* to know this). Does everything in the poem contribute to that intention, or did you try to squeeze in an extra good idea or so which ought to be saved for another poem? Does the poem repeat itself; are there two details which make the same point, one of which can be cut? (E.g., no need of saying "old and toothless" when "toothless" will convey the idea of age.)

Finally, is enough going on in the poem? I feel there ought to be more than one reason for every word in a poem; sound plus meaning is the most obvious consideration — but more is possible. Ambiguity is a fad, of course; but there is something in what the New Critics discovered: that the richest, most suggestive lines tend to reverberate with secondary intimations. "Gold" is a tiresomely frequent word in poetry, but when Keats says "Much have I travell'd in the realms of gold," its very overuse loads it with meaning — the sunny climes, the El Dorados of human aspiration, the realms of the imagination, and more and more, like a note struck in an echo chamber — so that when he develops the idea of exploration as an analogy for reading Homer or simply great poetry, we walk small in the valley of larger meaning. Similarly, *everything,* even the marks of punctuation, ought to be not only right but resonant. If you have simply said something, though you may have said it very well, the poem lies flat. Have you given it the dimensions of suggestiveness, of sound, rhythm, language, humanity, symbol, shape, which make it stand up round from the page, or, as Mr. Rago says, give it "vibration"?

It is true that magazines reject on the grounds of inappropriateness of subject matter and limitations of space; but these more often serve as rationalizations for poets who do not want to face the fact that they simply have not had an idea which can make a poem or, having had such an idea, have not brought it off. Nothing perhaps distinguished the poem from thousands of others which have crossed the editor's desk. It is difficult for a poet working in the solitude of his typewriter and thoughts to imagine how many other intelligent, original and sensitive people are similarly being reverent at that very moment before the altar of their own perceptions. It all comes out looking very much alike.

Or if he does realize this, a poet may resort to gimmicks — to astonishing language, peculiar line forms, bizarre titles, explosive openings and odd punctuation — to distinguish his own poem from all that grey matter. But this is also a dodge, and you might be surprised to know how many of the others have resorted to the same gimmicks.

There is, finally, no substitute for quality — and while, of course, some editors and some poets fail to recognize when they have hit upon quality, consistently good work is bound to be recognized. Most complaints about the narrowness or blindness or stupidity of editors (I know; I indulge in these myself) are tactics for putting off revision.

Mr. Rago adds that *POETRY* pays on publication, all manuscripts must be accompanied by stamped, self-addressed envelopes, or they can't be returned, but they need at least a month to consider most work, and they cannot consider book-length manuscripts. "Five, six or seven pages from most poets, especially new ones, would seem as big a packet as we ought to get. We're glad also to look at single poems, one-page. We wish we could write to each poet but we can't; the printed rejection slip is not meant to be a discouragement. We get as many as 70,000 poems a year (poems, not packets; one packet might have three or four or five poems)." It seems to me that everything he says would be endorsed by most poetry editors of quarterlies, little magazines, and probably such popular magazines as *Atlantic, Harper's* and *The New Yorker,* which are interested in quality poetry.

If you are serious about writing poetry — and there is very little reason to write it unless you are, as the pay, at best, is nominal — most market information is either obvious or unimportant. Those periodicals which publish "quality" poetry — as distinguished from the special interest verse outlets discussed below — will all tell you the same thing: we want nothing but the best. What constitutes the best varies, of course, from editor to editor and time to time, and the criteria are so subjective and relative that it is impossible to describe them in any useful way. Moreover, what is "best" for the editors is ultimately unimportant. The poet is much more apt to be concerned with what is best for himself — and what is best for the ages. If your motive in writing poetry is to second-guess editors and hit the top markets, you are probably in the wrong field.

The editor of a quality publication is in an honest dilemma when queried about what he wants. This comment by the poetry editor of *The New Yorker* is typical of what most would have to say:

> *The New Yorker* prints poetry and light verse. To characterize the nature of the poetry would seem to us impossible, since we publish poets as different as Theodore Roethke and Ogden Nash, Robert Graves and Marianne Moore, R. P. Lister and Elizabeth Bishop. . . . We would not be averse to publishing a kind of poem we never have published before, providing we liked it. We print many poems by people we have never heard of who send in manuscripts; we also try to get poems from poets whose work we admire. We print poems that are formal, and poems that are not. We do not really look for any particular "kind" of poetry, though many people seem to think so; we print the poems we like that we think are good.

Other periodicals may not be able to list such an auspicious group as examples, but most would like to be able to do so. If you read the work of Roethke, Nash, Graves, Moore, Lister and Bishop you will see the difficulty of generalizing.

One of the problems of definition which vexes people who want neat answers is the difference between poetry and verse. T. S. Eliot, in his essay on Kipling, suggests some lines along which a distinction may be made: verse is relatively more, rhythmic, puts more emphasis on rhyme, is more readily comprehensible, and is apt to be lighter in tone than poetry. There may, he says, be very great verse, and very poor poetry; the terms are not of quality but kind. However, the line between the kinds is itself blurred. Chaucer might so be classified as a verse-writer, and Anne Morrow Lindbergh as a poet. I think it more useful to stick to the technical definition of verse as a line of poetry, and admit anything as poetry which the author so designates, horrible as it may be. Poetry, then, might be defined as writing which employs the line — or verse — as a formal device; but that, of course, doesn't account for prose poems. Finally I think we must leave definition to the lexicographers and go back to writing poetry.

The periodicals of greatest interest to serious poets are those which have a national reputation of some duration for publication of excellent poetry. I have discussed *POETRY* as a prime example, but *The New York Quarterly* or *American Poetry Review* would serve as well. Some of the monthlies, such as *Harper's* would be included here; most of the quarterlies, such as *Yale Review, Hudson Review,* or *Virginia Quarterly Review;* some of the better established "little" magazines, such as *American Review, Carleton Miscellany, Chicago Review, Epoch,* or *Perspective.* One guide to such periodicals is the credit list in volumes of new poetry by poets you admire. Pay, of course, is no criterion: some, such as *Ladies' Home Journal,* pay as much as $10 a line; $.50 a line is more common — but some, such as *Prairie Schooner,* pay nothing at all.

The poet needs to recognize how much space these periodicals are able to give poems and what length poems are possible in their make-up. Short poems always have a much better chance than those over, say, twenty lines. And the odds favor "serious" poetry as opposed to light verse. (This is not, I think, because of any stuffiness on the part of the periodicals; it is easier to write a passable serious poem than to achieve a really distinctive style in humor.) Taboos of language and theme are about the same in poetry for these periodicals as they are for quality fiction — with the additional recognition that it is much more difficult to make shocking material work in a poem than it is in fiction.

The poet should also recognize that these periodicals receive hundreds of packets of poetry every week. There are surely more amateur poets than any other kind of writer — and much less space given to poetry than to any other kind of writing. The sooner a beginner develops some ability for realistic appraisal of what he writes — compared to the poetry he sees published — the better able he will be to save himself time and energy.

Unfortunately, no poet need go unpublished. Newspapers, church and other organizational organs, even trade journals, often use verse. There are, too, perennial little magazines appearing and disappearing on the literary scene. It is difficult to classify or comment on these. Some become important in time, and the part little magazines have played in American literary history is tremendous (in spite of the fact that Frost has said he would as soon make love in Lover's Lane as publish in little magazines). Some, such as *Epos,* devoted entirely to poetry, have respected age and reputation; all claim a standard of excellence comparable to that of their more esteemed competitors. Because they may not be so swamped with manuscripts as the better known periodicals, their editors are more often able to comment or be of direct help to poets and are therefore a good place for beginners to start submitting. Most important literary reputations begin in relatively ephemeral publications often edited by some of the most imaginative, talented and enthusiastic people in the field — so the poet should feel no loss of dignity in trying the relatively obscure outlets.

Those poets who write for money or merely to be published for the thrill of seeing their work in print should skip all the above and concentrate upon more specialized outlets. For example, they might examine *Arizona Highways,* whose rates are good, and try to write a short poem especially for them. Some poetry in publications directed toward special audiences or conveying creeds or programs is very fine, but excellence is not sufficient (nor always necessary) to win a place in their pages. In some cases they specify length limits, and usually the subject-matter must fall within a specified range. In a few cases the payment is quite high. In this case marketing of poetry is much like marketing fiction or articles; the premium is upon knowing the publication and its audience, and professional adaptation to external demands is required. If the idea of knocking out a verse in an odd hour and getting a few dollars from it appeals to you, study the little special-interest publications in the market list, and the best of luck to you. Or if you enjoy the prestige or self-satisfaction of seeing your name and work in print, but are not seriously concerned with making a career of poetry, there are many no-payment outlets — even local newspapers — which may appreciate and give a showing to your metrical observations, if they are appropriate to the publication's larger purpose.

A steady income from verse is almost impossible to come by, but there are some commercial outlets which have a steady enough demand to employ people with a facility with verse forms. Chief of these, of course, are the greeting-card publishers. Needless to say, the work is completely anonymous, and requires a high degree of expertness not only in poetic forms but knowledge of the field and of audience preferences. It is much like writing a very specialized variety of advertising copy, and this is no place for the idle rhymester unless he is willing to work hard at developing the skills and knowledge of an exacting trade.

Becoming a poet is quite another thing. If you want to compete with Shakespeare and Keats and Eliot, the specifications of periodicals must surely be a minor consideration. It is important for any poet to be heard, to be read, of course; but if you write good poetry you will not stifle for lack of publication. The periodicals of highest quality are flexible enough to respond to true and important talent of any variety. You may learn a great deal, of course, in the process of submission and rejection and from the comments of good editors. Almost no literary agents handle poetry unless the poet is also a commercial writer of another sort. So you go it alone. When it comes to publishing a book, you must notice which publishers do and do not publish poetry — and most don't. Some university presses are now bringing out volumes. But it is tough getting in. Much as I hate to say it, book publication almost requires a fairly established reputation and, if possible, influential friends. Nothing in the mails is quite so pathetic as a book-length poetry manuscript by an unknown writer. There are, of course, contests and competitions which give you some chance to rocket into prominence. But for most of us it is a long process of building up a reputation through consistently good publications in periodicals. It is hardly worth the trouble unless poetry matters more to you than anything else in life; and if it does, your concern is clearly with the learning what makes good poetry, not learning how to play the market like a speculator.

PART THREE:

READING POEMS

tradition and the individual talent

In a superb essay with that title T. S. Eliot points out how the voice of each new poet inescapably resonates with the overtones of his education and the culture which shaped him and how the most any individual can do is modify minimally the cultural stream. Part Three is a kind of short course in some of the traditions which bear upon the work of poets writing today. In the fifties and sixties most poets of the United States were college educated — most of them, in fact, teaching in colleges during at least part of their careers. In the seventies young people are increasingly choosing alternative modes of education as the attraction of professional, salaried, secure positions is declining — on the whole a healthy development both for them and for poetry. But there is a danger that the baby of traditional learning will be thrown out with the bathwater of credentials and requirements and formal, systematic schooling. Throughout this book, but especially in Part Three, I have tried to draw attention to some elements of our poetic heritage which I believe new talents should explore — on their own if they eschew university training.

It is absurd to think one can learn to write poetry by studying its abstract formal elements. One may learn to do mathematics that way — getting down the principles, and ignoring the errors and speculations and the discoveries of mathematicians of the past, though I should think that study of the tradition would be at least emotionally enriching if not downright useful in shaping and accelerating new work. If I were a mathematician I am sure that the detailed and anguished drama of mathematical knowledge unfolding in human history would be as exciting to me as my current work. Similarly, if I were a philosopher or painter or musician or architect, I would both want to learn from the past and participate in it as I empathized with the struggles and exhilarating moments of achievement of my predecessors. Certainly my notion of being a poet includes living the lives and feeling from the inside the poetry of others, of my contemporaries to some degree, but even more importantly the poets who shaped the culture I inherited.

Part Three only scratches the surface of that culture — examining in detail some few poems, part of the furniture of the mind which I think essential to any modern poet's education. These are reference points as, for an American, *Rhapsody in Blue* is likely to be, or the faces on Mount Rushmore, or the Golden Gate Bridge, or *Huckleberry Finn*. Because our national poetic history is so brief, these reference points reach back into English tradition which preceded it. These are poems that provide us with the dimensions and overtones of our thoughts and values and language, whether we know it or not. I conclude with consideration of the poetry of two little girls, one American, one French, who were surely innocent of any formal knowledge of most of the poetry I discuss here — but it has shaped their work, too, and as they become women they will become better poets as they understand more fully the influences working upon them.

CHAPTER SIXTEEN

Metaphysical and Cavalier

Immersed in modern poetry and in the issues of our breaking civilization, I begin to feel grey and transient as a newspaper — a soggy one, swept on the flood of the thaw, swirling along the gutter-tide of events, overwhelmed, sensing the only future lies downstream. Tomorrow is pounding the door, Gestapo-like, in the night. My nerves are screwed tight as piano wire. My ears are filled with sirens screaming . . . .

I wonder what renewal I can find in a day in my robe and slippers. Outside, somewhere, the traffic of the time snarls and honks, strident and harsh and swift in its oily air, but around me is a little space, the twittering of birds, a swinging bud and the garden's tentative green. I find myself considering, of all things, parallel strains of English love poetry in the seventeenth century: that of the metaphysical poet John Donne and the cavalier poet Sir John Suckling. I find in their world excitement, fun, wit, beauty, searching thought and rugged artfulness, much of which seems some-how more relevant to my own life in twentieth century America than is in much of the poetry of my contemporaries.

John Donne (1572-1631): the epitome of literary preciousness, the darling of the Mandarins, the supreme "metaphysical" poet — intensely cerebral, intellectual, twistingly witty and difficult. Sink in a deep chair. What has Donne to say to the world this morning?

THE SUNNE RISING

Busie old foole, unruly Sunne,
Why dost thou thus,
Through windowes, and through curtaines call on us?
Must to thy motions lovers seasons run?

So begins an aubade — a traditional dawn song in which a lover protests the daylight parting him from his mistress. It strikes my mood exactly. *Now* is an intrusion. Time drags me along like a mother pulling an unwilling child by the arm. Is there no private room — of love, of poetry, of thought or imagination — into which the calendar may not project its unwelcome beams?

> Sawcy pedantique wretch, goe chide
> Late schoole boyes, and sowre prentices,
> Go tell Court-huntsmen, that the King will ride,
> Call countrey ants to harvest offices;

Day breaks around the kingdom upon those with business: the sleepy scholar, lugging his books, running in fear of his teacher's rebuke; the grumpy apprentice sweeping the shop before his master arrives; the ambitious courtier pasting on a morning's smile to join the monarch's hunting party; the drudging farmer laboring to survive. This panorama included all who have something to fear, something to seek, something to acquire, but:

> Love, all alike, no season knowes, nor clyme,
> Nor houres, dayes, moneths, which are the rags of time.

That couplet concludes the first stanza with the claim that love is a kind of nirvana, a changeless state of grace to which the world's mutations are irrelevant. As the poet lies in bed with his mistress in his arms he has nothing to fear, seek or acquire — except continuation of his blessed condition.

In the next stanza he more-or-less accepts the presence of the sun, but attempts to ridicule it:

> Thy beames, so reverend, and strong
> Why shouldst thou thinke?
> I could eclipse and cloud them with a winke,
> But that I would not lose her sight so long:

How can your beams be so hallowed and powerful if I can close them off merely by shutting my eyes — which I will not do because I do not want to lose sight of my mistress even for the space of a blink. That thought reminds the poet of the brightness of the lady's eyes — which, according to the hyperbolic convention of Petrarchan poetry, is sufficient to outshine and blind the sun:

> If her eyes have not blinded thine,
> Looke, and to-morrow late, tell mee,
> Whether both the'India's of spice and Myne
> Be where thou leftst them, or lie here with mee.
> Aske for those Kings whom thou saw'st yesterday,
> And thou shalt heare, All here in one bed lay.

There is subtle humor lambent here: he has thought of a device for getting the sun off on an errand. The word "late" is slipped in wittily to tell the sun he needn't be in any hurry to return. In the humor is an implicit acknowledgment that the poet is aware of the sun's reality, that he knows he is spinning an elaborate fiction about love. But he goes on to spin it, nonetheless: our love is its own world; moreover, it is the real world, and that outer world which the sun warms must have disappeared. In my arms are contained the East Indies (of spices) and West Indies (where gold is mined). Perhaps Donne means to pun on *mine,* saying the Indias are now mine. He himself is the king of kings, containing them all.

> She'is all States, and all Princes, I,
> Nothing else is.
> Princes doe but play us; compar'd to this,
> All honor's mimique; All wealth alchimie.
> Thou sunne art halfe as happy'as wee,
> In that the world's contracted thus;
> Thine age askes ease, and since thy duties bee
> To warme the world, that's done in warming us.
> Shine here to us, and thou art every where;
> This bed thy center is, these walls, thy spheare.

The poem which began by telling the sun to go away ends by telling it to stick around — another way of making time stop. In possessing her, I possess all countries in the world. There is no reality other than ourselves. What appears to be real in that other world, outside our love, is an illusion. Those are not really kings out there, but people imitating us, the true kings. The honor between us is the only true honor — and that to which others pretend is mere mimicry. The wealth they claim is fraudulent, for the only true gold is our love.

With that thought the poet goes off on a new tangent: if we are the real world, the sun is doing its job in giving us its light and warmth. The sun should be grateful (half as happy as we are — because no one could be entirely as happy as we are) that all the world is contained in this bedroom. You're getting old, anyway, sun, so you can take it easy by warming the real world ("that's done," punning on Donne), ourselves. We are the world which in the Ptolemaic scheme is the center of the universe, surrounded by crystalline spheres belonging to the planets, stars, moon and sun.

Space is eradicated by the last stanza as time was by the first.

Essentially the poem asserts that the ideal — love — is real, and material "reality" is but an imitation or an illusion. But, as I said before, the poem is shot through with recognition that this is but fantasy: that the day indeed has come, that the workaday world grinds on with brutal inevitability, that time devours love as it does lovers and their brief night of escape. They have as little chance of escaping time as his mistress has of blinding the sun with her eyes. All this talk is poesy, elaborate flattery for the lady, extravagant postulation of an unattainable ideal. Beneath the fantasy is at first a bitter, then a rather comfortable acceptance of the facts of life. One can imagine the poet, at the end of the poem, smiling broadly, gesturing at the walls, and climbing from bed to put his pants on.

And as we look back over the poem we can see many clues to this double-edged tone. The opening line, while it is abusive, is also rather fond and indulgent. The sun may seem "unruly" as it interrupts their sleep, but it proceeds by inalterable rule more powerful than the rule of love. In the very language which rejects the outer world one can detect a love of the world, with its schoolboys, apprentices, huntsmen, laboring ants, spices, gold, Indias and kings. As the poet claims true "honor" for their presumably extramarital love, he is saying that is also of a piece with the deception, hyprocrisy and hollowness of honor in the streets. It's all a game — and one which occasionally rewards with delights. Constancy, the nirvana of love, in which time is frozen as it is for the figures on Keats' Grecian Urn, sometimes allures us in contemplation — but it would be a bore to live with — as Donne makes clear in this little poem:

WOMAN'S CONSTANCY

Now thou has lov'd me one whole day,
To morrow when thou leav'st, what wilt thou say?
Wilt thou then Antedate some new made vow?
    Or say that now
We are not just those persons, which we were?
Or, that oathes made in reverentiall feare
Of Love, and his wrath, any may forsweare?
Or, as true deaths, true maryages untie,
So lovers contracts, images of those,
Binde but till sleep, deaths image, them unloose?
    Or, your owne end to Justifie,

> For having purpos'd change, and falsehood; you
> Can have no way but falsehood to be true?
> Vaine lunatique, against these scapes I could
>   Dispute, and conquer, if I would,
>   Which I abstaine to doe,
> For by to morrow, I may thinke so too.

To protect himself against the anticipated inconstancy of his mistress he puts into her mouth a whole series of rationalizations she might use to leave him. She might, as one backdates a check, make up a claim that she had a prior commitment. Or she might use the relativistic argument that they have changed since she made her vow, and need not be true to vows made by slightly different people. Or she might claim to have been afraid of the wrath of the God of Love — and is no more bound than one would be who swore under torture. She might say that death unties marriage, so sleep (an imitation death) unties an agreement between lovers bound in imitation marriage. She might say she intended to be false, and now the only way to be true is to carry out her intention. "Vaine lunatique" (which, incidentally, means one who is moon-mad — as lovers often are) could apply to either the person addressed or to "I." With that phrase the poem swings round and denies its premise — that the poet objects to inconstancy. He will not protest because he, too, needs an exit route.

Such hearty, jocular, sometimes bitter and sometimes enthusiastic realism is characteristic of Donne's erotic verse. The logic-chopping mind in this poem is like the mythologizing mind in "The Sunne Rising." It spins out very ingenious propositions, but Donne will jerk it back if it gets too far from the facts of flesh-and-blood experience.

Contemporary with Donne was Sir John Suckling (1609-1641) — a very minor example of the Cavalier poets — that group which Pope, in the next century, described as a "mob of gentlemen who wrote with ease." Poetry of the metaphysical strain, such as that of Donne's, tends to be relatively crabbed, packed, intense, knobby, erudite and philosophical. The Cavaliers were much more classical in manner, seeking balance, lucidity, rationality and traditional values. The wit of Donne is like a tough and twisted briar. That of Suckling gleams like a sword.

The best known of Suckling's poems is this slight song:

Why so pale and wan fond Lover?
   prethee why so pale?
Will, when looking wel can't move her
   looking ill prevail?
   prethee why so pale?

Why so dull and mute young sinner?
   prethee why so mute?
Will, when speaking well can't win her,
   saying nothing do't?
   prethee why so mute?

Quit, quit for shame, this will not move,
   this cannot take her;
If of her self she will not love,
   nothing can make her:
   the divel take her.

I can imagine such a song, rendered by a rock group, becoming an international hit, except that its tough-minded, anti-romantic stance is perhaps stronger than even our sophisticated and unsentimental era is ready for. Compared with the lyrics of Simon and Garfunkle or Bob Dylan, this has a tighter, more ingenious form; it seems neater, more calculated than the prevailing style. But the language is modern enough — and the subject matter seems as relevant to our time as to any other. We still have mooning lovers who need to be kidded out of their drooping melancholy, haven't we? And do we not need reminders that love which results in slavish dependency and spiritual torpor is a kind of illness?

Like Donne and Carew and Jonson and Herrick (and Shakespeare in several of his sonnets and comedies), Suckling was in rebellion against the courtly love tradition which construed love as worship of a disdainful lady in a tower, the male vowing constancy, slaying dragons in her honor, suffering chills and fever of yearning, groveling as a slave before her power and purity. One of his favorite targets was the ideal of constancy:

Out upon it, I have lov'd
   Three whole days together;
And am like to love three more,
   If it prove fair weather.

Time shall moult away his wings
Ere he shall discover
In the whole wide world agen
Such a constant Lover.

But the spite on't is, no praise
Is due at all to me:
Love with me had made no staies,
Had it any been but she.

Had it any been but she
And that very Face,
There had been at least ere this
A dozen dozen in her place.

Beneath the ridicule of exaggerated rhetoric of conventional love poetry and its hypocritically held value of eternal devotion, one can also hear genial self-mockery and a hearty and sincere tenderness for the lady with the Face. If I were that lady I think I would be more flattered and pleased to receive this poem than many another which, with less candor, promised undying ardor and loyalty.

It will repay us to study the structure of that poem, for though the language and content seem casual and light-hearted, the stanzas are wrought and linked as by a jeweler. The first four lines neatly top one another with humor, each adding a new twist of wit to make his constancy appear more and more trivial. The second stanza is a glorious parody of the language and attitudes of courtly love poetry, revealing the egotism and extravagance of claims repeated so often they are acceptable clichés. In the middle of the poem there is a hinge, and the surprising motive of the poem — praise of his mistress — emerges. Egotism is cast aside as he pretends to accept the posture of the slave-of-love, inspired to heroism by the inescapable spell of her beauty. The repeated line (12 and 13) swings us into the climactic expression of adoration (understated — with no attempt to describe her peaches-and-cream-cherry-lips-bright-eyes, etc. — simply as "that very Face"), and the return in the last two lines of the theme of inconstancy. The greatest testimony to her attractions is that they have held a philandering scoundrel such as myself, he says, in line for three whole days.

These poems are clear, roundly proportioned, each line a unit of sense and grace. At times, perhaps influenced by his more baroque contemporaries, such as Donne, Suckling's poems are more complex, twisted, ragged, and more penetrating in thought than the ones I have quoted. For example, this song, a meditation on the theme that beauty is in the eye of the beholder, contains implications regarding contemporary semantics, psychology, and the emerging mechanistic, materialistic universe described by science:

> Of thee (kind boy) I ask no red and white
> to make up my delight,
> no odd becomming graces,
> Black eyes, or little know-not-whats, in faces;
> Make me but mad enough, give me good store
> Of Love, for her I Court,
> I ask no more,
> 'Tis love in love that makes the sport.
>
> There's no such thing as that we beauty call,
> it is meer cousenage all:
> for though some long ago
> Like't certain colours mingled so and so,
> That doth not tie me now from chusing new,
> If I fancy take
> To black and blue,
> That fancy doth it beauty make.
>
> Tis not the meat, but 'tis the appetite
> makes eating a delight,
> and if I like one dish
> More than another, that a Pheasant is;
> What in our watches, that in us is found,
> So to the height and nick
> We up be wound,
> No matter by what hand or trick.

In his prayer to Cupid (the "kind boy") he does not ask for the conventional mixture of red and white in his mistress' complexion, nor any other specific attributes. Rather, he asks that Cupid merely inflame him with desire (which he calls madness in the first stanza, fancy in the second, and, with blunt realism, appetite in the third). The last line of the first stanza might be paraphrased, "It is appetite which creates the fun in romance."

A philosopher or semanticist might call the second stanza nominalism, "a theory that there are no universal essences in reality and that the mind can frame no single concept or image corresponding to any universal or general term." "Cousenage" means deception or trickery. Words such as *beauty* trap us into believing that there is a thing outside us, in the world, which is beautiful, whereas the phenomenon is actually one of projection. Suckling associates the idealization of a classic variety of beauty with the past, "some long ago/ Like't certain coulours mingled so and so." We have, he implies, learned better. What determines beauty now is whimsical fancy.

It is the third stanza, however, which is the shocker, for though it says nothing the first two stanzas have not said, its two analogies for love — the primitive drive of hunger and the mechanistic conception of a watchspring — are reductive, deflating romance to a crude phenomenon of cause and effect. "Hunger is the best sauce," we say of food — and Suckling says the same of women. The last lines might be paraphrased: we are like our watches in that it is important that we be wound up tight ("to the height and nick"), but it doesn't really matter what hand winds us or what devices are used.

If that hard-headed behaviorism is too anti-idealistic for your taste, remember that it arises from protest against all the eloquent nonsense which for centuries has beguiled the world in the name of love. Many wedding nights would be happier if a strong dose of realism had been included in the ideological preparation of the bride and groom. Suckling's realism has a more genial face in "A Ballade. Upon a Wedding." This epithalamium in rural, folk dialect shows the positive side of Suckling's vision of the nature of sex and love. The "Ballade" begins this way:

> I tell thee *Dick* where I have been,
> Where I the rarest things have seen;
>   Oh things without compare!
> Such things again cannot be found
> In any place on English ground,
>   Be it at Wake, or Fair.

> At *Charing-Crosse,* hard by the way
> Where we (thou know'st) do sell our Hay,
>   There is a house with stairs;
> And there did I see comming down
> Such folks as are not in our Town,
>   Vorty at least, in Pairs.

Amongst the rest, one Pest'lent fine,
(His beard no bigger though then thine)
Walk't on before the rest:
Our landlord looks like nothing to him:
The King (God blesse him) 'twould undo him:
Should he go still so drest.

(Vorty is a northcountry pronunciation of *forty, Pest'lent,* or pestilent, is used merely as an expletive, as we might say "so infernally fine;" *still,* in the last line quoted above, means *always* — the King would go broke if he dressed every day in the way this young man was dressed.)

The bridegroom is fine enough ("the youth was going/ To make an end of all his woing"), but nothing compared to the bride. The pun in the first line below is intentional:

The maid (and thereby hangs a tale)
For such a maid no Whitson-ale
Could ever yet produce:
No Grape that's kindly ripe, could be
So round, so plump, so soft as she,
Nor half so full of Juyce.

Her finger was so small, the Ring
Would not stay on which they did bring,
It was too wide a Peck:
And to say truth (for out it must)
It lookt like the great Collar (just)
About our young Colts neck.

Her feet beneath her Petticoat,
Like little mice stole in and out,
As if they fear'd the light:
But oh! she dances such a way!
No Sun upon an Easter day
Is half so fine a sight.

He would have kist her once or twice,
But she would not, she was nice,
She would not do't in sight,
And then she lookt as who should say
I will do what I list to day;
And you shall do't at night.

Her Cheeks so rare a white was on,
No Dazy makes comparison,
  (Who sees them is undone)
For streaks of red were mingled there,
Such as are on a Katherne Pear,
  (The side that's next the Sun.)

Her lips were red, and one was thin,
Compar'd to that was next her chin;
  (Some Bee had stung it newly.)
But *(Dick)* her eyes so guard her face;
I durst no more upon them gaze,
  Then on the Sun in *July*.

Her mouth so small when she does speak,
Thou'dst swear her teeth her words did break,
  That they might passage get,
But she so handled still the matter,
They came as good as ours, or better,
  And are not spent a whit.

If wishing should be any sin,
The Parson himself had guilty bin;
  (She lookt that day so purely,)
And did the youth so oft the feat
At night, as some did in conceit,
  It would have spoil'd him, surely.

(Conceit, in the next to last line, means *imagination.)*

The gentleness and warmth of the humor take all sting out of
the satire and all ugliness out of the earthy, sensual view of love.
As in a painting by Brueghel, rosiness and vitality transform the
crude scene with radiance. This portrait of the bride seems to me
to be one of the most exquisite character sketches in our literature.

We turn from the bridal couple to the feast ("Before the
Parson could say Grace,/ The Company was seated"). Carousing,
dancing and toasting are described before the bride and her maids
withdraw, the groom noticing, and he himself "did not mean to
stay behind/ Above an hour or so."

When in he came *(Dick)* there she lay
Like new-faln snow melting away,
  ('Twas time I trow to part)

> Kisses were now the onely stay,
> Which soon she gave, as who would say,
> Good Boy! with all my heart.

At this critical moment the bridesmaids bring in the posset, the traditional drink of milk curdled with wine which newlyweds ceremonially drink in bed, sharing it with their company. The groom "in spight" gulps it down with dispatch.

> At length the candles out and out,
> All that they had not done, they do't:
> What that is, who can tell?
> But I beleeve it was no more
> Then thou and I have done before
> With *Bridget,* and with *Nell.*

When I say I find Suckling relevant to life today I do not mean, of course, that the details of life are the same. Weddings are not much like this one (and perhaps weren't when Suckling was writing). What I find relevant is a way of looking at human beings and human activities and human foibles which is sorely needed at the present time. For example, I have attended a number of student weddings in recent years, often done in the woods, the gathered friends in beautifully outlandish attire, with wine and guitars and bare feet, and often a good deal of poetry is written for such occasions — tending to read like reshuffled passages of Kahil Gibran's *The Prophet.* How gratifying it would be if someone could come up with an epithalamium having some of the quality of Suckling's "Ballade"! What we get instead is considerably more dreary, humorless, vaguely pretentious, falsely mystical — not "half so full of Juyce."

CHAPTER SEVENTEEN

Classic and Romantic

Pope's *Essay on Criticism* was written when the misshapen and tortured genius was about twenty, bringing him fame when it was published in 1711, and he was twenty-three. It is one of the most presumptuous poems in the language, setting out to do no less than tell critics how to criticize, and tells them in verse which dares their vengeance. It succeeds in providing a succinct and memorable summary of the canons of Neoclassical aesthetics. Though it was addressed to and is written about critics, it contains a great deal of incidental advice to poets, and many of its epigrams are often quoted for their embodiment of what seem fixed principles of good writing. Pope is often castigated for his respect for Rules — as though he thought good writing could be produced by formulae (he did not think so); it is ironic that we so often go to him, above all others, for his statement of rules we all find useful.

In the Neoclassical view, the world was in the latter stages of decay. Since Creation, since Eden, since the Classical age, civilization has been running steadily downhill. Poetry (or any art) is essentially an imitation of nature:

> First follow *Nature,* and your judgment frame
> By her just standard, which is still the same:
> Unerring *Nature,* still divinely bright,
> One clear, unchang'd, and universal light,
> Life, force, and beauty, must to all impart,
>   At once the source, and end, and test of Art.

But our vision of nature in modern times, he argues, is corrupted. Homer could see nature more clearly and imitate it more accurately. Therefore we study Homer's work and derive rules from it:

Those *Rules* of old discover'd, not devis'd,
Are Nature still, but Nature methodiz'd;
It is above all to the Greeks — to Homer and Aristotle, specifically — that we should go for guidance:
Learn hence for ancient rules a just esteem;
To copy nature is to copy them.
If we extend that concept of the Classics to include the great writers of all ages and cultures, it is still not bad advice for a poet. The opposite point of view is also not bad advice — for example, as expressed by Sir Philip Sidney:
But words came halting forth, wanting Invention's stay;
Invention, Nature's child, fled step-dame Study's blows;
And others' feet still seem'd but strangers in my way.
Thus, great with child to speak, and helpless in my throes,
Biting my truant pen, beating myself for spite —
Fool, said my Muse to me, Look in thy heart and write.
The precept of Sidney's muse is not one he followed himself assiduously. His greatest contribution to English literature was not his self-expression, but his adaptation to English of Continental and Classical forms and themes — including the theme expressed in those lines. Invention and learning are not really at war in great poetry; rather, they support one another — as Pope himself knew.

He also knew that the greatest art was ultimately inexplicable by rules. A mysterious element, a *je ne sais quoi,* inhabits the rational machine of the eighteenth century. Taste and Genius are themselves, for Pope, God-given attributes beyond man's power of understanding and explanation.
Some beauties yet no Precepts can declare,
For there's a happiness as well as care.
Happiness means what we would call luck — an accidental quality which a great artist knows enough to retain in his scrupulous revisions.
Thus Pegasus, a nearer way to take,
May boldly deviate from the common track.
From vulgar bounds with brave disorder part,
And snatch a grace beyond the reach of art.
Notice how the regular pentameter is altered to illustrate the point:

may **BOLD** ly _DE\ vi ate _FROM\ the_COM\ mon_TRACK\

A mid-line anapest may not seem particularly radical to us, but it was a bold deviation for Pope — and it somehow suggests Pegasus lurching off in an unexpected direction. *Art,* notice, means exactly what we would mean by *artistry* — and there is no real difference between the words for Pope. In modern usage the word *art* almost invariably shimmers with an aura of the mysterious, that aura which for Pope was *beyond* art.

The chief obstacle to good art or good criticism is pride:

> Whatever Nature has in worth deny'd,
> She gives in large recruits of needful Pride;
> For as in bodies, thus in souls, we find
> What wants in blood and spirits, swell'd with wind:
> Pride, where Wit fails, steps in to our defence,
> And fills up all the mighty Void of sense.

Wit in this period is a general word for intelligence, sometimes with an emphasis upon the creative intelligence or power of invention, at other times with the opposite emphasis upon judgment, or the restraining, critical faculty. The unfettered mind is subject to illusions, absurdities and dangerous aberrations:

> A *little learning* is a dang'rous thing;
> Drink deep, or taste not the Pierian spring:
> There shallow draughts intoxicate the brain,
> And drinking largely sobers us again.
> Fir'd at first sight with what the Muse imparts,
> In fearless youth we tempt the heights of Arts,
> While from the bounded level of our mind,
> Short views we take, nor see the lengths behind;
> But more advanc'd, behold with strange surprize
> New distant scenes of endless science rise!
> So pleas'd at first the tow'ring Alps we try,
> Mount o'er the vales, and seem to tread the sky,
> Th' eternal snows appear already past,
> And the first clouds and mountains seem the last:
> But, those attain'd, we tremble to survey
> The growing labours of the lengthen'd way,
> Th' increasing prospect tires our wand'ring eyes,
> Hills peep o'er hills, and Alps on Alps arise!

Samuel Johnson called that image of climbing the Alps the best simile in the English lanugage; it provides a good occasion for looking closely at the heroic couplet, the form which dominated English poetry with tyrannous sway for nearly a century and a half. Notice that the couplets are like bricks, each with distinct outlines, but blending easily into larger units and patterns. The first four lines of this quotation form a unit centering on the Pierian spring (Pieria is the region of Greece which is the legendary birthplace of Orpheus and of the Muses). The next six lines use "heights" as an abstraction, shifting the emotion of discovering there is more and more to learn from sobriety to wonder and "strange surprize." Finally, in the next eight lines, he takes a subtly different approach to the same discovery, taking us in some detail on a mountain-climbing expedition, complete with heady enthusiasm, a false sense of conquest, and then, as we scale one further height, a sudden fear and weariness mixed with awe, as we survey the endless ranges of un-explored learning.

Pope was, of course, already at this youthful age, the most polished poet in English literature. He tuned the heroic couplet, making it an instrument capable of the greatest delicacy and coarseness, of eloquence and rude colloquialism, of crisp, rational discourse and giddy flights of imagination, all within the tight bounds of closed pairs of rhymed pentameter lines. The couplet lends itself especially well to patterns of antithesis and balance. Notice how in each line the first half speaks to the second, and how the parts within the couplet as a whole speak to one another:

> *Fir'd at first* sight // with what the *Muse* imparts
> *In fearless youth* // we tempt the heights of Arts,

Study the close texture of sounds — the balance of the *f*'s and *r*'s with the *m*'s in the first line, the fricatives *(f, th)* of the second with the dental *t*'s. The phrases of the two halves of each line are balanced in rhythm and meaning. As you read on, the "views" seem short and the "lengths" long, "first clouds" balance "last" mountains, "growing labours" are heavy, and "the lengthen'd way" seems endless. Each sound, each word, each phrase, each line, each couplet is set like a jewel, jewels within jewels.

He manages astonishing variety within so tight a form, warning us against those poems which

> . . . . neither ebb, nor flow,
> Correctly cold, and regularly low,
> That shunning faults, one quiet tenour keep;
> We cannot blame indeed — but we may sleep.

He also warns us against concentrating on details to such an extent that we lose the overall effect:

> In Wit, as Nature, what affects our hearts
> Is not th'exactness of peculiar parts;
> 'Tis not a lip, or eye, we beauty call,
> But the joint force and full result of all.

Conceit means imagination in the 18th century:

> Some to *conceit* alone their taste confine,
> And glitt'ring thoughts struck out at ev'ry line;
> Pleas'd with a work where nothing's just or fit;
> One glaring Chaos and wild heap of wit.
> Poets, like painters, thus, unskill'd to trace
> The naked nature and the living grace,
> With gold and jewels cover ev'ry part,
> And hide with ornaments their want of art.
> True Wit is Nature to advantage dress'd,
> What oft was thought, but ne'er so well expressed;
> Something, whose truth convinc'd at sight we find,
> That gives us back the image of our mind.

In modern terms we call it overwriting — straining too hard to be original, to be effective, to be clever, and producing writing which is grotesquely over-decorated, laborious and, often, obscure.

He notes that some are more addicted to language than to sense. How often have you been frustrated by having someone read your poetry and praise its imagery, its language, its rhythms, and never give any indication he understands what you actually say? Pope nails such critics:

> Their praise is still, — the Style is excellent;
> The Sense, they humbly take upon content.

Both poets and critics are subject to this preoccupation with style at the expense of meaning — for example, to use archaic diction:

> Some by old words to fame have made pretence,
> Ancients in phrase, meer moderns in their sense;
> Such labour'd nothings, in so strange a style,
> Amaze th' unlearn'd, and make the learned smile.
>   . . .
> Be not the first by whom the new are try'd,
> Nor yet the last to lay the old aside.

The greatest *tour de force* in Pope's *Essay* is his discussion of versification. First he derides those who strive for too much harmony and regularity of sound ("as some to Church repair,/ Not for the doctrine, but the music there.")

These equal syllables alone require,
Tho' oft the ear the open vowels tire;
Circle the vowel sounds in that last line to see what he means.
An *expletive* is an extra word or syllable used merely to pad out the
meter; like this *do:*
While expletives their feeble aid do join;
And ten low words oft creep in one dull line:
While they ring round the same unvary'd chimes,
With sure returns of still expected rhymes.
Where-e'er you find "the cooling western breeze,"
In the next line, it "whispers thro' the trees":
If crystal streams "with pleasing murmurs creep,"
The reader's threaten'd (not in vain) with "sleep."
Then, at the last and only couplet fraught
With some unmeaning thing they call a thought,
A needless Alexandrine ends the song,
That, like a wounded snake, drags its slow length along.
As I have said in Chapter Seven, rhymes themselves do not become
clichés; the clichés are the phrases in which *breeze, trees,* etc., are
used; and Pope's prejudice against the Alexandrine (or hexameter)
variation, such as his last line quoted above, seems unnecessarily
harsh. But his wit in illustrating what he objects to is delightful.

He goes on to illustrate what he regards as good versification, in
which metrical variations, syllable lengths and sound combinations
are used to create an auditory image to reinforce ideas and visual
imagery:

True ease in writing comes from art, not chance,
As those move easiest who have learn'd to dance.
'Tis not enough no harshness gives offence,
The sound must seem an Echo to the sense:
Soft is the strain when Zephyr gently blows,
And the smooth stream in smoother numbers flows;
But when loud surges lash the sounding shore,
The hoarse, rough verse should like the torrent roar:
When Ajax strives some rock's vast weight to throw,
The line too labours, and the words move slow;
Not so, when swift Camilla scours the plain,
Flies o'er th' unbending corn, and skims along the main.

It is worth your time to analyze in detail the astonishing effects
of that passage: e.g., the unity of the phrase "Soft is the strain,"

achieved by alliteration and an initial trochee, the Ionic foot (uu//) at the beginning of the next line, the spondees ("loud surges," "rough verse," "vast weight") in the rough and heavy lines, the way the slow lines are retarded by monosyllables which must be drawn out in sound (e.g., the "too" in "The line too labours," which must be extended because of its grammatical situation). Much of the impression of speed and heaviness comes from length of syllables rather than metrical variation, but the race of three unaccented syllables together in the last line quoted above (achieved by the unusual combination of a trochee and an anapest at the beginning of the line) is a remarkable example of metrical acceleration.

He castigates the taste both of those too intent upon following fashion and those intellectual types:

> So much they scorn the croud, that if the throng
> By chance go right, they purposely go wrong:

He laments rapid linguistic change which carries poetry into obscurity:

> Our sons their fathers' failing language see,
> And such as Chaucer is, shall Dryden be.

And asks critics to be merciful:

> Good-nature and good-sense must ever join;
> To err is human, to forgive, divine.

(*Join* was pronounced *jine* in Pope's day.) He calls "Dullness" and "Obscenity" the major crimes of poetry and castigates the salacious drama of the Restoration period which immediately preceded Pope's own Augustan time of more elegant indecency. He gives critics a lesson in manners such as Lord Chesterfield might have given his son: "speak, tho' sure, with seeming diffidence," and:

> 'Tis not enough, your counsel still be true;
> Blunt truths more mischief than nice falshoods do;
> Men must be taught as if you taught them not,
> And things unknown propos'd as things forgot.

It is sometimes difficult to know when Pope is being ironic; apparently straight-faced advice such as that sometimes is pushed over the brink into pomposity:

> Be niggards of advice on no pretence;
> For the worst avarice is that of sense.

Pope would probably laugh at us if we took that too seriously. After telling us not to waste our time criticizing completely hopeless poets, he goes on to blast them with vicious satire for twenty lines ending with the old age of hacks who:

Still run on Poets, in a raging vein,
Ev'n to the dregs and squeezings of the brain,
Strain out the last dull droppings of their sense,
And rhyme with all the rage of Impotence.

He ends with a portrait of a good critic and a history of criticism from ancient to modern times.

One of the weaknesses of a reasonable position is its strength. Pope brilliantly, colorfully attacks excess in every direction, then retires to the doldrums of dead center, the Neoclassical heaven of moderation in which God, if he is a gentleman, is not oppressively good. All his advice for writers is excellent — for our age as for any other; but it does, finally, boil down to precepts which can never tell us when Pegasus should have taken a nearer way. It is in this poem that he tells us, "For Fools rush in where Angels fear to tread," which is more good advice — except that Angels, however harmoniously they choir around the throne of Reason, do not write poetry. At his best moments Pope was wise enough to be a Fool, to rush in with a fine flurry of excess. Precedents will never justify our foolishness, and we must be fools occasionally or never achieve art's sublime moments — those which redeem all its technical tedium. If you come to love the poetry of Pope as I do it will be for the way it refuses to be contained by its strictures. The God of Pope is absolute — but not unreasonably so.

While Pope deplored the degeneration of civilization as it drifted further and further from the pristine innocence and splendor of nature, the very reasonableness he embodied was the medium of science and progress, of industrialism, of artifice, and as it has dominated Western Civilization it has increasingly driven artists and poets into rebellion and flight. The stance of poets today is still primarily anti-reason, as it has been since the early nineteenth century, a hundred years after Pope. The word *poet* conjures up for many the image of a limp and tubercular young man with a flowing collar, velvet vest and long, fine hair — namely, John Keats. The stereotype is misleading, of course, but it captures something essential about poetry as it reaches the public imagination. Poets are thought of as sensitive, introspective; tormented, they yearn for unattainable absolutes, are "half in love with easeful Death" which will finally release them from harsh reality. What we do not often hear of is the poet's reconciliation with reality. But it is just such reconciliation which, again and again, is the burden of Keats' own poems.

His "Ode to a Nightingale" provides substance for the stereo-type — and for its correction. Its eight stanzas of ten lines each tell us how Keats himself felt about the poetic posture of rejection of life and romantic yearning for death. This is the first stanza:

> My heart aches, and a drowsy numbness pains
>   My sense, as though of hemlock I had drunk,
> Or emptied some dull opiate to the drains
>   One minute past, and Lethe-wards had sunk:
> 'Tis not through envy of thy happy lot,
>   But being too happy in thy happiness, —
>   That thou, light-wingèd Dryad of the trees,
>   In some melodious plot
>   Of beechen green, and shadows numberless,
>   Singest of summer in full-throated ease.

Contained here is almost a formula for romantic poetry. How do I feel at this moment? My heart aches. I am numb. It is as though I had committed suicide by drinking poison. No, that's not it. Perhaps it is more as though I had taken a narcotic drug and were drifting to forgetfulness. You, nightingale, might think I feel this way because I envy your happiness, but, no, it is because I am too deliriously happy that you are happy. I am happy that you, wood nymph, are singing your joy in the summer. The poet is engaging in a delicate examination of his own exuberance — I feel not exactly this way, but a little more like this . . . It is as though he were lost in his efforts to define the ineffable.

> O, for a draught of vintage! that hath been
>   Cool'd a long age in the deep-delvèd earth,
> Tasting of Flora and the country green,
>   Dance, and Provençal song, and sunburnt mirth!
> O for a beaker full of the warm South,
>   Full of the true, the blushful Hippocrene,
>   With beaded bubbles winking at the brim,
>   And purple-stainèd mouth;
>   That I might drink, and leave the world unseen,
>   And with thee fade away into the forest dim:

The imagery has now shifted from narcotics to wine, an idealization of wine which fuses the connotations of age, nature, the Renaissance, joy and sensuality. Hippocrene, the fountain on Olympus, is sacred to the Muses: he wants a wine to provide him with poetic inspiration. And all these accumulating connotations and desires are finally equated with slipping into anonymity and identifying totally with nature.

One might say that he wants to be delivered from selfness. The anguish (albeit one of happiness) in his breast at the beginning of the poem requires some way of extinguishing his personal identity — perhaps through poison or drugs, through drunkenness, through the past, through nature, through poetry, through following the bird into the dim forest to be absorbed finally and absolutely in feeling and beauty. The second stanza ended with a colon — and the third follows as an expansion of its concluding thought:

> Fade far away, dissolve, and quite forget
> What thou among the leaves hast never known,
> The weariness, the fever, and the fret
> Here, where men sit and hear each other groan;
> Where palsy shakes a few, sad, last grey hairs,
> Where youth grows pale, and spectre-thin, and dies;
> Where but to think is to be full of sorrow
> And leaden-eyed despairs,
> Where Beauty cannot keep her lustrous eyes,
> Or new Love pine at them beyond to-morrow.

This stanza creates the *here* from which the poet speaks: a world of sickness, decay and futility. What is the difference between the nightingale and the poet? Consciousness, reason, self-awareness. The bird, of course, is conscious, but (in the terms of this poem) not of himself or his mortal plight. Surely birds and animals suffer weariness, fever and fret; they grow old; they languish; their beauty fades and their passions are short-lived. But they don't "think" about it — and for a human being, "but to think is to be full of sorrow."

Here, then, is reality, as the poet sees it. All is transience; all is suffering; all our gift of awareness brings us is a sense of our tragic condition — doomed by our mortality to live with physical limitations and frustrated aspirations. The lines are particularly poignant when we know that Keats was himself pale and spectre-thin and dying; but he is not drawing attention to himself, now. His personal situation is but a paradigm of that of all men. We can conceive of Beauty, but it is irremediably decaying. We sometimes think we can be redeemed by love, but that, too, lasts only a day. Mortality is built-in. We cannot change our condition. At least we might hope to forget it — and, in doing so, dissolve into the nightingale's world of oblivion.

Away! away! for I will fly to thee,
    Not charioted by Bacchus and his pards,
But on the viewless wings of Poesy,
    Though the dull brain perplexes and retards:
Already with thee! tender is the night,
    And haply the Queen-Moon is on her throne,
        Cluster'd around by all her starry Fays;
            But here there is no light,
Save what from heaven is with the breezes blown
    Through verdurous glooms and winding mossy ways.

Pards means leopards, which draw the chariot of the god of wine.
The poet resolves to join the nightingale not by the use of wine but
flying on poetry's invisible wings. Reason, "the dull brain," makes
poetic flight difficult, but by the fifth line of the stanza above the
poet feels himself launched into the nightingale's blissful darkness.
That night might have been lighted by the moon and stars, but in
the new *here* in which the poet finds himself there is only an occasional glimmer illuminating the green gloom and mossy paths.

I cannot see what flowers are at my feet,
    Nor what soft incense hangs upon the boughs,
But, in enbalmèd darkness, guess each sweet
    Wherewith the seasonable month endows
The grass, the thicket, and the fruit-tree wild;
    White hawthorn, and the pastoral eglantine;
        Fast fading violets cover'd up in leaves;
            And mid-May's eldest child,
The coming musk-rose, full of dewy wine,
    The murmurous haunt of flies on summer eves.

Darkling I listen; and, for many a time
    I have been half in love with easeful Death,
Call'd him soft names in many a musèd rhyme,
    To take into the air my quiet breath;
Now more than ever seems it rich to die,
    To cease upon the midnight with no pain,
        While thou are pouring forth thy soul abroad
            In such an ecstasy!
Still wouldst thou sing, and I have ears in vain —
    To thy high requiem become a sod.

Having cast himself into the night, the poet finds himself not
soaring under the moon with the nightingale, but in a luscious, dark

garden. He guesses each flower by the scent and listens to the still distant song of the bird, reminded, now, of his own recurrent wish for death. His poetry is full, he says, of gentle references to Death, who often seems a welcome deliverer to one caught in the trammels of viney mortality. But now he reflects that if he were, indeed, to die, he could no longer hear the nightingale.

Death is no solution. If the nightingale symbolizes something like idealized beauty, something for which the poet is doomed hopelessly to yearn, his very power to hear and seek and desire is dependent upon his being alive. Ironically, his enjoyment is rooted in suffering. The ideal is outside life, but one cannot leave life to reach it, for as soon as he does so, the ideal is itself lost.

> Thou wast not born for death, immortal Bird!
> No hungry generations tread thee down;
> The voice I hear this passing night was heard
> In ancient days by emperor and clown:
> Perhaps the self-same song that found a path
> Through the sad heart of Ruth, when, sick for home,
> She stood in tears amid the alien corn;
> The same that oft-times hath
> Charm'd magic casements, opening on the foam
> Of perilous seas, in faery lands forlorn.
>
> Forlorn! the very word is like a bell
> To toll me back from thee to my sole self!
> Adieu! the fancy cannot cheat so well
> As she is fam'd to do, deceiving elf.
> Adieu! adieu! thy plaintive anthem fades
> Past the near meadows, over the still stream,
> Up the hillside; and now 'tis buried deep
> In the next valley-glades:
> Was it a vision, or a waking dream?
> Fled is that music: — do I wake or sleep?

When he says the nightingale was "not born for death" he is no longer speaking of the individual bird, which is, indeed, as mortal as he. The song of the nightingale is immortal, and it must have sounded in ancient ears as in his own. Because animals and birds (unless human beings capture them and make them pets) do not have names, they seem more purely amalgamated with their kind than humans do. The nightingale can slip away into anonymity and apparent immortality, but the poet must again resume his place on earth, embodied in a "sole self." The "fancy" or imagination (or *Poesy,* as he called it in the fourth stanza) cannot ultimately deliver him from himself. That very imagination which swept him like the nightingale's song through ancient days, to medieval courts, to Biblical Ruth "amid the alien corn," to castles overlooking perilous seas, to the land of fairies, also reminded him that in all places man is wretched and forlorn. When he consigns himself, as to a prison, to his "sole self," it is with reluctant realism. Dream as we may, we do not truly want death (and its necessary destruction of our ability to dream) and cannot otherwise escape the human plight.

We imagine the song of the bird diminishing as he drifts down the meadow, over a stream, up a hill and into some distant valley. It ceases upon the midnight with no pain — leaving the poet unsure of whether he heard it or dreamed it. At the end of the poem we are left, as Wordsworth remembered infancy, with intimations of immortality, a fine aura of idealism which seems to halo our beginnings and our destiny. But there is no question of where we are: on solid earth, with our weariness, fever and fret intact. However, hearing the nightingale has left us with certain overtones and unanswered questions. It may be that that other world of the imagination is the waking world, and in this one we are sleeping, unaware of an ideal reality which encompasses us.

Poetry, like the nightingale, stirs us to such questions. It expresses our futile desire to escape mortal bondage and sometimes seems to promise us such escape. If we let it, it would tease us into death, which is the opposite of the immortality we yearn for. If we heed the song closely, we find that it leads us only to a deepened awareness of our tragic condition. Its illumination only reveals the impossibility of escape.

Keats was reconciled to reality because he saw no options. A weaker poet (or less courageous man) might have stopped this poem after the seventh line of the fourth stanza — almost exactly halfway through the inexorable thought. The complement to vision is our acceptance of the lot of the visionary. Mere escapism inclines some to go flitting off with the nightingale into poetic oblivion, but Keats, throughout the second half of the poem, forces us back to cope with the inescapable facts of mortal life. Fancy is a "deceiving elf." Even our ability to reason — which was cursed in the first part of the poem — seems finally to be accepted; at least it does not deceive. Popular attitudes associate poetry with self-indulgence and escapism. Keats was as tempted as any poet is likely to be to abandon this harsh earth and to live in a dream world of imagination; but his integrity as a man told him of the delusions implied by such escape.

What happens if we stop this train of thought halfway through? A student once said to me (when I was talking about the hard work of writing) "You can be creative lying on your back in the sunny fields." It may be that as our culture abandons the Puritan ethic we will come to place much less value on achievement, and living may become for more people more of the time an end in itself. But the meaning of the word *creative* as I am conditioned to use it requires making something — a product for public scrutiny and use. Hart Crane used to get drunk so that he could write poetry. His counterpart today might take LSD as an end in itself. The experience is the product. The Cult of Experience which once drove writers to wash dishes in hamburger joints and pitch hay on mountain ranches has been transmuted to a cult of increasingly private experiences, symbolized by autonomous social dancing. It is interesting that many who are moving into the new world are becoming inarticulate, and when they create poetry at all are inclined to yearn for its extinction.

Compare this poem by Robert Creeley with Keats' ode:

THE MOUNTAINS IN THE DESERT

The mountains blue now
at the back of my head,
much geography of self and soul
brought to such limit of sight,

I cannot relieve it
nor leave it, my mind locked
in seeing it
as the light fades.

Tonight let me go
at last out of whatever
mind I thought to have,
and all the habits of it.

He is well on the way. The sentence — that old habit of mind — has degenerated (in the first two stanzas) and is gladly being abandoned. The mountains ("much geography of self and soul") function in this poem as the nightingale did in Keats', as an unattainable ideal, a teasing vision of the absolute, a beauty in the mind and

beyond the reach of mind. It attracts and torments. The solution
suggested by the poem is to wipe out the vision. In a way that is
like joining the nightingale, reaching the mountains, by going all the
way to easeful death.

I was talking a few years ago to a young lady of 17 who had
spent a good deal of her life in mental institutions and jail. She
started sniffing (not shooting) heroin, and got up to about sixteen
bags a day before she quit, afraid of addiction. She struck me as
a highly mature, intelligent and well-balanced person, generally
happy through the day. But she had trouble sleeping. "I just can't
bag my mind," she said. She could drink most men under the
table. Hashish didn't get to her. "How about sex?" I asked her.
"Sure: that does it fine," she answered, and told me about the
three acquaintances with whom she had shared bedrolls in the last
three nights.

So far as I could tell she was not tormented by any visions of
horror in her nightly search for oblivion. It was simply consciousness which was the enemy — and love (or simply sex) was the only
infallible rest she had discovered. Awareness of or relationship to
her partner did not seem to be a factor. What she wanted was
acceptance, which permitted self-acceptance, which permits self-
absorption and disappearance into sleep. It is ultimately a lonely,
passive orgy.

Listening compassionately to a tale like hers has helped me
understand what Creeley is talking about. I understand that need
to bag the mind. The only remaining mystery is why one should
write at all if what he desires is a coma of onanistic oblivion.

Keats gives us the answer. In the fourth stanza he pointedly
rejects wine and seeks "the viewless wings of Poesy" as the means
of joining the bird and finding deliverance from "The weariness,
the fever, and the fret" of mortal existence. The bird is both nature
and art, a Dryad, or wood nymph (adding suggestions of magic).
Poesy may help the poet transcend self and dwell in a magical,
immortal forest of perpetual sensation. Like Creeley, Keats dis-
dains "the dull brain" which "perplexes and retards" the soul which
would ascend on poetic wings.

Momentarily, then, the poet finds himself with the bird in the
tender night of a sensual paradise of intoxicating odors. The bird
has led him not to nature alone (for it is the mortal, natural state
he wishes to escape), but nature made immortal by art — as that
static world depicted on the Grecian Urn where the trees can never

he bare and love is "For ever warm and still to be enjoy'd." In both odes Keats recognizes that such an ideal state is to be equated only with death: "Cold Pastoral!"

Yearning for the ideal is yearning for death. It is the most profoundly human of our impulses, but a temptation to be reluctantly avoided. The nightingale's song is (like Frost's snowy woods) "lovely, dark and deep," but its appeal is ultimately sinister. The bird "not born for death" is an ideal; its song is immortal, repeated by nature's anonymous carolers in perpetuity. Two kinds of immortality are simultaneously embodied in the nightingale: that of nature's continual renewal and that of art's abstract beauty, which transcends its material incarnations.

But neither is for the poet himself, as a man. There is a neat pun on "forlorn," shifting from its sense of "lost" or "forgotten" to its suggestion of a wretched, pitiful condition, the sweet melancholy of romantic vision souring on the very mortal tongue. The self is nirvana for Creeley, but a disaster for Keats. The individual is doomed to what he calls, in "Ode on a Grecian Urn," a "breathing passion":

> That leaves a heart high-sorrowful and cloy'd,
> A burning forehead, and a parching tongue.

We cannot enter that "forest dim" to which the nightingale leads by imagination (or "fancy") alone; and to enter it truly, by death, means an end of the very consciousness which relishes its ease.

Thus the temptation to go out of his mind is rejected by Keats because he is courageous enough to recognize that the deliverance he seeks thereby does not, in fact, deliver what it promises. No one *really* wants to live paralyzed on a Grecian Urn, within reach of an unattainable mistress, or in a thicket of "embalmèd darkness" — not even Creeley, who preserves enough consciousness to mutter his poems. Keats faces up to the tragic situation of man, bound in his "sole self" (perhaps with an interesting pun on *sole*) in a social world where we are bound to "sit and hear each other groan," bound to yearn for an inaccessible ideal which — like the love of Isolde — can be achieved only in death.

But the song of Keats, like that of the nightingale, endures though the singer has departed. This may not be much compensation for us as we sit here eaten by the tuberculosis of time, unable at night to bag our minds, but it is all that is available. That is, man outlives himself by means of his works (not by the immortality of an afternoon in a sunny field). He endures by communication, his song winding through Ruth's sad heart. He may achieve immortality by stating beautifully his plight of inescapable mortality. The craft of the poem — the intricate stanzas of subtly altering rhymes and rhythms, the hewn and polished phrases, the concrete, intense rendering of profound emotion and thought — this craft enables us to soar above and speak to the "hungry generations" which tread upon the "sole self" of the mortal man.

It is the artistic product, then, which provides communion with men now and men unborn. If we look for such artistry, richness of language, profundity and teasing suggestiveness in Creeley's poem, we will be disappointed. Its appeal is immediate to people who seek reinforcement of their conviction that they may find happiness in self-absorption, since that is what it plainly (albeit ungrammatically) announces. But this is no news: the infant in his crib (when not hungry or wet) lives in those inner blue mountains by the hour. It takes more wisdom and courage to recognize the limits of that amusement.

Work has a bad name now for good reason: the work ethic is dysfunctional in a society which has to keep its citizens in the hothouses of schooling and retirement nearly half their lives. We define authenticity by employment — and then make it impossible for more than half our members — most women, most youth, many blacks, most old people, for example — to be employed. But it is misleading to confuse the concept of work with employment or the rat race for money and reputation. What will induce writers now to devote as much craft, effort and thought to a poem as Keats devoted to his ode?

He says the Grecian Urn will be, quite simply, "a friend to man," and I believe the drive behind his art was similarly to achieve communion with others, to embody ideals in the marble urn of concrete expression so that we palsied and pale ones may be linked in vision. Doomed to selfhood, we can at least achieve selfless utterance across the barriers of our skins. Cursed with awareness of our own mortality, we can at least state imperishably that fact of our condition.

Such needs, such drives do not shift with changing social patterns — though changing social patterns may temporarily obscure them. Some form of creative productivity is bound to persist — and to be more deeply satisfying than lying in a sunny field or any other means of bagging the mind.

CHAPTER EIGHTEEN

Type of the Modern

What is the difference between a nightingale and a locomotive — or a fly? If an answer were possible, it might tell us much about the meaning of twentieth century experience. Though Keats wrote to a grasshopper, it is inconceivable that he might have written a poem such as Emily Dickinson's "I heard a fly buzz when I died," (or "The Flea," by John Donne, whose sensibility was much closer to the modern temper in many ways than was that of Keats). Certainly he would not have written a deliberate celebration of a machine, as Whitman and Stephen Spender do in poems I will examine here. As many critics have pointed out, what we recognize as distinctively modern poetry begins in the mid-nineteenth century with such poets as Whitman and Dickinson. We can see in them themes and attitudes and techniques which were to flourish in and characterize poetry of our own century.

Just as painters repeatedly choose a classical subject — a nude woman, a still-life composition of fruit, flowers and a wine bottle — for their subjects, poets often deliberately select themes which have been treated by earlier poets. The subject matter is a constant in such poems; the play of the individual imagination and style is highlighted by the commonality of theme.

Walt Whitman's "To a Locomotive in Winter" and Stephen Spender's "The Express" are an obvious pair to illustrate this practice. Though I have never seen any explicit statement that this is so, I assume that Spender had Whitman's poem clearly in mind, perhaps even open before him as he wrote. This is in no sense plagiarism: it is acceptance of the challenge to treat the same theme, even in much the same form, that a great poet had treated earlier. Spender's poem is twenty-seven lines of loose blank verse; Whit-

man's is twenty-five longer and more limber lines. Both poets find
in the spectacle of the locomotive a madness, mystery and beauty
which transcend those of more conventional poetic subjects. "Type
of the modern," Whitman calls the machine; both poets are deliberately trying to bring the throbbing artifacts of industrial civilization
into the world of poetry.

"Thee for my recitative," Whitman begins. Often he takes the
posture of a singer, specifically of an operatic singer (he was a
great admirer of Wagner), in his poetry; and his Quaker habit of
using the archaic second person is more than poeticizing: it conveys
a reverence for the things of this world, especially for the ordinary,
neglected things and those regarded as ugly, which infuses all his
verse. Characteristically Whitman writes in a flowing, falling rhythm,
his key phrases and lines ending in a wave-like decrescendo of
trochees and dactyls:

> the winter-day declining,
> Thee in thy panoply
> thy beat convulsive
> tapering in the distance
> merrily following
> steadily careening

He places the locomotive ("even as now") in a winterscape,
buffeted by a snow storm, the "black cylindric body" a gross contrast to the gusting whiteness. Against the whirl and random
force of nature is placed an image of purpose and almost frightening order:

> Thy ponderous side-bars, parallel and connecting rods,
>   gyrating, shuttling at thy sides,
> Thy metrical, now swelling pant and roar, now tapering
>   in the distance,

Notice, in that last line, how the immediate scene is rounded off:
the poet is standing by the track in winter; in one line the train
surges toward him and passes; the exact word *tapering* takes it out
of sight.

The remainder of the poem is a meditation which is not bound
by the specific narrative setting — including images of the train
moving slow and fast, night and day, through mountain passages
and over plains, finally being released by the poet's imagination (one
gathers) into the vast West, across the wide and untamed continent:

> Launch'd o'er the prairies wide, across the lakes,
> To the free skies unpent and glad and strong.

Much of the poem is devoted to creating a very concrete sense of what the locomotive is like — sometimes in delicate observation ("the tremulous twinkle of thy wheels") and sometimes in broader strokes, the observer, almost like a camera, backing away ("Thy train of cars behind, obedient, merrily following,"). At quite a different level, the poet generalizes, elevating the concrete fact into symbol:

> Type of the modern — emblem of motion and power — pulse
>   of the continent,
> For once come serve the Muse and merge in verse, even as
>   here I see thee,
> With storm and buffeting gusts of wind and falling snow,

Notice that pull between the symbolic and the immediate experience. It is human conquest of nature, of the sprawling wilderness which excites the poet on one level. On the other it is the terror and admiration which man (who is, after all, a part of nature) feels for the Frankenstein he has created, the automaton now luminously, powerfully moving with a will of its own:

> Fierce-throated beauty!
> Roll through my chant with all thy lawless music, thy
>   swinging lamps at night,
> Thy madly-whistled laughter, echoing, rumbling like an
>   earthquake, rousing all,
> Law of thyself complete, thine own track firmly holding,

The word "beauty" suggests a female quality, but the locomotive seems overwhelmingly, almost rapaciously masculine. Whitman explicitly rejects the soft allure of other kinds of beauty:

> (No sweetness debonair of tearful harp or glib piano thine,)
> Thy trills of shrieks by rocks and hills return'd,

The music of the shriek has proved to be a keynote of twentieth century art; and Whitman was a bold pioneer in recognizing what fierce necessities lay ahead in making poetry of the environment of modern man.

While Whitman emphasizes the stark and fearsome contrast of the locomotive with the natural world, Spender seems almost to want to tame the monster, to civilize it and reabsorb it as an animate, almost spiritual being. We begin with thunderous emphasis in the round-house:

> After the first powerful, plain manifesto
> The black statement of pistons, without more fuss
> But gliding like a queen, she leaves the station.

Manifesto almost captures the sound as well as the meaning of that first release of steam in the confines of the station. The lines move laboriously as the train before they begin to "glide" with feminine and regal indifference past the human scene:

> Without bowing and with restrained unconcern
> She passes the houses which humbly crowd outside,
> The gasworks, and at last the heavy page
> Of death, printed by gravestones in the cemetery.

From dead and mechanical beginnings she rises to life in the "open country," she "acquires mystery,"

> The luminous self-possession of ships on ocean.
> It is now she begins to sing — at first quite low
> Then loud, and at last with a jazzy madness —
> The song of her whistle screaming at curves,
> Of deafening tunnels, brakes, innumerable bolts.
> And always light, aerial, underneath,
> Retreats the elate metre of her wheels.

As in Whitman's poem, one senses in this passage the approach and blasting presence and passing into the distance of the train. Like *tapering,* that word *Retreats* is precise for the sound's diminishment. Whitman heard the *metre* as the train approached; Spender hears it as a delicate gladness steadily sustaining the passing cars. *Elate* is a word selected by genius, conveying so exactly the sound, the rhythm and the sense (with etymological connotations of carrying and elevation as well as joy and pride). Whitman heard madness in the shrieking; Spender heard it in the "jazzy" frenzy of the building ecstasy of motion. The Express is transported (in both senses) in her power, alive and singing, clicking rhythmically off over the horizon.

As Whitman does, Spender turns (in the last eleven lines) to meditation and to symbol. The language as well as the imagery blurs:

> She plunges new eras of white happiness,
> Where speed throws up strange shapes, broad curves
> And parallels clean like trajectories from guns.

As Whitman's train disappeared into Western plains, Spender's crosses the horizon out of little Europe, "further than Edinburgh or Rome,/ Beyond the crest of the world." The horizon is phosphorescent as it disappears into night. The train embodies deliverance, transcendence; she is a goddess who transforms nuts and bolts and black smoke into flight.

And, again like Whitman, Spender insists on the supernal beauty of the machine, the beauty of power which is, at least for this poem, greater than all gentler or sweeter forms:

> Ah, like a comet through flame, she moves entranced,
> Wrapt in her music no bird song, no, nor bough
> Breaking with honey buds, shall ever equal.

Locomotives have roared into our poetry like fire-breathing dragons and departed like graceful swishing queens. In these days of ecological awareness, when man's long romance with power has come to seem a suicidal obsession, perhaps some poet among you should write another sort of hymn to the machine. The last locomotive I saw was quietly gigantic and gleaming in the Smithsonian Museum in Washington, D. C. It looked quite elegant and innocent in its huge impotence alongside the other scientific and mechanical exhibits there. I thought of Emily Dickinson's somewhat patronizing amusement at the beast, which she liked watching "lap the miles,/ And lick the valleys up." She had the feminine good sense not to take man's prideful contraptions too seriously, nor to be altogether beguiled by the locomotive's "horrid, hooting stanza," and to remember the paradox her bardic fellow poets ignored — that for all its apparent animation and autonomy, the monster stayed on the tracks, and though it might "neigh like Boanerges," ("sons of Thunder," as Jesus satirically called James and John when they wanted to call down fire on the Samaritans), it remained firmly under control:

> Then, punctual as a star
> Stop — docile and omnipotent —
> At its own stable door.

Had man retained some of Dickinson's wit and good sense about his mechanical gods, we might not be looking so desperately today for sprigs of America's greening.

By contrast with Dickinson, both Whitman and Spender wear elegaic robes. They speak as bards to what we might imagine as an assembled audience. Much more characteristic of modern poetry has been a humbler stance, in which the poet makes a quiet contract with the reader with as little posturing as possible. There is little orating. Rather, the poem comes as a whisper in the ear, as does this one of hers:

I heard a Fly buzz — when I died —
The Stillness in the Room
Was like the Stillness in the Air —
Between the Heaves of Storm —

The Eyes around — had wrung them dry —
And Breaths were gathering firm
For that last Onset — when the King
Be witnessed — in the Room —

I willed my Keepsakes — Signed away
What portion of me be
Assignable — and then it was
There interposed a Fly —

With Blue — uncertain stumbling Buzz —
Between the light — and me —
And then the Windows failed — and then
I could not see to see —

First, the opening is dramatic. The mere mention of something as homey and vulgar and insignificant as a fly catches our attention. How many poems do you know which mention a fly? And how quiet one must be to hear its buzz! We are prepared for the hush of the poem — and its intimate candor. Dash. Dickinson's dashes, capital letters and other unconventional practices in punctuation create in her poems a sense of breathless wonder. Unfortunately many editors in the late nineteenth and early twentieth centuries emended these — so most available editions are more conventionally punctuated, and sometimes even the wording is different from that in the manuscripts. It is important that a reader search out a recent edition in which the original texts are restored if he wants a true experience of her poetry. In this first line the dash sets off the astonishing dramatic twist (used several times by her): we are reading the words of one already dead. No fuss, no trumpets, but a flat and simple statement that she heard a fly buzz when she died. That line stands alone as a dramatic unit of the poem.

The next three lines take us into a flash-back to the period just before she heard the fly. We must have that stillness to hear the fly — but we are being subconsciously, rather than explicitly, prepared for the return to the fly at the end. We are in a Room. I repeat her capital to emphasize the awesomeness of each detail as it comes to the consciousness of the dying woman. The Stillness is like an object, something in the Air — like . . . like that eerie, sudden stillness that sometimes punctuates a tempest. We are between events — held in suspense after the throes of life have subsided and the impact of death remains unknown. That strange word *heaves* suggests *heavy,* emphasizing the surging power of the storm to come rather than its violence and turbulence.

Now we — and the dying woman — become conscious of people in the room, established by synecdoche, the use of *eyes* to represent persons. We stare up from the bed into dry, exhausted eyes. In the silence we become aware that even breaths are held, or are deliberately steady with foreboding — as though these relatives, friends, nurses, doctors (whoever they might be) awaited the presence of an awesome King. Three words build up the accumulating connotations of death: *Onset, King* and *witnessed. Onset* suggests an event of power, stress, an encounter with something terrible; *King* reinforces some of those feelings and adds suggestions of respect, ceremony, even reverence; *witnessed* emphasizes the helplessness and passivity of the observers, but it also has religious and judicial overtones, suggesting their perhaps unwilling sanction of the event, their testimony, their attestation of its finality, their presence before its mystery.

They — those disembodied eyes and breaths — clearly recognize the inevitability of death, and now, in the third stanza, the dying woman does likewise. The word *will* has an ironic meaning in regard to death, as it implies the extension of will into realms where the will cannot, in fact, intrude. She wills away what she has always willed to keep. She signs away whatever can be signed away. The abstract and official language *(portion, assignable,* the subjunctive *be)* evokes a muted shuffle of paper and scrupulous attention to detail — as though she could not be allowed to leave before these matters were attended to. Waiting just beyond the door is the King and his ominous Onset. Notice how this polysyllabic, administrative language picks up the tones of *witnessed* in the preceding stanza. We are mid-line in the third line of the third stanza when interrupted by the buzz.

It comes with the voiced *s* of *was,* is repeated in *interposed,* and is echoed by the other whispering sibilants of the last stanza. That elegant word *interposed* carries over the slightly stilted quality of *assignable.* (Note, by the way, that there are only three words in the poem with more than two syllables; *gathering* provides a slight ripple of uncertainty before *firm; assignable* and *interposed* take us to dry intellectual heights before our descent to the humming edge of lower consciousness in the last stanza.)

Among all the other aspects of death evoked by the poem — its stately finality, its reverent mystery, its busy termination of property, its aura of silence — there is the sheer fact of meat's mortality. We can think of the Angel of Death entering in kingly radiance for her spirit; but we must not forget the scavenger drawn by her carrion. The uncanny power of this poem derives in large part from the way that trivial fly mentioned in the first line and then forgotten looms larger and larger as an approaching vulture until it seems to blot out the light. What was it we were waiting for "Between the Heaves of Storm"? When it appears, it is the droning agent of nature's morbid cycle.

Its buzz is Blue. Synesthesia is the use of an image of one sense to describe an image of another sense — in this case the substitution of an image of sight for one of hearing. The displacement of the senses implied is appropriate to the state of semi-consciousness of the speaker. Similarly other impressions are dislocated by her dimming mind: the uncertainty of the buzz is actually her uncertainty; the failure of the windows is the failure of her own vision. That first line of the last stanza is relentless in its low-toned intensity. The dashes breaking up the lines come as gasps of panic suppressed in the dying woman's struggle to concentrate, to find explanations for the encroaching phenomenon of her own extinction. The repetition in the last line of *see* has the effect of a final stutter, of images receding in mirrors. The very moment of oblivion is dramatized and the poem ends with a dash of incompletion.

All the rhymes except in the last stanza are off-rhymes. The meter is placidly regular except for an occasional spondee *(buzz- when; last On*set; *me be)* and one anapest (gath*ering firm)*. The sentence structure is straight-forward and the language generally plain, without obscurities. Figurative language is similarly sparse and restrained. There is a matter-of-fact quality which — as in a good ghost story — heightens the terror and strangeness of the poem's experience.

It is like a good ghost story in other ways, too — especially structure. After the first hint the poem concentrates on creating an atmosphere of anticipation and dread. We are past grief ("The Eyes around — had wrung them dry —") and are preparing ourselves for the encounter with death itself. When it comes, it is in the unexpected form of that fly mentioned at the very beginning. Of course! Surprise in good fiction (or good poetry) is never complete surprise: it is always something carefully built-in and hidden which emerges unexpectedly after we have been subconsciously prepared.

Moreover vagueness is an important element of tales of the supernatural. We are expecting "the King," but have no clues as to what he will be like. And though we are taken to the very threshold of death and impelled across it by the poem. Dickinson does not try to tell us what it was really like. If she were to let her imagination create things utterly beyond human experience, our credibility would be strained. After the first premise, which we have to grant her, that she is speaking from beyond the grave, she remains carefully within the range of life. What further we supply about the experience of death must come from our own imaginations — and it will be all the more powerful for being wordless.

The principles of Dickinson's art are the principles of the art of Dylan Thomas or T. S. Eliot or Robert Lowell or of your own poetry when you are writing well. For instance, when I insist that poetry must have form, I am not talking about meter primarily — though meter is a part of it. A good poem has a dramatic structure: it is plotted as carefully as a play. The sequence of experiences is as important as their content. There is a definite, intentional relationship between sound and sense, word choice and tone, sentence structure and thought. I won't go into the argument as to whether the poet consciously plans all these relationships: that doesn't matter. The point is that consciously or not the poet has created elements related to one another. Good poems have form; bad poems do not.

This poem is not notable for originality, startling imagery, profundity or personal vision. Those qualities may characterize some good poetry — but they are not nearly so essential to it as structure, design, control — and veracity of experience. Living our way through these lines, our pulse beats faster and falters. We are not being *told* something; rather something is made to *happen* to us. No effort is being made to explain, to extract meaning, to moralize, to decorate: the concentration of the poet was upon providing us with the raw ingredients of an imagined experience — raw, but carefully selected, carefully arranged.

We might think of the poem as programming. The poet's intention was to seize your attention, hold it in rapt suspense, horrify you, elicit a gasp and release you with an impulse sending you on into the dark night of terror. Perhaps you would use other words to describe the sequence of experiences she puts you through, but I think you can recognize that there are these definite steps, this pattern: she picks you up at one point and lets you go at quite a different one.

Such programming is characteristic of all good poetry, of all ages, but increasingly so as poetry has become identified with intense, private experience in our own time. When all truth is relative, there is less point in addressing oneself to momentous issues or sculpting classic treatments of timeless themes. Whitman spreads his brawny arms to encompass all the world in its full variety and incongruity in his poetry, and Dickinson delved into her secret soul. Trampling old boundaries and breaking up old unities were to become the type of the modern, where limits are unknown — and anything goes.

CHAPTER NINETEEN

The Case for the Conventional Poem

it takes a heap o' wisdom in a verse t' make a poem

I have accepted the challenge of defending Edgar A. Guest's poem, "Home." I am not concerned to defend it from its detractors — of which I count myself one — but from its defenders — or from those who use this or similar poems as a banner for something they call "conventional" poetry — as opposed to something they call "modern" poetry, and who feel that their own verses are being rejected because editors are prejudiced against rhyme, rhythm, and plain sense.

Convention is, by and large, something poets cannot do without and is the source of strength of great poems. Attitudes like the now repugnant sentimentality and self-conscious folksiness of "Home" go out of fashion, but they are not bad because they are conventional. And technical conventions, like those of rhythm, are as essential to poetry as the diatonic scale is to music, which is present even when the composer rejects it, as a silent measure or norm against which music occurs. I hope that as an editor I would have the imagination to accept a poem as good as "Home" if I were to receive it in the mail tomorrow. Though it dates from the early part of the century, its strengths are timeless. It has sufficient artistic integrity and force to demand printing. This is easy to say now, of course, when there is hardly an American who cannot quote at least the first line (though often in contempt). But the poem's basis for such a long life is solid, as I hope to show. Craft without inspiration can endure, while inspiration without craft fades on the air like a sigh.

First we must set aside disagreement with the complacency and soggy spirituality which constitute its "message." Editors accept a good many poems they disagree with. Rhyme, rhythm and plain sense are the attractive and valuable aspects of the poem. The question is whether these compensate for its wordiness, clichés, its rather sickening indulgence of easy emotions, and the superficiality of its homiletic manner. These weaknesses are not poetic conventions — but rather products of a particular ethos and personality.

One of its difficulties is that the whole poem is contained in the excellent first line, "It takes a heap o' livin' in a house t'make it home." The distinction between house and home is neat and meaningful; the poem will be concerned with the transformation of one into the other, of a physical edifice into a spiritual concept. The alliteration of those key terms with *heap* provides the basic tonal unity of the line, and the surprising use of the colloquial "heap o' " with the abstraction "livin' " provides verve and twist. It is a perfect epigram in a memorable rhythm.

That rhythm is more complex than it at first appears. The heptameter — old fourteener-line — is the ancient source of the ballad stanza, and induces a natural break, or caesura, after the fourth beat, whether the sense calls for it or not. Moreover, the cadence of the poem is dipodic; that is, it tends to fall into two-foot units, a pyrrhic followed by an iamb (uu u/), making four strong beats to the line (rather than seven, which heptameter would seem to imply). Thus two stout conventions, the ballad stanza and the swinging dipodic line, are interwoven with the real stresses demanded by rhetoric and sense. If you were to break down each line of the poem in this form you would find a very artful employment of these cadences in relation to one another:

ballad: it TAKES a HEAP o'LIV in' IN // a HOUSE t'MAKE
it HOME

dipodic: it TAKES a heap o'LIV in' in a HOUSE t'make it
HOME

sense stresses: it takes a HEAP o'LIV in' in a HOUSE t'make
it HOME

In this first line the sense stresses underscore the dipodic beat — rightly, to establish it — but elsewhere the contrast between sense and the dipodic beat is quite effective, as in the last line of the first stanza:

dipodic: un TIL some how yer SOUL is sort o' WRAPPED
round ev ery THING
sense stresses: un til SOME how yer SOUL is SORT o'
WRAPPED ROUND EV ery thing

The pull of this line against the conventional base, especially in the three heavy beats and *r* alliterations, gives the line a rather uncanny effect as the simple, apparently sincere mind of the speaker strains to express an abstract, metaphysical idea against the background of his hillbilly language and folk cadence.

Good poetry grows out of such struggles. The remarkable popularity and persistence of the poem are due to more than a memorable first line and the poem's general appeal to a wide, public conviction in the sacredness of the family residence. The great danger, as I am sure Guest realized, was that the homey nuggets of familiar speech would reduce all to platitude. He attempts to offset this danger by playing the phrases against the rhythmic units within the lines and the line endings themselves. For example:

The old high chairs, the playthings, too, the little shoes they wore
Ye hoard: an' if ye could ye'd keep the thumbmarks on the door.

Running the sense over the end of the line throws a remarkable weight on the word *hoard,* particularly as it echoes the rhyme sound. The little words bunch, then, as the second line winds up (note the *k* sounds), and *thumbmarks* comes through big as release, emphasizing the symbolic effect of the marks. This couplet (ending the second stanza) also illustrates the way the poem pushes from material to immaterial considerations, from things to feelings, from house to home, from locality and furnishings to love.

That pattern is the central strategy of the poem and the deepest reason, I believe, for its success. While the statements seem to be merely an arbitrary catalogue of the qualities which make the house a home, their images actually take us progressively to more intense, personal, and more spiritual experiences. Stanza one concentrates on the physical simplicity of the home, the unimportance of luxury. Stanza two concerns mostly children, and ends with those thumbmarks which, in their material worthlessness and irrational value to affectionate parents, push us toward a conception of more altruistic love. Stanza three involves chiefly the death of a female loved one — I think of her as "Mother," possibly the speaker's wife — and brings us to a kind of religious apotheosis. Death is first personified, then brought on stage as a visitation from the supernatural, right in the house or home: "Death's angel."

Here our experience moves to a different imaginative level from the one it traveled before, and the only high-falutin word in the poem, *sanctified,* is used, the status of *home* finally being sealed on the house by the holy presence of the angel of death. Grief and memory of the departed immediately follow, and it is on this note that we enter the last stanza:

Ye've got t' sing an' dance fer years, ye've got t' romp an' play
An' learn t' love the things ye have by usin' 'em each day;
Even the roses 'round the porch must blossom year by year
Afore they 'come a part o' ye, suggestin' someone dear
Who used t' love 'em long ago, an' trained 'em jes' t' run
The way they do, so's they would get the early mornin' sun;
Ye've got t' love each brick an' stone from cellar up t' dome:
It takes a heap o' livin' in a house t' make it home.

The brief reminder of joy, the sense of passing time, modulates the grief of the preceding stanza into loving memory. The dead female is subtly present here, ghostlike, as (presumably) the person who tended the roses. The off-stage image of that remembered hand tenderly caring for the growing vine is reinforced by the tight little sounds of the line beginning, "Who used t' love 'em," and the delicate touch of the word *jes'* — emerging into broader sounds of the flowering result in the next line. The poem is resolved by a return to the physical fact of the home, its bricks and stones now sanctified, the whole transmuted into a kind of shrine. That word *dome* at the end appears insincere, labored — as houses nor homes are likely to have domes — used in a critical position for nothing more than an easy rhyme. But perhaps the poet felt it was justified for its association with cathedrals, conveying the height and hush of the now hallowed house.

Surely the poem derives its power from that shaping of experience, so that the familiar becomes touched with a sense of mystery and holy benediction. It is in the critical third stanza, however, that the poem and I most seriously part company. There the language becomes most trite, most painfully inadequate to deal with the moment summoned, and we get phrases like, "Death is nigh," "scenes that grip the heart," and "stillness o' the night." I can take hominess, colloquial ease, simplicity, even sentimentality, so long as they don't soar into pretentiousness, and that is what happens

here. My tears and piety are jerked, and I slip out in embarrassment as the organ wells up with mechanical chords, programmed by
an undertaker.

I hope this analysis has not seemed a parody of literary criticism, convincing you of nothing more than the fact that ingenuity
can make a case for anything. I read hundreds of poems each
week which all my ingenuity cannot make a case for. Most of
these are what you would call "modern" (free verse, free of sense,
melody and power), but the worst are what you would call "conventional." They are not conventional enough. They do not sufficiently exploit the rich traditions of English verse. Sure, they
rhyme and trot, but there is no complexity or magic — nothing
interesting to the mind or ear, and it is not traditional for English
verse to be uninteresting.

Though the fashion for dialect verse has passed — for good
reason, as it almost invariably seems stagy — Guest is consistent
and harmonious in his use of it, building up to that one fancy
word, *sanctified,* expertly. The carefully organized experience of
deepening love which he gives us is, like all good poetic experiences, largely unstated, implied by imagery and language, emerging through the string of homilies. And he does not sleep with
his metronome, but works gentle and various effects upon a fairly
complex metrical base. The major conception of the poem is
simple but solid. The language is fairly consistently corny, but he
is capable of an occasional provocative, true and creative phrase.
I wish those of you who use the term "conventional" as an apology
for verse devoid of thought, convincing emotion, imagination and
technical skill could write as well as Edgar Guest. I wish, of
course, that you could write a great deal better.

You may learn to do so by learning something about convention. The word has a stuffy sound to American ears, seeming to
imply mindless conformity to mediocre standards. But it need
not. We could not have even free verse without convention, for
free verse is, when it works, a patchwork of old harmonies, like
grandmother's quilt, relying heavily on the vivid scraps of old
designs for the vitality of the new. The best "experimental" writers
of the early part of the century — poets like Eliot, cummings,
Stevens, Crane, Yeats, Thomas — all were soundly grounded in
the conventions, and with their ears so tuned were able to improvise
with convincing control. What bad, ragged, meterless and obscure
verse you see, sloppy in the name of freedom, probably results from

insufficient tuning of the ears to conventional verse. I am particularly bitter that so many teachers and parents, still affected by the taste of the twenties, are embarrassed by rhyme and rhythm, are unable to read verse with attention to its music, and so fail to build in children a sense of the basic harmonies which have been and always will be the substance of good poetry.

Convention, though, is where you start; the tick tock of the metronome is not music, important as it is as an underlying measure. The tick tock of alternating meter, iambic verse, underlies all English poetry. The actual rhythm demanded by sense and rhetoric is, as it were, a comment on that substructure. If you get in two or more light syllables before an accent, the verse rushes. If you substitute heavy beats for light ones, the verse is impeded. If you deny the beat entirely for a passage (which may be very effective), you deliberately create tension in the ear yearning for regularity and order. But if you do that too much you have prose. Rhyme, besides pleasing the ear with harmony, shapes and points up the design of the poem; it may be a design deliberately at odds with the squirming, organic experience it contains (as is the case with Donne's elaborate stanza structures), or it may cohere and emphasize the sense, as in Pope's couplets.

Convention is no less important in providing us with phrasal units and rhetorical patterns with clear, long-established connotations, to be varied and juxtaposed and contradicted in the process of creating new verse. Each phrasal unit has its melody, which you may make to reinforce or pull against the syllabic rhythm. Inversions, periodic structures, parallelism, antithesis, all the rhetorical units and devices of sentences, have conventional uses and inescapable connotations. If you string a lot of things together with *and*'s you get simple-minded accumulation and speed. If you balance and contrast in your sentence-building, you awaken your reader's wit, sometimes at the expense of his emotion, and the verse becomes more ratiocinative, penetrating, analytical. If you use formal apostrophe and hortatory tones your poetry becomes elevated — sometimes inappropriately so, and sometimes the inappropriateness is ironic and deliberate. The cracker-barrel moralism of "Home" derives in large part from its consistent use of simple declarative sentences, each intended as a pungent statement of "truth," delivered by an omniscient poet to an anonymous "you." There is no ostensible dramatization, no raising of the voice, no variation of approach, just a rhymed, homey lecture, compounded of generalizations. The surprise is in the contrast of that flat manner with the interplay of images which make their own experience parallel to the line of statement.

The *kind* of poem is in itself a matter of convention. As we read any poem we are guided by our past experience to expect one of several fairly fixed and formal types. If something other than one of these traditional types is presented us as a poem, we stubbornly categorize it as satire, lyric, drama, or something else. We insist upon reading it as a *poem.*

DIRECTIONS FOR USE

Point valve toward
surface to be sprayed.
Hold can upright about
ten inches from surface.
Apply sufficient . . .

See what I mean? As you read you begin emphasizing rhythms, become aware of sound relationships, look for double-meanings, the significance of line-endings, prompted by your sense of what poets are likely to be doing. You may come to see those directions as a wry comment by someone on something totally unconnected with insect repellent. Actually there is a genre of poems called "found" poetry this example suggests — usually a slight rearrangement of the language of advertisements, business letters, signs or documents — a variety of parody, with surprising juxtapositions implying a bitterly ironic contemplation of false values — or some such standard poetic stance. Easy conventions quickly become clichés.

There are conventions of imagery, of attitudes, of poetic situations and themes. Petrarchan imagery for the whole freight of courtly love attitudes is perhaps the most persistent and viable system of conventions to permeate our poetry. Such conventions as the *carpe diem* motif (seize the day, for tomorrow we may die) will undoubtedly recur as long as poems do. The pastoral tradition of lovely shepherds with classical names ignoring their flocks for the shepherdesses, cavorting on blossomy greenswards and playing pipes, seems fairly to have exhausted itself, though poets still call upon their mistresses to come live with them and be their loves in some idealized setting.

The value of such conventions is that they provide an immediate frame of reference for what the poet wants to say. The basic situation of the love poem — lover appealing to or praising his mistress — is nothing more than a conventional, symbolic testing ground for ideas and values which apply to far more than sexual relations. Get "my dear" into the first line, and the reader recognizes the familiar, basic situation and readies his mind for the poet's comment on it. If you had to build each poem from scratch, inventing the language, attitudes, devices, forms and purposes which convention usually provides, you would not make much progress. Convention rightly understood is an assistance to originality. It provides the context in which individuality can be recognized and measured. If you undertake to write a sonnet you are stepping into the ring with Shakespeare, Milton, Wordsworth and e. e. cummings (who was very fond of the form). Okay, says the attending public, what can *you* do?

The mistake is in thinking that the convention is enough, that having stepped into the ring you have won the bout, or that in having achieved the remarkable feat of having gotten a sunset, a rose, Mother, God, a dog, a child and Abraham Lincoln into fourteen rhyming lines of iambic pentameter, you should be published — and that anyone who fails to appreciate you is against convention. No! Our reverence for convention is exactly what makes us shudder to see it so superficially employed.

For me the excitement comes in achieving something distinct and individual within the strictest confines of convention, in the subtle adaptation that makes a new form of an old one. In "Meeting and Passing," Frost imposes upon himself an inordinately tight form. It is basically an English sonnet, but with the same pair of rhymes used through the first two quatrains; the third quatrain shifts to another rhyme scheme, and the couplet uses identicals. But the meaning has its own form, which falls into a seven line structure. Two conventional lovers approach, meet in the middle of the poem, pause, and pass. The exact quality of their love is defined in the seventh and eighth lines, the decimal point just past the middle of the sonnet nailing down precisely the difference to be overcome as they move on and incorporate one another's experience in the way necessary to unite them. A great deal is said about love, originally observed and illustrated, and though the diction and meter never vary from a conventional norm, the flavor is exactly Frost's; he achieves the miracle of taking his distinct seat right in the middle of tradition:

MEETING AND PASSING

As I went down the hill along the wall
There was a gate I had leaned at for the view
And had just turned from when I first saw you
As you came up the hill. We met. But all
We did that day was mingle great and small
Footprints in summer dust as if we drew
The figure of our being less than two
But more than one as yet. Your parasol
Pointed the decimal off with one deep thrust.
And all the time we talked you seemed to see
Something down there to smile at in the dust.
(Oh, it was without prejudice to me!)
Afterward I went past what you had passed
Before we met and you what I had passed.

This poem is of about the same vintage as "Home," and is at least as conventional, or more so, for it escapes the novelty of dialect verse and American middle-class reference. But does it not make "Home" seem a tiresome, long motto by comparison? Achieve a poem such as "Meeting and Passing," poetasters, and you will have defeated modernity.

wanted: satirist

It is in one genre of poetry, especially, that a conventional, one might almost say reactionary, mind-set is essential — the writing of satire. In 1961, *Life* magazine announced the dawning of a new age of American satire, with such brilliant deflators as Mort Sahl, Mike Nichols and Elaine May, Bob Newhart, Shelley Berman, Dick Gregory, the staff of *Mad,* Jules Feiffer and Herb Gardner reaching an unprecedentedly large audience and growing rich on the conscience of the rich. To appreciate the significance of this surge of skepticism and dissent *Life* said, one must remember the Silence, when "the U.S., emerging shamefaced from the McCarthy era, strode boldly out of fear into apathy." The subsequent years have, indeed, been rich in satire, particularly in motion pictures, but also in cartoons, rock music, fiction, stage and nightclub entertainment. But satire is first and last a genre of poetry, and there has not yet emerged a talent comparable to Horace, Persius, Juvenal, Dryden, Pope, Swift, or even our own James Russell Lowell.

Satire comes from a Latin word meaning "fed up." Perhaps poets are not sufficiently disgusted yet with the state of their civilization, though it is hard to imagine this to be true. More likely, poets have lost touch with the tradition and conventions of satire, or see no way to adapt them to contemporary experience. Modern poetry, true enough, has a distinctive strain of wit and negation; but the wit is that of anguished doubt, and the negation is that of personal misery. Satire cannot well entertain uncertainty, and it is definitively a public art in which the world-weary groans of a subjective poet have little place. It is a poetry of reason rather than emotion, of realism rather than fantasy, of looking outward and speaking clearly — all characteristics very distinct from those we have come to associate with poetry. The poet may arouse amusement and anger in his audience, and inflict pain on his target, but he must himself remain cool. (Those cool cats, the Beats, were markedly bad at this, giving vent to a frenzied gibber of outrage, of egotistical self-involvement, which made their poems — though, true enough, often vituperative — the antithesis of satire.)

I think it is possible to extrapolate from the history of satire the qualifications that a new satirist, when he emerges, must have. They are quite specialized and demanding; it is not enough to stand on your hind legs and howl. In the hope that some poet somewhere may recognize himself in the portrait, or be helped to shape his forming talents, I would like to give here what I see as the most necessary characteristics.

First, of course, he must be knowledgeable. In the past, satirists have been close to the Court, close enough to observe at first hand the society and the political figures they hoped to depict. Now, of course, the Mandarins are not collected in a single place so convenient as Hampton Palace once was, but, in the U.S., are spread from Frisco pads to Madison Avenue. Belindas with yet unravaged locks rise at noon in Dallas, Achitophels are governors of southern states, MacFlecknoes teach in universities, and Senators are everywhere. Now, of course, we have photography, and publications like *Time* to catch kings in their stocking feet, as when it reports juicy tidbits like the following: "Throughout 90 minutes, Eichmann scarcely moved — except that once he picked his nose." With such massive communication as is now available, the poet need no longer attend state occasions, but may stay home and vomit.

He must have a firm base of values, an unhesitating opinion of what is right and wrong and some confidence that his values are shared by his public. It is this requirement, more than any other, which has heretofore made satire nearly impossible in the twentieth century. It has been a period of revision and re-examination of values rather than of assertion. Every good has seemed to have an evil worm at the core, and evils have seemed so relative they blur and disappear like optical illusions. Satire requires a sunny certainty, a faith in reason; but, alas, the myth of the reasonable animal has long since been exploded. There isn't time in satire to argue a judgment; its impact must be immediate, or else you find yourself in the painful position of explaining a joke. It will take genius to discover what it is the world agrees upon after all this chaos; it will require a simple mind.

Because the values must be fairly simple, clear and publicly agreed upon, the satirist is almost certain to be of a conservative temperament. He is more apt to be found criticizing the new than the old, disdaining the experimental in favor of the established. Clearly this presents another problem for the satirist in a country whose most dynamic literary and political tradition has always been liberal — to the extent that we completely lack any intelligent conservative force. Frost is an exception, and, indeed, might have been our satirist if he had had a mind to. Reactionaries like Pound and Eliot were exiles. The liberal tendency is to forgive rather than damn, to create rather than save what has been created. Liberalism thrives on newness, progress, humaneness — and satire, distrustful of any excess (even, of course, an excess of conservatism), almost invariably contrasts a noble, ancient tradition with the folly, vice and superficiality of modern life (modern, or modish, meaning whatever is going on at the time). The satirist is likely to see progress as impossible, the world rolling downhill, and he is not likely to dull his sword of justice with such degenerate considerations as mercy.

While satire is basically denunciation, of course, it must have as well an implicit or explicit affirmation; we have to know what the satirist approves of as well as what he damns. This is a frightening requirement for any able satirist. Pessimism easily becomes a habit, and the mordancy of a Swift can ultimately dissipate itself. Swift could satirize satire itself, and satire satirizing satire, ad infinitum, as in a hall of mirrors, and find himself ravaged by his own brilliance. These are tricky waters, for if any excess is a legitimate target, excess of moderation is one of the most obvious. Commitment to anything appears to be folly, and lack of commitment as absurd as any fanaticism. The satirist can find himself paralyzed in and scorched by his own fire.

Moreover, the expression of positive values always sounds so dreary, after the spicy, vicious excitement of attack. Because of insufficient affirmation, Horace sometimes sounds merely supercilious and blasé, Juvenal obsessed, Dryden sadistic, and Pope merely bad-tempered. The world wants to be entertained, not lectured to, and delights more in castigation than praise. Readers skip through the argumentative sections of Dryden's "Religio Laici" to get to the "good part" — where he lights out after the dissenters and the Catholics. Yet, unfairly, readers will be dissatisfied if they feel, finally, that they have been given much to hate and nothing to believe in.

The best tactic is to imply positive values rather than state them. The classical solution of the problem is for the satirist himself to step into his poem in the rhetorical posture of the reasonable man, the ordinary fellow, neither obsessed by his bleak view nor angered by his hatreds. Most American satire in the past has been in dialect for this reason — to suggest the cracker-barrel philosopher, the basically kindly and twinkly old fellow down at the general store, whose intolerance we sympathize with because we are fond of the old geezer and know he means no harm. One of our nightclub satirists, Mort Sahl, found excellent symbols for this function. He appeared in a sweater, clasping a rolled newspaper, a guy like you or me, automatically winning our sympathy, implying that what he said was plain common sense, and that he, for one, saw exactly where the trouble was, and wasn't going to let himself get worked-up over it. The relaxed, familiar posture is essential. It is the sangfroid of the skilled marksman. We must be convinced that the satirist's demands are not outrageous, that we cannot dismiss his judgments because he is fastidious, tendentious or impassioned. "Enthusiasm" was a derogatory word in the Age of Reason. A man possessed by gods is simply out of his wits, or so the man in the streets will judge him. However out of his wits the poet may actually be, he must establish in his satire an image of himself as a man able to slay dragons with a shrug.

Obviously he must be witty, partly for the same reason, for humor ingratiates as it punctures, and the most scandalous statements (witness Menken, Shaw) are forgiven when cleverly said. This has clear implications for the language of the poem. It must be of the middle-way, neither too earthy and colloquial, as that would suggest a mind too gross to be witty, to make fine distinctions and find exact words; nor must it be too fancy and intellectual, as that prevents our identification with the figure of the ordinary fellow. The satirist can use big words, but wryly — to show that the poet is conversant with the world of ideas but not taken in by it. He may use vulgar language, too, but with a wink to dissociate himself from vulgarity.

He must use rhyme and fairly conventional meter. Free verse is essentially romantic; it comes from the restless, undisciplined soul, impatient of all bondage, swirling and surging with the vagaries of passing emotion. The satirist must convey the sense that he is in perfect, exquisite control. Regular meter asserts this, but not sufficiently; it is rhyme that snaps home the raps. Song can endure without rhyme, for the musical qualities of rhyme are less important than its emphatic qualities (and humorous possibilities) — but satire must, I think, employ it. True, the Latin satirists, writing in another tradition, managed without rhyme, but now that we have this resource, we simply lose force if we neglect to use it. The rhythm may jolt and strain, the rhymes may be ridiculous; but there must always be the clear implication that the poet is so firmly in control that he can afford to play around. Like a comic on the slack-wire or the ice-rink, his performance must suggest a skill beyond grace — never less than grace.

Major satires are usually rather long poems with a narrative thread, usually transparently allegorical (as, even if there weren't problems of libel, the audience enjoys feeling in the know, penetrating an easy disguise). The language is generally very contemporary, packed with allusions to the people, ideas, events and details of current life, for part of the excitement of good satire is in its immediacy and topical reference. There is always the danger of smothering a poem with too much immediacy, or the opposite danger of ineffectuality because of over-abstractness. If an individual is denounced, for example, in such particular terms that the satire can apply to no one else, the poem may lose interest as soon as the individual leaves the contemporary scene. Moreover, personal satire is cruel. While we all love a little cruelty, an audience may switch its sympathy from the poet to the target if it feels his object is simply vilification of an individual. In other words, the poet should suggest that he is not damning Bishop X, or Secretary Y or Novelist Z so much as people *like* them; he is ridiculing human failings, as evidenced just now so deliciously by X, Y, and Z. On the other hand, if he makes his portrait too vague and generalized, his audience misses the spiteful joy of feeling that old X is getting his proper licking. He must find exactly the details which have both an immediate, personal reference and a general suggestiveness. His language and critical framework should imply that the criticism may be taken on several levels and that what he has to say will be important long after this particular pipsqueak X has left the scene. He wouldn't want to dignify his subject by suggesting that he, in himself, is worthy of attack.

In the greatest satire there are always dimensions beyond damnation, many of which require exceptions to the very criteria I have been suggesting. While the normal tone is crackling, brisk, jocular or acrimonious, there can be sudden moments of heart-rending sadness and profundity, passages of loveliness, of anguish or real bitterness — all of which would seem to undermine the essential nature of the satire.

We must go deeper. Irony has been described as a double commitment. Its sting or amusement arises from the fact that we recognize a crossing and contradiction of two (or more) values. As Cleanth Brooks has pointed out, Pope is half in love with Belinda in "The Rape of the Lock," for the vain little fool really *is,* after all, a sun that warms and lights her society. Frivolous as that society is, Pope cannot (or does not) quite disguise his own commitment to it, a society which fascinates, pleases and disgusts simultaneously, like an ingenious wax rose. Satirists often find themselves damning the things they love, and at such times emerges the richest, most poignant, and at the same time no less amusing and deadly satire. It is the whispered "alas" which escapes when a poet condemns with justice, his heart tugging against him, that gives satire the magnitude of great poetry, not just jingling, clever ridicule.

But satire, of course, is a mixture of rhetoric (the art of persuasion) and poetry (which I cannot define in parentheses), and even these moments or passages of glancing backwards, of self-revelation, have a calculable rhetorical function, for they establish that the ordinary fellow in the sweater, beneath his appearance of easy control and quick judgment, has moments of uncontrollable exasperation, of delicate sensibility, of mournful awareness of larger questions, of poignant despair, of doubt, of innocent glee, just like the rest of us. And a glimpse of these unsatirical characteristics makes all the more effective the usual manner of the hard grin and disciplined precision. (Nothing, I should warn, can be more quickly overdone, for sentiment of any sort, either for himself, mankind, or a pretty landscape, sours the satire in a moment, makes the humor seem nervous, the castigation hypocritical or merely mean.)

The heroic couplet, rhymed pairs of closed, balanced, antithetical and smoothly modulated pentameter lines, proved, of course, the perfect medium for the greatest age of English satire. It is still a splendid, inexhaustible form. The couplets, as Dryden said, are like bricks in a wall, neither losing their individuality entirely nor standing out too conspicuously from the general pattern. He might have added that they have something of the force, too, of bricks hurled — solid, square, inviolable and deadly. The audience gave out before the couplets. They had had a century of very hard use, often by mere versifiers, and seemed to begin to sing themselves, every sequence, every rhetorical twist, every rhyme and cadence having been rung so often by inexpert hands that readers became tone-deaf. Even now, after a long rest, many readers find themselves wearied by long passages of unrelieved couplets. I think, nevertheless, that another Pope could succeed again in the same form. We often blame innocent meter when we ought to blame bad poets.

But probably this satirist to emerge will find himself a new and somewhat more flexible form — my guess would be a versatile interweaving of various standard meters, taking advantage of songs, chants, now ballad tetrameter, now long galloping lines of anapests, maintaining frequency of rhyme and general regularity but with wrenching and dissonance more appropriate to our times than the elegant periods of the neoclassicists.

He will also have to find a new status quo to defend. This is a subtler task than it may sound, for what was liberal has become conservative. I can imagine, for example, a properly crotchety and crusty satirist defending nineteenth century liberalism and positivism against what might seem to him the metaphysical vagaries of more recent thought. Nowadays it is conservative to be an atheist in some quarters. Progressivism of the thirties in politics, morals and education seems a bit quaint now; and some youngster, yearning for a better past, might well build his fortress on that rock to blast more recent innovations. Mort Sahl said, "I'm not so much interested in politics as in overthrowing the government," and the statement rings of old gold. A rebellious satirist seems, on the face of it, a contradiction in terms; but, after all, rebellion is this country's oldest heritage, and talk of it now smacks more of the good old days than of the future. I cannot propose a platform for the satirist to come (being too deeply embroiled myself in the doubts, ambiguities and retreats which have made satire impossible in recent times); but I would predict that the platform will be built on a perception of and attachment to the strongest elements in the native grain.

I am, personally, as sick of sensitive, subjective lyrics as I imagine the world once was of heroic couplets and satire. We are in a state of peculiar bondage now, in which a poem is almost by definition a short, intense and anguished cry of the soul. We need longer forms, narrative forms, public commentary, a stable, durable prosody and the possibility of more variety of tone in order to escape the precious trammels of filler-poems and the standard tragic view. Perhaps satire may prove a way of breaking out. In the fields beyond lies a whole range of narrative and essay forms which, let us hope, can be rejuvenated and find meaningful contemporary expression.

CHAPTER TWENTY

Poetry and Children

the talent of naivety

Here is the title poem of a book published in 1968:

THE REAL TIN FLOWER

The old type lily has died.
It's so droopy now
    the old tiger
lily fell to its grave.
     The family
is sad. They are nuns who cannot sleep.

The old type lily was fashionable
in town.
    She sat on a golden stem.
Her servants carried her
      up in the air
in a sunburnt palm
     and gave her a bath.

They placed her
on the mantlepiece.
      She looked all around
      (couldn't hear thunder
      or the whippoorwill)
and died
   of envy.
Now she lives as the real tin flower.

I find mysef beguiled by the paradoxes of this poem and its gently
shaded humor and poignancy. It seems to be a poem about artifice

and nature. The natural flower was treated as though it were artifice, a work of art — and, of course, it drooped and died as a result of its elegant treatment. "Real" in the title and final line has a disturbing irony, for it means that artificial is real, perhaps that *only* the artificial is real, certainly that only the artificial can endure.

Why is the family called "nuns"? I assume they are people of conscience, grieving and perplexed by the passing of the natural flower. Are they the same people who reappear as "servants" in the next stanza? I assume so. They — perhaps people in general — worship and serve natural beauty. They pick the flower with "sunburnt palm," carry it inside to a "bath" in a vase, honor it by placing it on the altar of the living-room, the "mantlepiece." They have done all they know how to do in expressing their appreciation, love, reverence and subservience, but the flower, cut off from the sounds and nutriment of its natural environment, dies "of envy" for, I assume, the flowers left in the garden.

But it has served, at least, as a model for art. Someone has fashioned a "real tin flower" which will not droop and die; therefore, in a strange way the flower "lives," captured in an ideal, immortal, paralyzed existence in some ways superior to natural life of breathing passion, fevered brows and mortal consummation. The irony of that last line is unnerving: it exquisitely combines literal accuracy and celebration of art with the bitterest sarcasm concerning our futile and perverted efforts to trap natural beauty and somehow enshrine it on our mantlepiece.

Much of the magic and richness of that last line is embodied in the word "real," which has about it simultaneously an almost crude colloquial quality of enthusiasm (man, that's a real good flower!), a biting sarcasm, and a philosophical resonance which awakes our meditation and teases us out of thought. How does the poet prepare us to receive that word with all these reverberations? First, there is the free use of blatantly colloquial language: "old type lily," "so droopy," "in town." Second, simple images, ideas and expressions are juxtaposed with elements of much greater strangeness and sophistication, as the family's sadness is equated with the nuns' sleeplessness. The word *fashionable* nods heavily on its stem as the elegant blossom does, carried in state. The simple response of the flower looking "all around" is elaborated by the strange melancholy of "couldn't hear thunder/ or the whippoorwill." Third, the poem sparkles with fun — and the fun is sometimes devilish, so we cannot be sure whether the poet is *making* fun of the family, the flower, or human nature. Vanity in both senses elicits our snickers and our sympathy.

I neglected to include the epigraph, which appears under the title: "For Mummy as a Present," a phrase which brings us to compare the poem itself to the lily, a pretty object brought by sunburnt hands as an offering, hovering between its incarnation in nature and in art, because I didn't want you to know too soon that the poem was written by a nine-year-old, Aliki Barnstone.

It is almost impossible to think honestly about children's art. One remembers Dr. Johnson's remark on women preachers, whom he compared to talking dogs — the wonder is not whether they do it well, but that they do it at all. Is the kind of critical analysis to which I have subjected "The Real Tin Flower" appropriate? Knowing, now, the poet's age, are you inclined to believe that she could not have meant as much as I found, that the poem is, indeed, charming, but not, as I have implied, profound, skillful and premeditated? Or will you seize the opportunity to tell me that true poetry is, like this poem, sensitive, spontaneous, inspired — and intended to be felt rather than thought about.

After I read Aliki Barnstone's book I went back to one published by Harper in 1956: *First Poems by Minou Drouet,* written when the poet was eight. I have not heard of Miss Drouet since, but her first book was, like that of Aliki Barnstone, a kind of miracle. Minou's poems are much longer than those of Aliki: they tumble out in a torrent of rapid associations. I will quote a passage both in the original French and in English translation.

> Arbre je viens à toi
>   console-moi
>   d'être seulement moi.
> Léger, à pas de minet gris
>   le vent s'est levé
>   un vent coiffé
>   de nues
>   d'ouate molle
> un vent
>   à la jupe couleur d'étang
> et ses doigts curieux
>   ont ébouriffé les branches.

Tree I come to you
    console me
    for being only me.
With a light grey pussy-cat step
    the wind has risen
    a wind crowned
        of clouds
            with soft cotton wool
    a wind
        with a pond-coloured skirt
        and its prying fingers
        have rufflel the branches.

Both girls reach us first with their startlingly fresh imagery, their unspoiled impressions of the world — and, as Minou says, "Madame I truly believe/ that the impressionable is catching."

But their ability to produce metaphors is rooted in feeling and thought. Minou tells of a blow waking her in the morning:

        to punish me
            for grinding my teeth
            in my sleep

She thinks of growing up in terms of a black bundle being drawn from her on a string, and tells her dead dog:

    and when the little girl began to weep
    she was not weeping for you my friend
            it was because
                suddenly
            because of disgust
                and distress
        she felt
            she was afraid to feel
            that she was becoming
                she too
            a horrible
            grown-up person.

Elsewhere she describes her heart as "an airy boat" sailing very purposefully to nowhere in particular:

        my arms turn sadly away
            from what is here and now
        and yet so desired
            the moment before
            to look for tomorrow

which it will not want
when tomorrow comes.

The life she represents is not all pretty pictures seen by a cherub. She wrestles with her vanity, her identity transforming itself under her skin, her contemplation of the perishing world and our restlessness within it. Indeed, her capacity to see freshly and describe life vividly is inseparable from her ability to sense philosophical significance.

Minou plays the piano herself — and has a passionate love of intricate form in music. In a letter (printed in the collection of her poems) she writes:

Last night I heard some music by Bach on the radio . . . .
It made me feel quite ill, the music drew a big tree which
had its roots in my meat and it went up to the sky with
the marvellous voice of an angry forest, and when the
tree reached the clouds it crossed over its branches like
the arches in a church and the arches met in the sky like
two hands, and the music was so terrible that the two
hands were covered with blood.

The terror and illness she describes are surely only aspects of excruciating pleasure. Though the images are sensual and emotional — the tree, the forest, the arch, the hands, the blood — they are responses to form and archetechtonic thought.

Ah, how strong is the temptation to draw a curtain between us and the child's overheated little brain! Suppose we call her a "genius," as though that were a category of human being, like redhead, or pigmy, or twin, or paraplegic. The term protects us; we need not expect of ourselves such brilliance because we did not happen to be born with two heads. But these little girls keep reminding us of their ordinary humanity. Aliki Barnstone writes:

When I snooze with a gooey cold
I need Vicks Vapo-Rub's bluey world.

She tells about bugs going down the drain pipe where they

. . . crawl slowly on a far journey
to a wet jamboree,
a bug meeting under the world

There is no question she inhabits a world familiar to us all — and when she very simply announces:

I never see what I am looking at.
I see what I think.

she expresses a dilemma we all face, though few so frankly. Moreover, we know she sees *and* thinks a great deal.

Those last two lines are from this poem:

TIME

The calendars pile up in a neat stack.
I knew they would.

I tried to forget about them
yet the days . . .

I am older now and still a child
but time is a thirsty germ.

I have one year left to play in this lot
and am afraid.

Some people think about
what they do

or the school they are to lose.
Others just let a river go by.

I never see what I am looking at.
I see what I think.

At night life is blue waves,
piers with stairs going down,

people who jump off and frighten
fish who swim away,

boys who dive from the top of the rail.
This is my real life.

And we come round again to that word *real*. In this case it refers not to the natural lily nor the tin one, but to the lily of the inner life, of the subjective, thinking, dreaming self — the fear and excitement down by night's dark pier. Here is another escape from time — like that of the tin flower. The grey world of stacked calendars and outgrown play yards and schools is left behind as one enters the "real" world of the imagination. Her insistence upon the reality and importance of her own thoughts, impressions and visions may be what distinguishes her from you and me.

No, I would not classify these girls as geniuses, as "gifted" children — though they certainly are of unusual intelligence and use well the gifts we all have — our eyes and ears and vibrant skin, our kaleidoscopic ability to make surprising associations of our experiences. They are not women preachers or talking dogs or child artists: they are poets, from whom we can, if we are sufficiently modest, learn a great deal. Somehow they escaped or were not brain-damaged by that Procrustean bed we call our educational system. Somehow they realize more human potential than most of us do. To call them geniuses is, in a strange way, to dismiss them, to carry them up in the air in sunburnt hands, bathe them and place them on the mantlepiece to droop and die.

children as audience

Turning from poems written by children to those written for them, I think it is important to keep in mind the miracle of human potential. It is important for adult poets, too, to find the way to the dark pier by the blue waves where boys leap from the top rail. And children will know when poets have done so. When you get down to the bare bones of the greatest literature you find something that can be communicated to a child. The Bible, myths, the great epics, the plays of Shakespeare, all become familiar to us early in versions for children — which, though they lack the literary quality of the originals, convey somehow the essence, the primordial experience, which makes those works persist so forcefully in the human imagination.

Many great writers at some time in their careers have addressed themselves directly to children. Some, like Melville and Swift, have unwittingly (and, it seems to adults who know their works, grotesquely) been adopted by children. Others, like R. L. Stevenson, A. A. Milne, Lewis Carroll — and one might even add Charles Dickens — have largely been forgotten for their "serious" work, intended for adults, and have had their immortality insured by several loyal generations of children. It may be crass to measure literary success by popularity, but if you check the number of editions and translations of *Alice in Wonderland* in the Library of Congress catalogue, it may give you cause to wonder why you write what you write. All the logic and mathematics of the don Dodgson found its most valid and culturally valuable expression in the fantasy of Carroll. It is not easy to know how to aim our talent.

Clement Clarke Moore must have invested most of his energy and talent in his Biblical studies, his Greek and Hebrew lexicon, and yet it was the dog-trot "Visit from St. Nicholas," published in *Colliers* in 1823, which was his major contribution to Western civilization. Is there child or adult in the English-speaking world who cannot recite great patches of the poem? Is there a home without at least one copy? Children, cumulatively, are rather fine literary critics; we may be sure that what they have chosen to preserve and revere must be significant — in a way that should make us modest about our Wastelands and Godots.

"Visit from St. Nicholas" is a good poem for the reasons that most good poems are good. Its rattling anapestic tetrameter couplets are used with astonishing variety and movement. The homey, colloquial phrasing ("nestled all snug in their beds") gives way to heroic action ("More rapid than eagles his coursers they came") and imaginative delicacy ("As dry leaves . . .," etc.) with great facility and ease. There are the narrative design, the mystery, excitement, the sensory titillation, humor, and, above all, the celebratory, ritualistic quality; it is a poem which performs a function for family gatherings yearning for a ceremony to order their holiday feelings. It is, of course, absolutely pagan, and yet it defines a god, a "right jolly old elf," who has become astonishingly, nay disgustingly, central to the experience of winter, to the cheer of warmth and wealth in the home, the tribal victory over the season. I suspect that the pudgy little god of capitalism embodies a great deal more of our religious commitment than the sparer one whose birthday he usurped. Children know.

Since I have mentioned *The Wasteland,* it might be interesting to contrast it with Moore's poem. I suppose that in some sense Eliot's is greater — and I confess I enjoy reading it more — though it will never sell so well nor last as long as Moore's, and has very little about it communicable to children. (Will there be a Charles Lamb to write a *Tales from Eliot?*) Its basic complaint is of a lack of faith in modern society, which is amusing when one compares the adoration of Santa Claus with whatever enthusiasm has been generated for the Fisher King in whatever more primitive society. Eliot inspires much compassion for dispossessed aristocrats after World War I, and much contempt for the indifferent love affairs of secretaries and for people too poor to get their teeth fixed. Its allusive texture, both in form and direct reference, endears it to literary people who perhaps enjoy some suggested analogy between their own plight and that of dispossessed aristocrats. But, surely, the chief impact is the vision of the Wasteland itself, the rats and bones and dead trees and crickets that give no relief (one wonders what is expected of crickets). This is what we might call literary sensationalism; it is very reminiscent of the Jacobean gloom of Webster and Tourneur, the heavy horror and baroque ghastliness so influential for Eliot and other intellectuals sated on prosperity *(The Wasteland* is almost exactly a hundred years younger than "Visit from St. Nicholas"). Now horror is a staple quality of great literature — for good reason, as it pushes experience to the extremes, to force us to look over the foggy cliff-lip into the unknown. This, and the aristocratic sympathies and comic contempt for lower classes, the religious air, the sound of doom, the abracadabra to the tune of muted cellos, all are the ingredients of good literature for children or others.

What fails is the central metaphor. We are much more likely to drown in the juice of sentiment than to wither in spiritual aridity; London, wettest of cities, is simply in no way like a Wasteland. The damnation of our times is not that we fail to believe, but that we believe too freely and effusively, first this, then that. Our century is more like a gusher than a valley of dry bones. Visions of sugar plums (perhaps to our shame) are more familiar to us than those of bones in a "low dry garrett, / Rattled by the rat's foot only, year to year." Such a basic error — the complete irrelevance of a basic image to the experience of a world of people less dessicated than T. S. Eliot — would never be overlooked by a child, though it may be swallowed in the swill of literary fashion by leagues of us who are less aware of what life is about.

I mean no nonsense about the unspoiled imagination or clean vision of the uninformed. These, and lack of mental maturity, are disadvantages of children. But because they are free of literary fashion, they very often have a surer grasp of essential truth in literature. Most of us begin our literary education with Mother Goose rhymes, and there is not a one of them which is a bad poem. They are like pebbles in a stream, all the soft parts eroded away. Mostly they are in native English meter, pre-iambic — the pease-porridge-hot kind of insistent accent, the dissonant rhymes rediscovered by Emily Dickinson and other modern poets. They contain, in short, the native genius of the language, and ought to be studied and restudied by anyone learning to write poetry. They are also characterized by a lack of sentimentality and morality.

The mother who deals with excess progeny by whipping them all soundly and putting them to bed gets an affirming nod from wise kiddies who share from an early age this insight into adult behavior. If, for contrast, you look at the shelf of children's books or children's toys in most stores you get an impression of the cute and cuddly and sweet and benign world adults would like to wish on children, with so little relevance to the facts of life as children perceive them. The Mother Goose world is mysterious, arbitrary (what adults call nonsense), concrete and cantankerous. It is innocently wise.

I suppose that by the age of ten I must have known every poem in *A Child's Garden of Verses* by heart, and, again, for good reason. There is the same poetic sophistication in form as the Mother Goose rhymes exhibit, though, of course, Stevenson writes chiefly iambic rather than accentual verse. The penetrating power of these poems, however, is in the way they push the mind to wonder; I have a sense that each has in it somewhere a core of fear. (Maybe I was just an easily frightened child, but fear was an important literary experience for me; I was scared silly by "The Raven," the Alice books, by most of the children's classics — and that, of course, is why I loved them so.) Oh, how I like to go up in a swing, and while I am seeing so wide, beyond the garden wall, into the unknown, I have a knot of gasp in my chest. When *will* those boats come home? Why *does* that man keep galloping by on the windy night? And the shadow: make fun of him as I will, he clings along and leaps to unexpected size and diminishes like a ghost. And I, the giant great and still watching the world of counterpane, am busy wondering about the relative size of things, about the eyes looking on, and order imposed by unseen hands. The book grapples with life. As does the so-called nonsense of Edward Lear (Oh, wonderful pussy, you are, you are), the puzzling fun of Milne (when he doesn't go sentimental on us), the awe of De la Mare.

All these are English. An unfortunate shift in taste is apt to deprive our children of the poetry *we* grew up on with American roots. Riley and Eugene Field (not to be confused with a person named Rachel, who appears in so many recent anthologies) are the most obvious examples. Their poems are becoming hard to find. One anthology, over twenty years old now, instructs teachers and parents:

One of the outstanding developments in the field of verse for children is the comparatively recent change that has taken place in the choice of poetry considered suitable for children . . . An example is Eugene Field's "Little Boy Blue" which until fairly recently was commonly included in children's books. True, the poem speaks of a child and his toys, but its theme is a parent's grief and sorrow. Better understanding of children has brought marked changes . . . We have learned the value of starting with children *where they are.*

So teacher snatches "Little Boy Blue" from the child's loving hands and says "No, no, no! You must start where you *are!"* What incredible gall psychologists and educationists are apt to demonstrate. "Little Boy Blue" (which I also have by heart — as I imagine most of you do, too) is rather too childish for a child over ten, but it confronts death in a dignified and properly mysterious way, and if children continue to be as attracted by it as I was, I cannot imagine on what higher authority it ought to be denied them.

Dialect poses a similar problem. One almost has the impression that Riley and Field are excluded from collections of children's poetry because they use *ain't.* One of my favorite poems from childhood is Field's "Jest 'Fore Christmas," which has the integrity, wit, the guts of his best work. "Wynken, Blynken, and Nod," which is pleasant, though a bit gushy and silly, gets by, but "Jest 'Fore Christmas" is rarely reprinted now. "Little Orphant Annie," a real spine-tingler, still is accepted in the canon, though other Riley poems are not. Americans went through a phase of being embarrassed by their dialects — after a period of being proud of them. The kind of linguistic faithfulness Frost exhibits is probably better, in the long run, than the self-consciously rural dialects of the nineteenth century, but that should not keep us from sharing with our children the poems we cut our teeth on.

All this relates to the writing of poetry in two ways. First, of course, one must recognize and come to terms with his own literary inheritance; those rhythms were drummed into our heads early — and we should learn what they are and what they signify. There is a metrical education in Mother Goose, immensely valuable because we have it in our consciousness almost at the level of instinct. And the rollicking regularity of some of the longer children's poems similarly instructs us in song; if we do not lose entirely that sense of song, our poetry will be better, whatever form it takes.

The second value for poets in reconsidering children's poetry is in learning to write for children. Nothing, may I first warn you, is more demanding. The disciplines the task imposes on the poet — of vocabularly, rhythm, imagery, above all the pressure to make concepts vividly experiential — are healthy ones for their use in other work.

PART FOUR:

POETRY AND THE WORLD

CHAPTER TWENTY-ONE

The New Era

alternative futures

In Chapter Four I said that a poet should have six senses: a sense of self, a sense of fact, a sense of language, a sense of art, a sense of his age, and a sense of mystery. The last two of these senses are the most difficult to address in a book about how to become a poet — and yet are perhaps the most critical. By definition they require personal vision, which one writer cannot supply to another. In Chapter Three I described my own shift of vision as a dream of a planned society gave way to a vision of community. Prophecy is always a thankless and dangerous task, and yet an essential one for a poet, for he must put his psychic energies on the line — if not for the future he realistically anticipates, at least for the future he hopes may emerge.

We are told by our social analysts that we are already living in a "post-industrial" society. To some extent that is a "post-scientific" society as well. Not since the Renaissance has there been such widespread popular interest in what has been the dark side of the cultural moon, the products of the neglected and repressed right side of the brain (which governs emotion, intuition, artistic impulse and vision), interest in what Theodore Roszak has called the Old Gnosis, or primitive religious instinct, in such ancient modes of describing reality as astrology, in meditation, in the Tarot and I Ching and Tai Chi, in reawakened sensory experience, and in communal melding of mankind through achievement of higher consciousness. What these interests may mean for the future is, of course, impossible for any poet accurately to assess — but they are equally impossible for him to ignore.

The straight-line projections of the futurists of the sixties described a world much like that of present experience, except magnified, intensified, and accelerated, perhaps beyond human tolerance (the proposition of Alan Toffler in *Future Shock*). No serious questions were being raised about whether technology would continue to advance along the routes marked, the economy continue to expand (to keep pace with the population), and social institutions and services continue to encroach upon and determine more and more areas of human life. In the late sixties there was a reaction to such predictions — first on the political level, as the militants of the earlier years of the decade shifted their goals from those of organizing and seizing power to create a "just society" to those of creating an "alternative society," which would grow first parasitically upon the old system and then independently of it, at last to replace it — what Charles Reich called *The Greening of America*. Unexpected support for this direction of development came from ecologists and economists, a strong minority of whom, by the early seventies, were saying that a high-technological, high-growth solution to world problems was too dangerous, too exhaustive of resources, required an impractical (even if desirable) degree of centralization of authority and enforcement of regulations; they favored a "soft technology" based on low energy, self-sufficiency, community autonomy, and decentralization; the economists talked of "no growth."

We do not yet know which of these two directions the new era will take, but I think we can be confident that the seventies will be looked back upon as a period of mutation, one in which the style of civilization changed radically — as it did when the Enlightenment broke upon the Renaissance, or the Romantic era broke upon the Enlightenment. If you were Collins or Gray or Cowper or Goldsmith, writing at the end of the eighteenth century, how would you feel in your bones the forces which would soon burst forth with a Blake and a Burns, Wordsworth and Keats? How can you prepare yourself today if, tomorrow, the very premises of life and dimensions of human sensibility are largely unrecognizable in today's terms?

I will not take space here to argue that such a radical alteration in our culture is indeed upon us: the magazines are sufficiently full of apocalyptic utterances, and their essential validity is hard to deny. The end of the world we know, which cannot solve its problems of war and pollution and supply, will, if we are lucky, be the beginning of a new era of quite different quality. My concern here is what this means for the poet, particularly the poets emerging in our high schools and colleges at this moment. Some man or woman (I'll bet on woman) will transform poetry, and I would like to speculate on some of the directions change might take.

language

It is the difference in language we notice first when we compare Chaucer with Shakespeare, Donne with Dryden, Pope with Keats — not merely historical change in word forms and meanings, but metaphorical change, the terms poets seek to describe their experience in the world. The popular language today, for example, expresses a strange willingness for people to regard themselves as machines, as abstractions, as processes. "That turns me off," we say, as though we were gadgets. "We need a little feedback." "How do we plug into what they are doing?" The terms are borrowed from electronics, cybernetics, systems analysis. The language prepares us psychologically to surrender our individuality, to lay our names, as we lay our prejudices and our nationalities, on the altar of the planned society. Survival for the world's burgeoning population may depend upon the operation of networks, controls and calculations undreamed of a half-century ago — and emotionally intolerable to those of us conditioned to seek achievement, self-determination and personal significance. It is doubtful that many of the world's population have ever achieved much identity or control of their own lot, but individuality has persisted — at least in the Western World — as cultural ideal. Increasingly we are becoming numbers, cells in the bloodstream of transportation systems, communication systems, supply systems, governmental systems. It is as though we continued to speak the language of the plain, though we live in hives. The new poetry may be in the language of the hive.

If selfhood is eliminated, what tongue can poetry find? "John loves Mary" will not be carved on trees, but "76776XO relates to 982G001" may be programmed on tape. Can one make poetry of such Buck Rogers' stuff? I doubt it, except in satire, and great poets are less likely to be negators than affirmers. In all the years of the scientific revolution we have not found ways to incorporate the language of science comfortably into our verse, and I hesitate to prophecy that tomorrow's Shakespeare will do so. At least I would not expect him to include the technical terminology and quantitative mode of science in poetry. But he might use concepts we now associate with science — c.g., of storage and flow and feedback and circuits. He may think of a person not as a physical entity with a name and a history, but as a set of phenomena, a complex of relationships, connections, deficiencies, potentialities, a nodule in the processes of transmission and reception.

It is hard to imagine his celebrating anonymity and depersonalization, but he might be less troubled by these than we are, saddled with our archaic sensibilities. He might well find new sources of intensity and meaning as he comes to think of people not as individuals but as dividuals — divisible, that is, into their functions and organs and criss-crossing relationships. The image comes to mind of the black and white prisoners handcuffed together in a movie of the sixties, *The Defiant Ones:* they constituted a new individual — with four legs and two brains in orbit around one another as twin stars. They could chop off limbs more easily than they could break the bond between them. Cooperation became as instinctual as the coordination of the muscles of our eyes. I think of a cloud of gnats moving over water like a diffuse organism. I think of transplanted organs. I think of our voices recorded on tapes, our movements recorded on films — the thousand abstractions we make of ourselves, the way we multiply and divide ourselves — and realize that it is absurd to think of ourselves as indivisible units. We have, as Norbert Weiner said, the unity of the flame, not that of the stone. The poet of the future may describe life in terms of its currents, its waves, its pulses, its configurations, rather than in terms of the Tom's, Dick's and Harry's we now see as making up humanity.

Some loss of individuality seems to me inescapable. Whether our culture moves toward a centralized planned society, living in Soleri's hive-like superscrapers or Buckminster Fuller's airy spheres floating above the earth's surface, or toward a decentralized society of relatively autonomous and self-sufficient villages, there is bound to be a melding of small groups, if not all of humankind, into phases of what Teilhard de Chardin called "mass consciousness," the next evolutionary step in which we are more attuned to our involvement in one another. The concept of the individual was very largely a creature of industrial society, in which the fiction of "economic man," the alienated, isolated individual with purely personal drives and motivations, was a convenience of the factory as well as the marketplace. Increasingly we are aware of the vibrations that travel not only between us but between human beings and other living species, the informational network in which the universe sings. The imagery for that reality might be organic and valuative rather than mechanistic and quantitative, but the new romance is likely to be that of persons falling in love with their species and with the life force, with their new awareness of cosmic linkage.

form

The importance of superficial aspects of form can easily be exaggerated. The heroic couplet (rhymed iambic pentameter) served the purposes of Chaucer, Marlowe, Pope and Browning over six centuries of cultural revolution, and there is no reason to believe it would not serve a twenty-first century poet as well. On the other hand, there are enormous differences in how each of those poets used the couplet; it is this sort of difference in form we should concern ourselves with in attempting to predict the future. Will poetry tend toward harmony, order, regularity, closure? Or will it emphasize dissonance, tension, variety, openness? Will it seek elevation, grandeur? Will it be earthy, organic, realistic? Are, indeed, any of these terms relevant to the demands the future will place upon it?

I believe that free verse is already an exhausted tradition. It emphasizes individuality, uniqueness, spontaneity, the moment. We associate it, particularly in America, with our period of expansion and accumulation of world power. One can see it as a kind of implicit protest against the increasing industrialization, mass-production and uniformity of modern urban life (free verse poets are rarely bucolic). One conclusion might be that as life becomes more systematized and controlled, art will splash forth with ever-new forms of wildness and asymmetry. The drug culture might be taken as a similar symptom of the need to liberate ourselves in inner space when choice seems increasingly curtailed outside our minds. But free verse is as self-defeating as drugs in this respect. One only wakes up to constrictions in more and more disillusioning mornings after, and must dive back into the maelstrom to survive.

The life of the future may be exactingly programmed, but also be frighteningly free. Released from the bondage of time and place, perhaps even of mortality, even of identity, we will be, as it were, adrift in a Milky Way of phenomena, and the need of the spirit will be for order and limits. Free verse meant something to us as long as the old forms needed dismantling — from atoms to autocracies. But remember the enlargement in the film *Blow-Up,* which became eventually mere dots and blur. The mission of the new poet will be to reconcile man to existence in a reality blown into its apparently random parts. He will sing his awareness of intricate relationships, sustaining rhythms, patterns laced in patterns like the orbits of particles. The buzz in the hive trembles with modulations and meaning, for all its apparent uniformity. The poet's job will be to discover pattern where none seems to exist, to create the context in which signals may be transmitted. At such times ritual and regularity are more demanded than freedom and expressiveness. Today we associate art with the uniqueness of individual vision, but such egocentricity may disappear or change as selfhood is redefined or disregarded as a concept. Our art may come to resemble that of the mosaic or arabesque, our poetry that of the folk ballad or liturgical chant or epic. I hope it will not be so limited as those models imply, but whether poetry will serve more functions depends upon, in part, the kind of society in which it will occur.

the social context

When today's students finish college there will probably be a decreasing number of jobs for them. Full employment is one of the social goals which will surely be altered radically as the means of production absorb less and less human effort. Much of our life pattern, much of our ethics now depend upon notions of achievement and productivity — and these, too, will have to change. What we now call "leisure" will probably become the serious business of life for most; maintenance will be provided without regard to input into the social system. The means of conditioning, chemical control and surveillance of behavior may be such that freedom, as we now conceive it, will be unknown. I do not "advocate" this future: I simply repeat what the New York *Times* and most other mass media predict about tomorrow — and to advocate or object is as pointless as taking a position regarding an oncoming hurricane.

The new world might well be, as Orwell and Huxley and Burgess and others have warned, a totalitarian nightmare in which human life is meaningless. The challenge to poets (as to others) is to discover and define meaning in the interstices of social control. If the beagle sleeping on my couch were to wake to human consciousness and responsibilities he would no doubt complain that all meaning and freedom had disappeared from a dog's life. If my life has freedom and meaning, these have been created in the gaps left when "natural" life is rather fantastically structured, bounded and controlled. "Gaps" is too negative a word: I associate much of my sense of life's purpose, meaning, and even my freedom of action with the very constrictions I (and society) impose upon it.

The redirection of energy and imagination from economically productive goals will require a major refocusing of our culture — and I would imagine that poets will have a key role. There will, of course, be enormous changes in our patterns of processing, transmitting and storing information; the written word will probably not be used for many of its present informational tasks. One way of looking at the matter is to say there will be no reason to write anything *but* poetry — and I can easily imagine such things as personal letters and notes, diaries, and, of course, all fiction and drama being written — when they are written at all — in poetic form, just as *haiku* were once used by aristocratic Japanese as a means of social intercourse and entertainment. Once poetry was purely oral — and it might become oral again. Instead of thinking of a poem as words on paper, we might come to think of it as a film clip of the poet performing it, perhaps with the written words superimposed on the image. Or it is possible — and I hate to think this — that it might become as perishable as conversation, thought of, like the art of the "happening" as intended for the moment only, its function complete in its conception and first expression, with no need of storing and selecting and repeating.

Regardless of the physical forms of poetry's creation and transmission, the need of the spirit to which poetry speaks will surely be greater than it is in our present world. Tomorrow's Shakespeare will have the job of conceptualizing the terms and conditions of human experience and expressing these in ways that an overcrowded world can be reconciled to its constrictions and find promise in its new forms of freedom. In Huxley's *Brave New World* a savage rediscovered Shakespeare and learned from the old book what the glittering cities around him were lacking. Better we should keep something of the savage's vision, and of Shakespeare's, as we build tomorrow.

the new romanticism

Among poets and others these days there is a renewed interest in nature and natural processes. Perhaps the most chic word in Mad Ave's mod vocabulary is *organic,* used to advertise everything from plastic drink containers to cosmetics. More and more middle-class people, living in cities or suburbs, are buying up parcels of land in the country — to the extent that land-madness is driving up the prices of farmland in areas long since abandoned by family farms and agribusiness. A poet-friend commented that many of his friends seem to be building new exits for themselves, like prairie dogs who make sure they have an alternative tunnel to escape, by building little places in the country.

Why is it happening? I believe there is waning faith in the great liberal ideal of the Great Society, which was to solve all human problems by grand social planning, unlimited material progress, and more and more elaborate, comprehensive and universal institutions. There is waning faith in Western Civilization, in the gleaming beneficence of science, in man's ability (or even his right) to take dominion over the earth. Once we get serious about ecology, we realize that one of the implications is that we ourselves must assume a more modest and reverent relationship to the physical environment and the living things around us. These ideas are not new, of course; but they are getting a new, sometimes almost desperate stress as more and more people find it difficult to imagine, without a major shift in our attitudes, a livable planet or a tolerable future for many decades to come.

One of the prophets of the current trend was William Blake, who, in the early days of the industrial revolution was crying out against the blackening skies and expounding a creed of love and innocence, of intuition and mysticism, which is very harmonious with our contemporary interest in a return to nature and the retrieval of personal freedom from an over-institutionalized, over-regulated, over-rationalized culture.

When we think of romantic poets we are likely to associate

them with beautiful rhapsodies on nature or love. But there are two sides to their vision — not only did they write about what they favored, but what they were opposed to as well. Blake — again in tune with modern thought — was a very sharp and early analyst of the dangerous direction he saw his society going, epitomized by the swelling cities which were drawing more and more people from grinding rural poverty to equally destructive and more degrading urban poverty. When he walked the streets of the city, what did he see and hear?

LONDON

I wander thro' each chartered street,
Near where the chartered Thames does flow,
And mark in every face I meet
Marks of weakness, marks of woe.

In every cry of every Man,
In every Infant's cry of fear,
In every voice, in every ban,
The mind-forged manacles I hear.

How the Chimney-sweeper's cry
Every black'ning Church appalls;
And the hapless Soldier's sigh
Runs in blood down Palace walls.

But most thro' midnight streets I hear
How the youthful Harlot's curse
Blasts the new born Infant's tear,
And blights with plagues the Marriage hearse.

The tapestry is almost surrealistic, blending a range of images of the agonizing city which speak to the subconscious before they do to the rational mind. For example, the word *chartered* in the first stanza does not lend itself to merely logical paraphrase. Someone surely chartered, or authorized, the streets. They appear on charts. And just as surely — he notes with bitter irony — they have planned and determined the flow of the river Thames. But the word stands out from the stanza, almost an image in itself, as a suggestion of authority, reason, presumption, unnaturalness, all combined. Like *chartered, mark* is used rather innocently the first time, but in the fourth line it is repeated, a kind of pun. In our subconscious mind we are likely to picture marked faces, blackened, doomed, as by the sign of Cain, meeting each other on the streets, the poet as marked as the people he sees around him.

The word *ban* in the next stanza is, similarly, a kind of pun. In one sense it means a prohibition: the poet hears in every law, regulation, in every artificial restraint, the jangling of manacles invented by man's mind. In a more ancient sense, *ban* means a curse, a malediction; thus the word simultaneously suggests the confining stricture and the imprecation of those restrained by it. The phrase "mind-forged manacles" is often quoted from Blake, and it summarizes the central theme of the poem: most of the evil he associates with the city arises from reasoning man's tendency to manipulate and control himself and others. Blake's is an anarchistic position. Law itself is bad because it is unnatural and artificial; it results inevitably in human suffering.

Without breaking his sentence, Blake moves on in the third stanza to illustrate. The "mind-forged manacles" are expressed primarily in institutions — and the remainder of the poem attacks several: the Church, government, and the institution of marriage. His method continues to transcend the possibility of logical paraphrase. For example, *appalls* is another pun. In the first place, does the Church appall the cry, or the cry appall the Church? The sentence permits you to read it either way, as both meanings are relevant. *Appall* means to grow pale, to cast a pall over, to overcome with fear or dread. The sweeper sends out his "cry" to get business — or is it a cry of suffering? (Children were used as sweeps because of their small size, enabling them to crawl up through narrow shafts.) *Black'ning* also operates ambiguously: the Church grows black as it stands in the smoky city. But it also blackens the scene — with its bulk, with its repression. There is a subdued contrast between the image of blackness and that of whiteness, the innocence of the pallor, the white dread (of boy for Church or Church for boy). In spite of these ambiguities, the force of the statement is clear. The institution, which embodies the mind-forged manacles, oppresses and is wrought of oppression.

If the soldier is *hapless,* unfortunate, has no luck, we see also in that word that his fate is determined; it is not a matter of chance. To imagine a sigh running in blood down a palace wall requires, again, a surrealistic imagination; it is like a scene of Dali's. The Church and the Palace rule the spiritual and temporal worlds. They symbolize all institutions of the city and society. But Blake's major imprecation is withheld for last.

Blake's sympathy has clearly been with the Man, the Infant, the Chimney-Sweeper, the Soldier. In the next sentence, is it with the Harlot or the Infant blasted by her curse? I believe the answer is that he sympathizes with both, for they are both victims of another institution — marriage. How unnatural for a mother to curse her child. That unnaturalness arises from a most basic artifice: man's effort to regulate and control love and breeding. Instead of a wedding carriage trundling down this macabre street we see a *Marriage hearse*. Instead of a ceremony of life, marriage is a ceremony of burial — presumably burial of instinct, spontaneity, open and unregulated love. Marriage, if we may reason from the poem, creates harlotry, which in turn creates bastards and hatred of mother for the child, and, as well, creates disease. The marriage is itself infected, blighted with plague, from the harlot who would not exist if it were not for marriage.

As in all the social evils depicted in the poem, there is a circular pattern of cause and effect. The man who suffers is the man who forged the manacles. It is not the oppression of one class by another which Blake loathes, but man's oppression of himself through his arrogant efforts to control society by reason and institutions. The weakness and woe Blake finds everywhere in the city are the product of the intelligence man assumes to be his greatest strength.

The poem is almost dirge-like with its heavy syllables, its rhetorical repetitions and parallelisms, its pounding alliteration and heavily accented rhythm. On first reading it seems to be simple, straightforward, and in one sense it is; but closer examination reveals the play of wit, irony, ambiguity, around the thumping, primitive terms.

It is a poem of social protest quite in contrast to those which arise from political movements and class warfare. I believe Blake identified his cause with that of God and nature. It is as though he looked down from on high, then, indeed, walked the streets like God incarnate, to observe the catastrophe man has made of Creation by his efforts to control and improve upon it. That does not make the poem anti-man; for Blake also believed that in each man, no matter how distorted it may be, was a capacity for spiritual understanding, a mystical union with God, an ability to be humble and awed, and ultimately to celebrate the resplendent simplicity of life force as it surges in the world when man does not corrupt it with his mind-forged manacles.

Blake was a kind of prototype of the hippies, with his long

hair and idiosyncratic ways and artistic vision. Some might want to dismiss him (as they dismiss hippies) as anti-intellectual; and in a highly intellectual sense, ironically, he was. But the exercise of intelligence and artistic control and design are as evident in the poem as its message which denounces arrogant mind. I think he would argue that there is nothing wrong with intelligence, not even with that exceedingly narrow band of it called reason, so long as it is used in celebration and enhancement rather than domination of nature.

Such artistry does not always characterize those who object to civilization and its institutions. Much of the poetry of the new romanticism which I have read seems truly and ignominiously primitive in its simplicity and unbuttoned spontaneity. Blake may provide a useful model for poets who share his vision, as he illustrates through his highly crafted, powerful poems, that a reverence for the natural need not mean a disrespect for art.

a new breed of poets

Though you are probably familiar with the poetry of Irma Sikorski and that of Mel Romaine, you may not realize they are woman and husband. Except for this couple and Sylvia Plath and Ted Hughes, I cannot think of any marriages of poets since the Brownings. It is hard enough for poets to be married to anyone, let alone one another, and when I met these two recently I was intrigued at the way they reconciled, and failed to reconcile, their individuality with the demands of married life. Their discussion highlights some of the issues poets face in the new era.

Like Sylvia Plath, Irma retained her maiden name. She is strong on women's liberation and regards the acceptance by a wife of her husband's name as equivalent to becoming his chattel. She would be willing to adopt a tribal name, however. She and Mel are considering joining an agricultural commune dedicated to the worship of Kama, in which case they, like all other members of the tribe, would adopt the name of the god: Irma Kama, Mel Kama. I speculated that joining a commune might be even more threatening to self-ownership than marriage, but my language set Irma off on a tirade.

"The name thing is a big part of our problem in this society.

Like it's a bourgeois Western hang-up, attaching so much importance to your personal identity. You begin in the human family, in harmony. Individualism is discord. It means falling away from the state of union. I mean, you put too much emphasis upon personal survival."

"*I* do?" I asked.

"We all do. We think we can defeat death if our names continue. It makes us lean too heavily on our children — which is no good for them, growing up encumbered with our expectations and our need of surviving through them. Similarly, it distorts our art. Art becomes an ego-trip. We use it to become *known,* personally. We want to survive on the bookshelves after our bodies are gone. That's why in our society it is suicide for a woman to accept her husband's name. Symbolically she dies; her children do not bear her name; they are his. She is wiped out for posterity. This is, of course, madness: it would be much healthier if we would all surrender our names, become as anonymous as the animals, to free ourselves of these erroneous values."

"But you certainly sign your name to your books and poems, Irma," I said. "I don't think poets would write if they knew that publication would be anonymous. So we want to survive. That motive may seem selfish and ignoble, but it has produced our literature. If we weren't struggling to overcome death, would we produce any art at all?"

"Spoken like a capitalist!" Irma said. "My father always claimed people wouldn't work if they couldn't acquire private property. I believe just the opposite. Work is natural to man, especially artistic work, which is its own reward and becomes corrupt if done for any extrinsic reward. Private property makes men lazy because it conditions them to think only in terms of themselves. They won't work in a capitalist system unless it is for pay. Work and play become a dichotomy — and they might well be synonymous. Capitalists worry about leisure, vacation, retirement, about laying down their burdens and relaxing. They enslave others to do their work for them and deny themselves the satisfaction of an integrated life in which productive work is as necessary and pleasurable as eating. We are instinctually gregarious; we derive satisfaction from cooperation, from surrendering our personal interest to that of the herd. Capitalism perverts all that, alienating us from our brothers and training us to succeed personally at their expense."

"There has never been much worthwhile Communist art," I objected.

"Wait! I'm not talking about Communism. That is a very young political idea which may not have had an adequate chance yet — and may not be the answer to man's needs. But *most* of the world's art is anonymous. African art, Oriental art, folk art of all civilizations. It all comes from a natural, cooperative, creative drive. The artist works for the community — or to worship his tribal gods. It has nothing to do with the survival of his private self, his name, except insofar as his survival is linked to that of the tribe or the race. It is a celebration of life, not a struggle against death."

"I think you romanticize folk art, Irma," I said. "Sure, primitive carvings and medieval ballads are pleasant artifacts. But great art — that of Shakespeare or Beethoven or Rembrandt — comes from individuals. It expresses personal vision. It is eccentric, private, deeply linked to the artist's identity. You don't get *The Wasteland* written by a committee."

She laughed. "You picked a particularly bad example. *The Wasteland* was written by a committee of Pound and Eliot at the very least, but including Shakespeare and Goldsmith and Dante and Jessie Weston and dozens of other collaborators in its larger membership. Eliot was too good a Catholic to claim much for individual talent; the individual's contribution is a slight modification of the tradition in which he works. I don't think Shakespeare thought much about expressing *himself;* his job was to provide scripts for the company to work on together. The same goes for Mozart, El Greco — for most of the great artists before the twentieth century. Homer may have been a committee. Who designed Chartres? Art has always been dedicated to the community, to society, to God. But we are products of a privatistic, bourgeois, alienated, competitive disease of mind. *We* talk about the great significance of individual artists because we're conditioned to see the world as made up of individual achievements. We come out of Wall Street and project upon history this model that everyone is competing with everyone; only a few make it; most fail; all are perpetually anxious about success or failure. It is Hobbes' view of the State of Nature in which the life of man is solitary, poor, nasty, brutish and short. What a desperate world we have invented for ourselves!"

"Maybe we have discovered that it exists — that survival is basically a matter of competition . . . ."

"Equine offal! Survival of the fittest is a product of the mental illness of industrial England. At least equally important in survival is natural collaboration, harmony, ecological balance, symbiosis and all that. Sure, there is *some* individuality in nature and in art, but it is at least equally important that art be communal, a means of binding people together, of seeking coalescence of vision, of ritual, celebration, cooperation . . . ."

"You can't deny that there are some outstanding geniuses," I protested.

"Who needs to deny it?" she said. "It is an accident. Take science for a moment: the human rate of discovery is fairly predictable, and it is only incidental that we can look back and associate particular discoveries with particular names. Science is basically a cooperative enterprise, though it happens that specific breakthroughs occur in specific laboratories. Always someone is furthest north and somebody heaviest and somebody has the blondest hair. Somebody is secretary. Somebody sees something happen. I see you have a tape recorder running, but I'm doing the talking. If you write this up, which of us is the creative genius?"

"I'll give you credit . . . ."

"Who *cares?* If I sing soprano and you sing tenor, we can make music together. The point is the music, not the personal distinction. The point is truth, not the discoverer or spokesman of truth. Anonymity is an artist's greatest achievement. Listen, I saw it in one of *your* books, Jud — about how Tagore heard a peasant driving a cart, singing one of his songs, and how he felt it was the greatest possible reward to achieve anonymity in his own life time, to have his work accepted, absorbed into his nation's culture, without any deference to or memory of its creator. Suppose you had written the Lord's Prayer. Would you want your name printed at the bottom? Would you interrupt people praying to say, 'I wrote that!' Isn't it more satisfying to think what significance your words have in people's lives? Not even *your* words: the words you put together."

Mel had been listening to all this with some symptoms of restlessness. "I wish you wouldn't use religious examples so often, Irma," he finally said.

"I really don't see anything wrong with religion, Mel," she answered. "I mean, I think reason is another capitalistic invention: it divides, separates, undermines. Faith pulls people together . . . ."

"Sure! Often into madness!" Mel said.

"But our conflicts are of faith contending with faith, though many of us call their *own* faith reason. I'm getting over that. My faith is in the world revolution. I believe in overthrowing man's oppressive institutions, liberating him, restoring him to natural harmony with his fellow man and his environment. If that is religion, so be it. Christianity is evil and divisive, guilt-inducing, privatistic. But the counter-force must be another religion — which I call world revolution."

Mel spoke past Irma to me. "Irma was raised as an Orthodox Jew," he explained — in what even I took to be a condescending tone. "Her whole intellectual life is an attempt to regain the security of her lost faith, and to revenge her people for the injustices they have suffered in the Graeco-Latino-Christiano-Americano-Culture."

"How absolutely *male* of you!" she screamed. "You men talk together as though I were a prize specimen in a dog-show. You think you can explain me by discussing my pedigree!"

"Do you want us to acknowledge you as a personal, private *self?*" I asked.

"No! I don't want you to escape the revolution by cutting me down and using my carcass to feed your own egos."

"I think there is much in what Irma says," Mel went on, unruffled, "but her sense of mission, of the cause, contradicts much that she says about the communal nature of art. What she writes — and wants us all to write — is not poetry, but propaganda. She is so intent on what she calls the revolution that she utterly neglects art."

"By 'art' he means decadent, useless, egoistic . . . ."

"I agree with Irma that great art is anonymous. My ideal is the Grecian urn — the classical product, timeless, beyond personality, exquisite in artistry, symmetry, harmony — an imitation of the ideal. What has the Grecian urn to do with the world revolution? Political purpose is only an aggrandized form of individualism. What she calls faith I call partiality. Great art is a contemplation of Om. It transcends sectarianism, temporality, divisiveness, faction. The work of art is complete in itself, answerable only to itself, timeless as birdsong, urgent and endless as the surf, shaped as the stone by the sea. Alas that poetry must be written language — which is necessarily of a time and place of a people. I seek a language which approaches pure symbol, a poem which is pure design . . . ."

"Mel, you're making a fool of yourself," Irma warned, compassionately. She turned to me. "He's really not like that. I mean, he goes to demonstrations. We were in jail together in the South. We're into this commune thing — and it has a very activist edge. I mean, Mel," she pleaded, "you don't really mean to come on like Swinburne or someone. Not today. Refinement is obscene in our times."

"Wow!" he said with frightening glee. "Newspeak! Orwell really nailed it, didn't he? I mean, you can't conduct that revolution of yours without mind-washing. You are so desperate to have a family, a group, a club of members, a party, you can't *stand* divergence. There must be party discipline! There must be political unanimity. Individuality is a threat to you. You cannot tolerate the independent, critical mind . . . ."

"Don't you see, Mel," she said — almost in tears, "it is a threat to you, too. That's what they want — to separate you from the group, to encourage separateness, pride, ego. All those things that feel like strength to you are really weakness, for they take you out of the tribe and leave you subject to control by the System . . . ."

At that point I heard the *whisp, whisp, whisp* of the tape end whipping around the reel. The conversation went on another half-hour or so, ending not in resolution but tension and surface affection. "We are correctives to one another, like Yin and Yang," Mel said. "Truth is perfect stasis, containing all opposites, balancing all forces . . . ."

"Nonsense!" Irma said, pulling him out the door. "Life is emerging, becoming, actualizing. There must be progress, must be flow . . . ."

Alas, I must confess that Irma and Mel are fictitious. Their conversation is drawn from many I have had in the past few years with new professionals, young people in their twenties and early thirties whose graduate careers have been bounded by the Free Speech Movement and SDS and SNCC, by Viet Nam and radical and campus revolution. They assume of themselves and one another participation in the Movement just as naturally as we older academicians assumed membership in the American Association of University Professors. They are quite naturally, and with enormous dedication, preparing themselves for a new world. The new culture is not an exotic option for them: it is the fabric of their lives.

I should explain what I mean by the new culture. It has a political aspect of course, and the question of when and where violence is necessary as a tactic is a frequent topic of discussion. But behind the cutting edge is a whole hatchet head of ethics and metaphysics and life style. A good, brief summary is provided by Philip E. Slater in *The Pursuit of Loneliness — American Culture at the Breaking Point:*

> The old culture, when forced to choose, tends to give preference to property rights over personal rights, technological requirements over human needs, competition over cooperation, violence over sexuality, concentration over distribution, the producer over the consumer, means over ends, secrecy over openness, social reforms over personal expression, striving over gratification, Oedipal love over communal love, and so on. The new counterculture tends to reverse all these priorities.

Within the new culture there is an activist-hippie split (the Republican and Democratic parties of the future?) in which the task-oriented activists tend to take on the coloration of the old culture in order to achieve their goals (i.e., aggression, competitiveness, secrecy, etc.) and the hippies tend to be defeated by ineffectuality as they passionately hope that love will be catching (and get busted when it is not). There are, as Irma and Mel illustrate, many cross-currents and variations, but these terms are useful in understanding the new cultural context.

Many of the new professionals are quite accomplished poets. For example, I met a young man at a conference who was carrying his book-length collection of poetry, and it was, in my judgment, easily publishable — as good as any recent book I have seen. But he had not bothered even to submit many of the individual poems for publication, let alone send out his book. He was too busy. He was finishing another book on the history of the Students for a Democratic Society (of which he has been a member since its early days). His life is largely bound up with political action, but poetry is a necessity in his life: he writes for himself, for those he loves, and — eventually — for publication. He was carrying with him new books by William Meredith and Galway Kinnell. He "keeps up" with poetry as one might keep up with sports events or a hobby. But at this time in his life, poetry cannot be the central focus for his time and energy, and he is indifferent to the politics and back-scratching and scramble for positions, prizes and publication which characterize the world of those who are intent on making reputations as poets.

That, as they say, is where it's at. Those to whom we look for the next generation of significant poets are almost universally involved in political action and the emerging new culture. Women's Liberation is an important force, and I read much new work in a strikingly powerful genre of women's poetry, infused with a new consciousness of women's oppression, of changing women's roles, of the need for new, more intimate, more honest and more fulfilling personal relationships. Like the surge of poetry of black consciousness we have experienced, there is a new wave of poetry from women as they discover their own needs and potentialities and the possibility of organizing and acting to change society in order to permit greater fulfillment.

natural highs

The mind-expanding drugs are having a highly significant bearing on the emerging new consciousness. Young intellectuals casually share a pot culture and are familiar with (whether or not they experiment) a world in which acid and mescaline are an accepted and normal part of life. Those of us who have reputations as poets or teachers of poetry are, of course, aware of this culture, but we have not grown up with it as an accepted part of life. I have yet to see any poetry written about drug experiences (or, especially, written under the influence of drugs) which struck me as worthwhile, but that may be because I am simply out of it — that the good poetry has not reached my attention or that, if it did, I would not recognize its value. But whether or not people write about or with the use of drugs, mind-expansion is a phenomenon deeply affecting the artistic context in which emerging poets will work.

I wonder whether there is something innate in man which alternatively finds expression in his turning to drugs, his writing of poetry, and perhaps other activities (war? religion?) as well. We have heard a good deal about drug dependency, the use of drugs to escape, the self-perpetuating psychic and physical processes of addiction. I wonder what are the positive impulses which lead men to drugs — their sense of excitement, of exploration, of search for new awareness, their deep need of being off-balance, their dissatisfaction with states of adjustment and stasis, their predeliction for instability. Some talk of drug experiences as bringing inner peace and serenity and sublime passivity. That seems to me quite opposed to the search for a kick or a high. I once heard Allen Ginsberg say, after rhapsodizing on metrics, "Who knows? Maybe one day poetry will replace LSD!" Since drugs have some disadvantages — such as being dangerous, illegal and addictive — I wonder whether reading and writing poetry might not be a real source of alternative highs.

As I settle at my typewriter I check on the availability at arm's length of drugs — coffee and cigarettes — then turn my mind to the task. Pause. Sip a stimulant. Write another sentence. It is deeply imbedded in my pattern of life (as it is in that of most of us) habitually to ingest non-nutritive substances which alter mind and body, moods, feelings, kinds and intensities of awareness. The artificial substances or influences (for some music is a narcotic, or TV, or even the daily newspapers) have both good and bad effects, and sometimes both simultaneously. They may support and release human potential, improving on nature in what might be assumed to be nature's ends: health, energy, consciousness, happiness. On the other hand they may limit and destroy human potential, wasting and injuring the physical being, benumbing the mind or inducing states of madness. I would say that even when people take drugs which poison them they are motivated by authentic needs. Dysfunctioning of nature itself, of the social environment, of the personal psyche or organic being, may create dependency upon chemical or other support or means of relief. And that is merely the negative side: people seem to seek (and, indeed, to find) access to some kinds of self-fulfillment through adulteration of themselves which they cannot, or think they cannot, find otherwise. Today there are thousands of people around the country, many in their mid-twenties, who have been the drug route and are tired or afraid of it, who are actively seeking substitutes in religious meditation, yoga, exotic diets, more intense and more honest human relations, and in the arts. They are looking for what they call "natural highs" though some of the means they use are hardly more natural than drugs themselves. Poetry is no more artificial than some other devices — and it has the advantage of spreading the high from the poet to his readers.

I once read of a religious group in Tibet living around a mountain, with the head Lama in sanctuary on the very peak. According to this account, which is purported to be true, the Lama once a year, in a religious ceremony, ate a mushroom which turned him on. He then urinated into a bottle, which was passed down the mountain to the lesser monks, who drank the urine and, due to the peculiar chemical process induced by this particular drug, got an even greater high than the head Lama. They in turn passed down their urine, and imbibers at each level of descent were more numerous, had more liquid to share, and got increasingly wilder trips out of the experience, until, at the base of the mountain, the common people had the greatest abundance and greatest ecstasy of all. I would like to suggest that as an image for the influence of poetry. What could Shakespeare have read one half so precious as the stuff he wrote? The vintage seems to improve with age and use and traffic through other sensibilities. It is not only creative in itself, but the source of creativity in others (as the thousands of theatrical productions, books, essays, critical and scholarly articles and imitations exemplify). Shakespeare's own delirium must have been mild compared to that of a million school teachers at the base of the mountain quaffing the thousand fold distilled and re-distilled essence of the bard's effluence.

Lest the point be lost in levity, I would say that both drugs and poetry feed our need of transcendence. In a prose passage of *Hamlet* Shakespeare captured the syndrome:

> I have of late — but wherefore I know not — lost all my mirth, forgone all customs of exercises, and indeed it goes so heavily with my disposition that this goodly frame the earth seems to me a sterile promontory. This most excellent canopy, the air, look you, this brave o'erhanging firmament, this majestical roof fretted with golden fire — why, it appears no other thing to me than a foul and pestilent congregation of vapors. What a piece of work is a man! How noble in reason! How infinite in faculty! In form and moving how express and admirable! In action how like an angel! In apprehension how like a god! The beauty of the world! The paragon of animals! And yet, to me, what is this quintessence of dust? Man delights not me — no, nor woman neither, though by your smiling you seem to say so.

Wasted on the straight minds of Rosencrantz and Guildenstern, that paean to the potentiality of earth and of man mingled with existential despair is a futile attempt to lay out plainly what rational detectives can not see under their noses. Why, the detectives are sent to inquire, is Hamlet morose? He might give any number of reasons they could understand: his throne has been usurped, his mother whored, his father murdered. But deeper than any of these motivations is an inexplicable restlessness and dissatisfaction, an inborn heartache beyond the reach of objective inquiry.

I am writing on a perfect day of early summer, a light breeze swaying the leafy branches, singing insects and birds, buttery sun on the lawn and a rich blue overhead, girls sauntering by in bathing suits and beach towels as cool air teases my bare feet and legs, and I am overwhelmed, as often when hearing a tense, splendid passage of a string quartet, not with delight but an almost intolerable sense of melancholy, as though, in Keats' words, a "strenuous tongue" had "burst Joy's grape against my palate fine." Paradoxically, we languish in sensual opulence, the very intensity of satisfaction driving us to a heady poignancy — "but wherefore I know not."

We can see rationally that some human environments increase human need of drugs — from ant-hill ghettoes to garishly sensual and profligate metropolitan centers to empty-minded acres of prairie dog suburbs. Drug dependency is exacerbated by social conditions which can be changed — the punishing life of poverty, the vapid life of prosperity, the hectic, directionless, manic changes of a hopped-up civilization. We can ascribe to social and political conditions, to institutional and family patterns, the factors which undermine ego strength and make independence and self-actualization difficult. Studies of drug-users indicate a very low belief in the individual's power to control his own destiny. The worst pushers in a drug society are the advertisers of legitimate drugs from cigarettes to sleeping pills who pound into our consciousness that we can cope with our tensions and anxieties and discomforts simply by popping pills with speedy reactions in the blood stream. The Black Panthers (along with the anti-Communist Christians) are among the most aggressive enemies of drug use, for the Panthers suspect collaboration of the Mafia and the police to exploit the poor and keep them tractably doped.

But even if we could eliminate all the social problems which foster and grow out of drug dependency, I believe something would remain, rooted in the condition of being human, which leads men to toy with their minds, altering consciousness and sometimes escaping it. So far as I know, no culture has ever existed in which some kind of drug, be it alcohol or cannabis or some other, was not an accepted part of life, often sanctified (as in Christian Communion) by religious use.

Of course, I also know of no society which has been without religion and poetry. Drugs themselves are a side issue: I know of no *a priori* reason why any drug cannot be used for human benefit or that any cannot cause human harm. I assume that health, awareness, felicity, sensual and mental pleasure, religious illumination and ecstasy are good things, and the human search for these is to be respected and valued. I assume that the needs some people have for stimulation or depression, for relief from pain and boredom and social oppression are sometimes uncontrollable. I assume that physical deterioration, extended torpor, manic states, loss of coordination and self-control, irrationality and incoherence are, generally, bad. And I assume that drugs from cokes to cocaine serve variously in the achievement of those goods and extensions of those evils. Similarly, I assume that religion and poetry at times foster love, brotherhood, understanding, reverence for creation and insight into man's place in the universe — and that they at times foster delusion, intolerance, morbid escapism, passivity and other undesirable states of mind. They are not good nor bad in themselves. It is important that the motives people bring to them be understood and dealt with, that the protean human spirit, with its needs unfathomable to reason, be respected. In the process we should recognize that what speaks to our condition is often strange, unsettling, and even, at times, perverse.

Great tragedy, for example, is not a bummer, but a high. When we think of highs in poetry our imagination must go to celebrations of natural beauty of the earth, to human love, to the excitement when skis whisper through winter woods, to clanging adventure or uncanny encounters with the void. But we also have needs, which poetry can speak to, of dread and horror and revulsion, of despair, anxiety and sadness. Poetry which provides such highs will not comfort us when we have such emotions, but, indeed, will stimulate and evoke them. Such poetry will not explain our moods away: just as Hamlet recognizes that he does not truly understand the roots of his depression, so poetry must be honest enough to admit when it is uneasily in the presence of the unknown.

If poetry is to replace LSD (and I think this would be good), it will have to provide some of the highs that LSD is said to provide. I don't mean, like some pop lyrics and acid rock, it should imitate the weird hallucinations, dislocations, disproportions and jarring juxtapositions popularly associated with tripping. Such devices serve to remind drug users of what their trips were like, and probably drive them back to acid to experience the real thing. At best words are a pallid substitute for the vivid illusions of the drug experience. But, remaining true to its own strengths and characteristics, poetry might be able to satisfy more profoundly and lastingly the yearning for stimulation, revelation and liberation which chemical substitutes for good art can only fleetingly and dangerously supply.

toward a new poetry

A physicist in conversation with some humanists, including me, once expressed irritation over our tireless badgering of scientists for having contributed to the world's ills by producing the bomb. "The scientists did their job exactly right in producing it," he said. "Why have *you* not made it unnecessary?"

He was right. Humanists, particularly artists, have fallen down on their job in the twentieth century. We have fallen into a habit of auto-satisfaction (to disguise as politely as I can what I mean). By and large our aesthetics is one of solipsism. We have failed in our mission of humanizing the world. We have not taken that mission seriously — and the world has, with accurate intuition, not taken us seriously. We taught our audience not to read poetry for what it says but for the way it says it. And it should not be surprising if the world has developed a body, like that of the dinosaur, with frightening capacity — and with as little mind or conscience as those of the dinosaur. It is a world heading rapidly for the dinosaur's fate. A psychiatrist (Dr. Benson Snyder of M.I.T.) put it this way:

> . . . if you're talking about being strong enough to deal with your environment, and you're a dinosaur and you don't realize that the plains are turning to mud, and you keep getting stronger and stronger and that puts more and more weight on you, pretty soon you're up to your neck immobilized in mud.

In regard to poetry (and, more generally, to art) strength has disastrously been associated with freedom. In the face of any failure poets have tended to demand for themselves more and more freedom, for it is true that release from restraint gives a temporary feeling of success. But it is likely to take one further and further from poetry's serious goal — which the physicist symbolized succinctly as making the bomb unnecessary.

The cry of youth is always for liberty, and the answer of age is discipline. Too much emphasis upon either is, of course, destructive. What we need is a gut-level understanding of the relationship between the terms: a knowledge that lasting liberty is achieved only through discipline. Dante put it in religious terms: in God's will is our peace. Frost put it in an agricultural image: "moving easy in harness." Each of us must discover the way this principle makes sense to our private selves. I say, find the contract you will not violate. Find something you are willing to die for. Paradoxically that gives you something to live for, some reason why your death, when it occurs, will matter.

The poet Lew Turco pointed out to me that every great poet found his form early and stuck by it. Cummings' whole bag of tricks was in his first book, including his important themes. Whitman, who had long been foundering in conventional forms, suddenly in mid-life found his stride, changed his name from Walter to Walt, adopted his mode and swung out irrepressibly into literature. But the same is true of Shakespeare or Donne or Milton or Pope or Hopkins or Frost: they settled the question of form for themselves and more-or-less stuck by a limited set of containing principles. Of course they varied and experimented within the parameters they defined, and, of course, they sometimes broke through the parameters. At times poets such as Yeats and Eliot found, mature in their careers, new contracts. But the great ones have tended to find some manner which permitted them to put the question of form into the back of their minds so that they could give most of their attention to content. It is what poems have to say that matters.

That does not mean form is unimportant: without a container the content disperses like water into the soil. Respect for, acceptance of container walls is a measure of the poet's seriousness. Suppose, for example, that while writing "Song of Myself" Whitman had thought of an excellent iambic pentameter rhymed couplet which made his point beautifully — and, believing in the freedom of the artist, had put it into the poem. We would be likely to feel that a man who would do that would do anything, to lose all respect for his integrity. We would stop believing that he meant what he said.

A poem's form tells us what is and is not possible within it. It creates a context which limits, defines and shapes our expectations. Within the walls he builds, the poet, of course, surprises us, teases us, frustrates us and satisfies us by turns, but he never (if he is good) transgresses those invisible walls. He does not, for instance, stop his poem and include a photograph because that is the only way he can express what he means. We must sense that he accepts some self-evident harness, or we disregard him as trivial.

Let's call that *the principle of contract.* Combine it now with what I would like to call *the Ancient Mariner principle.* In some way the poem must seize the reader's elbow with skinny hand and demand to be heard. Pick up a magazine or book of poetry and ask yourself whether the poetry published there seizes you in that way. Much that is published (as well as most of that floating around in manuscript) seems not to give a damn whether anybody is listening. There is no air of necessity or urgency about it. Immortal poetry is at least as immediate as the news. If you don't feel that about what you write, if you don't feel that it is terribly important that many people read this, now, if you haven't gotten that need woven into the poem's fabric, I wish you would not clutter the mail. Our civilization has very little time, and it is important that we weed out our messages and state the essential ones carefully. I await the poem across the transom which says implicitly "I only have escaped alone to tell thee . . . ."

Contract. Ancient Mariner. Next, *the principle of the real rose.* I have heard that, before Franco, there was an annual Catalan poetry contest, the prizes for which were awarded on the steps of the cathedral in Barcelona. The third prize was a silver rose. The second prize was a golden rose. The first prize was, of course, a real rose. The poet's most difficult wrestling with his soul is learning never to be envious of the golden rose. The moment you concern yourself with fame and money rather than with writing the best poetry you know how to write you are being seduced by the golden rose. I realize it sounds distressingly moralistic and naive for me to say this, but I have been seduced and used too often, till my tender parts are leathery, and wish I could regain the innocence to rest firmly in the truth I have known all along: metallic roses are not worth the sacrifices they demand. What the great poet seeks is a kind of anonymity: that his work be incorporated in the literature and the language, though his name be "writ in water." When I find my guts in turmoil

> Wishing me like to one more rich in hope,
> Featur'd like him, like him with friends possest,
> Desiring this mans art, and that mans skope,
> With what I most injoy contented least,

I know I am once more in pursuit of the golden rose — and wish

I knew the words to warn others from that route. One of my poems says that the real rose "dies/ and recurs, recurs/ even in the kingdom of Midas." The only poetry which truly endures is that containing the principle of life, self-perpetuation. Everything our America touches turns to gold (or, rather, plastic) and the people starve in body and spirit. The poet's mission is to restore the real.

The principle of sailing: art achieves nothing except by indirection. You cannot sail directly into the wind: there is a ninety degree arc you must avoid, or your sails luff, the rigging slaps loose; you are in irons; you drift backwards. This prose is motoring into the wind: I am saying pretty nearly what I mean — but there is an annoying fume and noise of engine, and my supply of gas is limited. To proceed to art I would have to fall off till my sails filled, cut off the artificial power, and ride the edge of the wind's force. Most factors then — the wind, the currents, the onrush of time, the swell of sea, shape of hull and spread of canvas — are beyond my control, but a little intelligence at the tiller, a delicate setting of the sheets — these keep the great boat driving on this tack, then that, getting there, but never directly, too serious in intent to make the mistake of heading up too far so that the sails flap and the tiller goes dead in my hand. To sail well is to take full and sensitive account of the forces playing around you, to use them to their fullest by never mistaking the necessities they impose. In art that means tacking, boiling along full force about 45 degrees off-center from where you actually intend to go.

The principle of the game. Poetry is most serious when most a game. It creates artificial demands which draw out of the poet (and reader) feats he would never be capable of without the game's incitement, just as a tennis player could not, say, in his living room, make the leaps and twists and agile sweeps, recovering balance and darting to new positions, which are evoked by the demands of the court. In struggling to complete a line in some fixed measure, to find a rhyme, to produce one image which answers another, the poet often drags out of his depths things he never knew he knew or might not have the courage to say. Often the most powerful content of poetry is that most deeply buried, and we need the game, the contract of artificial demands, to free our best ideas from ourselves.

Finally, *the principle of driving.* In driving a car you do not think your way through the gears, are unaware of your delicate handling of the clutch and the accelerator and the wheel. Poetry requires the intelligent use of habit. Learning to drive you were conscious of each of these movements, but on a trip the burning point of your attention is on the road ahead, and your repertory of skills, relegated to habit, supplies you inexhaustibly with the fine movements and responses needed to keep the car safely progressing. A poet should read so much and write so much that he develops skills as unconscious habits; then, writing, he can keep his mind on where he is going, on remaining intact until he arrives. As you drive you don't think that now is time for third gear, now time to ease the clutch. That is not to say that the techniques are not present and rational; they don't come welling out of inspiration, but are learned, and then necessarily incorporated into a body of what seem intuitive responses.

Much of our current poetry is not true to these principles: *the contract* — an inviolable commitment to form; *the Ancient Mariner* — a clear thrust of intent and necessity; *of sailing* — an understanding of carefully directed indirection; *of the game* — the use of artifice to draw out strength; *of driving* — the conscious acquisition of skills which can be relegated to unconscious habit. But the crisis of our civilization may evoke a new poetry of rigor, commitment and dedication to the formation and transmission of humane values, just as the crisis is evoking discipline and commitment from those who are oppressed and outraged at the malfunctioning of the system.

The new poetry will be of social awareness, but not of propaganda, for that is sailing into the wind, speaking to those who need no persuasion and offending those who do not know the way. By "social awareness" I mean an implicit acceptance of poetry's social function, a recognition of its responsibility in the struggle for human survival. It will incorporate humane values in such a way that ordinary readers, not *literati,* will be engaged, will lock benevolent attitudes and sensitive language into their patterns of response and carry them into the arenas of discussion and the voting booths.

The turmoil of the breaking wave should not blind us to its surge of creative potential. At such a point in history it is urgent that we find the means of control, the way of staying steady and upright, riding the gathering strength.

CHAPTER TWENTY-TWO

Yin and Yang

sex and soul

According to Sigmund Freud, poetry (like all artistic expression) is a sublimation of sexual energy, the transmutation of a primitive drive into a more socially and ethically acceptable form. This insight was shocking in the nineteenth century, and still today some poets resist the implication that inspiration which seems to come from outer space in fact arises from a very inner, indeed glandular, source. We resist the idea because it seems reductive. Crudely put, it seems to say that art is "nothing but" sex. We have been conditioned to think of human functions in a hierarchical way, those associated with the heart, or, especially, the head, being "higher" and those associated with the rest of the body being "lower." But if we set aside moralistic prejudices, I think we can learn a great deal about what we do as poets by defining our task as the reconciliation of apparent opposites, of discovering the relationships and dependencies of head and heart, of psyche and flesh.

The "nothing but" frame-of-mind undermines poetic capacity. Do we think of the gentle light of the lamp as "nothing but" raw electricity generated at a noisy, distant plant? Whatever the energy source, we can be grateful for it, and can work effectively (and safely) with it only if we understand it in a neutral, non-judgmental way. We are equally seriously hampered as poets if we succumb to the opposite preference — for the "real" as opposed to the artificial. The prejudice inclines some to believe that since poetry is "really" sexual expression, it should come out in as frank and primitive a form as words can make it. This is a little like trying to light a home with the raw juice from the dynamo. Unsublimated sexuality can be a savage, violent force, destroying its object like a panther killing its dinner. Good poetry accepts and reconciles lust and tenderness, seeing that one is not more "real" than the other, and that the phenomenon of love encompasses both.

D. H. Lawrence captures the paradox in "The Elephant Is Slow To Mate":

> The elephant, the huge old beast,
>   is slow to mate;
> he finds a female, they show no haste
>   they wait
>
> for the sympathy in their vast shy hearts
>   slowly, slowly to rouse
> as they loiter along the river-beds
>   and drink and browse
>
> and dash in panic through the brake
>   of forest with the herd,
> and sleep in massive silence, and wake
>   together, without a word.

When they come together "in secret at last," these oldest and wisest of beasts demonstrate that they know:

> how to wait for the loneliest of feasts
>   for the full repast.
>
> They do not snatch, they do not tear;
>   their massive blood
> moves as the moon-tides, near, more near,
>   till they touch in flood.

Human beings, even with their power of sublimation, are often more "bestial" than such beasts. Western Civilization depends to a large extent upon the bottling up and channeling and selective explosion of sexual energy. Like the fossil fuels pressed and stored under the mantle of earth, the erotic drive is buried under strata of custom and contempt and (ironically) idealization. It is dark, subterranean, rather smelly and immensely volatile. It is capable of miracles. It generates cathedrals like petrified fountains; it tunnels under cities, propels the engines of commerce, and crochets the intricate lace of computation and calculation and rhetorical justification. It urges the artist's patient, silent brush. It organizes inert air into resonant symphonies. A great metropolis is a throbbing, erect concentration of diverted, sublimated, refined, pressurized libido, towering potential draining in glandular dusk the energies of the region to maintain a quivering salute to a Heaven of transcendental Yang.

Yang is the male principle in ancient Chinese thought, and (as the women seeking liberation have pointed out) our civilization is built upon exploitation of the Yin, or female principle, for the aggrandizement of the Yang. One of the functions of poetry may be to restore the balance, to bring about a great wilting, as of the Empire State Building, not as an aftermath of the ferocious discharge of war, but yet in orgasmic melding, a flowing of one into another, in which the urban Yang is relieved of its intolerable tension and the fallow Yin of the countryside is charged and renewed. The greatest contribution of poetry to civilization is its power of gentling brute force, of converting the armored might of the warrior into the palace politeness of chivalry; of responding to the "dark satanic mills" of industrialism with a reawakening of romantic vision. While England conquered the Spanish Armada on the seas, Shakespeare evoked the tragic terror of passion and vain power and the tender promise of young love in *Romeo and Juliet*.

But if the Yang dominance in our culture has caused a counterbalancing Yin force in our poetry, the ideal is nonetheless an integration of the two. Robert Frost's "To Earthward" compares the sensuality of youth to that of maturity. As a young man, Frost said, "Love at the lips was touch/ As sweet as I could bear; . . ."

> I craved strong sweets, but those
> Seemed strong when I was young;
> The petal of the rose
> It was that stung.
>
> Now no joy but lacks salt
> That is not dashed with pain
> And weariness and fault;
> I crave the stain
>
> Of tears, the aftermark
> Of almost too much love,

and he wished he had the weight and strength to press his whole length of body against the earth with the force he could exert leaning on a single palm.

That definition of pleasure combines pain and joy, and is nearer the mark as a guide to the kind of interaction of experience poetry embodies than a simple contrast of battlefield and bedroom, of urban and rural life. If we have overemphasized domination, rationality, individuality and order in our civilization, the correction is not overemphasis on submission, emotion, collectivism and spontaneity. It is not conflict of polarities, but a search for complementarity, as symbolized by the ancient Yin-Yang medallion. Discussing "complement dualism" in *The Faith of Other Men,* Wilfred Cantwell Smith says:

> We in the West are familiar with another type of dualism, which we may call conflict dualism. In this, two basic forces are in collision, as opposites that struggle and clash: good and evil, right and wrong, black and white, true and false. This type of dualism seems to have its origin about the middle of the first millenium B.C. in the Tigris-Euphrates valley or in Iran . . . . It found its way into the Jewish, Christian, and the Islamic traditions, and has been vigorously resuscitated in recent times on a world scale by Marxism.

The conflict model of dualism may be associated with original sin in the Edenic myth; "knowledge" or discrimination of Good and Evil is specifically that which separates humanity from the integrated life. A view of life in which opposites (man-woman, heaven-earth, hot-cold, dry-moist, active-passive) are seen as harmonious and necessary complements of one another prevails in Eastern thought and, (as Smith notes) is increasingly characteristic of Western science (e.g., in the wave-quantum theories of light, the physical principle of complementarity, matter and anti-matter, and acceptance of all fact statements as probalistic rather than absolute).

The Yin-Yang symbol is a circle combining tears of black and red nestled softly together, with a spot of red in the bulge of the black, a spot of black in the bulge of the red. Women are not Yin — only more Yin than Yang, and men are more Yang than Yin, but never absolutely Yang. The emphasis is on common humanity rather than sexual difference. But this is not the grey compromise that obliterates differences: the Yin-Yang distinguishes and celebrates the complementarity of femaleness in the male, maleness in the female.

I believe that it is in this sense that we can best understand the relationship of poetry to sexuality, of spirit to flesh. The term *sublimation* suggests a kind of lie, or hyprocrisy: a basic appetite is disguised in the lace draping of art. Freud himself seems to have held this prejudice: that the primal force was something to be contained and refined, albeit he recognized the neurotic byproducts of this process. Expression through sublimation was better than repression in the same sense that St. Paul believed it was better to marry than to burn, a practical and relatively harmless way of dealing with nature's unfortunately gross requirements. If a poet not only accepts but reveres the fact that spirit needs flesh and flesh needs spirit, he escapes the trap of hierarchy of values which *sublimation* implies.

The term *incarnation* more acutely suggests the paradox of poetic vision. Literally, the word refers to spirit's embodiment in flesh, indeed in meat, for the root is the same as that of *carnivorous*. The recognition that the abstract means nothing without the concrete, the spiritual means nothing without the carnal, is the basic source of poetic imagery — as in this poem, composed entirely of images — by the seventeenth century clergyman George Herbert:

PRAYER (1)

Prayer the Churches banquet, Angels age,
    Gods breath in man returning to his birth,
    The soul in paraphrase, heart in pilgrimage,
The Christian plummet sounding heav'n and earth;
Engine against th' Almightie, sinners towre,
    Reversed thunder, Christ-side-piercing spear,
    The six-daies world transposing in an houre,
A kind of tune, which all things heare and fear;
Softnesse, and peace, and joy, and love, and blisse,
    Exalted Manna, gladnesse of the best,
    Heaven in ordinarie, man well drest,
The milkie way, the bird of Paradise,
    Church-bels beyond the starres heard, the souls bloud,
    The land of spices; something understood.

That may seem some distance from sexuality, but is inextricable from it. Almost every image is a paradox, a necessary linking of Yin to Yang. Until Heaven walks the earth in ordinary dress and man invests himself with Sunday apparel, neither is complete. The flower cannot disdain its roots, nor the roots their flower.

A person in our civilization who wants to become a poet must somehow break the habit of linear, hierarchical thought, of what Smith calls "conflict dualism." One might call it breaking the prose habit. (The root of *prose* means "right on" in linear fashion.) It means acceptance of sexuality — not as the source, not as primary, but as a component of spirituality. It means developing the habit of paradoxical thought. (To the rationalist, paradox is merely fallacy.) It means finding the spot of Yin in Yang, of Yang in Yin. It means disgorging the apple, letting Good and Evil remain vividly distinct and complementary on the Tree of Knowledge. It means recovering tragic vision, depth perception, correcting the single-eyed simplicity of faith in Progress. It means finding liberation in the easy yoke of form.

This is very personal advice. Above all it means taking off the blinders that inhibit so many of us from seeing and using our whole selves in responding to the world. It means relating the lamp to the power source, acknowledging the connection: more than that, becoming able to celebrate it vigorously and joyously. Some poets are able to recover that innocence of vision by calling upon a childlike capacity for seeing things whole which they have somehow retained. Some use drugs. Some use religion. Many use poetry itself as the means of reawakening an innate capacity for releasing the springs of imagery. However you do it, find ways to let your flowers bloom, those ruddy incarnations, converting chemistry of soil into petals that illuminate the mind with beauty and touch the heart with perishability. From wholeness of self comes wholeness of vision. Sublimation does not mean denial of or substitution for flesh, but embodiment of the sublime.

the vacant vast surrounding

A long letter I received from a man named Irving R. Post of Sharon, Massachusetts, described his search for a "partial clue to that elusive thing called poetic language, poetic power, poetic impact in the modern world." He wrote:

> For the last few days I have been taking excerpts from *The Immense Journey,* a fascinating book by anthropologist Loren Eiseley. One of the passages which had caught my eye . . . tells how Eiseley discovered, by the shadow magnified on the sidewalk, a spider in late autumn spinning a web inside the globe of a street lamp. "Here was something that ought to be passed on to those who

will fight our final freezing battle with the void," he
writes. "I thought of setting it down carefully as a message to the future: IN THE DAYS OF THE FROST
SEEK A MINOR SUN. But as I hestitated, it became
plain that something was wrong. The marvel was escaping — a sense of bigness beyond man's power to grasp,
the essence of life in its great dealings with the universe.
It was better, I decided, for the emissaries returning from
the wilderness, even if they were merely descending from
a stepladder, *to record their marvel, not define its meaning. In that way it would go echoing on through the
minds of men, each grasping at that beyond out of which
the miracles emerge, and which, once defined, ceases to
satisfy the human need for symbols."* . . . I wrote at the
top of the page: The human hunger for epic symbols
makes another's definitions futile (re poetic language) . . .
I have found . . . phases in which I can observe the
thought and the words and the forms of the thoughts
and words going stale and brittle and tight — that I have
been . . . too often disengaged from elemental and meaningful experience, I haven't been out under the sky, perhaps, and into the middle of those changing conditions
that are the only things permanent in our lives, the conditions of sky and air and climate and season, and all the
sub-conditions which they orchestrate . . . . What I am
especially concerned about is establishing to my own satisfaction what can be the realm of significant poetry in our
own time: What must it do in order to reach out and
include? What must it be in order to say something worth
saying? How must it say these things in order to share a
concern about what we are and do? . . . What are the
clues to finding that group of symbols — the language, if
you will — with which to shape and share meaning in
this time where the clickety-clack of man's tools has
drowned out the chamber in which man must isolate
himself in order to find meaning, justification for his own
span of life?

In response to Mr. Post's search, let's start by considering the
way Eiseley shrinks from definition. What is this "beyond out of
which the miracles emerge?" Is it true that definition destroys its
ability to satisfy us? Is there a "human need for symbols?" While

these are good questions for Eiseley or anyone else to raise, I am inclined to be skeptical about their being raised in this context. There is nothing, on the face of it, very surprising or curious about a spider seeking heat, nor is there anything particularly oracular about the advice that we should find what comfort we can in inclement seasons. Eiseley's restraint in deciding not to deliver that advice (which he delivers in the process of deciding not to) strikes me as unnecessarily cautious. I don't think there is much danger of spoiling things for future generations by setting down that message. In fact I find the whole passage from Eiseley to be so much hokum, an attempt to blow a minor observation up, like the shadow of the spider, into something ominous and profound. The aura of mystery is, as it were, sprayed on like phosphorescent paint. Primitive man was easily able to convert his ignorance into a sense of miracle, but a modern anthropologist has to strain a bit to work up wonder, misty eyes and quasi-reverence.

Nonetheless, I think that Mr. Post is right in sensing that poetic language somehow must stop short of definition. Instead of talking about "poetry," let's see what a poem does. Here is one by Walt Whitman — about a spider:

A NOISELESS PATIENT SPIDER

A noiseless patient spider,
I mark'd where on a little promontory it stood isolated,
Mark'd how to explore the vacant vast surrounding,
It launch'd forth filament, filament, filament, out of itself,
Ever unreeling them, ever tirelessly speeding them.

And you O my soul where you stand,
Surrounded, detached, in measureless oceans of space,
Ceaselessly musing, venturing, throwing, seeking the spheres
    to connect them,
Till the bridge you will need be form'd, till the ductile anchor
    hold,
Till the gossamer thread you fling catch somewhere, O my soul.

The poem begins in detailed observation, creating the spider, asking us to contemplate it. For the most part the language is objective, factual; only the words "patient" and "tirelessly" go beyond fact to interpretation — and even these words are nearly verifiable. Where is the "poetry" in the first stanza? We might answer that it is in the sounds, the rhythms — the whispering silences of the first line, the liquid arcing of the repeated word *filament,* the balance (and subtle sound echoes) of the last two phrases. Or we might answer that it is in the suggestivity of the image itself, the speck of life in the "vacant vast surrounding," the futile reaching and reaching for something out there beyond the promontory. Those two ele-ments — the spider and the formless universe around it — set up the reverberations of larger meaning which we may regard as the "poetry" Mr. Post and Prof. Eiseley are seeking.

When we look at the second stanza, the reverberations con-tinue — but here we may feel that definition is, indeed, too specific. There is a haunting quality in the first stanza which diminishes some-what when Whitman tells us explicitly that the spider reminds him of his soul in its endless reaching for some grasp of firmness in the "measureless oceans of space." Why is it that we perversely do not want to be told the "meaning" of the initial image (if that is our reaction)? Why do we want to be haunted? Why do we relish mystery? That, I think, is the question Eiseley is raising and the question Mr. Post is responding to.

Part of the answer may be that any single meaning is bound to be partial. The spider is like *all* things which tirelessly toss futile strands of themselves into the void. I think of the hairy roots working the dark soil, the bird cries echoing in the empty summer, the rivulets of a wasted wave streaming and sinking in the sand, and, of course, too, the random gestures of loneliness, the mes-sages whispered to midnight pillows, the silent pandemonium of prayer . . . . If Whitman had taken some of the fine phrasing of the second stanza and incorporated it in the first, evoking the image of the spider so suggestively that we were impelled to think of the soul reaching, and all reaching things, perhaps the poem would be stronger.

The poet should resist the temptation to supply easy answers. Isn't that what Eiseley is saying? A reader has a tendency to write off what he thinks he has fully grasped, as a bite chewed and swal-lowed. (The poet's aim is to make the bites infinitely chewable and indigestible.) Of course it is often the reader's fault when he *thinks* he has grasped fully before he has done so. That second stanza of Whitman's poem is, after all, still more suggestive than explicit. Notice that it is an incomplete sentence. He addresses his soul elaborately, but never tells it what is on his mind — as though I were to say, "And you, Suzy, standing there in your pinafore, Oh Suzy . . ." The thought hangs in the air, as a filament spent into emptiness. Is he talking about the soul's need of communicating with others? Of the soul's need of verification of its view of the world? Of the soul's yearning for a spiritual answer to its probing? Of the soul's search for Heaven? Of its search for the good life? Of its attempts to understand? If the poem forced us to settle for any one of those (or other) possible interpretations, it would be less powerful.

One demand that any intelligent reader will make of a poem, however, is that its mysteriousness truly inheres in the material. It must not seem laid on. It must not be mere obfuscation of simplicity. The poem must force us to see very clearly and simply that things are not so clear and simple as they seem. Comparison is the root of it: on the one hand this object, this thing; on the other a vast range of phenomena illuminated by the particular. It makes us see unexpected equivalence — and unexpected non-equivalence. It asserts the fact of experience as one strikes a gong: for the sake of resonance that overwhelms and then slowly, imperceptibly fades to silence. The gong releases waves that permeate and connect all things, charging our nerves with sound and the sense that the sound dispersing is never-ending.

If that is what Eiseley means, resisting definition, it is, indeed, good guidance for poets. A modesty in the face of complexity, a surging awareness of the inexhaustible interconnectedness of the universe, an intuitive sense that we do an injustice to truth if we outline it too sharply — these are necessary responses if we want our poems to be more than pretty thoughts and self-confident morals.

Mr. Post wonders whether he is more apt to find the experiences which generate basic images if he were more often "under the sky." It is true that nature is our most ancient and best source of the imagery which seems to reach to archetypal truth, but in the remainder of his letter he asks "what can be the realm of significant poetry in our own time?" Most readers — like most poets — are out of touch with the processes of nature. I wonder whether we can discover elemental meaning in the grind and fume of the superhighway, the drifting faces of the television set, the beep and buzz of the computer, the pattering anonymity of the office. So far it hasn't happened. Little of our poetry conveys the sweat and grease and hard helmets of industry, the searing heats and clanks and humming lights, the stomach-biting tension of traffic, the swaying subway, the sterile slosh of laundromats and clinical array of supermarkets, the cell-blocks of classrooms and cannibalism of cocktail parties. When I think of a poet riding jets and conversing by telephone and recording his vacations on color film, then writing about clouds and daffodils, I am not surprised that many readers reject his poetry as precious.

One of the problems is the continuing battle of romanticism against artifice and civilization. Most of the things I have listed above have negative connotations for us, especially among poets. Though few of us are willing to relinquish our cars and wonder drugs and hi fi sets and typewriters, we talk (in our poetry) as though speed and convenience and comfort and sanitation were unwelcome intrusions on a life which, properly conducted, would be one of earthy toil and primitive simplicity. Since Blake complained of "these dark Satanic Mills" poets have tended to be horrified or repulsed by what ordinary citizens regard as progress. Mr. Post, writing of the "clickety-clack of man's tools," simply is not listening: today's tools are likely to move gearlessly with an electronic hum. Technology is more apparent on our landscape than the "meanest flower that grows," but we have found no poet to celebrate it.

I would like to return to Whitman's spider for suggestions as to how we might find language for modern experience. Life, as the mathematician Norbert Weiner described it, is an enclave of order in an entropic universe. With frightening acceleration we witness the disintegrating forms, the breaking down of order in figure drawing to the atom to university education to sexual mores to law in the streets. Not only is the universe expanding at the speed of light; the patterns of life on earth are exploding around us in chain reaction. In that "vacant vast surrounding" we are likely to feel more and more like the spider, desperately attempting with our ductile filaments to make at least transitory connections, to hold experience together another sweet while. Our consciousness glows like a luminous speck in the void: last week someone moved the horizon; yesterday they took out the promontory underfoot. And yet, until extinguished, we will send out our frail threads, our gossamer of inquiry; we will seek some tender linking as long as we can keep our electrons in orbit.

There, indeed, is a problem for poetry: how to keep signaling in the yawning darkness, how to find order in a universe blowing itself to silence, how to swing in the centerless night. The particles are flying outward. The poet's job is to attach himself to this one and that one, to spin an ever-expanding web.

science and poetry

An article in the New York *Times,* entitled "Scientist with an Artistic Beat," is the profile of Gerald Maurice Edelman, described as the "scientist from the Rockefeller University who headed the team that unraveled for the first time the complex chemical secrets of an antibody." In addition to biology, Dr. Edelman is interested in music, philosophy and poetry:

> In literature . . . Dr. Edelman's tastes run to the non-scientific. A poetry fan, particularly of Wallace Stevens and William Butler Yeats, the doctor said he likes to "riffle through literary magazines, especially the dusty academic poetry magazines.
>
> "I'm interested in poetry . . . because it is beautiful and useless. I like the sound of poetry and its corruptness." Dr. Edelman added, however, that he did not put stock in C. P. Snow's concept that art and science represent two distinct cultures.
>
> "Art and science are both imaginative," he said, "alike in the eccentricities of their creators.
>
> "The essential difference between the two," he went on, "is that poetry concerns itself with the particular, the arbitrary, and can look at many worlds at once, while science is concerned with the general, dealing with recurrent events in a world that has one value at a time."
>
> In the rare moments when he has spare time, Dr. Edelman writes poetry.

The literary or poetic imagination does seem to fix on the particular, the individual — not the behavior of enzymes in the brain, but the destiny of a "wee slicket" of a mouse turned up in plowing. And poetry often seems to discover worlds within worlds, values superimposed on values, as opposed to "recurrent events in a world that has one value at a time."

I would not want to put too much weight on the words of an interview, particularly as filtered through a newspaper reporter, but this quotation provides a good occasion to probe some fundamental questions.

First, I am not sure there is such a world which "has one value at a time," lest it be in the imagination of the scientist or artist. In my world an object simultaneously has weight and size and color and location and symbolic significance and an infinite range of other qualities. And the "worlds" of poetry are all, ultimately the real world of human experience. Fantasy is but truth seen from an unusual angle.

Nor, as I think about it, am I convinced that poets are any less concerned than scientists with abstract, general truth. If poets seem preoccupied with the particular and the arbitrary, it is only to insist that these cannot be disregarded in any inclusive theory. Tim Reynolds once wrote a poem which ran through the conventional approaches to autumn — regret at the departure of foliage, faith that green would be reborn; then he stubbornly ended by insisting on the undeniable, unpleasant, but important fact: "*These* leaves will rot." If you are Hamlet dying, there is only limited consolation in knowing the kingdom will be well-governed by Fortinbras. The audience's gratitude that evil has been purged and that order has been restored is tempered by grief that the hero had to be sacrificed. Poets keep discovering that the rule is compounded of a multitude of exceptions, as the drawing of the grasshopper in a biology text resembles no actual insect which ever hopped in grass.

Stevens and Yeats, Dr. Edelman's favorite poets, provide excellent illustrations. One of Wallace Stevens' most consistent themes is contained in this familiar poem:

ANECDOTE OF THE JAR

I placed a jar in Tennessee,
And round it was, upon a hill.
It made the slovenly wilderness
Surround that hill.

The wilderness rose up to it,
And sprawled around, no longer wild.
The jar was round upon the ground
And tall and of a port in air.

It took dominion everywhere.
The jar was gray and bare.
It did not give of bird or bush,
Like nothing else in Tennessee.

It is certainly very particular and arbitrary for a poet to place a jar on a hill in Tennessee. It is *artificial,* as is the jar itself. What are the qualities of artifice? The jar is round, regular in shape, erect, "of a port in air." That curious phrasing directs our attention to the word *port,* which is very important (no pun intended) in the "portry" (pun intended) of Wallace Stevens. It fuses three Latin roots: *portus,* haven; *porta,* door; and *portare,* to carry, all qualities of artifice. It *dominates* nature. It provides a focus. It is colorless — or worse: gray. It is sterile, empty. It does not reproduce itself. It tames the wilderness but does not participate in the vitality of the wilderness. It is like a thought or a formula. Its severe neutrality gives order but not life.

Only one more romantic than Stevens would think of it as bad. Art and science at their highest reaches are gravely objective, almost beyond value, certainly beyond human emotion. One thinks of George Meredith's Lucifer, restless in his dark dominion, setting out to regain Heaven:

> He reached a middle height, and at the stars,
> Which are the brain of heaven, he looked, and sank.
> Around the ancient track marched rank on rank,
> The army of unalterable law.

These are the laws of the universe or laws of nature. If one analyzes the sprawl of the wilderness of Tennessee, he finds evidence of such laws in the bottom of the test tube. Science and art are but alternate paths to the threshold of Awe. Nature is the rank growth, but roots suck at the pure water of principle. The human observer is stunned. "Biology," said Dr. Edelman, "is intriguing because it is matter observing itself." We are dumbfounded by our power to place a jar in Tennessee.

Similarly there is in Yeats a relentless pursuit of objectivity, of the serene truth beyond value, beyond nature's round of "Whatever is begotten, born, and dies." That line is from "Sailing to Byzantium," a poem which specifically rejects concrete and particular experience in pursuit of the abstract.

Yeats is regarded by many critics as having been silly or irresponsible in the realm of abstract thought. Not only did he toy with spiritualism and fascism naively, but he put on prophetic robes and delivered to us a complex system in prose — *A Vision* — purporting to be a philosophical and/or religious basis of his poetry, providing work for legions of industrious explicators and an almost deliberate barrier between any innocent reader and his work. Yet it is obvious that not many will read *A Vision,* and we will be lucky if we can keep a dozen or so of Yeats' poems in the anthologies during this second century of his reputation. If the poems are to survive at all, it must be without the system. Will we be left then with the judgment that Yeats was simply a bad thinker who luckily produced a handful of wonderful images? Would he have done better not to have thought at all?

"Sailing to Byzantium," though central to his system, has some chance of surviving in the culture just as Keats' "Ode on a Grecian Urn" survives.

Keats' poem is, incidentally, a good comparison, as it is addressed to the same philosophical problem — the limitations of mortality, the vision of an existence "out of nature," as Yeats puts it, or "all breathing human passion far above," in the phrase of Keats. Yeats starts with a comprehensive summary of our mortal state:

> That is no country for old men. The young
> In one another's arms, birds in the trees,
> — Those dying generations — at their song,
> The salmon-falls, the mackerel-crowded seas,
> Fish, flesh, or fowl, commend all summer long
> Whatever is begotten, born, and dies.
> Caught in that sensual music all neglect
> Monuments of unageing intellect.

Most of the language is abstract; even such images as appear are generalized — any young lovers, any birds in trees. We are not asked to see them but to think about them. The phrase "dying generations," combining as it does birth and death, making us think of the root of generation and the multitudinous dead, has purely intellectual impact and beauty. *Song* may evoke a sense image momentarily, and "The salmon-falls, the mackerel-crowded seas," with its specific references to kinds of fish, helps us visualize the mortal throng, leaping with tireless vitality, surging, slithering in silver clouds of infinite numbers of individuals, a spermy mob; but the next line moves quickly from the concrete to the highest plane of generality. *All* mortal beings "commend" (a dry, almost neutral verb) what? Themselves: "Whatever is begotten, born, and dies." The brilliance of the stanza is not in its feeling or imagination, but in its abstract thought: the antitheses (e. g., of *old* and *young), the brief, exact eloquence of the rounded phrases.

We may sense behind the statement an emotional commitment to the very mortal values being rejected — as though we caught a loving glimpse of the landscape of that country, populated by lovers, birds and teeming fish, all summery green with song — but the poem is rising granite and grand as a memorial enduring beyond the transitory and frail. *Caught* is a word of frightening power: the hypnotic mortal dance must be escaped. Over the green, oblivious plain stand grim and tall the "Monuments of unageing intellect," those products of pure mind (such as this poem) which are man's only salvation from the trap of age.

Since "That is no country for old men," the poem suggests what can be done about it in the second stanza:

> An aged man is but a paltry thing,
> A tattered coat upon a stick, unless
> Soul clap its hands and sing, and louder sing
> For every tatter in its mortal dress,
> Nor is there singing school but studying
> Monuments of its own magnificence;
> And therefore I have sailed the seas and come
> To the holy city of Byzantium.

As the plural "men" becomes "man," we feel the poem narrowing from generality to the specific case of "I" and sense the pathos and contempt with which the poet regards himself as a scarecrow. That image, "A tattered coat upon a stick," is the most specific, visual phrase which has occurred. The summer song of mortality is now contrasted with the shrill "sing, and louder sing" of the soul, counterpart of the intellect of the first stanza. In order for the old man not to be paltry, a scarecrow, his soul must clap its hands (suggesting warming oneself in the chill autumn as well as clapping hands to music) and express itself. How? As the mortal commends morality, so must the immortal commend "Monuments of its own magnificence," the products of soul which memorialize the soul and instruct the soul to sing its own praise. Therefore *I* (says the poet) "have crossed the seas" from the shores of mortality to the threshold of immortality. This is the dramatic situation of the poem: the poet is here, now, as it were, at the gates of heaven; but, of course, it is not life after death he is concerned with — rather, commitment of the immortal part of himself to those values and monuments which liberate it from mortality.

The third stanza is an invocation:

> O sages standing in God's holy fire
> As in the gold mosaic of a wall,
> Come from the holy fire, perne in a gyre,
> And be the singing-masters of my soul.
> Consume my heart away; sick with desire
> And fastened to a dying animal
> It knows not what it is; and gather me
> Into the artifice of eternity.

He appeals not to priests but to sages, to men whose stony wisdom endures past life. They are represented in the stiff, rather abstract medium of mosaic, the highly stylized art of Byzantium. Soul must learn to clap its hands and sing — and the sages are called upon as instructors. A *pern* is a honey buzzard: in making a verb out of the noun, Yeats seems to be asking the sages to circle, or spiral, like that variety of hawk. Gyres, or vortices, are important symbols in Yeats' poetry, suggesting among other things the interpenetrating revolutions of history, spiraling inward and outward and bringing mankind through regular sequences of contradictory phases. His prayer is that the sages participate in the immortal cycles of time, unlocked from their mosaic rigidity, to teach Yeats the secrets that transcend time.

He knows rather exactly what their lesson will be. He must surrender his passionate heart, which, like a foreign object, is hopelessly "fastened" to his mortal flesh, hence cannot know its own immortality. In being consumed, however, the heart seems not to be destroyed, but absorbed in, gathered into its native element — the "artifice of eternity." Art and nature are opposed. Nature is the world of the dying generations. Beyond that, standing monumentally over it, is the transcendent world of artifice.

The poem concludes with its fourth stanza:

> Once out of nature I shall never take
> My bodily form from any natural thing,
> But such a form as Grecian goldsmiths make
> Of hammered gold and gold enamelling
> To keep a drowsy Emperor awake;
> Or set upon a golden bough to sing
> To lords and ladies of Byzantium
> Of what is past, or passing, or to come.

He wishes to be delivered from nature, and then again to be incarnate, but not as a living being: rather he wishes to become a work of art — a golden bird upon a golden bough, whose song embodies past, present and future (note the echo of "begotten, born, and dies"). If the country he left behind is an oppressively sensual land, of total commitment to life, the Byzantium of his imagination seems to be no less so for its human inhabitants, its drowsy emperor and idle lords and ladies. But the art of that civilization — the intricate mosaics, the ingenious machines wrought of gold and enameling — is the stuff of enduring monuments. Ironically, that art, like all art, imitates nature: but in Yeats' view — at least in this poem — a golden bird is superior to one of flesh and blood because it is immortal.

The desperation one feels as he sees himself aging in the mirror and faces the absoluteness of mortality spurs many poets to dream of eternal embodiment in art as an answer to the frailty of flesh. But even as we read this poem, we know it is only half the story, a Yin without a Yang; and we are inescapably aware of the living, aging man who wrote it and know that for all he says here he will not relinquish easily the world of the young in one another's arms and of real birds in real trees. We know that the poet did not literally cross the seas to ancient Byzantium and probably never asked sages standing in holy fire to consume his heart.

Rather, the thought of the poem — that the only escape from death lies in commitment to art and intellect — is remarkably clear and free from the hocus-pocus of Yeats' religious, philosophical, anthropological and historical speculations. To delve into his system is to move *away* from, not into, the poem, and to becloud its golden precision.

Moreover, the poet represented here is essentially one who thinks rather than one who feels; he asks, even, to be delivered from feeling. If we want to know what Yeats the poet thinks, we should not turn to his mystic writings, essays, letters, autobiography, etc., but to the poems themselves, where he usually had the good sense to purge his images of the clutter of merely personal association ("perne in a gyre" is somewhat an exception). If we are interested in the *source* of his images, those other documents may be extremely useful — but in that case we are interested as amateur psychologists, not as poets or readers of poetry.

The thought of the poem is not, of course, original; the theme, as are the themes of most poems, is ancient. But its special quality, as rendered here, is in the toughness and realism with which Yeats faces the implications of the old idea. The mortal life is little more than a "mackerel-crowded sea" in which the individual is doomed to become "A tattered coat upon a stick" so long as he conceives of himself as primarily animal. Meanwhile, around him are monuments — disregarded by the young lovers — reminding him that artifice (he deliberately uses the word with negative connotations rather than the more easily acceptable *art)* transcends (at least a while) natural limitations. To wish oneself transformed into a golden bird on a golden bough is not to choose an immediately attractive alternative to life. Keats, for example, was seduced by an ideal of eternal youth ("For ever wilt thou love, and she be fair") which seems at first obviously more desirable than this life of "a heart high-sorrowful and cloy'd/A burning forehead, and a parching tongue." But Keats eventually recoils from that ideal vision: "Cold Pastoral!" Though the end of his poem is ambiguous, it seems to say that the consolation the urn brings to mortal man, wasted by age, is that beauty is in the mortal condition itself, in the realm of what is.

Yeats' rejection of mortal life seems to be more tough-minded and thorough — and yet there is a suggestion of reconciliation at the end of the poem. What function does art serve but to awaken mortals and remind them of eternity? In this respect, that golden bird Yeats would become is much like the Grecian urn, and its combination of a physical form, an imitation of nature, with the "artifice of eternity" similarly teases us "out of thought." Heaven is artificial life, but is still embodied — as he imagines it — in a physical, even a very sensual world, lush with luxury. Though he would leave "that country," he would not, finally, take leave of the world.

In every poet or scientist is this yearning for the realm of the absolute. Perhaps what we mean by *spirit* is our need to identify our essential selves with the unalterable, the permanent, the unnatural. "Artifice" is an unpleasant word for the young, caught in that sensual music of Tennessee or Ireland, but it is our deliverance from mutability and mortality. Our minds, if not our hearts, seek its glittering, cold security.

But none of us, especially not a full-blooded man like Yeats, is truly willing to relinquish flesh. There is a continual interaction between the individual and the absolute, between the mortal being and immortal truth which defines the conditions of his life. At times, in the poetry of Yeats, God intervenes in human affairs with frightful, impersonal and indifferent power, as in the rape of Leda by Zeus, as in the dread march of the aroused sphinx in "The Second Coming," "Slouching toward Bethlehem to be born." God is a kind of embodiment of those laws sought by both poet and scientist which exist without sympathy for the plight of individuals. In our myths of His incarnations we symbolize the disruptions of history by universal purposes as much beyond our understanding as were those of the Voice who spoke to Job from the whirlwind.

History is changed by man's traffic in the realm of ultimate truths. We can call it inspiration. It is the mind's escape from the moment.

It is thought pure as the jar in Tennessee. Yeats writes of three such moments which altered history:

LONG-LEGGED FLY

That civilisation may not sink,
Its great battle lost,
Quiet the dog, tether the pony
To a distant post;
Our master Caesar is in the tent
Where the maps are spread,
His eyes fixed upon nothing,
A hand under his head.
Like a long-legged fly upon the stream
His mind moves upon silence.

That the topless towers be burnt
And men recall that face,
Move most gently if move you must
In this lonely place.
She thinks, part woman, three parts a child,
That nobody looks; her feet
Practise a tinker shuffle
Picked up on a street.
Like a long-legged fly upon the stream
Her mind moves upon silence.

That girls at puberty may find
The first Adam in their thought,
Shut the door of the Pope's chapel,
Keep those children out.
There on that scaffolding reclines
Michael Angelo.
With no more sound than the mice make
His hand moves to and fro.
Like a long-legged fly upon the stream
His mind moves upon silence.

Such poetry is beautiful and corrupt, as Dr. Edelman contends. Whether Roman conquest is or is not in human interest, in the long run, is beside the point. Similarly Helen's adaptation of a slatternly walk to her own style of beauty may not easily be seen as contributing to human welfare. What fascinates Yeats is the *power* human affairs draw from divine intercourse. Helen's beauty,

Yeats speculates, stemmed from her divine conception when her mother was raped by Zeus in the form of a swan. We cannot say that Michael Angelo's sensual portrayal of Adam on the ceiling of the Sistine Chapel, and the erotic vision of man which it inspires, is good or bad in human terms. It is enormously powerful — and has its source, Yeats contends, in the artist's contemplation of the still, cold principles of unearthly truth.

Dr. Edelman speaks of "imagination" and "eccentricity" in art and science. I believe these are terms for our obsessive yearning to know and our capacity for transcending the normal considerations of experience and human welfare in our search for pattern, for what lies abstractly and immutably beyond appearance. C. P. Snow contended that the "two cultures" of science and the humanities had lost their ability to communicate with one another, to discover that they were, in fact, one culture. In my view, whether we recognize it or can communicate it, science, religion and art are engaged in a common quest, a doomed, tragic quest, to redeem us from individual mortality by identifying our essential selves with general truth, to transmute our fallible meat into what Yeats imagined as a golden bird upon a golden bough, "to sing/ To lords and ladies of Byzantium/ Of what is past, or passing, or to come." Perhaps in an ultimate sense that is the meaning of Yin and Yang, the mortal destiny and immortal conception, the actual and the abstract, the presence every moment in human life of both the immediate and the beyond.

CHAPTER TWENTY-THREE

Urgency—and Timelessness

as the sun sets over pinkville

Who, after Apollo 11, got very excited about the much more ambitious and more significant and dramatic flight of Apollo 12? Hiroshima is a symbol, but who remembers Nagasaki? Guernica, the first instance of bombing of a civilian population, is memorialized in Picasso's great painting which announces like a shriek in the night a new era of warfare, but the bombing of Guernica seems innocent indeed after the atomic bombs and after the pummeling of Dresden and the other cities of Europe. Lidice is a symbol that not only planes but footsoldiers slaughter the innocent, systematically wiping out a village. Mylai became a new symbol, for the same truth, for that incident made it impossible for Americans to pretend that atrocity is something committed by perverted Nazis and semi-human Orientals. We must own our membership in the human race.

But already minds are hardening, growing the necessary callus. The stark symbols of yesterday stand as dusty statues in a museum. Humanity seems to have an infinite capacity for healing its wounded conscience. It seems to have a deep need not to learn.

Like Picasso's *Guernica,* poetry has cried out in horror through the ages:
> Leaving the city
> one saw nothing, for the horror of the surroundings
> blotted out all else; everywhere
> the white bones of the dead were
> scattered and on the roads were starving women
> putting the children they could not feed
> into the grass to die.

That was written by a Chinese poet, Wang Tsan, who lived from 177-217.

> For I hear the sound of the trumpet, the alarm of war.
> Disaster follows hard on disaster, the whole land is laid waste.
> Suddenly my tents are destroyed, my curtains in a moment.
> How long must I see the standard, and hear the sound of the trumpet?

So wrote Jeremiah about 650 B. C., thinking he had visions of the end of the world.

> Those that were sent away they
> Knew, but now they receive back
> Not the faces they longed to see,
> Only a heap of ashes.

That was Aeschylus, writing about 500 B.C.

Each of those ancient wars, I'm sure, was "justified" in the name of protecting one people's view of civilization from the competing view of another people. Had they not stopped evil on those old battlefields, surely nation after nation would have toppled like a train of dominoes. It must often have been necessary to destroy villages to save them. Had those armies retreated, they would have left bloodpaths in their wake. Fathers would have been bitter that their sons had died in vain. In the taverns battered veterans would have muttered that in the good old days there was no surrendering.

Against the forces of "realism" poetry holds little sway, though the realism is often more illogical than any poet's fantasy. What we call realistic thinking often seems to be a projection of dark passions and mythology we hardly understand. Richard Lovelace, in the 1640's, told us a great deal about the human addiction to battle:

TO LUCASTA, GOING TO THE WARRES

> Tell me not (Sweet) I am unkinde,
>   That from the Nunnerie
> Of thy chaste breast, and quiet minde,
>   To Warre and Armes I flie.
>
> True; a new Mistresse now I chase,
>   The first Foe in the Field;
> And with a stronger Faith imbrace
>   A Sword, a Horse, a Shield.

Yet this Inconstancy is such,
As you too shall adore;
I could not love thee (Deare) so much,
Lov'd I not Honour more.

Lucasta's response has not been preserved, but when I watch co-ed cheerleaders flipping their bodies in ecstasy as their beefy heroes collide on the field, I can imagine Lucasta kissing him goodbye passionately, giving him a handkerchief to wear in his helm, batting her dewy eyes in hope that he will win some romantic wounds (not too disabling or unsightly) and medals. That notion of honor has been discredited, laughed at, rejected as an ideal of civilization — and yet it hovers over the negotiation table like an old ghost. One Easter I had this comment:

THE HITLER IN OUR HEARTS

reading all the grand old poems of war
resistance
                 my blood burns I feel renewed
cleaning and oiling my manhood
                                snapping my hammer.
I think of one bombed baby
                          and grow lewd
with brotherhood
                 something worth fighting for.
O dove of Peace on my banner
                            I could not love
thee half so much loved I not honor more.

justice shall overcome,
                       our tattered bands
storming the Winter Palace of Evil
                                hurling
flowers
           and non-negotiable demands . . .
I dream
           snarling at wife and kids when they
cling to me wanting
                   security and such.
hush darlings
              if it weren't for daddy's honor
he swears he could not love thee half so much.

    my hate is like a hard-on:
                   governments
    and economics —
              up against the wall!
    this very poem is an act
                of violence.
    My father started this:
              until he's beat
    at his own game I'll wage a daily war
    against myself
          all whom I love
               who love me
    for I love peace
          but peace with honor more.

In that poem my sarcasm is directed at the militant fighters for peace, the Weathermen and Crazies who intended to bring peace to this nation if they had to kill every man, woman and child to do so, who thought they might have to destroy the nation in order to save it. Once we associate Honor with our cause (fighting for Peace, for Justice, for Brotherhood, for Truth), we become capable of any atrocity; if we are willing to sacrifice ourselves, why should we hesitate to sacrifice anyone else — whether it be the enemy, a civilian population, or our own wives and children who must bear the burden of our obsession?

It is difficult to understand an appetite for killing except as some twisted form of sexual lust. The obscene terms for making love are conventionally used for killing, injuring, betraying, and it is difficult to know whether this is because we think of the sex act as a kind of violence or of violence as a kind of sex act or both. In the time of Lovelace the word *foe* was often used in lyrics of courtly love to refer to the poet's mistress. Lovelace makes the buried analogy quite explicit. His actual mistress, Lucasta, is chaste and quiet; his lust is for action and engagement. There are more kicks in a war than a nunnery. He calls this urge to ease his frustration with a substitute for sex "Honour."

All this is a preface to explaining the ultimate futility of a very powerful poem, one which has remained vividly in my mind since adolescence, which captures with scorching accuracy the disgusting horror of battle, and which falls helpless before the "old Lie" against which it beats its bloody fists. The title refers to the Latin tag at the end, which means "It is sweet and fitting to die for one's country."

DULCE ET DECORUM EST

Bent double, like old beggars under sacks,
Knock-kneed, coughing like hags, we cursed through sludge,
Till on the haunting flares we turned our backs,
And towards our distant rest began to trudge.
Men marched asleep. Many had lost their boots,
But limped on, blood-shod. All went lame, all blind;
Drunk with fatigue; deaf even to the hoots
Of gas-shells dropping softly behind.

Gas! Gas! Quick, boys! — An ecstasy of fumbling,
Fitting the clumsy helmets just in time,
But someone still was yelling out and stumbling
And floundering like a man in fire or lime. —
Dim through the misty panes and thick green light,
As under a green sea, I saw him drowning.

In all my dreams before my helpless sight
He plunges at me, guttering, choking, drowning.

If in some smothering dreams, you too could pace
Behind the wagon that we flung him in,
And watch the white eyes writhing in his face,
His hanging face, like a devil's sick of sin;
If you could hear, at every jolt, the blood
Come gargling from the froth-corrupted lungs,
Bitter as the cud
Of vile, incurable sores on innocent tongues, —
My friend, you would not tell with such high zest
To children ardent for some desperate glory,
The old Lie: Dulce et decorum est
Pro patria mori.

The author, Wilfred Owen, his awareness now scattered in the dust of the universe, knew of what he wrote. He was killed in action in 1918 at the age of 25.

As I hope I have implied, one cannot understand any art, including poetry, as though it were a mere collection of techniques. To read poetry well, just as to write it well, requires a total involvement of the sensibility, at least as much concern with *what* is being said as with *how* it is said. Picasso did not put an end to the

bombing of non-combatants with *Guernica,* nor did Owen put an end
to patriotism with "Dulce et Decorum Est," but we may be sure
these artists were not merely making pretty compositions on popular
themes. They hoped to have impact on human behavior. Wilfred
Owen was one of the thousands who died in vain in a dreadful year
with that pathetic hope.

The poem is as powerful as it is because the poet's emotion did
not impel him to spew a disorderly stream of invective. He cared
enough to be very precise, very artful, formal, and to rely on the
strength of understatement. The first quatrain is loaded with
heavy, fat syllables *(bent doub, old beg, knock-kneed)* of weary
marching, creating a silhouetted line of figures backlighted by the
"haunting flares." The second quatrain uses staccato statements,
short phrases, as the movement of the poem limps almost to a stop
and we hardly notice (as the soldiers hardly notice) the soft dropping
of the gas shells. The stanza break, like a gasp, prepares us for
the surprise of the exclaimed warning. An incomplete sentence
carries us to momentary relief "just in time" before we notice that
one man failed to get his mask on. Notice how those two lines
stretch out with *and's* and participles, dramatizing the plight of the
stumbling, drifting man. *(Lime* means *birdlime* — a sticky substance
used to trap birds; the poem was written before the invention of
napalm, however.)

The second quatrain of the second stanza pulls us inside the
safety of the poet's gasmask. The image is very vivid for me because
of experience I have had skin-diving, watching the struggling of
swimmers just out of reach. Owen seems to have imagined something like that, capturing briefly the suffocation, the blurring, the
weight of water and slowness of movement. Suddenly, unexpectedly,
in the last two lines of the second stanza, he jerks us forward to the
present. The memory of the gassed man is distant but returns in
nightmares. *Plunges* is a threatening word; one imagines waking in
fright from this recurrent dream of the dead man falling toward one
in grim accusation.

Narrative of the past experience, the jump to the present tormented state of mind of the speaker, and then, in the last stanza, the
accusation turned to an audience, a "you," someone who has not
been to the front and who can never, for all the strength and
accuracy of this description, know what it is like without direct
experience. He will not have the "smothering dreams" the poet
has of walking along behind the wagon staring at the dangling face

of the gassed man. The first two quatrains of the last stanza are much more intense in language than the rest of the poem. Adjective is piled on adjective to build an image sufficient to provoke a nauseous reaction. War is not exciting, frightening, glamorous: it is compounded of leaden-footed exhaustion and grotesque, disgusting ugliness which hangs in the mind as the gruesome stink of rotting flesh might cling to the nostrils. We hear and taste this ugliness in those lines.

An abbreviated line breaks down the orderly march of the closely rhymed quatrains. (Speaking of rhymes, notice the intensity achieved by repeating the word *drowning* in the second stanza — as though the poet were saying, with great effort, "There is no other word for it!") The emotion of the poem is finally breaking through its formal constraints (an effect which would be impossible if the constraints had not been firmly established in the first two stanzas). That last stanza is one long, rhetorical statement, swinging around in the last quatrain to the "friend" addressed. This is a rebuke — from one who has been there to one who has not been. If you had seen what I have seen, you would not encourage others to go to war; but, of course, you have not had my experience, and this poem can, at best, only suggest its full meaning. One can imagine the spitting, painful way the Latin words at the end are pronounced by the poet, and the hopelessness — for the children *are* ardent for some desperate glory, and the very antiquity of the lie tells us that it will still endlessly be repeated.

It will be repeated, I'm afraid, even by those who have witnessed the horror of war first-hand. I remember wandering over a battlefield near Naha on Okinawa about a year atfer the invasion, looking at the bunkers gutted by flame-throwers, walking among shards of bones scattered in volcanic rubble, finding little Japanese feet still in burned boots, scraps of puttees still swathed around the shins, the flesh hardened by the semi-tropical sun to a hardness of burnished leather. Climbing to a small shrine, I was startled by a rifle aimed at me over a parapet, and climbed up to find a little dead man, still in uniform and helmet, still kneeling to hold off the American invaders. In basic training I had whiffed gas, had crawled through dirt on my belly, a spray of live ammunition raking the air a foot overhead, mines bursting around me and showering dirt, had stabbed dummies with bayonets, searched huts for booby traps, practiced firing pistols, rifles and machine guns at cardboard human silhouettes. I had been systematically brutalized —

and if it did not work entirely on me, it worked well enough to make me associate manliness with toughness and murder with service of country. On Okinawa I snapped pictures like a tourist and collected souvenirs.

Art weeps tragically, its warnings muted, its deep experience nullified. Surely we cannot stop war with poems. We have not found anything else with which we *can* stop it. But a throbbing, angry, exquisite poem such as this one by Owen at least records recurrent human awareness. Perhaps — though there is little evidence of this — humane wisdom will eventually accumulate and have some effect on human behavior.

the present crisis

I write at a time when the nation is at war with its blacks and its young. The morning paper tells me that police at the University of Virginia are going to unaccustomed limits to stamp out rebellion: they swept through the dormitories and college buildings and arrested, among others, the father of a student, a man in a tuxedo, a gardener living in a cottage on campus, and a man delivering pizza to the home of the university president. I confess to being a provocateur: I have gone around the campuses urging students to take power into their own hands and make the universities and colleges over to their liking — and after the universities, the larger society.

It is increasingly difficult to separate myself as poet from myself as father, citizen, human being. And it is increasingly difficult to think in terms of the printed word. In view of the crisis in our civilization, books come low on anyone's list of priorities. Perhaps some will be found in the rubble. I have read few books in recent years, and I am finding that even the magazines are hopelessly dated before they reach my hands. Checking with others I find this is true of many: we are reading mimeographed reports, personal letters, carbons and Xerox copies of things not yet in print. It gives one a certain sense of futility being a writer. One man said, "I should write a book about that. No, it had better be an article. Come to think of it, I'd better just ditto it up and mail it out to friends. Nope. Better make a phone call." The next step is ESP, and not only print but words themselves become out of date.

Michael Vossick, who calls himself a "mendicant educator," traveling around the campuses helping students get themselves together, is perpetually writing poems wherever he happens to be sitting and passing them on to friends. He never makes copies. "I'd just rather write another poem," he says. The poem is a happening. He has rid himself of what he regards as the hang-up of writing for immortality.

A few years ago intellectuals argued about what really was and was not a poem. Such a discussion would sound fantastic and quaint today. Poetry is one of the many essential responses one may make in struggling for survival. It is what it is. It is here and gone. Written, it has served its purpose. If someone reads it and is moved or delighted or inspired by it, fine; but we may never know; we watch it drift away on the flotsam of a culture undergoing sea changes with a strange sense of detachment.

My library, which used to be precious to me, is more or less drifting away. I have talked to architects who wonder whether there is any point in designing and constructing buildings any more; they are preoccupying themselves with economic and temporary and infinitely flexible ways of enclosing space. I have talked to social scientists, lawyers, businessmen, who doubt that the concept of an institution continues to have relevance. All the forms of structure and organization seem to be moribund. Affairs are being managed, decisions are being made throughout our society in some vaguely participative, informal, unstructured way which no one understands. Survival requires one living in such a state of civilization to hang loose, adapt quickly, snip off memory, and maintain cheer.

Is there any point in writing poetry at all? I think the answer is, more than ever. There is not much point in writing anything else. Is there a point in writing? Expressing oneself is an inescapable human need — and doing so in words on paper has great value, as it permits one to reflect, organize, change, consider and perfect phrasing, achieve an exactness which weeping, for example, or spontaneous song, does not. There is no point in lying. There is no point in corrupting one's writing for money or fame. There is no time for documentation and argument. It may as well be poetry.

I hereby confer the title of poet upon every reader. As Jerry Rubin says — about everything — *Do it!* Power to the people. Daddy has left you his heritage: you have an endless checkbook to the Bank of Western Civilization (and of Eastern Civilization as well). Spend now, while the market is spiraling downward.

In this book I have been preoccupied with quality, with enduring value, with understanding and emulating the excellence of the past. I have implied that many who want to write poetry should go back to the books for a few years before inflicting any of their products on the mails. But my advice for spiritual survival in the seventies is to open up the gates of expression, spread the tidings, and don't look back.

In part I issue that advice in response to a couple of virulent letters I have received attacking me from left and right. Lucas Longo, who has published several books, attacks from the left, viewing me as an Establishment figure with a Sir in front of my name. He says, in part:

> A poet has to tell us we are mad and wherein our madness lies. Who does this? Could you send me a list of poets you think are doing this? Admit it, the best poets, aren't they hiding behind sound? My God — when you cut the cadaver in your column — it smells the whole joint up. Who are you fooling — a few thousand putzy poets who wouldn't recognize a poem if they fell into it. Which all brings me back to truth again. Our gangsters aren't all in the underworld. Quite a number reside in college campuses. The Sir in them makes of them real tyrants. They bull the public and average 20 grand per annum which isn't bad. Fortunately, the kids are getting wise to them and are showing up at weddings with smelly feet and smelly poetry. Why not? It's a kind of truth too . . .

> I have studied our American poets — and British friends — and they fall down in that one big dept. — truth telling. A poet like Stevens — who saw a lot of the black — dressed it too much in decor. Frost, for all of his direct and indirect honesty, is too much the cracker barrel philosopher. Eliot didn't write enough (for that matter all our poets don't write enough) and what he wrote has the smell of pew in it. Although now and then he caught some sublime modern images. I could go on and roast them all but to what avail? You cannot lie in a poem — that's one place you cannot lie. You can lie in religion and give the excuse that you want to save souls or bring solace for bleakness. But what excuse is there for distortion in

a poem — be the distortion in truth telling or word building? That you wanted 20 grand per annum and that Sir in
front of your name. No wonder the kids say — the Muse
sucks! What do you think?

Right on! I have to agree with much that he says. Currently there
is a lot of intellectual anti-intellectualism, of which this letter is
an example, and I understand the motivation. I hope he is wrong
about me, for though I was, in my fashion, a professor, that fashion
was a little unusual: I vowed long ago never to teach another
course, and devoted the remainder of my academic energy to
undermining current structures and liberating students from the
classroom, creating alternative modes of education to those of
curricula and classes. But I realized, after overcoming my indigna-
tion about the superficial points, that Lucas Longo was with the
necessary impudence saying what most needs to be said about
the academic establishment: the Emperor has no clothes.

From the right comes Ian MacAnally, writing from Konai,
Alaska, to the editor of *Writer's Digest:*

Although I never graduated from high school and am a
non-poet and non-writer, too (which you will see as I
go along), I read the *Writer's Digest* because I find it
interesting and informative. With one exception. Your
poetry Dept. annoys me no end. Don't you think it's high
time that you did something drastic about Mr. Judson
Jerome? . . . With typical arrogance, Mr. Jerome never
even considers that his lack of popularity might lie in the
sort of poetry he dishes up to the reading public. Perish
such a thought! Why, more than 200 of his poems have
been published in university quarterlies and such-like intellectual tomes. He must be good! And so he keeps on
in his lecture hall, teaching young Americans how to write
poetry, and continuing to write for the quarterlies. All
the while, likely enough, muttering darkly to himself
about pearls and swine . . . You must get him to bend
his head and listen for a change, even if you have to
use a baseball bat . . . . Tell him to forsake the campus,
and the company of the intellectual Pharisees that infest
it, these days. Let him go down among the silent majority (as they call it), that great mass of our people who
put the country to bed each night, and get it up again in
the morning. Tell him to get to know these people, the

office and factory workers, the truckers and railroaders,
the loggers and miners, the steel workers, the seamen and
fishermen, the farmers, foresters, wild life wardens, bush
pilots and all the rest of the teeming throng that make
America tick. Then, when he has mixed with these people, talked with them, eaten and drunk with them, heard
their hopes and dreams, their joys and sorrows, in short
learned about their America, let him begin writing poetry
again, about them. And let him write it proudly, because,
with all their faults, they inspire pride, as he will find. Let
this poetry of his be like the old true poetry, full of rhyme
and vigor and quotable. The kind of poetry one wants to
learn by rote, for the joy of saying it aloud. Let him write
sad and glad ballads to be sung, narrative poetry to be
read. Lusty, heady stuff, with swing and verve that plain
folk can appreciate. Let him try to be the poet of the
common people, as an American poet should be, for this
land of ours was founded (not by chance, but by plan)
by the common people, for the common people. In less
than 200 years we have done things for the good of the
common people that makes us the envy and hope of the
world. And we will continue to go on doing it. Now,
Mr. Editor, go on out and get that baseball bat. It's
your bounden duty to rescue him from himself. And who
knows, maybe a few knots on the head, and we will find
ourselves with the Robbie Burns of the U.S.A. . . .

There are some misconceptions here, of course. It was Richard
Nixon, not the "effete intellectual snobs," who popularized the
phrase "the Silent Majority." And if America is the most envied
nation in the world, I haven't heard of it: we seem to be currently
the most hated nation particularly among the cane cutters and
rice farmers and other common people of the Third World. I
haven't published primarily in the intellectual quarterlies — in fact,
have published in those only occasionally in recent years. And I
have published quite a few lusty ballads and narrative poems, and
am not the least unhappy — in fact, am surprised and gratified —
by my popular reception. But the sentiments behind this letter are
ones I deeply respect.

I wish our nation had popular poets such as Yevtushenko and
Voznesensky, whose books are eagerly awaited and consumed by
hundreds of thousands of readers in the Soviet Union. They don't

write like Robert Service or Robert Burns, either, but in free forms and sometimes difficult intellectual language. The bards of our nation — Whitman and Sandburg and Ginsberg — have not, in the peak periods of their influence, created comparable mass followings.

What Mr. MacAnally and Mr. Longo have in common (and may they lie down in peace together) is a deep-eyed resentment of the system and what it has come to represent, and they do not recognize in me an ally. When the red-neck whites and blacks and youth and women and elderly people of this country recognize that they have common cause, that they are *all* being oppressed by our present society, perhaps we will have the coalition which can effectively produce beneficial change.

But I agree with both of my critics that literature is properly in the dominion of the people — and that the academy has tried to stake it off from them and in a large part succeeded. If I have been part of that co-optation, I hereby disavow any further part in it. I will continue to write about the poetry I love and why I love it — and that of Suckling and Shakespeare and Frost and Stevens is part of what I love. But I also endorse strongly Mr. MacAnally's injunction that poets learn and write about the warp and woof of common life in ways that can be commonly understood. And I endorse Mr. Longo's injunction that poets tell truth and tell it abundantly. It is too late for any other mission to be worthwhile.

far out, man — cool!

Poetry. The word brings to mind a fat, sumptuously bound, prettily decorated, old, old book, with a limp marker half-way through to indicate the point at which *that* particular endeavor was abandoned: Anyone for brass-rubbing?

The New York *Times Magazine* told us in the sixties that Russia has some angry young poets. (Technical definition department: *angry,* used in regard to British writing, means attacking the upper class, or Establishment; *beat,* used in regard to American writing, means attacking the middle-class, or Audience; *angry* used in regard to Russian poetry apparently means attacking the official class, or rather, official dogma.) "The fact is that Moscow these days has become a town where a poet can tie up traffic for hours, just reading." I am inspired; I will open that fat book and try to stop traffic.

Although the "angry" development may have resulted from a temporary liberalization of party attitudes toward the arts, excitement about poetry is not new in Russia. Poetry is regularly published in editions of 20,000 and 30,000 copies; lines form outside bookstores, a printing often being sold out in a matter of days. (Compare with normal editions of 1,000 here, half of which will be remaindered.) This is not a phenomenon of the Communist regime, either. Literature seems always to have been much more central in Russian life than it has ever been in ours. One Russian-born scholar explained that literature was there, the "conscience of the culture." We may regard it as an inadequate conscience these days; but, consider, he is claiming for literature the function that banks have here.

I make no judgment about the quality of the poetry Russians find so exciting. The snippets translated in the *Times* are pretty dreary stuff — or are drearily translated. (Frost, remember, defines poetry as that which is left out in translation.) But in our culture poetry simply is not an important way of apprehending experience and conveying thought, and there is hardly a poet writing today able to convince more than a handful that it should be. We have much activity — jazz and coffee houses and paperback series and mutinous magazines — but for all the nervousness, there is very little sense of urgency in the world of poetry. I am not suggesting another variety of competition with Russia is in order. Even a government crash program wouldn't change the basic cultural fact; poets here, mostly by choice, are far out. Literature is way, way out. While the cultures of antiquity have defined themselves in literary expression, ours has not. We have had some good poets, true, some better novelists, and some worse dramatists. But while literacy (in terms of people being able to pronounce words they see written and to make marks others interpret as words) is higher in our civilization, surely, than it has even been in any other, we have probably the weakest literary production ever known in a major civilization. Renaissance England in less than a hundred years, with a population a fiftieth of ours, a public education hardly better, economic conditions operating even more severely against writers than our own, managed to produce a better literature than has the United States in its whole history. Discount the geniuses as accident — that is, even without Marlowe, Shakespeare, Spenser, Sidney, Donne, their literature is still better than ours. We have no excuse. We have had wealth, freedom, viable traditions both from England and our own country, inspiration, purpose and time. We simply have not come through.

The writers are to blame, not the civilization. Our best writers have almost unanimously declared their independence from readers — and have got it, with a vengeance. The whole concept of the artist as someone outside society, on the fringe, looking on critically at important events, is a curious, modern, Western development, the direct opposite of that prevailing in places and times when literature amounted to more. The writers of the English Renaissance were in spirit, if not actual position, at the center of their society looking outward. They would criticize deviation rather than celebrate it. They identified with the values, the ethics, the manners, the political and religious and philosophical views of their audience. It may be true that literature has always been, in Arnold's phrase, a "criticism of life," but that phrase has a more cosmic ring than a criticism of society. It is one thing to feel allied with mankind against the Universe — quite another to be against Washington or Madison Avenue. And even criticism of the Universe may be accompanied by a commitment to life. The much bemoaned human situation has probably always been the same, but it is only in recent times that our plight has obscured love and appreciation of the bounty and variety and spectacle of life, tenderness, enjoyment of and respect for one's cohabitants of the spinning dust.

Don't groan. Sure, I know we've had altogether too much affirmative literature from the dead center of society, supporting its values — all hack, sentimental, venal, mediocre and cowardly expression of little old ladies about birds and sunsets, or simian young men in charcoal suits, about tough executives with hearts of gold, or rosily potted Californians in sunglasses by swimming pools, about middle-aged middle-class midgets middling through on a middling wage. But this merely proves my point. If talent abandons the necessary themes and functions of literature, they will fall to the glib and the beaverish. Shakespeare, Marlowe, Jonson, got into developing popular theater and made it work. We have seen one enormous technical development after another, each of great potential for literary expression — newspapers, magazines, films, radio, television, even paperbacks — fall into the hands of the ad men. We have sneered and kept our hands clean. We can't blame it on the public, which is no more doltish than it has ever been. We can't blame it on sinister power complexes; those of the Renaissance were not inconsiderable. We might, in fact, find a variety of things to blame it on; but it is chastening to remember Shakespeare working as an actor, getting into the business, making the show go if he had to sew robes and hammer scenery. There was no such thing as a critical success; the measure was the crowd. There were no Guggenheims. Think of Fitzgerald falling to pieces in Hollywood. We blame it on Hollywood. We would blame the socio-economic conditions in the Garden of Eden. Eve was a victim of pressures.

While those Russians are stopping traffic, some of our poets are toying with mescaline to alter their perceptions, to get even farther out. The whole emphasis of our artistic climate is on the new, the different, the original, the bold and bright and batty, the advanced, the rare, the personal — exactly the qualities which separate artists from their culture. I do not deny that great writers have been original, that they have been ahead of their times, that they had personalities and, in fact, were sometimes rather odd. But, at least before the nineteenth century, oddity was not the point; originality was something that happened, not something to strive for. Quirks may have helped some be better writers. Kafka and Dostoevsky may have derived artistic benefit from their diseases, but we need not rush out to contract tuberculosis or epilepsy. Sickness is still something to be overcome, not to be achieved.

It is almost amusing (if it didn't hurt so much) that writers so often complain about conditions they seem bent on creating. They bring attention to the lack of coherency of values in our culture, but never to the large areas of agreement (that is, areas in which they themselves agree; I am not suggesting they should be hypocrites). Man's inability to communicate to others is perhaps the most characteristic theme of our literature, rendered in methods designed to prevent comprehension. They, who rejected society, complain of society's rejection of the artist. They, who permitted mass communications to develop in an artistic vacuum, complain of their vapidity and destructive effects. They, who have refused leadership, complain of the narrowness and selfcenteredness of the populace. Shelley's rather grand claim that poets are the unacknowledged legislators of the world may have an ironic truth, for poets have a large share of the responsibility for the anarchy of values, lack of communication, and they have done very little to educate the populace to better things. Science, the definitive development of the last century and this, has been almost totally ignored in literature except as the occasion for shudders and horror stories; rather than dealing with the world we find, like ostriches we bury our heads and exhibit our nether regions. I see a field of feathered rumps.

The genius of our civilization resides in the middle class. It may be an evil genius in some respects, but it has produced a civilization most of us prefer to live in over any other we have seen or read of. My advice to poets is to join the middle class. Bore from within. If you don't like it, improve it. For that purpose acid has its uses, but let us retain some humanity. That is, let us recognize virtue, however limited, where it exists. Let us remember that our poor benighted fellows are of flesh and blood, susceptible of error and difficulty in apprehending truth and justice. Let us remember how lonely we are without them.

I come back to the word humanity. Twentieth century art is by and large inhuman: narrow, intolerant, haughty, exclusive, often self-consciously and arrogantly obscure. These are the charges of the Philistines, of course; but they are also our clients, and their charges have considerable truth in them. If you but consider the awareness that created a Falstaff and Hotspur, you are brought up short by the over-specialization of the twentieth century literary imagination. We concentrate on turning out second-rate Hamlets and Malvolios. Or, better, we keep coming up with Richard II, the rather dissolute poet king, who just couldn't understand why he couldn't go on reigning by virtue of being himself, who felt the way to deal with power was to shake a symbol at it.

What we choose to ignore, the central values of our civilization and specifically, of our middle class, are neither contemptible nor easily achieved. I mean values like democracy, toleration, practicality, social welfare, social diversity and respect for differences, justice, and of course liberty. The last, particularly freedom of expression, is about all the artists ever concern themselves with — and then usually with very selfish and sometimes perverse emphasis upon freedom of certain people to express certain things, giving free rein to whatever is unintelligible, obscene or insulting to the rest of society. I am all in favor of expressing such things, but I think there is some disproportion in equating the whole democratic endeavor with that particular variety of liberty.

All this has several direct applications in the practice of poetry, but I will settle on one. Stop, dear poets, defining poetry in terms of the personal subjective lyric. Get some people in your poems besides yourself. The lyric, lovely and powerful as it may be, is a curious sub-type of the body of poetry. Tell stories; that is what poetry *really* is, if we would only remember. Narratives, of course, have much ground to regain before they can mean as they did for Chaucer's audience. There is a better chance in drama; in fact, I would predict that the next major poet to come along will be a dramatist. Yes, that means bucking Broadway, and all the impossible and destructive conditions that reign there; but among his virtues will not only be an ear for fine phrases, but, perhaps, some business sense and productive energy. The first popular poetic movie by someone other than Shakespeare will be the landmark, if such is ever to come, of literature's return to its ancient dignity.

CHAPTER TWENTY-FOUR

Where Do We Go From Here?

Dear You:

Having given up trying to be Jesus, I am now preparing to be John the Baptist. I am sitting here by the riverbank thinking up blessings for You.

It's noisy; both shores are lined with coke and souvenir shacks. Crowds are gathering, laden with paperbacks. Every ten minutes someone jumps in and anoints himself. There are overeager anointers, too, their sacramental oil in aerosol bombs, spraying the bullrushes. Every day droves of sport cars arrive; people put up little tents, erect aerials for hi-fis, and sit back reading *Playboy,* waiting. Hucksters wander through the camp villages selling do-it-yourself Prophecy Kits. Then at night, late, after everyone has turned his record player off and turned one another on, the dark air is split by a ghastly howl.

I have seen the best minds of my generation and found them wanting — and have greater faith in Yours. According to calculations, You were born about 23 years ago and are still in the Wilderness (probably college) but you should be about ready to tell Alternate Press to get behind Thee. Please hurry. All through the thirties we called You Lefty, and then changed Your name to Godot and waited more. People are becoming unreasonable. They would stop waiting if there were anything else to do. They are beginning to call You The Bomb.

You will be the Breakthrough. A Breakthrough is a scientific word for an explanation of past errors. It is always a simplification — something that will make sense again of the atom, that will make peace possible, make music bearable, painting viewable, poetry readable. Scientists know that progress comes through simplifications and unifications; but one of the obstacles you will find is that in the arts intelligibility is reactionary, that dispersion is always applauded (because art depends more on approval than on verification, and whenever one starts something new he confuses his critics and collects strange friends). But You will be so damned good that people will approve even if they understand and the waters will be still. The most revolutionary act possible in American poetry today would be for a radical press to publish something roughly comparable to the *Nonnes Preestes Tale* — a comic narrative, that is, in pentameter couplets — something so clearly eternal that fads would fall away like dominoes.

I do not mean that simplification would necessarily mean a return to the old forms. This is one of the things You will prove. Given any workable form, You will be able to make poetry. But just now such couplets would be a test case.

And I see, having said that, the need of more explanation. You will be an American poet, which calls for some fidelity to the native grain. To understand *that,* You need to take a long look at the poetry of the United States of America. (Such a country: how can it have a poetry when it hasn't even a name, only a catalogue description?) Let's move off some distance. Further. Don't complain that Lowell, from here, begins to look like Olson, and Olson (now we are farther) begins to look like Wilbur, and Wilbur (God! what distance!) begins to look like Whitman, and Whitman (I think we had better stop here, where the stars blur into a Milky Way) looks like Emily Dickinson. All you can tell about American poetry from here is that it sure as hell isn't English. Fine. Now, maybe, You can see something about the native grain.

I will give a short, absolutely biased history of our poetry. You already know the good points about our past. I will concentrate on our inadequacies.

After a couple of hundred years of European settlement we began to produce poets. We produced, in fact, three: Poe (born 1809), Whitman (born 1819), and Emily Dickinson (born 1830). Poe was never very red-blooded and American; he was too arty, vague and dandyish. Whitman — woolly giant — was American enough, all right, but he sprawled, he drooled, he slobbered, he yawped, he lacked art. Dickinson seemed destined only to lead little women. Except for Robinson (born 1869), the rest of American poets were born between 1875 and the beginning of our century, and this sudden, staggering list of Big Names, in their vast variety, almost succeeded in giving us the dimensions, if not the substance, of an American poetry: Frost, Sandburg, Lindsay, Stevens, Williams, Pound, Moore, Jeffers, Eliot, Ransom, Aiken, Millay, Macleish, cummings, Crane.

Some of these — Frost, Stevens, Williams, Eliot, cummings — continue to have a productive influence. (The influence of Pound, a special case, will come up later.) At first each of these poets appears to be *sui generis,* but if You look closely You can detect (in various mixtures) the dandyism and mystique, the sprawl and slobber, of American tradition. Dickinson's fey wit and wry discordance showed in Frost, who also, notably, had less Poe and Whitman in him than did the others. Frost and Eliot, the most important of the five, were the only two who seemed thoroughly to have digested the history of English verse. Verse may seem a relatively ignoble aim beside Poetry, but You have to start there like anyone else.

In case my drift is not clear, I mean to say that Emily Dickinson, E. A. Robinson (a lesser, bulkier genius), and Robert Frost represent a continuation of the tradition of poetry as it has been adapted to our continent. Of those five listed in the last paragraph, Frost was at once the most modern and the most difficult. He was the most modern because he alone took account of the scientific revolution; he understood science, he coped with its human meaning, and conveyed its steady skepticism and search for verification. He was the most difficult because he gave readers experience with its mystery hanging out, and his symbols — stars, darkness, artificial lights, leaves, snow, wasps, birds — were, in spite of their disarming simplicity, used in complex and contradictory ways which defy analysis. He was the most American and the most traditional; he shared not only the forms but largely the values of poets writing English from Chaucer to Yeats — and yet patently (and some even charge, vulgarly) showed the native grain of his nation and his region. It is, as will be clearer later, Dickinson and Frost upon whom You can build.

Meanwhile the landmark of all the *rest* of American poetry has been originality: everyone is so *different.* Chaucer, Shakespeare, Donne, Milton, Pope, Blake, Keats, Browning, Yeats, spread as they are over 600 years, have more in common than any two major American poets. I cannot think of much, for instance, Frost, Stevens, Williams, Eliot and cummings might agree upon, whereas it is quite easy to imagine an Olympian congress of the English poets chatting amiably through an eternal evening, toasting their feet on the sunset, and finding point after point at which their values (including aesthetic values) were reinforced. And Frost would be comfortable in their presence.

The variety in American poetry is most immediately obvious in form: the way poems look on the page. Flip through an anthology of American verse and then one of English; it will seem as though the American book is in technicolor, wired for sound, with all the wiggle and dash and irregularity of clever advertising copy, while the English will steadily preserve the margins like a celluloid collar. This is not merely because the bulk of American verse is of the twentieth century; the formal daring of, say, Hopkins, Lawrence, Edith Sitwell, Dylan Thomas, looks rather pallid beside the unpredictability of Sandburg, Lindsay, Stevens, Williams, Pound, well, all of them. American poets remind me of the Maine farmer who, finding a blank space at the end of a form marked, "Do Not Write in this Space," scrawled across it in giant letters, "I'LL WRITE WHERE I DAMN WELL PLEASE." Pound titled one of his books *Make It New,* and this empty-headed slogan should perhaps be incorporated in our national anthem (which, of course, should be rewritten in concrete music and never played the same way twice).

Our variety of content stems from an emphasis on personal vision. It is against our rules to say anything anyone else ever thought of. Black is not white but organdy. This is, like the variety in form, partly but not wholly a function of the relative modernity of our poetry. In the early twentieth century there was an aesthetic revolution in all arts that has encouraged a flight from reason, a sterile concentration on technique (by definition, *new* technique), and a celebration of individual perception and emotional response. But if you compare with the Americans born between 1875 and 1900 the following British poets born in the same years, you will see that disparity is an American speciality; Edward Thomas, James Masefield, James Stephens, D. H. Lawrence, Siegfried Sassoon, Rupert Brooke, Edith Sitwell, Wilfred Owen and Robert Graves. I think the American poets of that period are, on the whole, better — but not because they are disparate. It is incredible to think what they might have done if each hadn't felt obliged to start all over.

We have a bit of the criminal (Poe) and a bit of the pioneer (Whitman) in our heritage, which leads us always to want to be breaking something — at best, new ground. This is quite a different view of creation than that which, consciously or not, seems to have prevailed among British poets. Consider Chaucer's problem: to pull together the Norman and Saxon elements of his culture and his language into a workable relationship. Or Shakespeare's: to contribute to the violent yoking of classical drama with native drama, to make a new drama, indeed, but by making whole what he found in his culture. Americans seem to be impatient with such problems. With so much prairie, why not start fresh? And our culture, like our towns, sprawls in a slapdash, wasteful individualism across the wide ranges of the human spirit.

Except, I must keep excepting, for Frost. God knows he was Yankee enough, but he seemed to have escaped that particular inheritance. The opposite side of the MAKE IT NEW coin is MAKE IT DO, a very Yankee tendency to save and straighten old nails, patch together walls from old lumber, to get by with what one finds at hand. One can imagine a private moment in Frost's life when he realized he would like to write poetry. Well, he might have thought, I wonder how the fellers do *that*. So he read some poetry. And he did it. I have no idea whether this has any relation to what happened to Frost, or to Shakespeare, but I can easily imagine the latter looking around to see what the boys were doing down there in London, and setting to work doing the same, only better.

If we had a Minister of Poetry he would, I suppose, condemn Frost as a formalist — which is ironic in a way which would have appealed to Frost. For he, almost alone, escaped the Trap of Technique which obstructs most Poets' Progress. That is to say, of the poets of his generation, he fussed less with form. This is not to say he was careless or lacked formal invention; on the contrary, he was meticulous and subtly experimental (e.g., his "A Silken Tent" to name only one, advances the sonnet more than all cumming's violence; and watch the anapests throughout his verse from "Mowing" on). But his approach to technique was to master it and use it. Compare his contemporaries who, in all those years, never settled down to a flexible, useful form applicable to a variety of tones and purposes.

He also differs from his contemporaries in his refusal to show off his learning. There is a self-conscious display of exotic references in almost all American poetry — from Poe and Whitman on as the frontiersman attempts to demonstrate he's "edicated" in spite of hell. Pound, among other things, was the world's worst pendant, and the rough-talk of much modern verse is splattered with arcane illuminations from abroad. Even a belligerently American poet like William

Carlos Williams kept pulling Frenchmen out of his sleeve. None of that for Frost. Not that he mightn't, but, probably, because it hardly seemed relevant to getting something said (particularly if you include allusions not to evoke something in your audience but to astonish them, knowing very well they haven't read the same books you have).

As I implied earlier, there have been no major poets (as one may judge today) to emerge except those born before 1900. Another generation of poets born before and during the first World War has established itself as Good and Grey, but no member of that generation has anything like the stature of those of the preceding generation. I mean those collected and represented in John Ciardi's anthology, *Mid-Century American Poets* — an immensely valuable collection — including Richard Wilbur, Peter Viereck, Muriel Rukeyser, Theodore Roethke, Karl Shapiro, William Townley Scott, John Frederick Nims, Robert Lowell, Randall Jarrell, John Holmes, Richard Eberhart, John Ciardi, Elizabeth Bishop, and Delmore Schwartz. These poets are, on the whole, Frostian, with a dash of Dickinson for ambiguity. Ciardi, in his introduction, calls them "sane," and recognizes the passing of the wilder years, the twenties, of experiment, discovery and blinding madness, Almost all these poets were college professors, of which more later. They were the most influential body of opinion in poetry, advising on fellowships, granting prizes, editing periodicals, teaching at conferences, giving readings. Young poets could learn from them and build on their achievement. But, sadly, they look not merely sane but tame today. None has yet (there is still time — many are vigorous) set his foot upon the sill of immortality.

Wilbur and Roethke seemed to me "most likely to succeed." I have heard one of Lowell's books referred to as the long-awaited Breakthrough, and have seen him apply the same term to W. D. Snodgrass. Shapiro made noise as a very brave critic (of the Eliot-Pound Axis), but seems to have lapsed into silence. Ciardi has been a clear, popular and (to my mind) sensible enunciator of theory, as well as a brilliant translator. But where is another "Sunday Morning" or "Prufrock" or "Mending Wall"? It is not, I think, merely that time and anthologies have canonized the poems of that magnificent generation. The mid-century poets simply did not come up with the symbols of their time. There were symbols, symbols everywhere, but not a drop to drink.

Meanwhile, of course, they worked and explored the very

best of what their American heritage gave them, and if You haven't read them, You'd better dig in. Above all, dig Wilbur. If You are going to go on, You will go on from there.

You are looking, of course, for a workable manner, a stance that will enable You to act, a range of values which will enable You to deal with life as it happens in Your time. Remember that it is silly to try to build these things for Yourself. You aren't so proud when You want to go somewhere: You buy a car or a ticket on a plane, or stick out Your thumb. Borrow, and what You can't borrow, steal. What You have to do is too important to worry about Your petty pride.

But let's get back to the story. Undergraduates of all ages resent, quite naturally, professors; and the professorial cast of the mid-century poets inspired a rebellion. Beats are a figure of fun by now — those middle-aged men in blue-jeans. But the rebellion was much more significant and dangerous than the mass media made it look. Donald Allen called an anthology *The New American Poetry: 1945-1960.* There had been developing for some time a New Dichotomy between the Academics and All the Rest, and this anthology collected everyone (except Kenneth Rexroth and Kenneth Patchen) who had been left out of Ciardi's volume (e.g., Charles Olson, Robert Creeley) and a number of people who had appeared since then with no significant academic connections (some were students, some teachers, but they liked to pretend colleges didn't happen). Now of course, the Academics were never in the very academic; and the Others, so non-conventional, seemed rather desperately searching for a convention, and glutted their work with second-hand literary experience . . . but, for all that, we must climb them, for, like hairy old Everest, they are there.

The gods of the anti-academicists were Whitman and Pound. Whitman chiefly as reincarnated in Williams. The lessons from their masters seem to have amounted to "unrepressed wordslinging," Jack Kerouac's phrase, which is among other things, a beastly insult to Whitman and even to Pound. It is fun enough to sling words or anything else without repression, but for it to be art one needs a rationale. For this they seem, most of them, to go to the Thinker, Charles Olson, and particularly to an essay of his published in 1950 in *Poetry-New York,* called "Projective Verse." It is rather hard to tell what this essay says, it being written in a combination of American-tough and Manhattan-mystic tongues (Olson was something of a linguist), but it seems chiefly to be based on the aesthetic principle of let'errip. He calls it OPEN verse written in FIELD COMPOSITION (caps his) in which "ONE PERCEP- TION MUST IMMEDIATELY AND DIRECTLY LEAD TO A FURTHER PERCEPTION. It means exactly what it says, is a matter of, at *all* points (even, I should say, of our management of daily reality as of the daily work) get on with it, keep moving, keep in, speed, the nerves, their speed, the perceptions, theirs, the act, the split second acts, the whole business, keep it moving as fast as you can, citizen. And if you also set up as a poet, USE, USE, USE the process at all points, in any given poem always, always one perception must must must MOVE, INSTANTER, ON AN- OTHER!"

This quality of mind infected other cultists who left the poundy feet at St. Elizabeth's to set up White Citizens' Councils. Only now can we see the full horror of what the Bollingen Award for the Pisan Cantos meant: you absolve art of responsibility, then turn it like a spew of acid on society; for never had Pound nor have his many-headed disciples ever laid off society and never have they failed to scurry off from the riot squad under a Wildean cloak of Art. Listen, I was *for* the Bollingen Award, and sympathetically suffered the good fight for the liberation of art. Sure, I said in those days, Jews may be burned on the Altar of Poetry. But the 1950's changed my mind. The only explanation of this artless artiness, this anti-intellectual pedantry, hobo snobbery, genital mys- ticism, slovenly aestheticism, this revolting revolution, is that if you keep moving FROM ONE PERCEPTION TO THE NEXT LIKE A HOUSEWIFE IN A SUPERMARKET you haven't time to think.

But the sad thing is that the anti-academic rebellion of the sixties was the most notable and influential event in American poetry since *The Wasteland*. And as the rebels aged, and one by one the elders died or stopped producing, no really significant new poets came along to replace them. This conversation was over- heard in Harvard Yard after the death of Frost:

STUDENT: Mr. Lowell, since Frost died, you are the Major
   American Poet.
LOWELL: Nonsense. There's Auden.
STUDENT: Oh, no one reads Auden any more.
LOWELL: Hmm.

Another anecdote I have on good authority is of James Dickey, drunk in a hotel room in Manhattan in the middle of a night in the mid-sixties calling Robert Lowell in Boston. "Ah'm goin ta *git* chew, Lowell!" was all he said. So far as I know, it hasn't happened. Lowell continues nodding as the Dean of the Academy, followed by a line of disciples such as W. D. Snodgrass, Anne Sexton — and for her fiery moment, Sylvia Plath (a talent as great as that of Emily Dickinson's, burned out tragically soon). There was a vogue of raw confessional poetry in which near scandalous self-revelations replaced most other resources of aesthetic impact. The succession of waves of youth rebellion, counter-culture, militancy and the search for alternatives has so far produced little in the way of significant poetry, though rich sources — Eastern religion, American Indian heritage, psychic and esoteric thought, drug experiences, ecological awareness, communalism — have been opened up and made available to some new synthesis. Never has there been a greater cultural readiness for You. We pant and wait.

MAKE IT NEW and MAKE IT DO. One element of the American heritage induces an hysteria of consumption, use, novelty, belligerent barbarianism nervously combined with effete exoticism, the narrowed eyes and untrimmed beard, obscurantism combined with rudeness, hauteur combined with crumbiness, the open-road, the get-away, the fly-by-night, the opportunistic, the ulcer-ridden dyspepsia of businessmen and poets who don't have time to have a past. It is from this You must save us — and save the world, which shivers in the shadows of our gadget-happy gat-twirling. We were settled by criminals and Puritans. Let us look to the lean fellows, the wry fellows who regard Life as an understatement, who mend walls, but not without questioning, who grow corn in granite fields. History, the human condition, the iambic yoke, are all we have. Let's make them do.

But I don't have to tell You. You are a Puritan. You are conservative (I mean You'd like to conserve life and intelligence and harmony and direction as long as they'll let You). You understand You are not called upon to invent poetry, only to practice it.

You will start, of course, by ignoring all this flurry and drink at the cool springs. Poetry is making. It is the old mother of fiction: the creation of people, of life, of events, of meaning. It tells stories. It makes Hamlets who are realer than people. It runs rings around Hell and Paradise. It catches Creseyde flirting and Satan consorting with Eve. It has very little to do, in short, with the filler material in the quarterlies or the contents of *POETRY*. It is less ecstasy or revelation or confession or castigation than a steady voice that makes fiction so compelling that hearts are moved and people live by it. It seeks out the order life obscures, and articulates the values life may aspire to. (There is, interestingly, more *agreement* in poetry's long discourse than in the annals of science or philosophy.) It has told us how little life is, and how much that little means.

I am quite serious, You see. We are Rome, about to go down without having had our Virgil. The impulse to chaos in our civilization is so strong, and its means are so enormous, I have no hope of Your stopping it. But it would be sweet to have You come to the last year or years, to hear from Your lips what it all meant before we die. And here, by the riverbank, the best are all involved in committee-work, and the worst, as usual, are full of passionate intensity.

Read Dickinson. Read Frost. And tell us what we meant.

Yours sincerely,

Jud Jerome